NON-LEAGUE FOOTBALL TABLES 1889-2003

EDITOR
Michael Robinson

British Library Cataloguing in Publication Data
A catalogue record for this book is available from the British Library

ISBN 1-86223-078-1

Copyright © 2003,   Soccer Books Limited

Printed by The Cromwell Press

FOREWORD

In selecting the Leagues to be included in this second edition of Non-League Football Tables we have again chosen those forming the pinnacle of the Non-League Football Pyramid, i.e. The Football Conference and it's three direct feeders.

In addition we have once more included the briefly-lived Football Alliance which became, effectively, the 2nd Division of the Football League in 1892 together with the five leagues for the North-West part of the country. In future editions we expect to include leagues for other parts of the country.

Furthermore, as league sponsors change frequently, we have not used sponsored names (eg. Rymans League) other than in an indicative way on the cover.

We are indebted to Mick Blakeman for providing tables for the five North Western Leagues included in this publication.

CONTENTS

FOOTBALL ALLIANCE

1889-90

Sheffield Wednesday	22	15	2	5	70	39	32
Bootle	22	13	2	7	66	39	28
Sunderland Albion	21	12	2	7	64	39	28
Grimsby Town	22	12	2	8	58	47	26
Crewe Alexandra	22	11	2	9	68	59	24
Darwen	22	10	2	10	70	75	22
Birmingham St George	21	9	3	9	62	49	21
Newton Heath	22	9	2	11	40	44	20
Walsall Town Swifts	22	8	3	11	44	59	19
Small Heath	22	6	5	11	44	67	17
Nottingham Forest	22	6	5	11	31	62	17
Long Eaton Rangers	22	4	2	16	35	73	10

Sunderland Albion record includes 2 points awarded when
Birmingham St George refused to fulfil a fixture which the Alliance
committee had ordered to be replayed.

1890-91

Stoke	22	13	7	2	57	39	33
Sunderland Albion	22	12	6	4	69	28	30
Grimsby Town	22	11	5	6	43	27	27
Birmingham St George	22	12	2	8	64	62	26
Nottingham Forest	22	9	7	6	66	39	25
Darwen	22	10	3	9	64	59	23
Walsall Town Swifts	22	9	3	10	34	61	21
Crewe Alexandra	22	8	4	10	59	67	20
Newton Heath	22	7	3	12	37	55	17
Small Heath	22	7	2	13	58	66	16
Bootle	22	3	7	12	40	61	13
Sheffield Wednesday	22	4	5	13	39	66	13

1891-92

Nottingham Forest	22	14	5	3	59	22	33
Newton Heath	22	12	7	3	69	33	31
Small Heath	22	12	5	5	53	36	29
Sheffield Wednesday	22	12	4	6	65	35	28
Burton Swifts	22	12	2	8	54	52	26
Grimsby Town	22	6	6	10	40	39	18
Crewe Alexandra	22	7	4	11	44	49	18
Ardwick	22	6	6	10	39	51	18
Bootle	22	8	2	12	42	64	18
Lincoln City	22	6	5	11	37	65	17
Walsall Town Swifts	22	6	3	13	33	59	15
Birmingham St George	22	5	3	14	34	64	13

SOUTHERN LEAGUE

1894-95

First Division

Millwall Athletic	16	12	4	0	68	19	28
Luton Town	16	9	4	3	36	22	22
Southampton St Mary's	16	9	2	5	34	25	20
Ilford	16	6	3	7	26	40	15
Reading	16	6	2	8	33	38	14
Chatham	16	4	5	7	22	25	13
Royal Ordnance Factories	16	3	6	7	20	30	12
Clapton	16	5	1	10	22	38	11
Swindon Town	16	4	1	11	24	48	9

Second Division

New Brompton	12	11	0	1	57	10	22
Sheppey United	12	6	1	5	25	23	13
Old St Stephen's	12	6	0	6	26	26	12
Uxbridge	12	4	3	5	14	20	11
Bromley	12	4	1	7	23	30	9
Chesham	12	3	3	6	20	42	9
Maidenhead	12	2	4	6	19	33	8

1895-96

First Division

Millwall Athletic	18	16	1	1	75	16	33
Luton Town	18	13	1	4	68	14	27
Southampton St Mary's	18	12	0	6	44	23	24
Reading	18	11	1	6	45	38	23
Chatham	18	9	2	7	43	45	20
New Brompton	18	7	4	7	30	37	18
Swindon Town	18	6	4	8	38	41	16
Clapton	18	4	2	12	30	67	10
Royal Ordnance Factories	18	3	3	12	23	44	9
Ilford	18	0	0	18	10	81	0

Second Division

Wolverton L & NW Railway	16	13	1	2	43	10	27
Sheppey United	16	11	3	2	60	19	25
1st Scots Guards	16	8	5	3	37	22	21
Uxbridge	16	9	1	6	28	23	19
Old St Stephen's	16	6	3	7	34	21	15
Guildford	16	7	1	8	29	41	15
Maidenhead	16	4	1	11	20	49	9
Chesham	16	2	3	11	15	48	7
Bromley	16	2	2	12	16	49	6

1896-97

First Division

Southampton St Mary's	20	15	5	0	63	18	35
Millwall Athletic	20	13	5	2	63	24	31
Chatham	20	13	1	6	54	29	27
Tottenham Hotspur	20	9	4	7	43	29	22
Gravesend United	20	9	4	7	35	34	22
Swindon Town	20	8	3	9	33	37	19
Reading	20	8	3	9	31	49	19
New Brompton	20	7	2	11	32	42	16
Northfleet	20	5	4	11	24	46	14
Sheppey United	20	5	1	14	34	47	11
Wolverton L & NW Railway	20	2	0	18	17	74	4

Second Division

Dartford	24	16	4	4	83	19	36
Royal Engineers Training Battalion	24	11	9	4	49	37	31
Freemantle	24	12	4	8	58	40	28
Uxbridge	24	11	5	8	62	37	27
Wycombe Wanderers	24	10	6	8	37	54	26
Chesham	24	11	3	10	41	55	25
Southall	24	9	6	9	55	52	24
1st Scot Guards	24	9	6	9	49	50	24
West Herts	24	11	1	12	41	49	23
Warmley (Bristol)	24	10	2	12	44	43	22
Old St Stephen's	24	5	7	12	36	52	17
Maidenhead	24	4	8	12	33	64	16
1st Coldstream Guards	24	3	6	15	30	66	12

1897-98

First Division

Southampton	22	18	1	3	53	18	37
Bristol City	22	13	7	2	67	33	33
Tottenham Hotspur	22	12	4	6	52	31	28
Chatham	22	12	4	6	50	34	28
Reading	22	8	7	7	39	31	23
New Brompton	22	9	4	9	37	37	22
Sheppey United	22	10	1	11	40	49	21
Gravesend United	22	7	6	9	28	39	20
Millwall Athletic	22	8	2	12	48	45	18
Swindon Town	22	7	2	13	36	48	16
Northfleet	22	4	3	15	29	60	11
Wolverton L & NW Railway	22	3	1	18	28	82	7

Second Division

Royal Artillery (Portsmouth)	22	19	1	2	75	22	39
Warmley (Bristol)	22	19	0	3	108	15	38
West Herts	22	11	6	5	50	48	28
Uxbridge	22	11	2	9	39	57	24
St Albans	22	9	5	8	47	41	23
Dartford	22	11	0	11	68	55	22
Southall	22	8	2	12	49	61	18
Chesham	22	8	2	12	38	48	18
Olsd St Stephen's	22	7	2	13	47	66	16
Wycombe Wanderers	22	7	2	13	37	55	16
Maidenhead	22	4	4	14	27	81	12
Royal Engineers Training Battalion	22	4	2	16	26	62	10

1898-99

First Division

Southampton	24	15	5	4	54	24	35
Bristol City	24	15	3	6	55	12	33
Millwall Athletic	24	12	6	6	59	35	30
Chatham	24	10	8	6	32	23	28
Reading	24	9	8	7	31	24	26
New Brompton	24	10	5	9	38	30	25
Tottenham Hotspur	24	10	4	10	40	36	24
Bedminster	24	10	4	10	35	39	24
Swindon Town	24	9	5	10	43	49	23
Brighton United	24	9	2	13	37	48	20
Gravesend United	24	7	5	12	42	52	19
Sheppey United	24	5	3	16	23	53	13
Royal Artillery (Portsmouth)	24	4	4	16	17	60	12

Second Division (London Section)

Thames Ironworks	22	19	1	2	64	16	39
Wolverton L & NW Railway	22	13	4	5	88	43	30
Watford	22	14	2	6	62	35	30
Brentford	22	11	3	8	59	39	25
Wycombe Wanderers	22	10	2	10	55	57	22
Southall	22	11	0	11	44	55	22
Chesham	22	9	2	11	45	62	20
St Albans	22	8	3	11	45	59	19
Shepherds Bush	22	7	3	12	37	53	17
Fulham	22	6	4	12	36	44	16
Uxbridge	22	7	2	13	29	48	16
Maidenhead	22	3	2	17	33	86	8

Second Division (South West Section)

Cowes	10	10	0	0	58	8	20
Ryde	10	7	0	3	30	11	14
Freemantle	10	4	1	5	18	31	9
Sandown	10	4	0	6	20	29	8
Eastleigh	10	2	1	7	17	37	5
Andover	10	2	0	8	14	41	4

1899-1900

First Division

Tottenham Hotspur	28	20	4	4	67	26	44
Portsmouth	28	20	1	7	58	27	41
Southampton	28	17	1	10	70	33	35
Reading	28	15	2	11	41	28	32
Swindon Town	28	15	2	11	50	42	32
Bedminster	28	13	2	13	44	45	28
Millwall Athletic	28	12	3	13	36	37	27
Queens Park Rangers	28	12	2	14	49	57	26
Bristol City	28	9	7	12	43	47	25
Bristol Rovers	28	11	3	14	46	55	25
New Brompton	28	9	6	13	39	49	24
Gravesend United	28	10	4	14	38	58	24
Chatham	28	10	3	15	38	58	23
Thames Ironworks	28	8	5	15	30	45	21
Sheppey United	28	3	7	18	24	66	13

Second Division

Watford	20	14	2	4	57	25	30
Fulham	20	10	4	6	44	23	24
Chesham Town	20	11	2	7	43	37	24
Wolverton L & NW Railway	20	9	6	5	46	36	24
Grays United	20	8	6	6	63	29	22
Shepherds Bush	20	9	4	7	45	37	22
Dartford	20	8	3	9	36	44	19
Wycombe Wanderers	20	8	3	9	35	50	19
Brentford	20	5	7	8	31	48	17
Southall	20	6	3	11	21	44	15
Maidenhead	20	1	2	17	16	64	4

1900-01

First Division

Southampton	28	18	5	5	58	26	41
Bristol City	28	17	5	6	54	27	39
Portsmouth	28	17	4	7	56	32	38
Millwall Athletic	28	17	2	9	55	32	36
Tottenham Hotspur	28	16	4	8	55	33	36
West Ham United	28	14	5	9	40	28	33
Bristol Rovers	28	14	4	10	46	35	32
Queens Park Rangers	28	11	4	13	43	48	26
Reading	28	8	8	12	24	25	24
Luton Town	28	11	2	15	43	49	24
Kettering	28	7	9	12	33	46	23
New Brompton	28	7	5	16	34	51	19
Gravesend United	28	6	7	15	32	85	19
Watford	28	6	4	18	24	52	16
Swindon Town	28	3	8	17	19	47	14

Second Division

Brentford	16	14	2	0	63	11	30
Grays United	16	12	2	2	62	12	26
Sheppey United	16	8	1	7	44	26	17
Shepherds Bush	16	8	1	7	30	30	17
Fulham	16	8	0	8	38	26	16
Chesham Town	16	5	1	10	26	39	11
Maidenhead	16	4	1	11	21	49	9
Wycombe Wanderers	16	4	1	11	23	68	9
Southall	16	4	1	11	22	68	9

1901-02

First Division

Portsmouth	30	20	7	3	67	24	47
Tottenham Hotspur	30	18	6	6	61	22	42
Southampton	30	18	6	6	71	28	42
West Ham United	30	17	6	7	45	28	40
Reading	30	16	7	7	57	24	39
Millwall Athletic	30	13	6	11	48	31	32
Luton Town	30	11	10	9	31	35	32
Kettering	30	12	5	13	44	39	29
Bristol Rovers	30	12	5	13	43	39	29
New Brompton	30	10	7	13	39	38	27
Northampton	30	11	5	14	53	64	27
Queens Park Rangers	30	8	7	15	34	56	23
Watford	30	9	4	17	36	60	22
Wellingborough	30	9	4	17	34	75	22
Brentford	30	7	6	17	34	61	20
Swindon Town	30	2	3	25	17	93	7

Second Division

Fulham	16	13	0	3	51	19	26
Grays United	16	12	1	3	49	14	25
Brighton & Hove Albion	16	11	0	5	34	17	22
Wycombe Wanderers	16	7	3	6	36	30	17
West Hampstead	16	6	4	6	39	29	16
Shepherds Bush	16	6	1	9	31	31	13
Southall	16	5	2	9	28	52	12
Maidenhead	16	3	1	12	23	59	7
Chesham Town	16	2	2	12	24	64	6

1902-03

First Division

	P	W	D	L	F	A	Pts
Southampton	30	20	8	2	83	20	48
Reading	30	19	7	4	72	30	45
Portsmouth	30	17	7	6	69	32	41
Tottenham Hotspur	30	14	7	9	47	31	35
Bristol Rovers	30	13	8	9	46	34	34
New Brompton	30	11	11	8	37	35	33
Millwall Athletic	30	14	3	13	52	37	31
Northampton Town	30	12	6	12	39	48	30
Queens Park Rangers	30	11	6	13	34	42	28
West Ham United	30	9	10	11	35	49	28
Luton Town	30	10	7	13	43	44	27
Swindon Town	30	10	7	13	38	46	27
Kettering	30	8	11	11	33	40	27
Wellingborough	30	11	3	16	36	56	25
Watford	30	6	4	20	35	87	16
Brentford	30	2	1	27	16	84	5

Second Division

	P	W	D	L	F	A	Pts
Fulham	10	7	1	2	27	7	15
Brighton & Hove Albion	10	7	1	2	34	11	15
Grays United	10	7	0	3	28	12	14
Wycombe Wanderers	10	3	3	4	13	19	9
Chesham Town	10	2	1	7	9	37	5
Southall	10	1	0	9	10	35	2

1903-04

First Division

	P	W	D	L	F	A	Pts
Southampton	34	22	6	6	75	30	50
Tottenham Hotspur	34	16	11	7	54	37	43
Bristol Rovers	34	17	8	9	66	42	42
Portsmouth	34	17	8	9	41	38	42
Queens Park Rangers	34	15	11	8	53	37	41
Reading	34	14	13	7	48	35	41
Millwall	34	16	8	10	64	42	40
Luton Town	34	14	12	8	38	33	40
Plymouth Argyle	34	13	10	11	44	34	36
Swindon Town	34	10	11	13	30	42	31
Fulham	34	9	12	13	33	34	30
West Ham United	34	10	7	17	38	43	27
Brentford	34	9	9	16	34	48	27
Wellingborough	34	11	5	18	44	63	27
Northampton Town	34	10	7	17	36	69	27
New Brompton	34	6	13	15	26	43	25
Brighton & Hove Albion	34	6	12	16	45	79	24
Kettering	34	6	7	21	30	78	19

Second Division

	P	W	D	L	F	A	Pts
Watford	20	18	2	0	70	15	38
Portsmouth Reserves	20	15	2	3	85	25	32
Millwall Reserves	20	9	4	7	35	39	22
Southampton Reserves	20	9	3	8	59	35	21
Grays United	20	9	3	8	25	55	21
Fulham Reserves	20	8	4	8	40	34	20
Swindon Town Reserves	20	8	3	9	50	44	19
Reading Reserves	20	8	2	10	43	42	18
Wycombe Wanderers	20	5	5	10	29	64	15
Southall	20	4	2	14	25	62	10
Chesham Town	20	1	2	17	19	65	4

1904-05

First Division

	P	W	D	L	F	A	Pts
Bristol Rovers	34	20	8	6	74	36	48
Reading	34	18	7	9	57	38	43
Southampton	34	18	7	9	54	40	43
Plymouth Argyle	34	18	5	11	57	39	41
Tottenham Hotspur	34	15	8	11	53	34	38
Fulham	34	14	10	10	46	34	38
Queens Park Rangers	34	14	8	12	51	46	36
Portsmouth	34	16	4	14	61	56	36
New Brompton	34	11	11	12	40	41	33
West Ham United	34	12	8	14	48	42	32
Brighton & Hove Albion	34	13	6	15	44	45	32
Northampton Town	34	12	8	14	43	54	32
Watford	34	14	3	17	41	44	31
Brentford	34	10	9	15	33	38	29
Millwall	34	11	7	16	38	47	29
Swindon Town	34	12	5	17	41	59	29
Luton Town	34	12	3	19	45	54	27
Wellingborough	34	5	3	26	25	104	13

Second Division

	P	W	D	L	F	A	Pts
Fulham Reserves	22	16	4	2	78	25	36
Portsmouth Reserves	22	14	2	6	75	28	30
Swindon Town Reserves	22	12	3	7	54	47	27
Grays United	22	11	3	8	61	40	25
Southampton Reserves	22	10	5	7	52	35	25
Brighton & Hove Albion	22	9	3	10	48	49	21
West Ham United Reserves	22	8	5	9	45	47	21
Clapton Orient	22	7	7	8	47	56	21
Watford Reserves	22	5	6	11	30	62	16
Southall	22	7	2	13	31	66	16
Wycombe Wanderers	22	6	2	14	37	70	14
Reading Reserves	22	4	4	14	24	57	12

1905-06

First Division

	P	W	D	L	F	A	Pts
Fulham	34	19	12	3	44	15	50
Southampton	34	19	7	8	58	39	45
Portsmouth	34	17	9	8	61	35	43
Luton Town	34	17	7	10	64	40	41
Tottenham Hotspur	34	16	7	11	46	29	39
Plymouth Argyle	34	16	7	11	52	33	39
Norwich City	34	13	10	11	46	38	36
Bristol Rovers	34	15	5	14	56	56	35
Brentford	34	14	7	13	43	52	35
Reading	34	12	9	13	53	46	33
West Ham United	34	14	5	15	42	39	33
Millwall	34	11	11	12	38	41	33
Queens Park Rangers	34	12	7	15	58	44	31
Watford	34	8	10	16	38	57	26
Swindon Town	34	8	9	17	31	52	25
Brighton & Hove Albion	34	9	7	18	30	55	25
New Brompton	34	7	8	19	20	62	22
Northampton Town	34	8	5	21	32	79	21

Second Division

	P	W	D	L	F	A	Pts
Crystal Palace	24	19	4	1	66	14	42
Leyton	24	16	6	2	61	18	38
Portsmouth Reserves	24	12	8	4	52	24	32
Fulham Reserves	24	11	6	7	52	39	28
Southampton Reserves	24	7	9	8	39	41	23
Southern United	24	8	7	9	45	49	23
St Leonard's United	24	9	4	11	54	50	22
Watford Reserves	24	8	5	11	43	47	21
West Ham United Reserves	24	7	5	12	46	48	19
Grays United	24	8	3	13	24	77	19
Reading Reserves	24	6	5	13	36	49	15
Swindon Town Reserves	24	5	5	14	36	51	15
Wycombe Wanderers	24	5	3	16	36	83	13

1906-07

First Division

Fulham	38	20	13	5	58	32	53
Portsmouth	38	22	7	9	64	36	51
Brighton & Hove Albion	38	18	9	11	53	43	45
Luton Town	38	18	9	11	52	52	45
West Ham United	38	15	14	9	60	41	44
Tottenham Hotspur	38	17	9	12	63	45	43
Millwall	38	18	6	14	71	50	42
Norwich City	38	15	12	11	57	48	42
Watford	38	13	16	9	46	43	42
Brentford	38	17	8	13	57	56	42
Southampton	38	13	9	16	49	56	35
Reading	38	14	6	18	57	47	34
Leyton	38	11	12	15	38	60	34
Bristol Rovers	38	12	9	17	55	54	33
Plymouth Argyle	38	10	13	15	43	50	33
New Brompton	38	12	9	17	47	59	33
Swindon Town	38	11	11	16	43	54	33
Queens Park Rangers	38	11	10	17	47	55	32
Crystal Palace	38	8	9	21	46	66	25
Northampton Town	38	5	9	24	29	88	19

Second Division

Southend United	22	14	5	3	58	23	33
West Ham United Reserves	22	14	3	5	64	30	31
Portsmouth Reserves	22	11	6	5	53	24	28
Fulham Reserves	22	11	4	7	47	32	26
Hastings & St Leonards	21	10	4	7	46	31	24
Tunbridge Wells Rangers	22	10	1	11	46	36	21
Salisbury City	22	9	2	11	40	42	20
Southampton Reserves	22	8	2	12	37	56	18
Swindon Town Reserves	22	7	3	12	35	43	17
Reading Reserves	22	6	4	12	32	47	16
Royal Engineers (Aldershot)	21	5	4	12	27	58	14
Wycombe Wanderers	22	4	6	12	28	68	14

The match between Tunbridge Wells Rangers and Royal Engineers (Aldershot) was not completed.

1907-08

First Division

Queens Park Rangers	38	21	9	8	82	57	51
Plymouth Argyle	38	19	11	8	50	31	49
Millwall	38	19	8	11	49	32	46
Crystal Palace	38	17	10	11	54	51	44
Swindon Town	38	16	10	12	55	40	42
Bristol Rovers	38	16	10	12	59	56	42
Tottenham Hotspur	38	17	7	14	59	48	41
Northampton Town	38	15	11	12	50	41	41
Portsmouth	38	17	6	15	63	52	40
West Ham United	38	15	10	13	47	48	40
Southampton	38	16	6	16	51	60	38
Reading	38	15	6	17	55	50	36
Bradford Park Avenue	38	12	12	14	53	54	36
Watford	38	12	10	16	47	49	34
Brentford	38	14	5	19	49	52	33
Norwich City	38	12	9	17	46	49	33
Brighton & Hove Albion	38	12	8	18	46	59	32
Luton Town	38	12	6	20	33	56	30
Leyton	38	8	11	19	51	73	27
New Brompton	38	9	7	22	44	75	25

Second Division

Southend	18	13	3	2	47	16	29
Portsmouth Reserves	18	10	5	3	39	22	25
Croydon Common	18	10	3	5	35	25	23
Hastings & St Leonard's	18	10	2	6	43	29	22
Southampton Reserves	18	7	4	7	54	46	18
Tunbridge Wells Rangers	18	7	3	8	42	38	17
Salisbury City	18	6	4	8	35	46	16
Swindon Town Reserves	18	5	5	8	36	40	15
Brighton & Hove Albion Reserves	18	4	4	10	34	47	12
Wycombe Wanderers	18	1	1	16	16	72	3

1908-09

First Division

Northampton Town	40	25	5	10	90	45	55
Swindon Town	40	22	5	13	96	55	49
Southampton	40	19	10	11	67	58	48
Portsmouth	40	18	10	12	68	60	46
Bristol Rovers	40	17	9	14	60	63	43
Exeter City	40	18	6	16	56	65	42
New Brompton	40	17	7	16	48	59	41
Reading	40	11	18	11	60	57	40
Luton Town	40	17	6	17	59	60	40
Plymouth Argyle	40	15	10	15	46	47	40
Millwall	40	16	6	18	59	61	38
Southend United	40	14	10	16	52	54	38
Leyton	40	15	8	17	52	55	38
Watford	40	14	9	17	51	64	37
Queens Park Rangers	40	12	12	16	52	50	36
Crystal Palace	40	12	12	16	62	62	36
West Ham United	40	16	4	20	56	60	36
Brighton & Hove Albion	40	14	7	19	60	61	35
Norwich City	40	12	11	17	59	75	35
Coventry City	40	15	4	21	64	91	34
Brentford	40	13	7	20	59	74	33

Second Division

Croydon Common	12	10	0	2	67	14	20
Hastings & St Leonard's	12	8	1	3	42	18	17
Depot Battalion Royal Engineers	12	8	1	3	23	22	17
2nd Grenadier Guards	12	5	0	7	21	33	10
South Farnborough Athletic	12	2	4	6	20	39	8
Salisbury City	12	3	1	8	24	36	7
Chesham Town	12	2	1	9	17	52	5

1909-10

First Division

Brighton & Hove Albion	42	23	13	6	69	28	59
Swindon Town	42	22	10	10	92	46	54
Queens Park Rangers	42	19	13	10	56	47	51
Northampton Town	42	22	4	16	90	44	48
Southampton	42	16	16	10	64	55	48
Portsmouth	42	20	7	15	70	63	47
Crystal Palace	42	20	6	16	69	50	46
Coventry City	42	19	8	15	71	60	46
West Ham United	42	15	15	12	69	56	45
Leyton	42	16	11	15	60	46	43
Plymouth Argyle	42	16	11	15	61	54	43
New Brompton	42	19	5	18	76	74	43
Bristol Rovers	42	16	10	16	37	48	42
Brentford	42	16	9	17	50	58	41
Luton Town	42	15	11	16	72	92	41
Millwall	42	15	7	20	45	59	37
Norwich City	42	13	9	20	59	78	35
Exeter City	42	14	6	22	60	69	34
Watford	42	10	13	19	51	76	33
Southend United	42	12	9	21	51	90	33
Croydon Common	42	13	5	24	52	96	31
Reading	42	7	10	25	38	73	24

Second Division - Section A

Stoke	10	10	0	0	48	9	20
Ton Pentre	10	4	2	4	17	21	10
Merthyr Town	9	4	1	4	16	21	9
Salisbury City	8	2	1	5	7	18	5
Burton United	6	2	0	4	8	21	4
Aberdare	7	1	0	6	6	11	2

Second Division - Section B

Hastings & St Leonard's	9	6	3	0	26	11	15
Kettering	10	6	0	4	34	19	12
Chesham Town	10	5	2	3	25	25	12
Peterborough City	10	4	2	4	16	23	10
South Farnborough Athletic	10	4	1	5	23	19	9
Romford	9	0	0	9	7	33	0

1910-11

First Divison

Swindon Town	38	24	5	9	80	31	53
Northampton Town	38	18	12	8	54	27	48
Brighton & Hove Albion	38	20	8	10	58	35	48
Crystal Palace	38	17	13	8	55	48	47
West Ham United	38	17	11	10	63	46	45
Queens Park Rangers	38	13	14	11	52	41	40
Leyton	38	16	8	14	57	52	40
Plymouth Argyle	38	15	9	14	54	55	39
Luton Town	38	15	8	15	67	63	38
Norwich City	38	15	8	15	46	48	38
Coventry City	38	16	6	16	65	68	38
Brentford	38	14	9	15	41	42	37
Exeter City	38	14	9	15	51	53	37
Watford	38	13	9	16	49	65	35
Millwall	38	11	9	18	42	54	31
Bristol Rovers	38	10	10	18	42	55	30
Southampton	38	11	8	19	42	67	30
New Brompton	38	11	8	19	34	65	30
Southend United	38	10	9	19	47	64	29
Portsmouth	38	8	11	19	34	53	27

Second Division

Reading	22	16	3	3	55	11	35
Stoke	22	17	1	4	72	21	35
Merthyr Town	22	15	3	4	52	22	33
Cardiff City	22	12	4	6	48	29	28
Croydon Common	22	11	3	8	61	26	25
Treharris	22	10	3	9	38	31	23
Aberdare	22	9	5	8	38	33	23
Ton Pentre	22	10	3	9	44	40	23
Walsall	22	7	4	11	37	41	18
Kettering	22	6	1	15	34	68	13
Chesham Town	22	1	3	18	16	93	5
Salisbury City	22	0	3	19	16	92	3

1911-12

First Divison

Queens Park Rangers	38	21	11	6	59	35	53
Plymouth Argyle	38	23	6	9	63	31	52
Northampton Town	38	22	7	9	82	41	51
Swindon Town	38	21	6	11	82	50	48
Brighton & Hove Albion	38	19	9	10	73	35	47
Coventry City	38	17	8	13	66	54	42
Crystal Palace	38	15	10	13	70	46	40
Millwall	38	15	10	13	60	57	40
Watford	38	13	10	15	56	68	36
Stoke	38	13	10	15	51	63	36
Reading	38	11	14	13	43	69	36
Norwich City	38	10	14	14	40	60	34
West Ham United	38	13	7	18	64	69	33
Brentford	38	12	9	17	60	65	33
Exeter City	38	11	11	16	48	62	33
Southampton	38	10	11	17	46	63	31
Bristol Rovers	38	9	13	16	41	62	31
New Brompton	38	11	9	18	35	72	31
Luton Town	38	9	10	19	49	61	28
Leyton	38	7	11	20	27	62	25

Second Division

Merthyr Town	26	19	3	4	60	14	41
Portsmouth	26	19	3	4	73	20	41
Cardiff City	26	15	4	7	55	26	34
Southend United	26	16	1	9	73	24	33
Pontypridd	26	13	6	7	39	24	32
Ton Pentre	26	12	3	11	56	45	27
Walsall	26	13	1	11	44	41	27
Treharris	26	11	5	10	44	47	27
Aberdare	26	10	3	13	39	44	23
Kettering	26	11	0	15	37	62	22
Croydon Common	26	8	2	15	43	45	18
Mardy	26	6	6	12	37	51	18
Cwm Albion	26	5	1	16	27	70	11
Chesham Town	26	1	0	25	18	131	2

1912-13

First Division

Plymouth Argyle	38	27	6	10	77	36	50
Swindon Town	38	20	8	10	66	41	48
West Ham United	38	18	12	8	66	43	48
Queens Park Rangers	38	18	10	10	46	35	43
Crystal Palace	38	17	11	10	55	36	45
Millwall	38	19	7	12	62	43	45
Exeter City	38	18	8	12	48	44	44
Reading	38	17	8	13	59	55	42
Brighton & Hove Albion	38	13	12	13	48	47	38
Northampton Town	38	12	12	14	61	48	36
Portsmouth	38	14	8	16	41	49	36
Merthyr Town	38	12	12	14	42	60	36
Coventry City	38	13	8	17	53	59	34
Watford	38	12	10	16	43	50	34
Gillingham	38	12	10	16	36	53	34
Bristol Rovers	38	12	9	17	55	64	33
Southampton	38	10	11	17	40	72	31
Norwich City	38	10	9	19	39	50	29
Brentford	38	11	5	22	42	55	27
Stoke	38	10	4	24	39	75	24

Second Division

Cardiff City	24	18	5	1	54	15	41
Southend United	24	14	6	4	43	23	34
Swansea Town	24	12	7	5	29	23	31
Croydon Common	24	13	4	7	51	29	30
Luton Town	24	13	4	7	52	39	30
Llanelly	24	9	6	9	33	39	24
Pontypridd	24	6	11	7	30	28	23
Mid Rhondda	24	9	4	11	33	31	22
Aberdare	24	8	6	10	38	40	22
Newport County	24	7	5	12	29	36	19
Mardy	24	6	3	15	38	38	15
Treharris	24	5	2	17	18	60	12
Ton Pentre	24	3	3	18	22	69	9

1913-14

First Division

Swindon Town	38	21	8	9	81	41	50
Crystal Palace	38	17	16	5	60	32	50
Northampton Town	38	14	19	5	50	37	47
Reading	38	17	10	11	43	36	44
Plymouth Argyle	38	15	13	10	46	42	43
West Ham United	38	15	12	11	61	60	42
Brighton & Hove Albion	38	15	12	11	43	45	42
Queens Park Rangers	38	16	9	13	45	43	41
Portsmouth	38	14	12	12	57	48	40
Cardiff City	38	13	12	13	46	42	38
Southampton	38	15	7	16	55	54	37
Exeter City	38	10	16	12	39	38	36
Gillingham	38	13	9	16	48	49	35
Norwich City	38	9	17	12	49	51	35
Millwall	38	11	12	15	51	56	34
Southend Unied	38	10	12	16	41	66	32
Bristol Rovers	38	10	11	17	46	67	31
Watford	38	10	9	19	50	56	29
Merthyr Town	38	9	10	19	38	61	28
Coventry City	38	6	14	18	43	68	26

Second Division

Croydon Common	30	23	5	2	76	14	51
Luton Town	30	24	3	3	92	22	51
Brentford	30	20	4	6	80	18	44
Swansea Town	30	20	4	6	66	23	44
Stoke	30	19	2	9	71	34	40
Newport County	30	14	8	8	49	38	36
Mid Rhondda	30	13	7	10	55	37	33
Pontypridd	30	14	5	11	43	38	33
Llanelly	30	12	4	14	45	39	28
Barry	30	9	8	13	44	70	26
Abertillery	30	8	4	18	44	57	20
Ton Pentre	30	8	4	18	33	61	20
Mardy	30	6	6	18	30	60	18
Caerphilly	30	4	7	19	21	103	15
Aberdare	30	4	5	21	33	87	13
Treharris	30	2	4	24	19	106	8

1914-15

First Division

Watford	38	22	8	8	68	46	52
Reading	38	21	7	10	68	43	49
Cardiff City	38	22	4	12	72	38	48
West Ham United	38	18	9	11	58	47	45
Northampton Town	38	16	11	11	56	51	43
Southampton	38	19	5	14	78	74	43
Portsmouth	38	16	10	12	54	42	42
Millwall	38	16	10	12	50	51	42
Swindon Town	38	15	11	12	77	59	41
Brighton & Hove Albion	38	16	7	15	46	47	39
Exeter City	38	15	8	15	50	41	38
Queens Park Rangers	38	13	12	13	55	56	38
Norwich City	38	11	14	13	53	56	36
Luton Town	38	13	8	17	61	73	34
Crystal Palace	38	13	8	17	47	61	34
Bristol Rovers	38	14	3	21	53	75	31
Plymouth Argyle	38	8	14	16	51	61	30
Southend United	38	10	8	20	44	64	28
Croydon Common	38	9	9	20	47	63	27
Gillingham	38	6	8	24	43	82	20

Second Division

Stoke	24	17	4	3	62	15	38
Stalybridge Celtic	24	17	3	4	47	22	37
Merthyr Town	24	15	5	4	46	20	35
Swansea Town	24	16	1	7	48	21	33
Coventry City	24	13	2	9	56	33	28
Ton Pentre	24	11	6	7	42	43	28
Brentford	24	8	7	9	35	45	23
Llanelly	24	10	1	13	39	32	21
Barry	24	6	5	13	30	35	17
Newport County	24	7	3	14	27	42	17
Pontypridd	24	5	6	13	31	58	16
Mid Rhondda	24	3	6	15	17	40	12
Ebbw Vale	24	3	1	20	23	88	7

1919-20

First Division

Portsmouth	42	23	12	7	73	27	58
Watford	42	26	6	10	69	42	58
Crystal Palace	42	22	12	8	69	43	56
Cardiff City	42	18	17	7	70	43	53
Plymouth Argyle	42	20	10	12	57	29	50
Queens Park Rangers	42	18	10	14	62	50	46
Reading	42	16	13	13	51	43	45
Southampton	42	18	8	16	72	63	44
Swansea Town	42	16	11	15	53	45	43
Exeter City	42	17	9	16	57	51	43
Southend United	42	13	17	12	46	48	43
Norwich City	42	15	11	16	64	57	41
Swindon Town	42	17	7	18	65	68	41
Millwall	42	14	12	16	52	55	40
Brentford	42	15	10	17	52	59	40
Brighton & Hove Albion	42	14	8	20	60	72	36
Bristol Rovers	42	11	13	18	61	78	35
Newport County	42	13	7	22	45	70	33
Northampton Town	42	12	9	21	64	103	33
Luton Town	42	10	10	22	51	76	30
Merthyr Town	42	9	11	22	47	78	29
Gillingham	42	10	7	25	34	74	27

Second Division

Mid Rhondda	20	17	3	0	79	10	37
Ton Pentre	20	12	7	1	50	14	31
Llanelly	20	10	5	5	47	30	25
Pontypridd	20	10	3	7	33	29	23
Ebbw Vale	20	7	7	6	38	40	21
Barry	20	7	5	8	32	27	19
Mardy	20	7	5	8	29	30	19
Abertillery	20	6	5	9	29	40	17
Porth Athletic	20	4	4	12	30	74	12
Aberaman Athletic	20	4	3	13	28	48	11
Caerphilly	20	1	3	16	20	74	5

1920-21

English Section

Brighton & Hove Albion Reserves	24	16	3	5	65	29	35
Portsmouth Reserves	24	13	7	4	44	20	33
Millwall Reserves	24	12	4	8	46	24	28
Southampton Reserves	24	10	7	7	53	35	27
Boscombe	24	10	6	8	25	40	26
Reading Reserves	24	11	3	10	41	34	25
Luton Town Reserves	24	8	8	8	38	35	24
Charlton Athletic	24	8	8	8	41	41	24
Watford Reserves	24	9	4	11	43	45	22
Norwich City Reserves	24	7	7	10	31	39	21
Gillingham Reserves	24	6	5	13	32	47	17
Chatham	24	5	6	13	24	47	16
Thornycrofts	24	4	6	14	29	74	14

Welsh Section

Barry	20	13	4	3	35	12	30
Aberdare Athletic	20	12	3	5	29	23	27
Ebbw Vale	20	10	5	5	34	23	25
Pontypridd	20	10	3	7	34	23	23
Mid Rhondda	20	10	3	7	26	18	23
Abertillery Town	20	8	5	7	35	24	21
Ton Pentre	20	7	5	8	32	34	19
Aberaman Athletic	20	5	7	8	30	33	17
Llanelly	20	7	2	11	28	46	16
Mardy	20	2	6	12	18	39	10
Porth Athletic	20	3	3	14	28	54	9

1921-22

English Section

Plymouth Argyle Reserves	36	22	5	9	91	38	49
Bristol City Reserves	36	18	8	10	73	50	44
Portsmouth Reserves	36	17	10	9	63	41	44
Southampton Reserves	36	19	5	12	70	47	43
Gillingham Reserves	36	17	9	10	65	47	43
Charlton Athletic Reserves	36	18	6	12	69	54	42
Boscombe	36	17	5	14	38	55	39
Luton Town Reserves	36	17	4	15	50	54	38
Watford Reserves	36	15	7	14	65	53	37
Brighton & Hove Albion Reserves	36	12	13	11	60	52	37
Bath City	36	16	5	15	55	53	37
Swindon Town Reserves	36	14	7	15	59	46	35
Bristol Rovers Reserves	36	13	7	16	50	82	33
Millwall Reserves	36	13	4	19	49	53	30
Reading Reserves	36	11	7	18	46	59	29
Exeter City Reserves	36	10	9	17	42	63	29
Guildford United	36	11	6	19	44	56	28
Norwich City Reserves	36	10	6	20	47	86	26
Southend United Reserves	36	9	3	24	47	92	21

Welsh Section

Ebbw Vale	16	11	3	2	33	11	25
Ton Pentre	16	9	4	3	35	14	22
Aberaman Athletic	16	7	5	4	25	19	19
Porth Athletic	16	6	6	4	31	20	18
Pontypridd	16	7	4	5	28	19	18
Swansea Town Reserves	16	7	4	5	24	17	18
Barry	16	3	3	10	14	35	9
Abertillery Town	16	3	2	11	21	45	8
Mardy	16	2	3	11	14	43	7

1922-23

English Section

Bristol City Reserves	38	24	5	9	84	39	53
Boscombe	38	22	7	9	67	34	51
Portsmouth Reserves	38	23	3	12	93	51	49
Bristol Rovers Reserves	38	20	8	10	59	41	48
Plymouth Argyle Reserves	38	20	7	11	74	41	47
Torquay United	38	18	8	12	63	38	44
Brighton & Hove Albion Reserves	38	20	3	15	95	60	43
Luton Town Reserves	38	16	11	11	67	56	43
Southend United Reserves	38	18	6	14	69	68	42
Southampton Reserves	38	18	5	15	65	54	41
Millwall Reserves	38	15	10	13	61	55	40
Coventry City Reserves	38	15	8	15	56	61	38
Guildford Town Reserves	38	15	7	16	65	59	37
Swindon Town Reserves	38	13	6	19	54	73	32
Bath City	38	10	8	20	44	71	28
Watford Reserves	38	11	6	21	34	79	28
Yeovil & Petters United	38	10	6	22	56	104	26
Norwich City Reserves	38	9	7	22	42	68	25
Exeter City Reserves	38	10	5	23	43	81	25
Reading Reserves	38	7	6	25	43	95	20

Welsh Section

Ebbw Vale	12	6	5	1	22	15	17
Aberaman Athletic	12	7	2	3	30	19	16
Swansea Town Reserves	12	6	2	4	25	14	14
Pontypridd	12	6	2	4	18	18	14
Barry	12	4	3	5	15	11	11
Bridgend Town	12	4	2	6	15	21	10
Porth Athletic	12	0	2	10	18	24	2

1923-24

Eastern Section

Peterborough & Fletton United	30	20	2	8	54	31	42
Leicester City Reserves	30	19	3	8	72	30	41
Southampton Reserves	30	18	5	7	60	36	41
Millwall Reserves	30	18	3	9	56	38	39
Portsmouth Reserves	30	16	2	12	66	37	34
Brighton & Hove Albion Reserves	30	13	7	10	55	42	33
Norwich City Reserves	30	13	6	11	46	34	32
Folkestone	30	12	5	13	61	51	29
Coventry City Reserves	30	10	8	12	39	4	28
Watford Reserves	30	11	6	13	36	48	28
Reading Reserves	30	11	6	13	32	43	28
Northampton Town Reserves	30	9	10	11	32	47	28
Luton Town Reserves	30	10	7	13	40	49	27
Guildford United	30	7	5	18	38	72	19
Kettering	30	5	8	17	30	67	18
Bournemouth Reserves	30	4	5	21	40	85	13

Western Section

Yeovil & Petters United	34	25	3	6	71	30	53
Plymouth Argyle Reserves	34	21	5	8	74	37	47
Pontypridd	34	19	8	7	81	44	46
Torquay United	34	19	7	8	59	25	45
Bristol City Reserves	34	17	9	8	63	39	43
Swansea Town Reserves	34	19	5	10	62	38	43
Bristol Rovers Reserves	34	17	6	11	69	43	40
Cardiff City Reserves	34	15	4	15	55	31	34
Exeter City Reserves	34	11	11	12	48	47	33
Weymouth	34	15	3	16	48	60	33
Llanelly	34	14	5	15	47	62	33
Swindon Town Reserves	34	11	6	17	36	60	28
Bridgend Town	34	11	5	18	57	72	27
Newport County Reserves	34	10	7	17	57	79	27
Ebbw Vale	34	8	8	18	38	62	24
Bath City	34	6	9	19	32	71	21
Barry	34	6	7	21	36	74	19
Aberaman Athletic	34	6	4	24	41	87	16

1924-25

Eastern Section

Southampton Reserves	32	17	10	5	65	30	44
Kettering Town	32	17	6	9	67	39	40
Brighton & Hove Albion Reserves	32	15	10	7	68	42	40
Millwall Reserves	32	15	10	7	65	48	40
Peterborough & Fletton United	32	15	9	8	56	29	39
Bournemouth Reserves	32	15	9	8	66	48	39
Leicester City Reserves	32	15	7	10	61	45	37
Portsmouth Reserves	32	15	7	10	51	40	37
Folkestone	32	13	11	8	55	46	37
Norwich City Reserves	32	13	8	11	65	58	34
Coventry City Reserves	32	12	9	11	51	41	33
Luton Town Reserves	32	15	2	15	48	63	32
Northampton Town Reserves	32	10	5	17	38	59	25
Watford Reserves	32	7	7	18	44	71	21
Nuneaton Town	32	8	2	22	37	62	18
Reading Reserves	32	8	1	23	38	87	17
Guildford United	32	4	3	25	40	107	11

Western Section

Swansea Town Reserves	38	25	4	9	73	26	54
Plymouth Argyle Reserves	38	22	10	6	97	35	54
Pontypridd	38	24	4	10	81	39	52
Bridgend Town	38	20	11	7	74	52	51
Mid Rhondda United	38	21	6	11	79	48	48
Weymouth	38	21	4	13	77	50	46
Cardiff City Reserves	38	18	6	14	56	44	42
Newport County Reserves	38	17	8	13	71	60	42
Swindon Town Reserves	38	17	8	13	48	46	42
Bristol City Reserves	38	15	5	13	51	43	41
Yeovil & Petters United	38	15	10	13	49	50	40
Exeter City Reserves	38	16	6	16	78	55	38
Taunton Unied	38	15	6	17	55	51	36
Bristol Rovers Reserves	38	13	6	19	45	50	32
Torquay United	38	9	11	18	41	73	29
Llanelly	38	6	12	20	49	94	24
Ebbw Vale	38	9	6	23	40	91	24
Bath City	38	8	8	22	28	85	24
Barry	38	8	6	24	38	82	22
Aberaman Athletic	38	6	7	25	39	95	19

1925-26

Eastern Section

Millwall Reserves	34	24	6	4	106	37	54
Leicester City Reserves	34	23	2	9	105	60	48
Brighton & Hove Albion Reserves	34	21	4	9	105	69	46
Kettering Town	34	19	5	10	98	68	43
Peterborough & Fletton United	34	19	3	12	76	62	41
Portsmouth Reserves	34	17	5	12	76	67	39
Norwich City Reserves	34	17	4	13	85	90	38
Bournemouth Reserves	34	15	7	12	76	67	37
Southampton Reserves	34	14	7	13	65	72	35
Fulham Reserves	34	13	6	15	86	77	32
Grays Thurrock United	34	13	5	16	63	77	31
Guildford United	34	11	8	15	71	87	30
Watford Reserves	34	12	2	20	62	94	26
Luton Town Reserves	34	11	3	20	70	78	25
Folkestone	34	9	6	19	67	93	24
Reading Reserves	34	10	3	21	58	84	23
Coventry City Reserves	34	9	5	20	54	93	23
Nuneaton Town	34	7	3	24	61	113	17

Western Section

Plymouth Argyle Reserves	26	20	1	5	67	31	41
Bristol City Reserves	26	16	4	6	48	28	36
Bristol Rovers Reserves	26	13	4	9	51	35	30
Swindon Town Reserves	26	13	4	9	57	49	30
Ebbw Vale	26	13	3	10	60	46	29
Torquay United	26	12	5	9	59	46	29
Yeovil & Petters United	26	9	8	9	43	48	26
Mid Rhondda	26	12	1	13	47	49	25
Weymouth	26	10	3	13	64	60	23
Exeter City Reserves	26	8	5	13	40	49	21
Barry	26	8	4	14	47	55	20
Taunton United	26	9	2	15	44	60	20
Pontypridd	26	7	5	14	44	77	19
Bath City	26	7	1	18	38	86	15

1926-27

Eastern Section

Brighton & Hove Albion Reserves	32	21	6	5	86	47	48
Peterborough & Fletton United	32	18	9	5	80	39	45
Portsmouth Reserves	32	19	6	7	95	65	44
Kettering Town	32	15	10	7	66	41	40
Millwall Reserves	32	16	5	11	67	56	37
Bournemouth Reserves	32	14	6	12	69	64	34
Norwich City Reserves	32	14	5	13	79	74	33
Dartford	32	13	7	12	60	71	33
Reading Reserves	32	12	8	12	75	79	32
Luton Town Reserves	32	10	11	11	75	70	1
Leicester City Reserves	32	12	5	15	94	72	29
Watford Reserves	32	10	8	14	74	84	28
Southampton Reserves	32	10	6	16	57	77	26
Poole	32	9	6	17	55	86	24
Grays Thurrock United	32	10	3	19	49	66	23
Guildford United	32	6	7	19	57	106	19
Folkestone	32	7	4	21	57	98	18

Western Section

Torquay United	26	17	4	5	63	30	38
Bristol City Reserves	26	14	10	2	77	37	38
Plymouth Argyle Reserves	26	15	4	7	56	38	34
Ebbw Vale	26	14	2	10	67	45	30
Bristol Rovers Reserves	26	12	4	10	51	43	28
Swindon Town Reserves	26	11	5	10	60	57	27
Barry	26	11	4	11	65	50	26
Essex City Reserves	26	10	6	10	62	49	26
Weymouth	26	12	2	12	48	65	26
Newport County Reserves	26	9	6	11	57	53	24
Bath City	26	7	9	10	44	52	23
Yeovil & Petters United	26	9	5	12	49	66	23
Taunton United	26	4	4	18	36	83	12
Mid Rhondda United	26	2	5	19	22	89	9

1927-28

Easter Section

Kettering Town	34	23	6	5	90	39	52
Peterborough & Fletton United	34	21	3	10	73	43	45
Northfleet United	34	17	7	10	83	54	41
Brighton & Hove Albion Reserves	34	20	0	14	90	63	40
Norwich City Reserves	34	17	6	11	69	69	40
Southampton Reserves	34	16	7	11	92	70	39
Aldershot Town	34	17	5	12	85	66	39
Sittingbourne	34	16	5	13	64	70	37
Millwall Reserves	34	15	6	13	66	59	36
Poole	34	15	5	14	69	84	35
Folkestone	34	12	6	16	71	91	30
Guildford City	34	12	5	17	65	89	29
Dartford	34	12	4	18	46	49	28
Gillingham Reserves	34	10	7	17	72	84	27
Sheppey United	34	11	3	20	57	87	25
Chatham	34	10	4	20	49	70	24
Grays Thurrock United	34	10	3	21	48	88	23
Bournemouth Reserves	34	9	4	21	48	62	22

Western Section

Bristol City Reserves	30	20	3	7	95	51	43
Exeter City Reserves	30	18	4	8	104	56	40
Bristol Rovers Reserves	30	16	3	11	80	64	35
Plymouth Argyle Reserves	30	16	2	12	88	53	34
Newport County Reserves	30	13	8	9	99	70	34
Ebbw Vale	30	15	3	12	67	74	33
Swindon Town Reserves	30	13	4	13	80	74	30
Aberdare & Aberaman	30	12	6	12	62	68	30
Yeovil & Petters United	30	11	7	12	64	57	29
Torquay United Reserves	30	11	6	13	51	67	28
Bath City	30	12	3	15	64	68	27
Taunton Town	30	11	5	14	60	65	27
Weymouth	30	10	6	14	50	83	26
Merthyr Town Reserves	30	9	4	17	50	77	22
Barry	30	8	6	16	45	87	22
Mid Rhondda United	30	7	6	17	36	81	20

1928-29

Eastern Section

Kettering Town	36	24	4	8	96	46	52
Peterborough & Fletton United	36	21	5	10	86	44	47
Brighton & Hove Albion Reserves	36	19	9	8	91	56	47
Millwall Reserves	36	21	4	11	90	67	46
Bournemouth Reserves	36	20	5	11	82	58	45
Aldershot Town	36	18	5	13	68	52	41
Sheppey United	36	17	7	12	58	58	41
Folkestone	36	17	6	13	83	80	40
Northfleet United	36	17	4	15	87	65	38
Gillingham Reserves	36	15	8	13	68	70	38
Guildford City	36	13	11	12	85	78	37
Southampton Reserves	36	14	6	16	86	79	34
Poole	36	13	8	15	62	66	34
Thames Association	36	13	5	18	67	74	31
Dartford	36	10	6	20	55	106	26
Chatham	36	8	8	20	47	81	24
Sittingbourne	36	11	1	24	59	98	23
Norwich City Reserves	36	8	6	22	48	96	22
Grays Thurrock United	36	6	6	24	47	91	18

Western Section

Plymouth Argyle Reserves	26	15	6	5	69	27	36
Newport County Reserves	26	15	2	9	64	58	32
Bristol Rovers Reserves	26	14	3	9	54	45	31
Bristol City Reserves	26	14	2	10	70	46	30
Torquay United Reserves	26	13	4	9	52	42	30
Bath City	26	13	4	9	43	59	30
Exeter City Reserves	26	11	6	9	69	53	28
Lovells Athletic	26	11	6	9	54	48	28
Swindon Town Reserves	26	11	5	10	68	74	27
Yeovil & Petters United	26	11	2	13	49	57	24
Taunton Town	26	9	5	12	58	66	23
Ebbw Vale	26	9	5	12	56	66	23
Barry	26	6	3	17	38	66	15
Merthyr Town Reserves	26	3	1	22	37	92	7

1929-30

Eastern Section

Aldershot Town	32	21	6	5	84	39	48
Millwall Reserves	32	21	3	8	75	56	45
Thames Association	32	17	6	9	80	60	40
Peterborough & Fletton United	32	18	3	11	66	39	39
Northampton Town Reserves	32	17	4	11	86	60	38
Southampton Reserves	32	14	7	11	73	62	35
Sheppey United	32	15	5	12	76	69	35
Kettering Town	32	13	7	12	70	69	33
Dartford	32	14	5	13	57	59	33
Norwich City Reserves	32	14	3	15	69	69	31
Guildford City	32	13	2	17	65	97	28
Bournemouth Reserves	32	10	7	15	59	63	27
Brighton & Hove Albion Reserves	32	12	2	18	56	79	26
Folkestone	32	13	0	19	56	82	26
Sittingbourne	32	10	5	17	55	59	25
Northfleet United	32	6	7	19	53	77	19
Grays Thurrock United	32	7	2	23	54	101	16

Western Section

Bath City	28	16	6	6	85	52	38
Bristol Rovers Reserves	28	16	4	8	66	50	36
Taunton Town	28	14	7	7	50	40	35
Barry	28	15	3	10	65	55	33
Yeovil & Petters United	28	12	7	9	63	47	31
Plymouth Argyle Reserves	28	14	3	11	68	52	31
Newport County Reserves	28	13	4	11	68	76	30
Lovells Athletic	28	13	2	13	59	57	28
Exeter City Reserves	28	11	6	11	49	54	28
Bristol City Reserves	28	11	5	12	59	63	27
Swindon Town Reserves	28	10	6	12	69	67	26
Torquay United Reserves	28	10	6	12	76	77	26
Llanelly	28	10	4	14	55	52	24
Ebbw Vale	28	5	6	17	52	97	16
Merthyr Town Reserves	28	5	1	22	48	93	11

1930-31

Eastern Section

	P	W	D	L	F	A	Pts
Dartford	16	9	5	2	39	18	23
Aldershot Town	16	10	3	3	50	28	23
Norwich City Reserves	16	9	1	6	47	38	19
Peterborough & Fletton United	16	6	5	5	35	29	17
Thames Association Reserves	16	7	2	7	38	31	16
Millwall Reserves	16	7	0	9	47	40	14
Folkestone	16	4	3	9	31	46	11
Guildford City	16	5	1	10	28	53	11
Sheppey United	16	4	2	10	31	63	10

Western Section

	P	W	D	L	F	A	Pts
Exeter City Reserves	22	15	2	5	59	28	32
Llanelly	22	10	8	4	72	39	28
Merthyr Town	22	12	3	7	62	49	27
Plymouth Argyle Reserves	22	12	2	8	55	34	26
Bath City	22	10	6	6	47	39	26
Torquay United Reserves	22	9	5	8	66	49	23
Swindon Town Reserves	22	7	7	8	48	52	21
Bristol Rovers Reserves	22	7	6	9	58	64	20
Barry	22	7	5	10	29	39	19
Taunton Town	22	5	7	10	36	62	17
Newport County Reserves	22	6	2	14	36	66	14
Ebbw Vale	22	5	1	16	32	79	11

1931-32

Eastern Section

	P	W	D	L	F	A	Pts
Dartford	18	12	3	3	53	18	27
Folkestone	18	12	2	4	58	27	26
Guildford City	18	11	1	6	33	24	23
Norwich City Reserves	18	9	2	7	46	33	20
Millwall Reserves	18	9	2	7	41	39	20
Tunbridge Wells Rangers	18	7	5	6	23	25	19
Bournemouth Reserves	18	6	4	8	43	61	16
Peterborough & Fletton United	18	4	5	9	28	29	13
Aldershot Town	18	3	5	10	17	30	11
Sheppey United	18	2	1	15	16	72	5

Western Section

	P	W	D	L	F	A	Pts
Yeovil & Petters United	24	16	4	4	65	31	36
Plymouth Argyle Reserves	24	15	5	4	81	31	35
Bath City	24	12	7	5	50	33	31
Llanelly	24	12	4	8	65	46	28
Taunton Town	24	13	2	9	53	58	28
Newport County Reserves	24	10	6	8	70	51	26
Exeter City Reserves	24	9	7	8	59	43	25
Merthyr Town	24	9	4	11	66	73	22
Bristol Rovers Reserves	24	8	4	12	54	47	20
Swindon Town Reserves	24	8	4	12	54	95	20
Barry	24	7	3	14	58	76	17
Torquay United Reserves	24	5	6	13	43	66	16
Ebbw Vale	24	3	2	19	34	102	8

1932-33

Eastern Section

	P	W	D	L	F	A	Pts
Norwich City Reserves	14	9	2	3	34	22	20
Dartford	14	8	2	4	26	23	18
Folkestone	14	7	1	6	35	32	15
Bournemouth Reserves	14	5	4	5	36	33	14
Tunbridge Wells Rangers	14	5	2	7	23	24	12
Guildford City	14	5	2	7	22	28	12
Millwall Reserves	14	5	1	8	27	31	11
Aldershot Reserves	14	3	4	7	24	34	10

Western Section

	P	W	D	L	F	A	Pts
Bath City	20	13	4	3	62	34	30
Exeter City Reserves	20	12	3	5	62	46	27
Torquay United Reserves	20	12	1	7	56	37	25
Plymouth Argyle Reserves	20	11	2	7	68	38	24
Yeovil & Petters United	20	11	2	7	59	44	24
Llanelly	20	10	2	8	53	33	22
Bristol Rovers Reserves	20	7	3	10	53	65	17
Newport County Reserves	20	6	4	10	42	55	16
Merthyr Tydfil	20	7	1	12	39	58	15
Barry	20	3	4	13	30	72	10
Taunton Town	20	4	2	14	21	63	10

1933-34

Eastern Section

	P	W	D	L	F	A	Pts
Norwich City Reserves	16	9	4	3	41	15	22
Margate	16	8	3	5	23	20	19
Millwall Reserves	16	7	4	5	28	28	18
Clapton Orient Reserves	16	8	1	7	33	34	17
Bournemouth Reserves	16	6	3	7	28	30	15
Tunbridge Wells Rangers	16	6	2	8	25	36	14
Folkestone	16	5	3	8	26	26	13
Guildford City	16	5	3	8	27	33	13
Dartford	16	4	5	7	15	24	13

Western Section

	P	W	D	L	F	A	Pts
Plymouth Argyle Reserves	20	13	6	1	62	22	32
Bristol Rovers Reserves	20	14	3	3	56	27	31
Bath City	20	11	3	6	43	25	25
Torquay United Reserves	20	9	4	7	54	36	22
Yeovil & Petters United	20	10	1	9	35	39	21
Exeter City Reserves	20	8	3	9	54	47	19
Merthyr Town	20	8	2	10	39	50	18
Llanelly	20	8	1	11	25	39	17
Barry	20	4	5	11	37	64	13
Newport County Reserves	20	4	3	13	36	54	11
Taunton Town	20	5	1	14	27	65	11

Central Section

	P	W	D	L	F	A	Pts
Plymouth Argyle Reserves	18	16	1	1	47	14	33
Clapton Orient Reserves	18	9	3	6	35	25	21
Norwich City Reserves	18	8	4	6	41	27	20
Yeovil & Petters United	18	7	4	7	34	38	18
Bath City	18	7	3	8	31	36	17
Dartford	18	6	4	8	28	26	16
Tunbridge Wells Rangers	18	7	1	10	26	37	15
Llanelly	18	6	2	10	28	39	14
Folkestone	18	6	1	11	30	41	13
Guildford City	18	6	1	11	28	45	13

1934-35

Eastern Section

	P	W	D	L	F	A	Pts
Norwich City Reserves	18	12	1	5	52	21	25
Dartford	18	8	6	4	36	22	22
Margate	18	7	6	7	38	30	20
Bournemouth Reserves	18	8	3	8	34	26	19
Guildford City	18	7	5	6	41	34	19
Aldershot Reserves	18	7	3	8	29	43	17
Folkestone	18	5	6	7	30	39	16
Tunbridge Wells Rangers	18	6	4	8	32	56	16
Clapton Orient Reserves	18	5	4	9	33	35	14
Millwall Reserves	18	3	6	9	26	45	12

Western Section

	P	W	D	L	F	A	Pts
Yeovil & Petters United	16	11	2	3	49	18	24
Newport County Reserves	16	8	5	3	45	29	21
Plymouth Argyle Reserves	16	7	5	4	40	24	19
Exeter City Reserves	16	7	2	7	38	32	16
Bath City	16	6	4	6	35	32	16
Bristol Rovers Reserves	16	5	5	6	33	37	15
Barry	16	6	3	7	30	40	15
Torquay United Reserves	16	5	3	8	24	29	13
Taunton Town	16	1	3	12	13	66	5

Central Section

	P	W	D	L	F	A	Pts
Folkestone	20	11	4	5	43	31	26
Guildford City	20	11	4	5	43	39	26
Plymouth Argyle Reserves	20	6	9	5	40	28	21
Torquay United Reserves	20	7	6	7	34	35	20
Bristol Rovers Reserves	20	8	4	8	38	46	20
Margate	20	8	3	9	40	34	19
Dartford	20	8	3	9	43	38	19
Aldershot Reserves	20	8	3	9	33	44	19
Tunbridge Wells Rangers	20	8	2	10	37	37	18
Yeovil & Petters United	20	8	1	11	45	51	17
Bath City	20	6	3	11	34	43	15

1935-36

Eastern Section

Margate	18	13	2	3	49	16	28
Folkestone	18	11	3	4	46	23	25
Dartford	18	9	3	6	47	25	21
Tunbridge Wells Rangers	18	9	1	8	26	41	19
Clapton Orient Reserves	18	7	4	7	39	31	18
Millwall Reserves	18	7	3	8	42	39	17
Norwich City Reserves	18	8	0	10	39	38	16
Guildford City	18	6	3	9	32	52	15
Aldershot Reserves	18	6	1	11	24	45	13
Bournemouth Reserves	18	3	2	13	25	59	8

Western Section

Plymouth Argyle Reserves	16	12	3	1	51	18	27
Bristol Rovers Reserves	16	8	3	5	35	30	19
Newport County Reserves	16	8	3	5	29	30	19
Torquay United Reserves	16	7	1	8	25	28	15
Bath City	16	5	5	6	18	26	15
Cheltenham Town	16	6	2	8	32	28	14
Yeovil & Petters United	16	5	3	8	31	35	13
Barry	16	5	2	9	29	41	12
Exeter City Reserves	16	4	2	10	24	38	10

Central Section

Margate	20	14	3	3	57	18	31
Bristol Rovers Reserves	20	13	1	6	51	37	27
Plymouth Argyle Reserves	20	12	2	6	53	32	26
Aldershot Reserves	20	9	4	7	37	37	22
Folkestone	20	9	3	8	51	36	21
Tunbridge Wells Rangers	20	7	4	9	40	41	18
Dartford	20	7	3	10	34	42	17
Guildford City	20	7	3	10	33	47	17
Cheltenham Town	20	5	5	10	32	45	15
Bath City	20	5	5	10	34	52	15
Yeovil & Petters United	20	3	5	12	40	75	11

1936-37

Ipswich Town	30	19	8	3	68	35	46
Norwich City Reserves	30	18	5	7	70	35	41
Folkestone	30	17	4	9	71	62	38
Margate	30	15	4	11	64	49	34
Guildford City	30	15	4	11	54	60	34
Bath City	30	14	5	11	65	55	33
Yeovil & Petters United	30	15	3	12	77	69	33
Plymouth Argyle Reserves	30	11	8	11	64	58	30
Newport County Reserves	30	11	8	11	72	68	30
Barry	30	12	4	14	58	72	28
Cheltenham Town	30	10	4	16	61	70	24
Dartford	30	9	5	16	41	55	23
Exeter City Reserves	30	8	7	15	57	78	23
Tunbridge Wells Rangers	30	8	6	16	62	64	22
Torquay United Reserves	30	8	5	17	46	76	21
Aldershot Reserves	30	7	6	17	47	74	20

Midweek Section

Margate	18	12	1	5	48	24	25
Bath City	18	10	5	3	38	28	25
Norwich City Reserves	18	9	5	4	44	27	23
Folkestone	18	7	6	5	32	36	20
Millwall Reserves	18	8	3	7	44	47	19
Portsmouth Reserves	18	6	5	7	40	27	17
Tunbridge Wells Rangers	18	5	4	9	30	41	14
Aldershot Reserves	18	6	2	10	20	30	14
Guildford City	18	3	6	9	24	36	12
Dartford	18	4	3	11	19	43	11

1937-38

Guildford City	34	22	5	7	94	60	49
Plymouth Argyle Reserves	34	18	9	7	98	58	45
Ipswich Town	34	19	6	9	89	54	44
Yeovil & Petters United	34	14	14	6	72	45	42
Norwich City Reserves	34	15	11	8	77	55	41
Colchester United	34	15	8	11	90	58	38
Bristol Rovers Reserves	34	14	8	12	63	62	36
Swindon Town Reserves	34	14	7	13	70	76	35
Tunbridge Wells Rangers	34	14	6	14	68	74	34
Aldershot Reserves	34	10	12	12	42	55	32
Cheltenham Town	34	13	5	16	72	68	31
Exeter City Reserves	34	13	5	16	71	75	31
Dartford	34	9	11	14	51	70	29
Bath City	34	9	9	16	45	65	27
Folkestone	34	10	6	18	58	82	26
Newport County Reserves	34	10	6	18	56	86	26
Barry	34	8	7	19	50	88	23
Torquay United Reserves	34	8	7	19	46	81	23

Midweek Section

Millwall Reserves	18	13	3	2	59	21	29
Colchester United	18	13	1	4	42	23	27
Aldershot Reserves	18	11	3	4	38	29	25
Norwich City Reserves	18	9	1	8	45	39	19
Portsmouth Reserves	18	5	5	8	31	30	15
Dartford	18	6	3	9	32	35	15
Folkestone	18	6	3	9	34	38	15
Tunbridge Wells Rangers	18	5	4	9	28	36	14
Bath City	18	5	3	10	27	45	13
Guildford City	18	4	0	14	21	61	8

1938-39

Colchester United	44	31	5	8	110	37	67
Guildford City	44	30	6	8	126	52	66
Gillingham	44	29	6	9	104	57	64
Plymouth Argyle Reserves	44	26	5	13	128	63	57
Yeovil & Petters United	44	22	10	12	85	70	54
Arsenal Reserves	44	21	9	14	92	57	51
Cardiff City Reserves	44	24	3	17	105	72	51
Tunbridge Wells Rangers	44	22	6	16	93	76	50
Norwich City Reserves	44	23	4	17	86	76	50
Chelmsford City	44	18	8	18	74	73	44
Bath City	44	16	12	16	58	74	44
Barry	44	18	7	19	76	90	43
Cheltenham Town	44	16	9	19	76	105	41
Ipswich Town Reserves	44	14	12	18	64	76	40
Worcester City	44	13	14	17	72	90	40
Folkestone	44	16	6	22	74	85	38
Newport County Reserves	44	13	10	21	74	108	36
Exeter City Reserves	44	12	9	23	51	107	33
Torquay United Reserves	44	12	8	24	53	89	32
Swindon Town Reserves	44	11	9	24	66	101	31
Aldershot Reserves	44	12	6	26	69	92	30
Bristol Rovers Reserves	44	9	11	24	66	85	29
Dartford	44	8	5	31	53	119	21

Midweek Section

Tunbridge Wells Rangers	16	8	7	1	37	18	23
Colchester United	16	9	2	5	36	21	20
Norwich City Reserves	16	7	4	5	40	26	18
Millwall Reserves	16	7	4	5	33	23	18
Portsmouth Reserves	16	5	4	7	21	29	14
Guildford City	16	4	6	6	24	39	14
Aldershot Reserves	16	4	5	7	22	25	13
Folkestone	16	4	5	7	24	35	13
Dartford	16	4	3	9	24	45	11

1939-40

Eastern Section

Chelmsford City	7	5	0	2	29	9	10
Guildford City	8	4	1	3	26	13	9
Tunbridge Wells Rangers	7	2	3	2	21	16	7
Dartford	7	2	1	4	17	30	5
Norwich City Reserves	7	2	1	4	9	34	5

Western Section

Lovells Athletic	14	11	1	2	53	22	23
Worcester City	14	9	2	3	55	30	20
Hereford United	14	8	0	6	45	31	16
Yeovil & Petters United	14	7	2	5	30	24	16
Gloucester City	14	5	0	9	35	49	10
Barry	14	4	1	9	31	56	9
Cheltenham Town	13	3	2	8	21	38	8
Bath City	13	3	2	8	21	41	8

1945-46

Chelmsford City	18	15	1	2	66	23	34
Hereford United	20	13	3	4	59	31	29
Bath City	20	12	2	6	62	32	26
Cheltenham Town	18	9	1	8	35	54	22
Barry Town	20	8	4	8	42	42	20
Yeovil & Petters United	18	7	1	10	57	52	18
Worcester City	20	8	2	10	60	58	18
Colchester United	20	7	3	10	29	47	17
Bedford Town	16	4	1	11	30	49	15
Swindon Town Reserves	18	4	3	11	36	65	14
Cardiff City Reserves	20	4	5	11	39	60	13

1946-47

Gillingham	31	20	6	5	103	45	47
Guildford City	32	21	4	7	86	39	46
Merthyr Tydfil	31	21	2	8	104	37	45
Yeovil Town	32	19	6	7	100	49	44
Chelmsford City	31	17	3	11	90	60	38
Gravesend & Northfleet	32	17	4	11	82	58	38
Barry Town	30	14	6	10	89	61	36
Colchester United	31	15	4	12	65	60	35
Cheltenham Town	31	14	3	14	68	75	32
Millwall	24	8	5	11	59	57	29
Dartford	32	10	5	17	71	100	25
Bedford Town	32	8	8	16	63	98	24
Hereford United	32	8	7	17	37	85	23
Worcester City	31	8	5	18	55	90	22
Exeter City Reserves	32	10	2	20	69	126	22
Bath City	32	7	7	18	52	93	21
Gloucester City	32	8	1	23	57	120	17

1947-48

Merthyr Tydfil	34	23	7	4	84	38	53
Gillingham	34	21	5	8	81	43	47
Worcester City	34	21	3	10	74	45	45
Colchester United	34	17	10	7	88	41	44
Hereford United	34	16	10	8	77	53	42
Lovells Athletic	34	17	6	11	74	50	40
Exeter City Reserves	34	15	7	12	65	57	37
Yeovil Town	34	12	11	11	56	50	35
Chelmsford City	34	14	7	13	62	58	35
Cheltenham Town	34	13	9	12	71	71	35
Bath City	34	12	8	14	55	62	32
Barry Town	34	10	9	15	60	70	29
Gravesend & Northfleet	34	11	6	17	52	81	28
Guildford City	34	11	4	19	69	74	26
Dartford	34	10	6	18	35	62	26
Gloucester City	34	8	6	20	45	78	22
Torquay United Reserves	34	6	9	19	43	95	21
Bedford Town	34	6	3	25	41	104	15

1948-49

Gillingham	42	26	10	6	104	48	62
Chelmsford City	42	27	7	8	115	64	61
Merthyr Tydfil	42	26	8	8	133	54	60
Colchester United	42	21	10	11	94	61	52
Worcester City	42	22	7	13	87	56	51
Dartford	42	21	9	12	73	53	51
Gravesend & Northfleet	42	20	9	13	60	46	49
Yeovil Town	42	19	9	14	90	53	47
Cheltenham Town	42	19	9	14	71	64	47
Kidderminster Harriers	42	19	6	17	77	96	44
Exeter City Reserves	42	18	7	17	83	73	43
Hereford United	42	17	6	19	83	84	40
Bath City	42	15	8	19	72	87	38
Hastings United	42	14	10	18	69	93	38
Torquay United Reserves	42	15	7	20	73	93	37
Lovells Athletic	42	14	8	20	73	74	36
Guildford City	42	12	12	18	58	85	36
Gloucester City	42	12	10	20	78	100	34
Barry Town	42	12	10	20	55	95	34
Tonbridge	42	9	7	26	54	105	25
Chingford Town	42	6	9	27	43	94	21
Bedford Town	42	5	8	29	32	101	18

1949-50

Merthyr Tydfil	46	34	3	9	143	62	71
Colchester United	46	31	9	6	109	51	71
Yeovil Town	46	29	7	10	104	45	65
Chelmsford City	46	26	9	11	121	64	61
Gillingham	46	23	9	14	92	61	55
Dartford	46	20	9	17	70	65	49
Worcester City	46	21	7	18	85	80	49
Guildford City	46	18	11	17	79	73	47
Weymouth	46	19	9	18	80	81	47
Barry Town	46	18	10	18	78	72	46
Exeter City Reserves	46	16	14	16	73	83	46
Lovells Athletic	46	17	10	19	86	78	44
Tonbridge	46	16	12	18	65	76	44
Hastings United	46	17	8	21	92	450	42
Gravesend & Northfleet	46	16	9	21	88	81	41
Torquay United Reserves	46	14	12	20	80	89	40
Bath City	46	16	7	23	61	78	39
Gloucester City	46	14	11	21	72	101	39
Hereford United	46	15	8	23	74	76	38
Cheltenham Town	46	13	11	22	75	96	37
Headington United	46	15	7	24	72	97	37
Bedford Town	46	12	11	23	63	79	35
Kidderminster Harriers	46	12	11	23	64	108	35
Chingford Town	46	10	6	30	63	151	26

1950-51

Merthyr Tydfil	44	29	8	7	156	66	66
Hereford United	44	27	7	10	110	69	61
Guildford City	44	23	8	13	88	60	54
Chelmsford City	44	21	12	11	84	58	54
Llanelly	44	19	13	12	89	73	51
Cheltenham Town	44	21	8	15	91	61	50
Headington United	44	18	11	15	84	83	47
Torquay United Reserves	44	20	6	18	93	79	46
Exeter City Reserves	44	16	12	16	90	94	44
Weymouth	44	16	12	16	82	88	44
Tonbridge	44	16	12	16	79	87	44
Gloucester City	44	16	11	17	81	76	43
Yeovil Town	44	13	15	16	72	72	41
Worcester City	44	15	11	18	69	78	41
Bath City	44	15	10	19	66	73	40
Dartford	44	14	11	19	61	70	39
Bedford Town	44	15	9	20	64	94	39
Gravesend & Northfleet	44	12	14	18	83	88	38
Kettering Town	44	13	11	20	87	87	37
Lovells Athletic	44	12	13	19	81	93	37
Kidderminster Harriers	44	13	9	22	58	103	35
Barry Town	44	13	7	24	54	104	33
Hastings United	44	11	6	27	91	143	28

1951-52

Merthyr Tydfil	42	27	6	9	128	60	60
Weymouth	42	22	13	7	81	42	57
Kidderminster Harriers	42	22	10	10	70	40	54
Guildford City	42	18	16	8	66	47	52
Hereford United	42	21	9	12	80	59	51
Worcester City	42	23	4	15	86	73	50
Kettering Town	42	18	10	14	83	56	46
Lovells Athletic	42	18	10	14	87	68	46
Gloucester City	42	19	8	15	68	55	46
Bath City	42	19	6	17	75	67	44
Headington United	42	16	11	15	55	53	43
Bedford Town	42	16	10	16	75	64	42
Barry Town	42	18	6	18	84	89	42
Chelmsford City	42	15	10	17	67	80	40
Dartford	42	15	9	18	63	65	39
Tonbridge	42	15	6	21	63	84	36
Yeovil Town	42	12	11	19	56	76	35
Cheltenham Town	42	15	4	23	59	85	34
Exeter City Reserves	42	13	7	22	76	106	33
Llanelly	42	13	6	23	70	111	32
Gravesend & Northfleet	42	12	7	23	68	88	31
Hastings United	42	3	5	34	41	131	11

1952-53

Headington United	42	23	12	7	93	50	58
Merthyr Tydfil	42	25	8	9	117	66	58
Bedford Town	42	24	8	10	91	61	56
Kettering Town	42	23	8	11	88	50	54
Bath City	42	22	10	10	71	46	54
Worcester City	42	20	11	11	100	66	51
Llanelly	42	21	9	12	95	72	51
Barry Town	42	22	3	17	89	69	47
Gravesend & Northfleet	42	19	7	16	83	76	45
Gloucester City	42	17	9	16	50	78	43
Guildford City	42	17	8	17	64	60	42
Hastings United	42	18	5	19	75	66	41
Cheltenham Town	42	15	11	16	70	89	41
Weymouth	42	15	10	17	70	75	40
Hereford United	42	17	5	20	76	73	39
Tonbridge	42	12	9	21	62	88	33
Lovells Athletic	42	12	8	22	68	81	32
Yeovil Town	42	11	10	21	75	99	32
Chelmsford City	42	12	7	23	58	92	31
Exeter City Reserves	42	13	4	25	71	94	30
Kidderminster Harriers	42	12	5	25	54	85	29
Dartford	42	6	5	31	40	121	17

1953-54

Merthyr Tydfil	42	27	8	7	97	55	62
Headington United	42	22	9	11	68	43	53
Yeovil Town	42	20	8	14	87	76	48
Bath City	42	17	12	13	73	67	46
Kidderminster Harriers	42	18	9	15	62	59	45
Weymouth	42	18	8	16	83	72	44
Barry Town	42	17	9	16	108	91	43
Bedford Town	42	19	5	18	80	84	43
Gloucester City	42	16	11	15	69	77	43
Hastings United	42	16	10	16	73	67	42
Kettering Town	42	15	12	15	65	63	42
Hereford United	42	16	9	17	66	62	41
Llanelly	42	16	9	17	80	85	41
Guildford City	42	15	11	16	56	60	41
Gravesend & Northfleet	42	16	8	18	76	77	40
Worcester City	42	17	6	19	66	71	40
Lovells Athletic	42	14	11	17	62	60	39
Tonbridge	42	15	9	18	85	91	39
Chelmsford City	42	14	10	18	67	71	38
Exeter City Reserves	42	11	13	18	61	72	35
Cheltenham Town	42	11	12	19	56	83	34
Dartford	42	6	13	23	42	89	25

1954-55

Yeovil Town	42	23	9	10	105	66	55
Weymouth	42	24	7	11	105	84	55
Hastings United	42	21	9	12	94	60	51
Cheltenham Town	42	21	8	13	85	72	50
Guildford City	42	20	8	14	72	59	48
Worcester City	42	19	10	13	80	73	48
Barry Town	42	16	15	11	82	87	47
Gloucester City	42	16	13	13	66	54	45
Bath City	42	18	9	15	73	80	45
Headington Town	42	18	7	17	82	62	43
Kidderminster Harriers	42	18	7	17	84	86	43
Merthyr Tydfil	42	17	8	17	97	94	42
Exeter City Reserves	42	19	4	19	67	78	42
Lovells Athletic	42	15	11	16	71	68	41
Kettering Town	42	15	11	16	70	69	41
Hereford United	42	17	5	20	91	72	39
Llanelly	42	16	7	19	78	81	39
Bedford Town	42	16	3	23	75	103	35
Tonbridge	42	11	8	23	69	91	30
Dartford	42	9	12	21	55	76	30
Chelmsford City	42	11	6	25	73	111	28
Gravesend & Northfleet	42	9	9	24	62	97	27

1955-56

Guildford City	42	26	8	8	74	34	60
Cheltenham Town	42	25	6	11	82	53	56
Yeovil Town	42	23	9	10	98	55	55
Bedford Town	42	21	9	12	99	69	51
Dartford	42	20	9	13	78	62	49
Weymouth	42	19	10	13	83	63	48
Gloucester City	42	19	9	14	72	60	47
Lovells Athletic	42	19	9	14	91	78	47
Chelmsford City	42	18	10	14	67	55	46
Kettering Town	42	16	11	15	105	86	43
Exeter City Reserves	42	17	9	16	75	76	43
Gravesend & Northfleet	42	17	8	17	79	75	42
Hereford United	42	17	7	18	90	90	41
Hastings United	42	15	10	17	90	76	40
Headington United	42	17	6	19	82	86	40
Kidderminster Harriers	42	14	7	21	86	108	35
Llanelly	42	14	6	22	64	98	34
Barry Town	42	11	11	20	91	108	33
Worcester City	42	12	9	21	66	83	33
Tonbridge	42	11	11	20	53	74	33
Merthyr Tydfil	42	7	10	25	52	127	24
Bath City	42	7	10	25	43	107	24

1956-57

Kettering Town	42	28	10	4	106	47	66
Bedford Town	42	25	8	9	89	52	58
Weymouth	42	22	10	10	92	71	54
Cheltenham Town	42	19	15	8	73	46	53
Gravesend & Northfleet	42	21	11	10	74	58	53
Lovells Athletic	42	21	7	14	99	84	49
Guildford City	42	18	11	13	68	49	47
Hereford United	42	19	8	15	96	60	46
Headington United	42	19	7	16	64	61	45
Gloucester City	42	18	8	16	74	72	44
Hastings United	42	17	9	16	70	58	43
Worcester City	42	16	10	16	81	80	42
Dartford	42	16	10	16	79	88	42
Chelmsford City	42	16	9	17	73	85	41
Tonbridge	42	14	12	16	74	65	40
Yeovil Town	42	14	11	17	83	85	39
Bath City	42	15	8	19	56	78	38
Exeter City Reserves	42	10	10	22	52	89	30
Merthyr Tydfil	42	9	11	22	72	95	29
Barry Town	42	6	11	25	39	84	23
Kidderminster Harriers	42	7	10	25	60	83	20
Llanelly	42	5	8	29	39	123	18

1957-58

	P	W	D	L	F	A	Pts
Gravesend & Northfleet	42	27	5	10	109	71	59
Bedford Town	42	25	7	10	112	64	57
Chelmsford City	42	24	9	9	93	57	57
Weymouth	42	25	5	12	90	61	55
Worcester City	42	23	7	12	95	59	53
Cheltenham Town	42	21	10	11	115	66	52
Hereford United	42	21	6	15	79	56	48
Kettering Town	42	18	9	15	99	76	45
Headington Town	42	18	7	17	90	83	43
Poole Town	42	17	9	16	82	81	43
Hasting United	42	13	15	14	78	77	41
Gloucester City	42	17	7	18	70	70	41
Yeovil Town	42	16	9	17	70	84	41
Dartford	42	14	9	19	66	92	37
Lovells Athletic	42	15	6	21	60	83	36
Bath City	42	13	9	20	65	64	35
Guildford City	42	12	10	20	58	92	34
Tonbridge	42	16	7	22	77	100	33
Exeter City Reserves	42	12	8	22	60	94	32
Barry Town	42	11	9	22	72	101	31
Kidderminster Harriers	42	10	10	22	60	101	30
Merthyr Tydfil	42	9	3	30	69	137	21

1958-59

North-Western Zone

	P	W	D	L	F	A	Pts
Hereford United	34	22	5	7	80	37	49
Kettering Town	34	20	7	7	83	63	47
Boston United	34	18	8	8	73	47	44
Cheltenham Town	34	20	4	10	65	47	44
Worcester City	34	19	4	11	74	47	42
Bath City	34	17	5	12	89	62	39
Wellington Town	34	15	9	10	74	58	39
Nuneaton Borough	34	17	5	12	76	66	39
Wisbech Town	34	16	5	13	77	54	37
Headington United	34	16	3	15	76	61	35
Barry Town	34	15	5	14	64	67	35
Merthyr Tydfil	34	16	3	15	54	59	35
Gloucester City	34	12	6	16	50	65	30
Corby Town	34	10	8	16	59	79	28
Lovells Athletic	34	10	3	21	51	70	23
Rugby Town	34	7	6	21	45	93	20
Kidderminster Harriers	34	7	3	24	42	94	17
Burton Albion	34	3	3	28	41	104	9

South-Eastern Zone

	P	W	D	L	F	A	Pts
Bedford Town	32	21	6	5	90	41	48
Gravesend & Northfleet	32	21	2	9	79	54	44
Dartford	32	20	3	9	77	41	43
Yeovil Town	32	17	8	7	60	41	42
Weymouth	32	13	11	8	61	43	37
Chelmsford City	32	12	12	8	74	53	36
King's Lynn	32	14	5	13	70	63	33
Poole Town	32	12	8	12	60	65	32
Cambridge City	32	12	7	13	61	54	31
Hastings United	32	13	5	14	60	59	31
Tonbridge	32	14	3	15	51	59	31
Cambridge United	32	11	8	13	55	77	30
Trowbridge Town	32	12	4	16	53	75	28
Exeter City Reserves	32	7	12	13	47	71	26
Guildford City	32	7	6	19	45	67	20
Clacton Town	32	6	7	19	44	81	19
Yiewsley	32	3	7	22	36	78	13

1959-60

Premier Division

	P	W	D	L	F	A	Pts
Bath City	42	32	3	7	116	50	67
Headington United	42	23	8	11	78	61	54
Weymouth	42	22	9	11	93	69	53
Cheltenham Town	42	21	6	15	82	68	48
Cambridge City	42	18	11	13	81	72	47
Chelmsford Town	42	19	7	16	90	70	45
Bedford Town	42	21	3	18	97	85	45
King's Lynn	42	17	11	14	89	78	45
Boston United	42	17	10	15	83	80	44
Wisbech Town	42	17	10	15	81	84	44
Yeovil Town	42	17	8	17	81	73	42
Hereford United	42	15	12	15	70	74	42
Tonbridge	42	16	8	18	79	73	40
Hastings United	42	16	8	18	63	77	40
Wellington Town	42	13	11	18	63	78	37
Dartford	42	15	7	20	64	82	37
Gravesend & Northfleet	42	14	8	20	69	84	36
Worcester City	42	13	10	19	72	89	36
Nuneaton Borough	42	11	11	20	64	78	33
Barry Town	42	14	5	23	78	103	33
Poole Town	42	10	8	24	69	96	28
Kettering Town	42	9	10	23	60	90	28

First Division

	P	W	D	L	F	A	Pts
Clacton Town	42	27	5	10	106	69	59
Romford	42	21	11	10	65	40	53
Folkestone Town	42	23	5	14	93	71	51
Exeter City Reserves	42	23	3	16	85	62	49
Guildford City	42	19	9	14	79	56	47
Sittingbourne	42	20	7	15	66	55	47
Margate	42	20	6	16	88	77	46
Trowbridge Town	42	18	9	15	90	78	45
Cambridge United	42	18	9	15	71	72	45
Yiewsley	42	17	10	15	83	69	44
Bexleyheath & Welling	42	16	11	15	85	77	43
Merthyr Tydfil	42	16	10	16	63	65	42
Ramsgate Athletic	42	16	8	18	83	84	40
Ashford Town	42	14	12	16	61	70	40
Tunbridge Wells United	42	17	5	20	77	73	39
Hinckley Athletic	42	14	8	20	62	75	36
Gloucester City	42	13	9	20	56	84	35
Dover	42	14	6	22	59	85	34
Kidderminster Harriers	42	14	6	22	59	97	34
Corby Town	42	15	3	24	75	91	33
Burton Albion	42	11	10	21	52	79	32
Rugby Town	42	10	11	21	67	91	31

1960-61

Premier Division

	P	W	D	L	F	A	Pts
Oxford United	42	27	10	5	104	43	64
Chelmsford City	42	23	11	8	91	55	57
Yeovil Town	42	23	9	10	109	54	55
Hereford United	42	21	10	11	83	67	52
Weymouth	42	21	9	12	78	63	51
Bath City	42	18	14	10	74	52	50
Cambridge City	42	16	12	14	101	71	44
Wellington Town	42	17	9	16	66	68	43
Bedford Town	42	18	7	17	94	97	43
Folkestone Town	42	18	7	17	75	86	43
King's Lynn	42	13	16	13	68	66	42
Worcester City	42	15	11	16	69	69	41
Clacton Town	42	15	11	16	82	83	41
Romford	42	13	15	14	66	69	41
Guildford City	42	14	11	17	65	62	39
Tonbridge	42	16	6	20	79	85	38
Cheltenham Town	42	15	7	20	81	81	37
Gravesend & Northfleet	42	15	7	20	75	101	37
Dartford	42	13	11	18	57	90	37
Hastings United	42	8	9	25	60	100	25
Wisbech Town	42	9	6	27	58	112	24
Boston United	42	6	8	28	62	123	20

Oxford United were previously known as Headington United.

First Division

Kettering Town	40	26	7	7	100	55	59
Cambridge United	40	25	5	10	100	53	55
Bexleyheath & Welling	40	22	8	10	93	46	52
Merthyr Tydfil	40	23	6	11	88	65	52
Sittingbourne	40	21	10	9	77	63	52
Hinckley Athletic	40	17	13	10	74	59	47
Ramsgate Athletic	40	19	7	14	77	56	45
Rugby Town	40	18	9	13	89	71	45
Corby Town	40	16	10	14	82	73	42
Poole Town	40	18	5	17	71	65	41
Barry Town	40	16	9	15	65	74	41
Yiewsley	40	17	7	16	65	76	41
Trowbridge Town	40	14	10	16	71	73	38
Ashford Town	40	14	8	18	61	67	36
Margate	40	11	12	17	62	75	34
Dover	40	12	7	21	67	74	31
Canterbury City	40	10	10	20	52	75	30
Nuneaton Borough	40	11	7	22	60	91	29
Burton Albion	40	12	4	24	63	85	28
Tunbridge Wells United	40	8	5	27	56	115	21
Gloucester City	40	7	7	26	40	102	21

1961-62

Premier Division

Oxford United	42	28	5	9	118	46	61
Bath City	42	25	7	10	102	70	57
Guildford City	42	24	8	10	79	49	56
Yeovil Town	42	23	8	11	97	59	54
Chelmsford City	42	19	12	11	74	60	50
Weymouth	42	20	7	15	80	64	47
Kettering Town	42	21	5	16	90	84	47
Hereford United	42	21	2	19	81	68	44
Cambridge City	42	18	8	16	70	71	44
Bexleyheath & Welling	42	19	5	18	69	75	43
Romford	42	15	9	18	63	70	39
Cambridge United	42	13	12	17	76	78	38
Wellington United	42	14	10	18	75	78	38
Gravesend & Northfleet	42	17	4	21	59	92	38
Bedford Town	42	16	5	21	73	79	37
Worcester City	42	15	7	20	51	64	37
Merthyr Tydfil	42	13	11	18	62	80	37
Clacton Town	42	13	10	19	74	91	36
Tonbridge	42	10	14	18	71	92	34
King's Lynn	42	12	8	22	59	74	32
Folkestone Town	42	12	6	24	64	103	30
Cheltenham	42	9	7	26	48	86	25

First Division

Wisbech Town	38	21	11	6	76	42	53
Poole Town	38	23	6	9	81	47	52
Dartford	38	21	8	9	89	50	50
Rugby Town	38	20	9	9	82	49	49
Margate	38	20	6	12	73	55	46
Corby Town	38	19	6	13	82	60	44
Sittingbourne	38	16	12	10	69	51	44
Dover	38	19	6	13	66	55	44
Yiewsley	38	18	6	14	64	51	42
Barry Town	38	14	11	13	55	51	39
Ashford Town	38	14	11	13	66	70	39
Hinckley Athletic	38	15	8	15	75	65	38
Burton Albion	38	16	5	17	70	79	37
Nuneaton Borough	38	12	12	14	63	69	36
Tunbridge Wells United	38	12	7	19	60	85	31
Canterbury City	38	11	8	19	60	82	30
Ramsgate Athletic	38	10	9	19	48	70	29
Trowbridge Town	38	9	9	20	45	69	27
Gloucester City	38	6	4	28	46	104	16
Hastings United	38	5	4	29	45	115	14

1962-63

Premier Division

Cambridge City	40	25	6	9	99	64	56
Cambridge United	40	23	7	10	74	50	53
Weymouth	40	20	11	9	82	43	51
Guildford City	40	20	11	9	70	50	51
Kettering Town	40	22	7	11	66	49	51
Wellington Town	40	19	9	12	71	49	47
Dartford	40	19	9	12	61	54	47
Chelmsford City	40	18	10	12	63	50	46
Bedford Town	40	18	8	14	61	45	44
Bath City	40	18	6	16	58	56	42
Yeovil Town	40	15	10	15	64	54	40
Romford	40	14	11	15	73	68	39
Bexleyheath & Welling	40	13	11	16	55	63	37
Hereford United	40	14	7	19	56	66	35
Merthyr Tydfil	40	15	4	21	54	71	34
Rugby Town	40	14	5	21	65	76	33
Wisbech Town	40	15	3	22	64	84	33
Worcester City	40	12	9	19	47	65	33
Poole Town	40	10	12	18	54	66	32
Gravesend & Northfleet	40	10	3	27	62	91	23
Clacton Town	40	3	7	30	50	135	13

First Division

Margate	38	21	13	4	86	47	55
Hinckley Athletic	38	22	9	7	66	38	53
Hastings United	38	22	8	8	86	36	52
Nuneaton Borough	38	21	10	7	82	41	52
Tonbridge	38	22	8	8	81	51	52
Dover	38	22	7	9	78	56	51
Corby Town	38	19	8	11	79	50	46
King's Lynn	38	19	7	15	76	66	45
Cheltenham Town	38	18	7	13	83	52	43
Folkestone Town	38	15	10	13	79	57	40
Canterbury City	38	14	8	16	42	56	36
Yiewsley	38	11	10	17	63	71	32
Ramsgate Athletic	38	12	7	19	58	82	31
Trowbridge Town	38	11	9	18	50	81	31
Burton Albion	38	10	10	18	48	76	30
Gloucester City	38	9	11	18	42	78	29
Sittingbourne	38	12	3	23	56	75	27
Ashford Town	38	9	6	23	58	76	24
Barry Town	38	6	5	27	35	75	17
Tunbridge Wells United	38	6	2	30	43	118	14

1963-64

Premier Division

Yeovil Town	42	29	5	8	93	36	63
Chelmsford City	42	26	7	9	99	55	59
Bath City	42	24	9	9	88	51	57
Guildford City	42	21	9	12	90	55	51
Romford	42	20	9	13	71	58	49
Hastings United	42	20	8	14	75	61	48
Weymouth	42	20	7	15	65	53	47
Bedford Town	42	19	9	14	71	68	47
Cambridge United	42	17	9	16	92	77	43
Cambridge City	42	17	9	16	76	70	43
Wisbech Town	42	17	8	17	64	68	42
Bexley United	42	16	10	16	70	77	42
Dartford	42	16	8	18	56	71	40
Worcester City	42	12	15	15	70	74	39
Nuneaton Borough	42	15	8	19	58	61	38
Rugby Town	42	15	8	19	68	86	38
Margate	42	12	13	17	68	81	37
Wellington Town	42	12	9	21	73	85	33
Merthyr Tydfil	42	12	8	22	69	108	32
Hereford United	42	12	7	23	58	86	31
Kettering Town	42	10	5	27	49	89	25
Hinckley Athletic	42	7	6	29	51	104	20

First Division

Team	P	W	D	L	F	A	Pts
Folkstone Town	42	28	7	7	82	38	63
King's Lynn	42	28	5	9	94	44	61
Cheltenham Town	42	25	10	7	92	49	60
Tonbridge	42	24	11	7	98	54	59
Corby town	42	24	7	11	114	56	55
Stevenage Town	42	21	6	15	70	59	48
Ashford Town	42	19	9	14	73	57	47
Burton Albion	42	19	8	15	76	70	46
Poole Town	42	17	11	14	75	61	45
Dover	42	18	9	15	86	75	45
Canterbury City	42	16	12	14	66	66	44
Crawley Town	42	20	2	20	81	71	42
Trowbridge Town	42	16	9	17	71	78	41
Clacton Town	42	19	1	22	76	88	39
Gloucester City	42	17	4	21	88	89	38
Yiewsley	42	15	8	19	63	77	38
Sittingbourne	42	15	8	19	52	70	38
Ramsgate Athletic	42	13	9	20	57	55	35
Tunbridge Wells Rangers	42	10	8	24	47	89	28
Gravesend & Northfleet	42	7	9	26	43	96	23
Deal Town	42	5	7	30	48	106	17
Barry Town	42	3	6	33	33	137	12

1964-65

Premier Division

Team	P	W	D	L	F	A	Pts
Weymouth	42	24	8	10	99	50	56
Guildford City	42	21	12	9	73	49	54
Worcester City	42	22	6	14	100	62	50
Yeovil Town	42	18	14	10	76	55	50
Chelmsford City	42	21	8	13	86	77	50
Margate	42	20	9	13	88	79	49
Dartford	42	17	11	14	74	64	45
Nuneaton Borough	42	19	7	16	57	55	45
Cambridge United	42	16	11	15	78	66	43
Bedford Town	42	17	9	16	66	70	43
Cambridge City	42	16	9	17	72	69	41
Cheltenham Town	42	15	11	16	72	78	41
Folkstone Town	42	17	7	18	72	79	41
Romford	42	17	7	18	61	70	41
King's Lynn	42	13	13	16	56	79	39
Tonbridge	42	10	16	16	66	75	36
Wellington Town	42	13	10	19	63	78	36
Rugby Town	42	15	6	21	71	98	36
Wisbech Town	42	14	6	22	75	91	34
Bexley United	42	14	5	23	67	74	33
Hastings United	42	9	14	19	58	86	32
Bath City	42	13	3	26	60	86	29

First Division

Team	P	W	D	L	F	A	Pts
Hereford United	42	34	4	4	124	39	72
Wimbledon	42	24	13	5	108	52	61
Poole Town	42	26	6	10	92	56	58
Corby Town	42	24	7	11	88	55	55
Stevenage Town	42	19	13	10	83	43	51
Hillingdon Borough	42	21	7	14	105	63	49
Crawley Town	42	22	5	15	83	52	49
Merthyr Tydfil	42	20	9	13	75	59	49
Gloucester City	42	19	10	13	68	65	48
Burton Albion	42	20	7	15	83	75	47
Canterbury City	42	13	16	13	73	53	42
Kettering Town	42	14	13	15	74	64	41
Ramsgate Athletic	42	16	8	18	51	59	40
Dover	42	14	10	18	54	59	38
Hinckley Athletic	42	13	9	20	56	81	35
Trowbridge Town	42	13	5	24	68	106	31
Ashford Town	42	11	8	23	60	98	30
Barry Town	42	11	7	24	47	103	29
Deal Town	42	7	13	22	61	127	27
Tunbridge Wells Rangers	42	10	6	26	51	107	26
Gravesend & Northfleet	42	9	7	26	57	101	25
Sittingbourne	42	8	5	29	58	103	21

1965-66

Premier Division

Team	P	W	D	L	F	A	Pts
Weymouth	42	22	13	7	70	35	57
Chelmsford City	42	21	12	9	74	50	54
Hereford United	42	21	10	11	81	49	52
Bedford Town	42	23	6	13	80	57	52
Wimbledon	42	20	10	12	80	47	50
Cambridge City	42	19	11	12	67	52	49
Romford	42	21	7	14	87	72	49
Worcester City	42	20	8	14	69	54	48
Yeovil Town	42	17	11	14	91	70	45
Cambridge United	42	18	9	15	72	64	45
King's Lynn	42	18	7	17	75	72	43
Corby Town	42	16	9	17	66	73	41
Wellington Town	42	13	13	16	65	70	39
Nuneaton Borough	42	15	8	19	60	74	38
Folkstone Town	42	14	9	19	53	75	37
Guildford City	42	14	8	20	70	84	36
Poole Town	42	14	7	21	61	75	35
Cheltenham Town	42	13	9	20	69	99	35
Dartford	42	13	7	22	62	69	33
Rugby Town	42	11	10	21	67	95	32
Tonbridge	42	11	6	25	63	101	28
Margate	42	8	10	24	66	111	26

First Division

Team	P	W	D	L	F	A	Pts
Barnet	46	30	9	7	114	49	69
Hillingdon Borough	46	27	10	9	101	46	64
Burton Albion	46	28	8	10	121	60	64
Bath City	46	25	13	8	88	50	63
Hastings United	46	25	10	11	104	59	60
Wisbech Town	46	25	9	12	98	54	59
Canterbury City	46	25	8	13	89	66	58
Stevenage Town	46	23	9	14	86	49	55
Kettering Town	46	22	9	15	77	74	53
Merthyr Tydfil	46	22	6	18	95	68	50
Dunstable Town	46	15	14	17	76	72	44
Crawley Town	46	17	10	19	72	71	44
Bexley United	46	20	4	22	65	71	44
Trowbridge Town	46	16	11	19	79	81	43
Dover	46	17	8	21	59	62	42
Barry Town	46	16	10	20	72	94	42
Gravesend & Northfleet	46	16	9	21	84	86	41
Gloucester City	46	14	12	20	75	98	40
Sittingbourne	46	11	12	23	77	121	34
Ramsgate Athletic	46	9	15	22	35	76	33
Hinckley Athletic	46	10	12	24	59	93	32
Tunbridge Wells Rangers	46	12	8	26	47	88	32
Ashford Town	46	9	10	27	44	92	28
Deal Town	46	3	4	39	29	165	10

1966-67

Premier Division

Team	P	W	D	L	F	A	Pts
Romford	42	22	8	12	80	60	52
Nuneaton Borough	42	21	9	12	82	54	51
Weymouth	42	18	14	10	64	40	50
Wimbledon	42	19	11	12	88	60	49
Barnet	42	18	13	11	86	66	49
Guildford City	42	19	10	13	65	51	48
Wellington Town	42	20	7	15	70	67	47
Cambridge United	42	16	13	13	75	67	45
Chelmsford City	42	15	15	12	66	59	45
Hereford United	42	16	12	14	79	61	44
King's Lynn	42	15	14	13	78	72	44
Cambridge City	42	15	13	14	66	70	43
Cheltenham Town	42	16	11	15	60	71	43
Yeovil Town	42	14	14	14	66	72	42
Burton Albion	42	17	5	20	63	71	39
Corby Town	42	15	9	18	60	75	39
Poole Town	42	14	11	17	52	65	39
Hillingdon Borough	42	11	13	18	49	70	35
Bath City	42	11	12	19	51	74	34
Worcester City	42	11	8	23	59	79	30
Bedford Town	42	8	13	21	54	72	29
Folkestone Town	42	6	15	21	44	81	27

First Division

Dover	46	29	12	5	92	35	70
Margate	46	31	7	8	127	54	69
Stevenage Town	46	29	8	9	90	32	66
Hastings United	46	25	16	5	89	45	66
Kettering Town	46	27	9	10	105	62	63
Canterbury City	46	26	8	12	81	48	60
Ramsgate Athletic	46	23	8	15	79	62	54
Dartford	46	19	15	12	92	67	53
Tonbridge	46	21	10	15	91	69	52
Trowbridge Town	46	20	12	14	73	60	52
Ashford Town	46	18	8	20	74	68	44
Merthyr Tydfil	46	17	9	20	81	71	43
Gloucester City	46	18	6	22	69	83	42
Canterbury City	46	17	8	21	57	75	42
Wisbech Town	46	16	9	21	87	93	41
Bexley United	46	13	15	18	53	69	41
Banbury United	46	13	14	19	88	100	40
Rugby Town	46	15	7	24	57	77	37
Dunstable Town	46	14	6	26	55	87	34
Barry Town	46	11	11	24	62	89	33
Gravesend & Northfleet	46	11	9	26	63	106	31
Hinckley Athletic	46	10	8	28	44	100	28
Tunbridge Wells Rangers	46	4	15	27	31	96	23
Sittingbourne	46	5	10	31	44	136	20

1967-68

Premier Division

Chelmsford City	42	25	7	10	85	50	57
Wimbledon	42	24	7	11	85	47	55
Cambridge United	42	20	13	9	73	42	53
Cheltenham Town	42	23	7	12	97	67	53
Guildford City	42	18	13	11	56	43	49
Romford	42	20	8	14	72	60	48
Barnet	42	20	8	14	81	71	48
Margate	42	19	8	15	80	71	46
Wellington Town	42	16	13	13	70	66	45
Hillingdon Borough	42	18	9	155	53	54	45
King's Lynn	42	18	8	16	66	57	44
Yeovil Town	42	16	12	14	45	43	44
Weymouth	42	17	8	17	65	62	42
Hereford United	42	17	7	18	58	62	41
Nuneaton Borough	42	13	14	15	62	64	40
Dover	42	17	6	19	54	56	40
Poole Town	42	13	10	19	55	74	36
Stevenage Town	42	13	9	20	57	75	35
Burton Albion	42	14	6	22	51	73	34
Corby Town	42	7	13	22	40	77	27
Cambridge City	42	10	6	26	51	81	26
Hastings United	42	4	8	30	33	94	16

First Division

Worcester City	42	23	14	5	92	35	60
Kettering Town	42	24	10	8	88	40	58
Bedford Town	42	24	7	11	101	40	55
Rugby Town	42	20	15	7	72	44	55
Dartford	42	23	9	10	70	48	55
Bath City	42	21	12	9	78	51	54
Banbury United	42	22	9	11	79	59	53
Ramsgate Athletic	42	17	7	8	70	37	51
Merthyr Tydfil	42	18	13	11	80	66	49
Tonbridge	42	18	9	15	76	71	45
Canterbury City	42	16	11	15	66	63	43
Ashford Town	42	18	6	18	73	78	42
Brentwood Town	42	16	9	17	63	73	41
Bexley United	42	12	13	17	56	64	37
Trowbridge Town	42	12	11	19	64	70	35
Gloucester City	42	12	9	21	54	68	33
Wisbech Town	42	11	10	21	43	78	32
Crawley Town	42	10	8	24	54	85	28
Folkestone Town	42	10	7	25	49	80	27
Dunstable Town	42	8	10	24	44	94	26
Barry Town	42	7	12	23	36	81	26
Gravesend & Northfleet	42	6	7	29	28	112	19

1968-69

Premier Division

Cambridge United	42	27	5	10	72	39	59
Hillingdon Borough	42	24	10	8	68	47	58
Wimbledon	42	21	12	9	66	48	54
King's Lynn	42	20	9	13	68	60	49
Worcester City	42	19	11	12	53	47	49
Romford	42	18	12	12	58	52	48
Weymouth	42	16	15	11	52	41	47
Yeovil Town	42	16	13	13	52	50	45
Kettering Town	42	18	8	16	51	55	44
Dover	42	17	9	16	66	61	43
Nuneaton Borough	42	17	7	18	74	58	41
Barnet	42	15	10	17	72	66	40
Chelmsford City	42	17	6	19	56	58	40
Hereford United	42	15	9	18	66	62	39
Telford United	42	14	10	18	62	61	38
Poole Town	42	16	6	20	75	76	38
Burton Albion	42	16	5	21	55	71	37
Margate	42	14	7	21	79	90	35
Cheltenham Town	42	15	5	22	55	64	35
Bedford Town	42	11	12	19	46	63	34
Rugby Town	42	10	6	26	38	83	26
Guildford City	42	7	11	24	41	73	25

First Division

Brentwood Town	42	26	12	4	44	37	64
Bath City	42	26	10	6	96	40	62
Gloucester City	42	25	9	8	100	53	59
Crawley Town	42	21	13	8	65	32	55
Corby Town	42	22	6	14	81	65	50
Dartford	42	20	8	14	79	51	48
Ramsgate Athletic	42	19	9	14	72	57	47
Salisbury	42	20	6	16	69	52	46
Cambridge City	42	18	10	14	73	63	46
Banbury United	42	16	12	14	67	72	44
Trowbridge Town	42	15	8	19	70	60	44
Folkestone Town	42	19	5	18	53	59	43
Canterbury City	42	17	7	18	67	63	41
Ashford Town	42	16	8	18	72	73	40
Bexley United	42	15	9	18	62	75	39
Hastings United	42	15	9	18	58	69	39
Wisbech Town	42	11	13	18	57	70	35
Dunstable Town	42	14	6	22	73	99	34
Merthyr Tydfil	42	10	7	25	49	101	27
Barry Town	42	8	10	24	39	78	26
Gravesend & Northfleet	42	8	9	25	51	79	25
Tonbridge	42	2	6	34	36	137	10

1969-70

Premier Division

Cambridge United	42	26	6	10	86	49	58
Yeovil Town	42	25	7	10	78	48	57
Chelmsford City	42	20	11	11	76	58	51
Weymouth	42	18	14	10	59	37	50
Wimbledon	42	19	12	11	64	52	50
Hillingdon Borough	42	19	12	11	56	50	50
Barnet	42	16	15	11	71	54	47
Telford United	42	18	10	14	61	62	46
Brentwood Town	42	16	13	13	61	38	45
Hereford United	42	18	9	15	74	65	45
Bath City	42	18	8	16	63	55	44
King's Lynn	42	16	11	15	72	68	43
Margate	42	17	8	17	70	64	42
Dover	42	15	10	17	51	50	40
Kettering Town	42	18	3	21	64	75	39
Worcester City	42	14	10	18	35	44	38
Romford	42	13	11	18	50	62	37
Poole Town	42	8	19	15	48	57	35
Gloucester City	42	12	9	21	53	73	33
Nuneaton Borough	42	11	10	21	52	74	32
Crawley Town	42	6	15	21	53	101	27
Burton Albion	42	3	9	30	24	82	15

First Division

Bedford Town	42	26	9	7	93	37	61
Cambridge City	42	26	8	8	104	43	60
Dartford	42	24	11	7	33	46	58
Ashford Town	42	19	15	8	71	43	53
Rugby Town	42	20	10	12	82	66	50
Trowbridge Town	42	20	8	14	72	65	48
Hastings United	42	18	11	13	67	51	47
Guildford City	42	19	9	14	68	58	54
Cheltenham Town	42	20	5	17	78	81	45
Canterbury City	42	15	13	14	61	57	43
Corby Town	42	14	15	13	58	53	43
Folkestone Town	42	19	5	18	57	55	43
Ramsgate Athletic	42	14	13	15	53	57	41
Salisbury	42	13	13	16	48	53	39
Gravesend & Northfleet	42	13	11	18	62	71	37
Bexley United	42	10	11	21	58	76	31
Dunstable Town	42	11	9	22	52	82	31
Merthyr Tydfil	42	9	11	22	40	80	29
Barry Town	42	11	6	25	39	76	28
Wisbech Town	42	8	9	25	58	116	25
Tonbridge	42	4	10	28	46	101	18

1971-72

Premier Division

Chelmsford City	42	28	6	8	109	46	62
Hereford United	42	24	12	6	68	30	60
Dover	42	20	11	11	67	45	51
Barnet	42	21	7	14	80	57	49
Dartford	42	20	8	14	75	68	48
Weymouth	42	21	5	16	69	43	47
Yeovil Town	42	18	11	13	67	51	47
Hillingdon Borough	42	20	6	16	64	58	46
Margate	42	19	8	15	74	68	46
Wimbledon	42	19	7	16	75	64	45
Romford	42	16	13	13	54	49	45
Guildford City	42	20	5	17	71	65	45
Telford United	42	18	7	17	83	68	43
Nuneaton Borough	42	16	10	16	46	47	42
Bedford Town	42	16	9	17	59	66	41
Worcester City	42	17	7	18	46	57	41
Cambridge City	42	12	14	16	68	71	38
Folkestone	42	14	7	21	58	64	35
Poole Town	42	9	11	22	43	72	29
Bath City	42	11	4	27	45	86	26
Merthyr Tydfil	42	7	8	27	29	93	22
Gravesend & Northfleet	42	5	6	31	30	110	16

1970-71

Premier Division

Yeovil Town	42	25	7	10	66	31	57
Cambridge City	42	22	11	9	67	38	55
Romford	42	23	9	10	63	42	55
Hereford United	42	23	8	11	71	53	54
Chelmsford City	42	20	11	11	61	32	51
Barnet	42	18	14	10	69	49	50
Bedford Town	42	20	10	12	62	46	50
Wimbledon	42	20	8	14	72	54	48
Worcester City	42	20	8	14	61	46	48
Weymouth	42	14	16	12	64	48	44
Dartford	42	15	12	15	53	51	42
Dover	42	16	9	17	64	63	41
Margate	42	15	10	17	64	70	40
Hillingdon Borough	42	17	6	19	61	68	40
Bath City	42	13	12	17	48	68	38
Nuneaton Borough	42	12	12	18	43	66	36
Telford United	42	13	8	21	64	70	34
Poole Town	42	14	6	22	57	75	34
King's Lynn	42	11	7	24	44	67	29
Ashford Town	42	8	13	21	52	86	29
Kettering Town	42	8	11	23	48	84	27
Gloucester City	42	6	10	26	34	81	21

First Division

Guildford City	38	22	10	6	76	36	54
Merthyr Tydfil	38	19	12	7	52	33	50
Gravesend & Northfleet	38	19	10	9	74	42	48
Folkestone	38	20	8	10	83	53	48
Burton Albion	38	19	10	9	56	37	48
Rugby Town	38	17	14	7	58	40	48
Ramsgate Athletic	38	20	5	13	83	54	45
Trowbridge Town	38	19	7	12	78	55	45
Bexley United	38	17	11	10	57	45	45
Crawley Town	38	15	11	12	84	68	41
Hastings United	38	13	12	13	51	50	38
Banbury United	38	13	11	14	58	53	37
Corby Town	38	14	8	16	57	60	36
Salisbury	38	13	7	18	56	60	33
Cheltenham Town	38	8	15	15	44	58	31
Stevenage Athletic	38	12	7	19	55	79	21
Tonbridge	38	8	8	22	48	83	24
Barry Town	38	9	6	23	35	82	24
Dunstable Town	38	8	4	26	32	81	20
Canterbury City	38	5	4	29	37	105	14

First Division (North)

Kettering Town	34	23	6	5	70	27	52
Burton Albion	34	18	13	3	58	27	49
Cheltenham Town	34	20	4	10	72	51	44
Rugby Town	34	18	7	9	52	36	43
Wellingborough Town	34	15	10	9	73	44	40
Stourbridge	34	13	14	7	59	42	40
King's Lynn	34	14	11	9	62	45	39
Corby Town	34	15	9	10	47	35	39
Ilkeston Town	34	14	11	9	44	38	39
Banbury United	34	14	5	15	54	46	33
Bury Town	34	14	5	15	47	44	33
Wealdstone	34	14	5	15	51	58	33
Lockheed Leamington	34	15	3	16	41	52	33
Gloucester City	34	8	8	18	46	61	24
Stevenage Athletic	34	8	8	18	41	69	24
Bletchley	34	7	7	20	36	70	21
Dunstable Town	34	5	7	22	29	75	17
Barry Town	34	1	7	26	22	84	9

First Division (South)

Waterlooville	30	15	9	6	40	22	39
Ramsgate Athletic	30	14	11	5	42	27	39
Maidstone United	30	14	10	6	48	28	38
Crawley Town	30	15	5	10	67	55	35
Metropolitan Police	30	15	3	12	48	41	33
Tonbridge	30	12	9	9	37	34	33
Bexley United	30	14	4	12	52	46	32
Basingstoke Town	30	14	4	12	37	36	32
Andover	30	11	9	10	32	34	31
Ashford Town	30	12	4	14	43	48	28
Salisbury	30	10	7	13	45	44	27
Winchester City	30	10	7	13	40	47	27
Hastings United	30	10	7	13	28	42	27
Trowbridge Town	30	8	7	15	41	49	23
Canterbury City	30	7	8	15	39	56	22
Woodford Town	30	4	6	20	22	52	14

1972-73

Premier Division

Kettering Town	42	20	17	5	74	44	57
Yeovil Town	42	21	14	7	67	61	56
Dover	42	23	9	10	61	68	55
Chelmsford City	42	23	7	12	75	43	53
Worcester City	42	20	13	9	68	47	53
Weymouth	42	20	12	10	72	51	52
Margate	42	17	15	10	80	60	49
Bedford Town	42	16	15	11	43	36	47
Nuneaton Borough	42	16	14	12	51	41	46
Telford United	42	12	20	10	57	47	44
Cambridge City	42	14	15	13	64	53	43
Wimbledon	42	14	14	14	50	50	42
Barnet	42	15	11	16	60	59	41
Romford	42	17	5	20	51	65	39
Hillingdon Borough	42	16	6	20	52	58	38
Dartford	42	12	11	19	49	63	35
Folkestone	42	11	11	20	41	72	33
Guildford City	42	10	11	21	59	84	31
Ramsgate	42	9	13	20	35	61	31
Poole Town	42	10	10	22	50	88	30
Burton Albion	42	9	7	26	43	81	25
Waterlooville	42	4	16	22	33	63	24

First Division (North)

Grantham	42	29	8	5	113	41	66
Atherstone Town	42	23	11	8	82	48	57
Cheltenham Town	42	24	8	10	87	47	56
Rugby Town	42	20	10	12	60	47	50
Kidderminster Harriers	42	19	12	11	67	56	50
Merthyr Tydfil	42	17	12	13	51	40	46
Corby Town	42	14	16	12	62	56	44
Stourbridge	42	16	11	15	70	64	43
Gloucester City	42	18	7	17	55	64	43
Bromsgrove Rovers	42	17	8	17	63	54	42
Redditch United	42	18	6	18	58	59	42
Banbury United	42	18	5	19	60	53	41
Wellingborough Town	42	17	7	18	58	71	41
King's Lynn	42	14	12	16	45	49	40
Lockheed Leamington	42	13	12	17	51	58	38
Enderby Town	42	12	14	16	50	61	38
Stevenage Athletic	42	12	13	17	50	63	37
Tamworth	42	14	8	20	45	65	36
Bury Town	42	13	9	20	52	69	35
Barry Town	42	11	10	21	45	71	32
Ilkeston Town	42	9	6	27	35	68	24
Bedworth United	42	10	3	29	42	94	23

First Division (South)

Maidstone United	42	25	12	5	90	38	62
Tonbridge	42	26	7	9	70	44	59
Ashford Town	42	24	7	11	90	40	55
Bideford	42	19	14	9	70	43	52
Minehead	42	20	12	10	65	47	52
Gravesend & Northfleet	42	22	7	13	81	55	51
Bath City	42	18	11	13	56	54	47
Wealdstone	42	16	12	14	81	61	44
Bletchley Town	42	14	13	15	54	51	41
Hastings United	42	14	13	15	53	53	41
Andover	42	15	11	16	62	70	41
Canterbury City	42	14	12	16	51	59	40
Basingstoke Town	42	14	12	16	48	57	40
Crawley Town	42	14	11	17	59	76	39
Metropolitan Police	42	15	8	19	82	75	38
Trowbridge Town	42	15	8	19	65	77	38
Bexley United	42	12	14	16	54	64	38
Salisbury	42	14	10	18	49	60	38
Bognor Regis Town	42	12	9	21	41	66	33
Dorchester Town	42	10	12	20	47	73	32
Winchester City	42	7	11	24	41	79	25
Dunstable Town	42	4	10	28	38	105	18

1973-74

Premier Division

Dartford	42	22	13	7	67	37	57
Grantham	42	18	13	11	70	49	49
Chelmsford City	42	19	10	13	62	49	48
Kettering Town	42	16	16	10	62	51	48
Maidstone United	42	16	14	12	54	43	46
Yeovil Town	42	13	20	9	45	39	46
Weymouth	42	19	7	16	60	41	45
Barnet	42	18	9	15	55	46	45
Nuneaton Borough	42	13	19	10	54	47	45
Cambridge City	42	15	12	15	45	54	42
Atherstone Town	42	16	9	17	61	59	41
Wimbledon	42	15	11	16	50	56	41
Telford United	42	12	16	14	51	57	40
Dover	42	11	17	14	41	46	39
Tonbridge	42	12	15	15	38	45	39
Romford	42	11	17	14	39	52	39
Margate	42	15	8	19	56	63	38
Guildford City	42	13	11	18	48	67	37
Worcester City	42	11	14	17	53	67	36
Bedford Town	42	11	14	17	38	51	36
Folkestone	42	11	12	19	56	65	34
Hillingdon Borough	42	9	15	18	44	65	33

First Division (North)

Stourbridge	42	29	11	2	103	36	69
Burton Albion	42	27	9	6	88	32	63
Cheltenham Town	42	24	9	10	75	51	56
AP Leamington	42	21	12	9	82	45	54
Enderby Town	42	19	14	9	60	36	52
Witney Town	42	20	10	12	69	55	50
Stevenage Athletic	42	19	11	12	65	46	49
Banbury United	42	19	11	12	69	57	49
King's Lynn	42	19	10	13	65	50	48
Kidderminster Harriers	42	15	14	13	67	53	44
Merthyr Tydfil	42	16	12	14	70	61	44
Redditch United	42	14	11	17	56	73	39
Bromsgrove Rovers	42	14	10	18	54	61	38
Bedworth United	42	14	10	18	50	77	38
Tamworth	42	13	11	18	42	51	37
Corby Town	42	12	11	19	40	57	35
Bletchley Town	42	10	15	17	47	71	35
Barry Town	42	10	8	24	53	85	29
Bury Town	42	10	6	26	57	84	26
Gloucester City	42	10	6	26	52	81	26
Wellingborough Town	42	7	9	26	42	87	23
Dunstable Town	42	5	11	26	26	83	21

First Division (South)

Wealdstone	38	26	7	5	75	35	59
Bath City	38	20	8	10	55	34	48
Waterlooville	38	16	15	7	55	38	47
Minehead	38	16	15	7	69	52	47
Bideford	38	17	12	9	61	51	46
Poole Town	38	18	9	11	67	47	45
Bexley United	38	18	7	13	50	42	43
Hastings United	38	16	9	13	45	36	41
Basingstoke Town	38	14	11	13	55	44	39
Gravesend & Northfleet	38	13	13	12	58	52	39
Bognor Regis Town	38	13	12	13	48	54	38
Ashford Town	38	14	8	16	41	42	36
Ramsgate	38	13	9	16	46	44	35
Dorchester Town	38	10	13	15	40	48	33
Canterbury City	38	9	12	17	37	46	30
Trowbridge Town	38	8	14	16	44	61	30
Salisbury	38	10	9	19	40	60	29
Metropolitan Police	38	9	11	18	37	61	29
Andover	38	11	3	24	38	70	25
Crawley Town	38	6	9	23	35	79	21

1974-75

Premier Division

	P	W	D	L	F	A	Pts
Wimbledon	42	25	7	10	63	33	57
Nuneaton Borough	42	23	8	11	56	37	54
Yeovil Town	42	21	9	12	64	34	51
Kettering Town	42	20	10	12	73	41	50
Burton Albion	42	18	13	11	54	48	49
Bath City	42	20	8	14	63	50	48
Margate	42	17	12	13	64	64	46
Wealdstone	42	17	11	14	62	61	45
Telford United	42	16	13	13	55	56	45
Chelmsford City	42	16	12	14	62	51	44
Grantham	42	16	11	15	70	62	43
Dover	42	15	13	14	43	53	43
Maidstone United	42	15	12	15	52	50	42
Atherstone Town	42	14	14	14	48	53	42
Weymouth	42	13	13	16	66	58	39
Stourbridge	42	13	12	17	56	70	38
Cambridge	42	11	14	17	51	56	36
Tonbridge	42	11	12	19	44	66	34
Romford	42	10	13	19	46	62	33
Dartford	42	9	13	20	52	70	31
Barnet	42	10	9	23	44	76	29
Guildford & Dorking United	42	10	5	27	45	82	25

First Division (North)

	P	W	D	L	F	A	Pts
Bedford Town	42	28	9	5	85	33	65
Dunstable Town	42	25	8	9	105	61	58
AP Leamington	42	25	7	10	68	48	57
Redditch United	42	22	12	8	76	40	56
Worcester City	42	24	8	10	84	50	56
Cheltenham Town	42	21	9	12	72	53	51
Tamworth	42	21	8	13	74	53	50
King's Lynn	42	19	10	13	71	64	48
Enderby Town	42	17	12	13	61	48	46
Banbury United	42	18	10	14	52	51	46
Stevenage Athletic	42	16	13	13	62	48	45
Bromsgrove Rovers	42	18	9	15	63	52	45
Merthyr Tydfil	42	11	15	16	53	64	37
Witney Town	42	16	4	22	57	76	36
Corby Town	42	11	13	18	60	57	35
Kidderminster Harriers	42	12	11	19	50	66	35
Gloucester City	42	13	8	21	55	75	34
Wellingborough Town	42	9	13	20	42	61	31
Barry Town	42	10	10	22	49	73	30
Bedworth United	42	9	9	24	60	91	27
Milton Keynes City	42	7	5	30	48	100	19
Bury Town	42	5	7	30	36	119	17

First Division (South)

	P	W	D	L	F	A	Pts
Gravesend & Northfleet	38	24	12	2	70	30	60
Hillingdon Borough	38	22	8	8	87	45	52
Minehead	38	21	9	8	74	33	51
Ramsgate	38	19	11	8	70	37	49
Bexley United	38	19	7	12	61	44	45
Waterlooville	38	17	11	10	67	49	45
Ashford Town	38	16	12	10	64	55	44
Basingstoke Town	38	16	11	11	64	50	43
Canterbury City	38	16	9	13	54	43	41
Hastings United	38	13	14	11	54	45	40
Poole Town	38	11	13	14	50	60	35
Metropolitan Police	38	11	13	14	54	66	35
Folkestone & Shepway	38	10	14	14	53	57	34
Andover	38	12	8	18	52	71	32
Bognor Regis Town	38	10	11	17	49	64	31
Salisbury	38	9	11	18	45	66	29
Trowbridge Town	38	10	9	19	48	76	29
Bideford	38	10	8	20	40	71	28
Dorchester Town	38	8	10	20	40	63	26
Crawley Town	38	3	5	30	31	102	11

1975-76

Premier Division

	P	W	D	L	F	A	Pts
Wimbledon	42	26	10	6	74	29	62
Yeovil Town	42	21	12	9	68	35	54
Atherstone Town	42	18	15	9	56	55	51
Maidstone United	42	17	16	9	52	39	50
Nuneaton Borough	42	16	18	8	41	33	50
Gravesend & Northfleet	42	16	18	8	49	47	50
Grantham	42	15	14	13	56	47	44
Dunstable Town	42	17	9	16	52	43	43
Bedford Town	42	13	17	12	55	51	43
Burton Albion	42	17	9	16	52	53	43
Margate	42	15	12	15	62	60	42
Hillingdon Borough	42	13	14	15	61	54	40
Telford United	42	14	12	16	54	51	40
Chelmsford City	42	13	14	15	52	57	40
Kettering Town	42	11	17	14	48	52	39
Bath City	42	11	16	15	62	57	38
Weymouth	42	13	9	20	51	67	35
Dover	42	8	18	16	51	60	34
Wealdstone	42	12	9	21	61	82	33
Tonbridge AFC	42	11	11	20	45	70	33
Cambridge City	42	8	15	19	41	67	31
Stourbridge	42	10	9	23	38	72	29

First Division (North)

	P	W	D	L	F	A	Pts
Redditch United	42	29	11	2	101	39	69
AP Leamington	42	27	10	5	85	31	64
Witney Town	42	24	9	9	66	40	57
Worcester City	42	24	8	10	90	49	56
Cheltenham Town	42	20	10	12	87	55	50
Barry Town	42	19	10	13	52	47	48
King's Lynn	42	17	14	11	52	48	48
Tamworth	42	18	11	13	65	43	47
Barnet	42	15	12	15	56	50	42
Oswestry Town	42	16	8	18	63	71	40
Enderby Town	42	16	6	20	48	51	38
Banbury United	42	15	8	19	58	67	38
Merthyr Tydfil	42	11	15	16	59	67	37
Bromsgrove Rovers	42	13	11	18	49	65	37
Milton Keynes City	42	15	6	21	51	63	36
Bury Town	42	12	11	19	52	72	35
Gloucester City	42	13	9	20	49	78	35
Kidderminster Harriers	42	13	8	21	54	70	34
Bedworth United	42	8	18	16	41	66	34
Corby Town	42	11	10	21	50	65	32
Wellingborough Town	42	9	11	22	42	68	29
Stevenage Athletic	42	6	6	30	46	105	18

First Division (South)

	P	W	D	L	F	A	Pts
Minehead	38	27	8	3	102	35	62
Dartford	38	26	4	8	84	46	56
Romford	38	21	9	8	66	37	51
Salisbury	38	17	11	10	73	53	45
Hastings United	38	15	15	8	67	51	45
Poole United	38	20	2	16	57	57	42
Bexley United	38	14	13	11	62	53	41
Waterlooville	38	13	13	12	62	54	39
Basingstoke Town	38	13	12	13	69	71	38
Ashford Town	38	14	8	16	67	73	36
Canterbury City	38	11	13	14	53	60	35
Folkestone & Shepway	38	10	14	14	36	51	34
Metropolitan Police	38	9	14	15	46	58	32
Trowbridge Town	38	11	10	17	48	75	32
Guildford & Dorking United	38	9	13	16	43	50	31
Bognor Regis Town	38	6	17	15	44	72	29
Ramsgate	38	9	10	19	57	76	28
Crawley Town	38	9	10	19	46	66	28
Andover	38	9	10	19	42	62	28
Dorchester Town	38	11	6	21	45	69	28

1976-77

Premier Division

Wimbledon	42	28	7	7	64	22	63
Minehead	42	23	12	7	73	39	58
Kettering Town	42	20	16	6	66	46	56
Bath City	42	20	15	7	51	30	55
Nuneaton Borough	42	20	11	11	52	35	51
Bedford Town	42	17	14	11	54	47	48
Yeovil Town	42	15	16	11	54	42	46
Dover	42	13	16	13	46	43	42
Grantham	42	14	12	16	55	50	40
Maidstone United	42	13	14	15	46	50	40
Gravesend & Northfleet	42	13	13	16	38	43	39
AP Leamington	42	12	15	15	44	53	39
Redditch United	42	12	14	16	45	54	38
Wealdstone	42	13	12	17	54	66	38
Hillingdon Borough	42	14	10	18	45	59	38
Atherstone Town	42	14	9	19	41	49	37
Weymouth	42	16	5	21	53	73	37
Dartford	42	13	10	19	52	57	36
Telford United	42	11	12	19	36	50	34
Chelmsford City	42	9	13	20	56	68	31
Burton Albion	42	10	10	22	41	52	30
Margate	42	9	10	23	47	85	28

First Division (North)

Worcester City	38	32	5	1	97	22	69
Cheltenham Town	38	23	8	7	85	35	54
Witney Town	38	21	8	9	48	31	50
Bromsgrove Rovers	38	20	8	10	61	37	48
Barry Town	38	19	8	11	62	45	46
Cambridge City	38	17	10	11	68	43	44
Stourbridge	38	17	9	12	48	35	43
Kidderminster Harriers	38	17	6	15	74	65	40
Banbury United	38	15	10	13	51	47	40
Gloucester City	38	18	4	16	70	81	40
Enderby Town	38	15	9	14	50	44	39
King's Lynn	38	13	11	14	47	53	37
Corby Town	38	11	13	14	56	64	35
Tamworth	38	11	13	14	49	58	35
Merthyr Tydfil	38	12	6	20	60	69	30
Oswestry Town	38	8	10	20	30	60	26
Wellingborough Town	38	8	7	23	37	73	23
Dunstable	38	7	7	24	38	84	21
Bedworth United	38	5	10	23	28	68	20
Milton Keynes City	38	7	6	25	31	76	20

First Division (South)

Barnet	34	23	8	3	65	25	54
Hastings United	34	18	11	5	47	18	47
Waterlooville	34	19	6	9	50	25	44
Dorchester Town	34	16	11	7	48	30	43
Salisbury	34	15	11	8	57	39	41
Romford	34	18	5	11	47	32	41
Poole Town	34	17	7	10	40	35	41
Trowbridge Town	34	15	8	11	47	39	38
Crawley Town	34	14	9	11	53	42	37
Folkestone & Shepway	34	12	11	11	39	42	35
Basingstoke Town	34	12	10	12	51	43	34
Canterbury City	34	6	16	12	36	46	28
Bognor Regis Town	34	9	9	16	33	50	27
Tonbridge AFC	34	9	9	16	33	50	27
Metropolitan Police	34	5	12	17	37	61	22
Andover	34	4	11	19	17	49	19
Ashford Town	34	5	8	21	32	65	18
Aylesbury United	34	5	6	23	27	68	16

1977-78

Premier Division

Bath City	42	22	18	2	83	32	62
Weymouth	42	21	16	5	64	36	58
Maidstone United	42	20	11	11	59	41	51
Worcester City	42	20	11	11	67	50	51
Gravesend & Northfleet	42	19	11	12	57	42	49
Kettering Town	42	18	11	13	58	48	47
Barnet	42	18	11	13	63	58	47
Wealdstone	42	16	14	12	54	48	46
Telford United	42	17	11	14	52	45	45
Nuneaton Borough	42	15	14	13	38	36	44
Dartford	42	14	15	13	57	65	43
Yeovil Town	42	14	14	14	57	49	42
Hastings United	42	15	9	18	49	60	39
Cheltenham Town	42	12	14	16	43	52	38
Hillingdon Borough	42	13	9	20	45	54	35
Atherstone Town	42	10	15	17	41	56	35
Redditch United	42	15	5	22	40	55	35
AP Leamington	42	11	13	18	34	57	35
Minehead	42	11	12	19	43	48	34
Dover	42	9	13	20	41	63	31
Bedford Town	42	8	13	21	51	75	29
Grantham	42	11	6	25	40	66	28

First Division (North)

Witney Town	38	20	15	3	54	27	55
Bridgend Town	38	20	9	9	59	45	49
Burton Albion	38	17	11	10	48	32	45
Enderby Town	38	17	10	11	59	44	44
Bromsgrove Rovers	38	16	12	10	56	41	44
Banbury United	38	17	10	11	52	47	44
Kidderminster Harriers	38	16	11	11	58	41	43
Merthyr Tydfil	38	18	6	14	85	62	42
Cambridge City	38	14	12	12	56	45	40
Barry Town	38	14	11	13	58	48	39
Wellingborough Town	38	11	15	12	47	43	37
King's Lynn	38	12	13	13	55	55	37
Gloucester City	38	14	8	16	68	75	36
Corby Town	38	9	17	12	46	48	35
Dunstable Town	38	11	13	14	49	59	35
Stourbridge	38	9	15	14	52	53	33
Tamworth	38	10	11	17	37	48	31
Bedworth United	38	8	14	16	36	58	30
Milton Keynes City	38	5	11	22	26	74	21
Oswestry Town	38	6	8	24	29	85	20

First Division (South)

Margate	38	24	10	4	92	32	58
Dorchester Town	38	23	10	5	67	31	56
Salisbury	38	21	10	7	60	27	52
Waterlooville	38	19	13	6	66	36	51
Romford	38	17	15	6	58	37	49
Aylesbury United	38	20	7	11	56	42	47
Trowbridge Town	38	16	11	11	65	59	43
Chelmsford City	38	15	11	12	58	46	41
Folkestone & Shepway	38	16	9	13	64	56	41
Taunton Town	38	15	10	13	57	54	40
Addlestone	38	14	10	14	57	60	38
Crawley Town	38	14	9	15	61	60	37
Basingstoke Town	38	11	11	16	44	50	37
Tonbridge AFC	38	13	5	20	64	77	31
Ashford Town	38	9	13	16	39	60	31
Hounslow	38	10	10	18	43	62	30
Bognor Regis Town	38	9	8	21	52	69	26
Poole Town	38	8	10	20	43	68	26
Andover	38	4	12	22	30	68	20
Canterbury City	38	2	6	30	31	113	10

1978-79

Premier Division

	P	W	D	L	F	A	Pts
Worcester City	42	27	11	4	92	33	65
Kettering Town	42	27	7	8	109	43	61
Telford United	42	22	10	10	60	39	54
Maidstone United	42	18	18	6	55	35	54
Bath City	42	17	19	6	59	41	53
Weymouth	42	18	15	9	71	51	51
AP Leamington	42	19	11	12	65	53	49
Redditch United	42	19	10	13	70	57	48
Yeovil Town	42	15	16	11	59	49	46
Witney Town	42	17	10	15	53	52	44
Nuneaton Borough	42	13	17	12	59	50	43
Gravesend & Northfleet	42	15	12	15	56	55	42
Barnet	42	16	10	16	52	64	42
Hillingdon Borough	42	12	16	14	50	41	40
Wealdstone	42	12	12	18	51	59	36
Atherstone Town	42	9	17	16	46	65	35
Dartford	42	10	14	18	40	56	34
Cheltenham Town	42	11	10	21	38	72	32
Margate	42	10	9	23	44	75	29
Dorchester Town	42	7	11	24	46	86	25
Hastings United	42	5	13	24	37	85	23
Bridgend Town	42	6	6	30	39	90	18

First Division (North)

	P	W	D	L	F	A	Pts
Grantham	38	21	10	7	70	45	52
Merthyr Tydfil	38	22	7	9	90	53	51
Alvechurch	38	20	10	8	70	42	50
Bedford Town	38	19	9	10	74	49	47
King's Lynn	38	17	11	10	57	46	45
Oswestry Town	38	18	8	12	63	43	44
Gloucester City	38	18	8	12	76	59	44
Burton Albion	38	16	10	12	51	40	42
Kidderminster Harriers	38	13	14	11	70	60	40
Bedworth United	38	13	14	11	41	34	40
Tamworth	38	15	8	15	47	45	38
Stourbridge	38	15	7	16	64	61	37
Barry Town	38	14	9	15	51	53	37
Enderby Town	38	14	8	16	46	55	36
Banbury United	38	10	13	15	42	58	33
Wellingborough Town	38	13	6	19	50	71	32
Cambridge City	38	9	9	20	37	62	27
Bromsgrove Rovers	38	6	14	18	33	61	26
Milton Keynes City	38	7	9	22	37	87	23
Corby Town	38	5	6	27	40	85	16

First Division (South)

	P	W	D	L	F	A	Pts
Dover	40	28	9	3	88	20	65
Folkestone & Shepway	40	22	6	12	84	50	50
Gosport Borough	40	19	11	10	62	47	49
Chelmsfor d City	40	20	7	13	65	61	47
Minehead	40	16	13	11	58	39	45
Poole Town	40	15	15	10	48	44	45
Hounslow	40	16	12	12	56	45	44
Waterlooville	40	17	10	13	52	43	44
Trowbridge Town	40	15	12	13	65	61	42
Aylesbury United	40	16	9	15	54	52	41
Taunton Town	40	16	9	15	53	51	41
Bognor Regis Town	40	17	7	16	58	58	41
Dunstable	40	18	4	18	57	55	40
Tonbridge AFC	40	15	10	15	43	47	40
Salisbury	40	13	10	17	47	51	36
Basingstoke Town	40	12	11	17	49	62	35
Addlestone	40	12	9	19	56	64	33
Andover	40	12	6	22	47	69	30
Ashford Town	40	10	10	20	28	53	30
Crawley Town	40	9	9	22	44	75	27
Canterbury City	40	6	3	31	31	98	15

1979-80

Midland Division

	P	W	D	L	F	A	Pts
Bridgend Town	42	28	6	8	85	39	62
Minehead	42	22	15	5	70	42	59
Bedford Town	42	20	12	10	71	42	52
Kidderminster Harriers	42	23	6	13	81	59	52
Merthyr Tydfil	42	20	11	11	70	47	51
Enderby Town	42	21	8	13	62	50	50
Stourbridge	42	19	11	12	67	49	49
Alvechurch	42	17	14	11	78	60	48
Trowbridge Town	42	19	9	14	62	61	47
Bromsgrove Rovers	42	18	10	14	67	56	46
Barry Town	42	15	12	15	64	58	42
King's Lynn	42	15	11	16	48	55	41
Banbury United	42	13	14	15	56	56	40
Taunton Town	42	16	8	18	55	62	40
Witney Town	42	10	19	13	43	45	39
Bedworth United	42	12	15	15	40	42	39
Milton Keynes City	42	15	7	20	46	59	37
Gloucester City	42	10	14	18	55	68	32
Cheltenham Town	42	13	5	24	49	70	31
Wellingborough Town	42	9	7	26	54	106	25
Cambridge City	42	6	9	27	30	73	21
Corby Town	42	5	9	28	40	94	19

Southern Division

	P	W	D	L	F	A	Pts
Dorchester Town	46	25	12	9	81	53	62
Aylesbury United	46	25	11	10	73	40	61
Dover	46	22	13	11	78	47	57
Gosport Borough	46	21	15	10	70	50	57
Dartford	46	21	14	11	66	45	56
Bognor Regis Town	46	20	15	11	66	38	55
Hillingdon Borough	46	19	16	11	64	41	54
Dunstable	46	17	19	10	93	64	53
Addlestone	46	20	13	13	72	57	53
Hastings United	46	19	15	12	74	65	53
Fareham Town	46	16	16	14	61	53	48
Waterlooville	46	17	12	17	67	64	46
Andover	46	16	13	17	65	65	45
Poole Town	46	16	13	17	49	64	45
Canterbury City	46	15	15	17	56	60	44
Hounslow	46	14	14	17	44	57	43
Margate	46	17	8	21	51	62	42
Folkestone & Shepway	46	14	11	21	54	63	39
Ashford Town	46	12	14	20	54	71	38
Crawley Town	46	13	11	22	55	72	37
Chelmsford City	46	9	18	19	47	69	36
Basingstoke Town	46	9	15	22	48	79	33
Salisbury	46	10	12	24	47	59	32
Tonbridge AFC	46	3	9	34	30	128	15

1980-81

Midland Division

	P	W	D	L	F	A	Pts
Alvechurch	42	26	9	7	76	40	61
Bedford Town	42	25	11	6	63	32	61
Trowbridge Town	42	24	9	9	69	39	57
Kidderminster Harriers	42	23	9	10	67	41	55
Barry Town	42	21	9	12	60	40	51
Stourbridge	42	17	16	9	75	49	50
Enderby Town	42	21	8	13	71	47	50
Cheltenham Town	42	18	12	12	70	59	48
Bromsgrove Rovers	42	19	9	14	65	50	47
Corby Town	42	19	7	16	69	58	45
Bridgend Town	42	19	7	16	74	64	45
Minehead	42	19	7	16	54	60	45
Gloucester City	42	19	6	17	82	72	44
Merthyr Tydfil	42	15	12	15	60	50	42
Bedworth United	42	14	12	16	49	46	40
Banbury United	42	11	11	20	51	65	33
Taunton Town	42	10	9	23	48	68	29
Cambridge City	42	8	12	22	46	87	28
Witney Town	42	9	9	24	44	65	27
Wellingborough Town	42	10	7	25	43	91	27
Redditch United	42	11	4	27	54	92	26
Milton Keynes City	42	3	7	32	28	103	13

Southern Division

Dartford	46	26	14	6	76	39	66
Bognor Regis Town	46	25	13	8	95	43	63
Hastings United	46	24	14	8	87	43	62
Gosport Borough	46	24	12	10	84	52	60
Waterlooville	46	19	21	6	67	50	59
Dorchester Town	46	21	13	12	84	56	55
Dover	46	22	10	14	70	50	54
Poole Town	46	19	14	13	70	56	52
Addlestone & Weybridge	46	21	9	16	66	57	51
Dunstable	46	19	13	14	73	68	51
Aylesbury United	46	20	10	16	66	60	50
Hounslow	46	17	13	16	65	55	47
Hillingdon Borough	46	16	15	15	50	49	47
Basingstoke Town	46	16	14	16	69	58	46
Crawley Town	46	18	4	24	64	78	40
Ashford Town	46	12	15	19	55	76	39
Tonbridge AFC	46	12	15	19	44	68	39
Chelmsford City	46	13	12	21	54	78	38
Canterbury City	46	12	13	21	40	59	37
Salisbury	46	14	8	24	57	76	36
Folkestone	46	11	11	24	47	65	33
Margate	46	11	7	28	65	117	29
Fareham Town	46	5	18	23	31	73	28
Andover	46	6	10	30	41	94	22

1982-83

Premier Division

AP Leamington	38	25	4	9	78	50	79
Kidderminster Harriers	38	23	7	8	69	40	76
Welling United	38	21	6	11	63	40	69
Chelmsford City	38	16	11	11	57	40	59
Bedworth United	38	16	11	11	47	39	59
Dartford	38	16	8	14	48	38	56
Gosport Borough	38	14	13	11	47	43	55
Fareham Town	38	16	7	15	73	82	55
Dorchester Town	38	14	12	12	52	50	54
Gravesend & Northfleet	38	14	12	12	49	50	54
Gloucester City	38	13	12	13	61	57	51
Witney Town	38	12	13	13	60	48	47
Alvechurch	38	13	8	17	60	66	47
Stourbridge	38	12	11	15	48	54	47
Corby Town	38	12	11	15	58	67	47
Hastings United	38	11	11	16	48	61	44
Enderby Town	38	11	9	18	44	62	42
Waterlooville	38	10	9	19	62	83	39
Poole Town	38	9	9	20	57	73	36
Addlestone & Weybridge	38	5	10	23	24	62	25

1981-82

Midland Division

Nuneaton Borough	42	27	11	4	88	32	65
Alvechurch	42	26	10	6	79	34	62
Kidderminster Harriers	42	22	12	8	71	40	56
Stourbridge	42	21	10	11	69	47	52
Gloucester City	42	21	9	12	64	48	51
Bedworth United	42	20	10	12	59	40	50
Enderby Town	42	20	10	12	79	66	50
Witney Town	42	19	8	15	71	49	46
Barry Town	42	16	14	12	59	46	46
Corby Town	42	19	8	15	70	59	46
Merthyr Tydfil	42	16	12	14	63	54	44
Wellingborough Town	42	15	12	15	50	45	42
Bridgend Town	42	13	13	16	50	62	39
Bromsgrove Rovers	42	15	8	19	57	63	38
Bedford Town	42	12	13	17	45	54	37
Cheltenham Town	42	11	14	17	65	68	36
Taunton Town	42	12	8	22	46	76	32
Banbury United	42	11	8	23	63	91	30
Minehead	42	12	6	24	38	69	30
Cambridge City	42	10	8	24	38	80	28
Milton Keynes City	42	6	11	25	34	70	23
Redditch United	42	8	5	29	37	103	21

Midland Division

Cheltenham Town	32	22	5	5	65	29	71
Sutton Coldfield Town	32	21	7	4	62	24	70
Forest Green Rovers	32	21	3	8	68	32	66
Merthyr Tydfil	32	17	7	8	64	45	58
Willenhall Town	32	17	6	9	74	49	57
Oldbury United	32	16	6	10	52	49	54
Banbury United	32	15	3	14	59	55	48
Bridgend Town	32	12	11	9	46	37	47
Wellingborough Town	32	13	7	12	49	37	46
Bromsgrove Rovers	32	13	5	14	47	47	44
Dudley Town	32	12	7	13	40	45	43
Bridgwater Town	32	12	6	14	42	43	42
Aylesbury United	32	12	5	15	37	51	41
Redditch United	32	8	6	18	51	73	30
Taunton Town	32	5	7	20	30	64	22
Minehead	32	5	7	20	24	62	22
Milton Keynes City	32	0	4	28	22	90	4

Southern Division

Wealdstone	46	32	8	6	100	32	72
Hastings United	46	31	9	6	79	34	71
Dorchester Town	46	21	18	7	76	41	60
Gosport Borough	46	26	8	12	76	45	60
Fareham Town	46	20	14	12	58	48	54
Poole Town	46	19	15	12	92	63	53
Waterlooville	46	22	9	15	75	53	53
Welling United	46	19	13	14	70	48	51
Addlestone & Weybridge	46	17	17	12	71	53	51
Chelmsford City	46	20	11	15	64	53	51
Aylesbury United	46	19	12	15	79	61	50
Basingstoke Town	46	18	12	16	75	61	48
Dover	46	19	8	19	61	63	46
Ashford Town	46	16	14	16	52	56	46
Tonbridge AFC	46	19	7	20	62	70	45
Dunstable	46	18	8	20	63	68	44
Salisbury	46	16	10	20	64	81	42
Hounslow	46	15	11	20	59	83	41
Hillingdon Borough	46	14	10	22	46	58	38
Canterbury City	46	10	16	20	49	78	36
Crawley Town	46	9	12	25	46	81	30
Folkestone	46	10	6	30	49	101	26
Andover	46	4	11	31	39	100	19
Thanet United	46	5	7	34	37	110	17

Southern Division

Fisher Athletic	34	23	5	6	79	34	74
Folkestone	34	22	6	6	79	41	72
RS Southampton	34	21	7	6	66	30	70
Dunstable	34	19	5	10	57	39	62
Hillingdon Borough	34	14	11	9	41	30	53
Salisbury	34	14	10	10	59	49	52
Crawley Town	34	14	9	11	51	43	51
Ashford Town	34	13	10	11	51	41	49
Tonbridge AFC	34	14	5	15	57	57	47
Hounslow	34	11	12	11	46	47	45
Canterbury City	34	12	9	13	52	63	45
Cambridge City	34	12	5	17	56	63	41
Dover	34	11	7	16	35	52	40
Thanet United	34	10	5	19	50	61	35
Basingstoke Town	34	8	10	16	37	56	34
Woodford Town	34	6	9	19	29	57	27
Andover	34	6	8	20	28	53	26
Erith & Belvedere	34	5	9	20	26	62	24

1983-84

Premier Division

Dartford	38	23	9	6	67	32	78
Fisher Athletic	38	22	9	7	80	42	75
Chelmsford City	38	19	9	10	67	45	66
Gravesend & Northfleet	38	18	9	11	50	38	63
Witney Town	38	18	6	14	75	50	60
King's Lynn	38	18	6	14	42	45	60
Folkestone	38	16	9	13	60	56	57
Cheltenham Town	38	16	7	15	63	56	55
Gloucester City	38	13	15	10	55	50	54
Hastings United	38	15	9	14	55	57	54
Bedworth United	38	15	9	14	51	55	54
Welling United	38	15	7	16	61	61	52
AP Leamington	38	14	9	15	73	83	51
Corby Town	38	12	14	12	55	54	50
Fareham Town	38	13	11	14	65	70	50
Alvechurch	38	12	12	14	56	62	48
Sutton Coldfield Town	38	10	14	14	49	53	44
Gosport Borough	38	6	15	17	31	64	33
Dorchester Town	38	4	8	26	40	69	20
Stourbridge	38	4	7	27	30	82	19

Midland Division

Willenhall Town	38	27	4	7	100	44	85
Shepshed Charterhouse	38	25	5	8	88	37	80
Bromsgrove Rovers	38	20	8	10	73	43	68
Dudley Town	38	18	13	7	71	43	67
Aylesbury United	38	17	15	6	62	35	66
Moor Green	38	18	12	8	63	44	66
Rushden Town	38	17	12	9	68	42	63
Merthyr Tydfil	38	18	8	12	63	44	62
Redditch United	38	17	9	12	67	67	60
VS Rugby	38	15	12	11	68	51	57
Forest Green Rovers	38	15	12	11	67	51	57
Bridgnorth Town	38	16	9	13	64	52	57
Leicester United	38	12	9	17	58	58	45
Oldbury United	38	10	13	15	53	51	43
Coventry Sporting	38	11	7	20	40	67	40
Bridgwater Town	38	10	8	20	39	65	38
Wellingborough Town	38	7	9	22	43	80	30
Banbury United	38	6	11	21	37	78	29
Milton Keynes City	38	3	9	26	31	110	18
Tamworth	38	2	7	29	25	118	13

Southern Division

RS Southampton	38	26	6	6	83	35	84
Crawley Town	38	22	9	7	68	28	75
Basingstoke Town	38	20	9	9	54	36	69
Tonbridge AFC	38	20	9	9	61	44	69
Addlestone & Weybridge	38	19	11	8	58	34	68
Poole Town	38	20	7	11	68	42	67
Hillingdon Borough	38	18	11	9	43	20	65
Ashford Town	38	19	5	14	65	47	62
Salisbury	38	17	8	13	61	48	59
Cambridge City	38	13	9	16	43	53	48
Canterbury City	38	12	9	17	44	52	45
Waterlooville	38	12	9	17	56	69	45
Dover Athletic	38	12	9	17	51	74	45
Chatham Town	38	11	10	17	46	56	43
Andover	38	12	6	20	35	54	42
Erith & Belvedere	38	11	9	18	43	68	42
Dunstable	38	10	8	20	38	65	38
Thanet United	38	9	8	21	40	65	35
Woodford Town	38	7	8	23	30	69	29
Hounslow	38	4	12	22	30	58	24

1984-85

Premier Division

Cheltenham Town	38	24	5	9	83	41	77
King's Lynn	38	23	6	9	73	48	75
Crawley Town	38	22	8	8	76	52	74
Willenhall Town	38	20	8	10	57	38	68
RS Southampton	38	21	4	13	76	52	67
Welling United	38	18	11	9	55	38	65
Folkestone	38	19	6	13	70	54	63
Fisher Athletic	38	19	5	14	67	57	62
Chelmsford City	38	17	10	11	52	50	61
Shepshed Charterhouse	38	18	5	15	67	50	59
Corby Town	38	15	6	17	56	54	51
Bedworth United	38	14	8	16	48	52	50
Gravesend & Northfleet	38	12	12	14	46	46	48
Fareham Town	38	13	8	17	52	55	47
Alvechurch	38	11	7	20	53	59	40
Hastings United	38	11	7	20	46	71	40
Witney Town	38	9	12	17	51	58	39
Gloucester City	38	10	6	22	49	74	36
Trowbridge	38	10	5	23	45	83	35
AP Leamington	38	2	5	31	22	112	11

Midland Division

Dudley Town	34	21	8	5	70	36	71
Aylesbury United	34	20	7	7	62	30	67
Hednesford Town	34	18	7	9	58	42	61
Moor Green	34	17	9	8	63	43	60
VS Rugby	34	17	9	8	59	41	60
Bromsgrove Rovers	34	16	10	8	53	42	58
Stourbridge	34	15	11	8	52	45	56
Redditch United	34	12	11	11	68	57	47
Sutton Coldfield Town	34	13	6	15	50	56	45
Bridgnorth Town	34	13	5	16	67	65	44
Coventry Sporting	34	11	9	14	45	52	42
Merthyr Tydfil	34	10	11	13	43	46	41
Rushden Town	34	10	7	17	42	52	37
Forest Green Rovers	34	9	10	15	49	65	37
Wellingborough Town	34	10	7	17	39	63	37
Oldbury United	34	10	6	18	52	66	36
Banbury United	34	9	5	20	33	59	32
Leicester United	34	3	6	25	17	62	15

Southern Division

Basingstoke Town	38	24	9	5	61	22	81
Gosport Borough	38	22	6	10	78	41	72
Poole Town	38	20	12	6	69	38	72
Hillingdon	38	19	10	9	51	23	67
Thanet United	38	19	9	10	63	47	66
Salisbury	38	19	5	14	55	54	62
Sheppey United	38	18	6	14	49	45	60
Addlestone & Weybridge	38	16	9	13	68	54	57
Waterlooville	38	15	10	13	71	63	55
Canterbury City	38	15	7	16	61	64	52
Woodford Town	38	13	13	12	46	53	52
Tonbridge AFC	38	16	3	19	59	62	51
Andover	38	15	5	18	54	54	50
Dorchester Town	38	13	7	18	45	60	46
Cambridge City	38	11	11	16	59	71	44
Chatham Town	38	12	8	18	44	66	44
Ashford Town	38	10	9	19	54	69	69
Dunstable	38	8	10	20	35	56	64
Dover Athletic	38	7	7	24	39	78	28
Erith & Belvedere	38	6	8	24	36	65	26

1985-86

Premier Division

Welling United	38	29	6	3	95	31	93
Chelmsford City	38	20	10	8	68	41	70
Fisher Athletic	38	20	7	11	67	45	67
Alvechurch	38	19	9	10	71	56	66
Worcester City	38	19	9	10	64	50	66
Crawley Town	38	18	5	15	76	59	59
Shepshed Charterhouse	38	19	1	18	51	52	58
Aylesbury United	38	14	10	14	52	49	52
Folkestone	38	14	10	14	56	56	52
Bedworth United	38	14	8	16	44	49	50
Willenhall Town	38	12	13	13	51	44	49
Dudley Town	38	15	4	19	58	62	49
Corby Town	38	14	7	17	61	67	49
King's Lynn	38	12	10	16	39	42	46
Basingstoke Town	38	13	4	21	36	67	43
RS Southampton	38	11	9	18	44	61	42
Witney Town	38	11	6	21	44	74	39
Gosport Borough	38	10	8	20	42	66	38
Fareham Town	38	8	13	17	40	62	37
Gravesend & Northfleet	38	9	9	20	29	55	36

Midland Division

Bromsgrove Rovers	40	29	5	6	95	44	92
Redditch United	40	23	6	11	70	42	75
Merthyr Tydfil	40	21	10	9	60	40	73
VS Rugby	40	17	14	9	41	31	65
Stourbridge	40	15	14	11	62	49	59
Rusden Town	40	17	7	16	69	74	58
Bilston Town	40	15	12	13	60	48	57
Bridgnorth Town	40	13	18	9	56	45	57
Gloucester City	40	15	12	13	61	57	57
Grantham	40	16	7	17	46	59	55
Wellingborough Town	40	15	9	16	56	56	54
Sutton Coldfield Town	40	13	14	13	60	45	53
Hednesford Town	40	14	9	17	67	70	51
Forest Green Rovers	40	14	9	17	52	56	51
Mile Oak Rovers	40	14	8	18	56	73	50
Leicester United	40	13	10	17	41	48	49
Banbury United	40	13	8	19	38	55	47
Coventry Sporting	40	10	15	15	42	48	45
Moor Green	40	12	6	22	63	91	42
Leamington	40	10	6	24	40	77	36
Oldbury United	40	8	7	25	50	87	31

Southern Division

Cambridge City	40	23	11	6	87	41	80
Salisbury	40	24	8	8	84	51	80
Hastings Town	40	23	9	8	83	51	78
Dover Athletic	40	23	6	11	89	53	75
Corinthian	40	20	9	11	79	45	69
Tonbridge AFC	40	17	13	10	65	51	64
Dunstable	40	17	11	12	70	61	62
Ruislip	40	17	6	17	67	66	57
Erith & Belvedere	40	14	12	14	35	40	54
Waterlooville	40	16	6	18	52	58	54
Burnham & Hillingdon	40	16	6	18	44	59	54
Canterbury City	40	13	13	14	58	58	52
Trowbridge Town	40	13	13	14	57	63	52
Sheppey United	40	14	10	16	43	53	52
Thanet United	40	13	7	20	58	63	46
Woodford Town	40	12	10	18	49	62	46
Poole Town	40	12	7	21	55	63	43
Ashford Town	40	10	12	18	45	65	42
Chatham Town	40	8	15	17	53	70	39
Andover	40	10	8	22	52	92	38
Dorchester Town	40	5	8	27	35	94	23

1986-87

Premier Division

Fisher Athletic	42	25	11	6	72	29	86
Bromsgrove Rovers	42	24	11	7	82	41	83
Aylesbury United	42	24	11	7	72	40	83
Dartford	42	19	12	11	76	43	69
Chelmsford City	42	17	13	12	48	45	64
Cambridge City	42	14	20	8	68	52	62
Redditch United	42	16	14	12	59	54	62
Alvechurch	42	18	8	16	66	62	62
Corby Town	42	14	17	11	65	51	59
Worcester City	42	16	11	15	62	55	59
Shepshed Charterhouse	42	16	10	16	59	59	58
Bedworth United	42	15	12	15	55	51	57
Crawley Town	42	14	11	17	59	60	53
Fareham Town	42	11	17	14	58	49	50
Willenhall Town	42	13	11	18	48	57	50
Basingstoke Town	42	12	12	18	53	78	48
Witney Town	42	12	12	18	29	56	48
Gosport Borough	42	11	13	18	42	57	46
Salisbury	42	12	7	23	52	82	43
King's Lynn	42	9	13	20	48	72	40
Dudley Town	42	9	9	24	39	76	36
Folkestone	42	8	11	23	36	79	35

Midland Division

VS Rugby	38	25	5	8	81	43	80
Leicester United	38	26	1	11	89	49	79
Merthyr Tydfil	38	23	6	9	95	54	75
Moor Green	38	22	6	10	73	55	72
Halesowen Town	38	19	12	7	72	50	69
Hednesford Town	38	21	5	12	84	56	68
Gloucester City	38	19	5	14	77	59	62
Coventry Sporting	38	17	8	13	55	54	59
Forest Green Rovers	38	16	9	13	65	53	57
Stourbridge	38	16	7	15	56	56	55
Grantham	38	15	9	14	74	54	54
Banbury United	38	14	7	17	55	65	49
Buckingham Town	38	13	9	16	55	59	48
Bridgnorth Town	38	12	9	17	59	63	45
Wellingborough Town	38	13	6	19	55	76	45
Mile Oak Rovers	38	11	10	17	50	63	43
Sutton Coldfield Town	38	8	10	20	56	78	34
Bilston Town	38	8	7	23	37	76	31
Leamington	38	4	13	21	37	80	25
Rushden Town	38	1	10	27	42	124	13

Southern Division

Dorchester Town	38	23	8	7	83	42	77
Ashford Town	38	23	7	8	63	32	76
Woodford Town	38	22	6	10	72	44	72
Hastings Town	38	20	10	8	74	54	70
Dover Athletic	38	20	6	12	66	43	66
Gravesend & Northfleet	38	18	7	13	67	46	61
Tonbridge AFC	38	16	10	12	73	67	58
Erith & Belvedere	38	15	12	11	57	50	57
Chatham Town	38	16	9	13	53	46	57
Thanet United	38	14	14	10	56	50	56
Waterlooville	38	16	8	14	66	65	56
Trowbridge Town	38	15	9	14	77	65	54
Dunstable	38	13	9	16	60	57	48
Corinthian	38	11	12	15	56	65	45
Sheppey United	38	9	12	17	43	65	39
Andover	38	9	9	20	51	80	36
Burnham & Hillingdon	38	7	11	20	32	62	32
Poole Town	38	8	6	24	50	90	30
Ruislip	38	6	12	20	35	75	30
Canterbury City	38	8	5	25	46	82	29

1987-88

Premier Division

Aylesbury United	42	27	8	7	79	35	89
Dartford	42	27	8	7	79	39	89
Cambridge City	42	24	8	10	84	43	80
Bromsgrove Rovers	42	22	11	9	65	39	77
Worcester City	42	22	6	14	58	48	72
Crawley Town	42	17	14	11	73	63	65
Alvechurch	42	17	13	12	54	52	64
Leicester United	42	15	14	13	68	59	59
Fareham Town	42	16	11	15	51	59	59
Corby Town	42	16	8	18	61	64	56
Dorchester Town	42	14	14	14	51	57	56
Ashford Town	42	12	16	14	45	54	52
Shepshed Charterhouse	42	13	11	18	53	62	50
Bedworth United	42	12	14	16	49	64	50
Gosport Borough	42	10	17	15	39	49	47
Burton Albion	42	11	14	17	62	74	47
VS Rugby	42	10	16	16	52	57	46
Redditch United	42	10	13	19	55	63	43
Chelmsford City	42	11	10	21	60	75	43
Willenhall Town	42	9	12	21	39	76	39
Nuneaton Borough	42	8	13	21	58	77	37
Witney Town	42	8	11	23	45	71	35

Midland Division

Merthyr Tydfil	42	30	4	8	102	40	94
Moor Green	42	26	8	8	91	49	86
Grantham Town	42	27	4	11	97	53	85
Atherstone United	42	22	10	10	93	56	76
Sutton Coldfield Town	42	22	6	14	71	47	72
Halesowen Town	42	18	15	9	75	59	69
Gloucester City	42	18	14	10	86	62	68
Dudley Town	42	20	5	17	64	55	65
Forest Green Rovers	42	14	16	12	67	54	58
Banbury United	42	17	7	18	48	46	58
Bridgnorth Town	42	16	7	19	59	75	55
Buckingham Town	42	15	9	18	74	75	54
King's Lynn	42	16	6	20	53	63	54
Wellingborough Town	42	14	10	18	67	70	52
Rushden Town	42	14	9	19	69	85	51
Trowbridge Town	42	14	3	25	53	82	45
Bilston Town	42	12	8	22	52	87	44
Hednesford Town	42	11	10	21	50	81	43
Mile Oak Rovers	42	9	14	19	43	65	41
Coventry Sporting	42	11	8	23	46	83	41
Stourbridge	42	10	10	22	46	79	40
Paget Rangers	42	10	9	23	49	89	39

Southern Division

Dover Athletic	40	28	10	2	81	28	94
Waterlooville	40	27	10	3	88	33	91
Salisbury	40	24	11	5	71	33	83
Gravesend & Northfleet	40	20	12	8	60	32	72
Thanet United	40	17	13	10	60	38	64
Andover	40	17	13	10	64	58	64
Dunstable	40	17	12	11	78	56	63
Burnham	40	17	10	13	61	45	61
Bury Town	40	17	7	16	80	67	58
Erith & Belvedere	40	16	9	15	52	56	57
Sheppey United	40	14	10	16	58	52	52
Hastings Town	40	14	10	16	62	70	52
Tonbridge AFC	40	14	8	18	51	56	50
Poole Town	40	13	10	17	69	70	49
Baldock Town	40	12	12	16	44	53	48
Hounslow	40	11	8	21	41	76	41
Folkestone	40	9	11	20	47	76	38
Corinthian	40	9	10	21	49	67	37
Ruislip	40	5	13	22	33	80	28
Canterbury City	40	7	6	27	33	87	27
Chatham Town	40	7	5	28	39	88	26

1988-89

Premier Division

Merthyr Tydfil	42	26	7	9	104	58	85
Dartford	42	25	7	10	79	33	82
VS Rugby	42	24	7	11	64	43	79
Worcester City	42	20	13	9	72	49	73
Cambridge City	42	20	10	12	72	51	70
Dover Athletic	42	19	12	11	65	47	69
Gosport Borough	42	18	12	12	73	57	66
Burton Albion	42	18	10	14	79	68	64
Bath City	42	15	13	14	66	51	58
Bromsgrove Rovers	42	14	16	12	68	56	59
Wealdstone	42	16	10	16	60	53	59
Crawley Town	42	14	16	12	61	56	59
Dorchester Town	42	14	16	12	56	61	59
Alvechurch	42	16	8	18	56	59	56
Moor Green	42	14	13	15	58	70	55
Corby Town	42	14	11	17	55	59	53
Waterlooville	42	13	13	16	61	63	52
Ashford Town	42	13	13	16	59	76	52
Fareham Town	42	15	6	21	43	68	51
Leicester United	42	6	11	25	46	84	29
Redditch United	42	5	7	30	36	105	22
Bedworth United	42	4	7	31	36	102	19

Midland Division

Gloucester City	42	28	8	6	95	37	92
Atherstone United	42	26	9	7	85	38	87
Tamworth	42	26	9	7	85	45	87
Halesowen Town	42	25	10	7	85	42	85
Grantham Town	42	23	11	8	66	37	80
Nuneaton Borough	42	19	9	14	71	58	66
Rushden Town	42	19	8	15	71	50	65
Spalding United	42	17	13	12	72	64	64
Dudley Town	42	16	13	13	73	62	61
Sutton Coldfield Town	42	18	7	17	56	56	61
Willenhall Town	42	16	12	14	65	71	60
Forest Green Rovers	42	12	16	14	64	67	52
Bilston Town	42	15	7	20	63	71	52
Ashtree Highfield	42	12	15	15	57	62	51
Hednesford Town	42	12	15	15	49	57	51
Banbury United	42	10	14	18	53	74	44
Bridgnorth Town	42	12	7	23	59	77	43
Stourbridge	42	11	10	21	37	65	43
King's Lynn	42	7	13	22	31	67	34
Coventry Sporting	42	6	13	23	39	91	31
Wellingborough Town	42	5	15	22	39	72	30
Mile Oak Rovers	42	5	10	27	46	98	25

Southern Division

Chelmsford City	42	30	5	7	106	38	95
Gravesend & Northfleet	42	27	6	9	70	40	87
Poole Town	42	24	11	7	98	48	83
Bury Town	42	25	7	10	75	34	82
Burnham	42	22	13	7	78	47	79
Baldock Town	42	23	5	14	69	40	74
Hastings Town	42	21	11	10	75	48	74
Hounslow	42	21	6	15	75	60	69
Salisbury	42	20	5	17	79	58	65
Trowbridge Town	42	19	7	16	59	52	64
Folkestone	42	17	8	17	62	65	59
Corinthian	42	13	13	16	59	69	52
Canterbury City	42	14	8	20	52	60	50
Witney Town	42	13	11	18	61	71	50
Dunstable	42	11	14	17	42	57	47
Buckingham Town	42	12	10	20	56	79	46
Erith & Belvedere	42	11	10	21	48	63	43
Andover	42	11	9	22	56	90	42
Sheppey United	42	10	8	24	50	90	38
Thanet United	42	7	15	20	47	95	36
Tonbridge AFC	42	7	6	29	50	98	27
Ruislip	42	6	8	28	47	112	26

1989-90

Premier Division

	P	W	D	L	F	A	Pts
Dover Athletic	42	32	6	4	87	27	102
Bath City	42	30	8	4	81	28	98
Dartford	42	26	9	7	80	35	87
Burton Albion	42	20	12	10	64	40	72
VS Rugby	42	19	12	11	51	35	69
Atherstone United	42	19	10	13	60	52	67
Gravesend & Northfleet	42	18	12	12	44	50	66
Cambridge City	42	17	11	14	76	56	62
Gloucester City	42	17	11	14	80	68	62
Bromsgrove Rovers	42	17	10	15	56	48	61
Moor Green	42	18	7	17	62	59	61
Wealdstone	42	16	9	17	55	54	57
Dorchester Town	42	16	7	19	52	67	55
Worcester City	42	15	10	17	62	63	54
Crawley Town	42	13	12	17	53	57	51
Waterlooville	42	13	10	19	63	81	49
Weymouth	42	11	13	18	50	70	46
Chelmsford City	42	11	10	21	52	72	43
Ashford Town	42	10	7	25	43	75	37
Corby Town	42	10	6	26	57	77	36
Alvechurch	42	7	5	30	46	95	26
Gosport Borough	42	6	5	31	28	93	23

Midland Division

	P	W	D	L	F	A	Pts
Halesowen Town	42	28	8	6	100	49	92
Rushden Town	42	28	5	9	82	39	89
Nuneaton Borough	42	26	7	9	81	47	85
Tamworth	42	22	8	12	82	70	74
Barry Town	42	21	8	13	67	53	71
Spalding United	42	20	7	15	73	63	67
Sutton Coldfield Town	42	18	10	14	72	69	64
Stourbridge	42	17	12	13	73	61	63
Dudley Town	42	18	9	15	69	64	63
Stroud	42	16	13	13	75	62	61
Leicester United	42	17	5	20	66	77	56
Bridgnorth Town	42	13	14	15	68	73	53
King's Lynn	42	16	5	21	57	69	53
Grantham Town	42	14	10	18	57	63	52
Bedworth United	42	14	9	19	50	60	51
Hednesford Town	42	11	14	17	50	62	47
Bilston Town	42	11	14	17	40	54	47
Redditch United	42	11	13	18	57	64	46
Racing Club Warwick	42	11	11	20	45	66	44
Willenhall Town	42	9	9	24	37	66	36
Banbury United	42	9	9	24	46	83	34
Sandwell Borough	42	6	12	24	46	79	30

Southern Division

	P	W	D	L	F	A	Pts
Bashley	42	25	7	10	80	47	82
Poole Town	42	23	8	11	85	60	77
Buckingham Town	42	22	10	10	67	46	76
Dunstable	42	20	14	8	56	38	74
Salisbury	42	21	9	12	72	50	72
Hythe Town	42	20	12	10	69	48	72
Trowbridge Town	42	20	9	13	79	64	69
Hastings Town	42	20	9	13	64	54	69
Bury Town	42	18	12	12	76	62	66
Baldock Town	42	18	11	13	69	52	65
Burnham	42	17	11	14	77	52	62
Fareham Town	42	14	14	14	49	53	56
Yate Town	42	16	6	20	53	52	54
Witney Town	42	16	6	20	54	56	54
Canterbury City	42	14	10	18	52	52	52
Margate	42	12	15	15	46	45	51
Folkestone	42	14	9	19	61	83	51
Andover	42	13	11	18	54	70	50
Hounslow	42	11	5	26	39	82	38
Erith & Belvedere	42	8	11	23	34	73	35
Corinthian	42	6	10	26	44	93	28
Sheppey United	42	6	7	29	35	83	25

1990-91

Premier Division

	P	W	D	L	F	A	Pts
Farnborough Town	42	26	7	9	79	43	85
Gloucester City	42	23	14	5	86	49	83
Cambridge City	42	21	14	7	63	43	77
Dover Athletic	42	21	11	10	56	37	74
Bromsgrove Rovers	42	20	11	11	68	49	71
Worcester City	42	18	12	12	55	42	66
Burton Albion	42	15	15	12	59	48	60
Halesowen Town	42	17	9	16	73	67	60
VS Rugby	42	16	11	15	56	46	59
Bashley	42	15	12	15	56	52	57
Dorchester Town	42	15	12	15	47	54	57
Wealdstone	42	16	8	18	57	58	56
Dartford	42	15	9	18	61	64	54
Rushden Town	42	14	11	17	64	66	53
Atherstone United	42	14	10	18	55	58	52
Moor Green	42	15	6	21	64	75	51
Poole Town	42	12	13	17	56	69	49
Chelmsford City	42	11	15	16	37	68	48
Crawley Town	42	12	12	18	45	67	48
Waterlooville	42	11	13	18	51	70	46
Gravesend & Northfleet	42	9	7	26	46	91	34
Weymouth	42	4	12	26	50	88	24

Midland Division

	P	W	D	L	F	A	Pts
Stourbridge	42	28	6	8	80	48	90
Corby Town	42	27	4	11	99	48	85
Hednesford Town	42	25	7	10	79	47	82
Tamworth	42	25	5	12	84	45	80
Nuneaton Borough	42	21	11	10	74	51	70
Barry Town	42	20	7	15	61	48	67
Newport AFC	42	19	6	17	54	46	63
King's Lynn	42	17	9	16	53	62	60
Grantham Town	42	17	7	18	62	56	56
Redditch United	42	16	10	16	66	75	58
Hinckley Town	42	16	9	17	72	68	57
Sutton Coldfield Town	42	15	11	16	56	65	56
Bedworth United	42	15	9	18	57	73	54
Bilston Town	42	14	9	19	69	79	51
Leicester United	42	14	10	18	65	77	51
Racing Club Warwick	42	12	13	17	56	65	49
Bridgnorth Town	42	13	9	20	61	74	48
Stroud	42	11	14	17	51	64	47
Dudley Town	42	11	13	18	48	73	46
Alvechurch	42	10	8	24	54	92	38
Willenhall Town	42	10	10	22	58	69	37
Spalding United	42	8	9	25	35	70	33

Southern Division

	P	W	D	L	F	A	Pts
Buckingham Town	40	25	8	7	73	38	83
Trowbridge Town	40	22	12	6	67	31	78
Salisbury	40	22	11	7	63	39	77
Baldock Town	40	21	9	10	66	52	72
Ashford Town	40	22	5	13	82	52	71
Yate Town	40	21	8	11	76	48	71
Hastings Town	40	18	11	11	66	46	65
Hythe Town	40	17	9	14	55	44	59
Andover	40	16	6	18	69	76	54
Margate	40	14	11	15	52	55	53
Burnham	40	12	16	12	57	49	52
Bury Town	40	15	5	20	58	74	50
Sudbury Town	40	13	0	17	60	68	49
Newport IOW	40	13	9	18	56	62	48
Gosport Borough	40	12	11	17	47	58	47
Witney Town	40	12	11	17	57	75	47
Dunstable	40	9	15	16	48	63	42
Canterbury City	40	12	6	22	60	83	42
Erith & Belvedere	40	10	0	24	46	73	36
Fareham Town	40	9	9	22	46	74	36
Corinthian	40	5	12	23	34	78	27

1991-92

Premier Division

Bromsgrove Rovers	42	27	9	6	78	34	90
Dover Athletic	42	23	15	4	66	30	84
VS Rugby	42	23	11	8	70	44	80
Bashley	42	22	8	12	70	44	74
Cambridge City	42	18	14	10	71	53	68
Dartford	42	17	15	10	62	45	66
Trowbridge Town	42	17	10	15	69	51	61
Halesowen Town	42	15	15	12	61	49	60
Moor Green	42	15	11	16	61	59	56
Burton Albion	42	15	10	17	59	61	55
Dorchester Town	42	14	13	15	66	73	55
Gloucester City	42	15	9	18	67	70	54
Atherstone United	42	15	8	19	54	66	53
Corby Town	42	13	12	17	66	81	51
Waterlooville	42	13	11	18	43	56	50
Worcester City	42	12	13	17	56	59	49
Crawley Town	42	12	12	18	62	67	48
Chelmsford City	42	12	12	18	49	56	48
Wealdstone	42	13	7	22	52	69	46
Poole Town	42	10	13	19	46	77	43
Fisher Athletic	42	9	11	22	53	89	38
Gravesend & Northfleet	42	8	9	25	39	87	33

1992-93

Premier Division

Dover Athletic	40	25	11	4	65	23	86
Cheltenham Town	40	21	10	9	76	40	73
Corby Town	40	20	12	8	68	43	72
Hednesford Town	40	21	7	12	72	52	70
Trowbridge Town	40	18	8	14	70	66	62
Crawley Town	40	16	12	12	68	59	60
Solihull Borough	40	17	9	14	68	59	60
Burton Albion	40	16	11	13	53	50	59
Bashley	40	18	8	14	60	60	59
Halesowen Town	40	15	11	14	67	54	56
Waterlooville	40	15	9	16	59	62	54
Chelmsford City	40	15	9	16	59	69	54
Gloucester City	40	14	11	15	66	68	53
Cambridge City	40	14	10	16	62	73	52
Atherstone United	40	13	14	13	56	60	50
Hastings Town	40	13	11	16	50	55	50
Worcester City	40	12	9	19	45	62	45
Dorchester Town	40	12	6	22	52	74	42
Moor Green	40	10	6	24	58	79	36
VS Rugby	40	10	6	24	40	63	36
Weymouth	40	5	10	25	39	82	23

Bashley had 3 points deducted

Midland Division

Solihull Borough	42	29	10	3	92	40	97
Hednesford Town	42	26	13	3	81	37	91
Sutton Coldfield Town	42	21	11	10	71	51	74
Barry Town	42	21	6	15	88	56	69
Bedworth United	42	16	15	11	67	63	63
Nuneaton Borough	42	17	11	14	68	53	62
Tamworth	42	16	12	14	66	52	60
Rushden Town	42	16	12	14	69	63	60
Stourbridge	42	17	8	17	85	62	59
Newport AFC	42	15	13	14	72	60	58
Yate Town	42	14	15	13	65	64	57
Bilston Town	42	15	10	17	56	67	55
Grantham Town	42	11	17	14	59	55	50
King's Lynn	42	13	11	18	61	68	50
Hinckley Town	42	14	8	20	61	87	50
Leicester United	42	12	13	17	56	63	49
Bridgnorth Town	42	12	12	18	61	74	48
Racing Club Warwick	42	11	14	17	45	61	47
Stroud	42	14	4	24	66	88	46
Redditch United	42	12	8	22	52	92	44
Alvechurch	42	11	10	21	54	88	43
Dudley Town	42	8	9	25	41	92	33

Midland Division

Nuneaton Borough	42	29	5	8	102	45	92
Gresley Rovers	42	27	6	9	94	55	87
Rushden & Diamonds	42	25	10	7	85	41	85
Barri	42	26	5	11	82	49	83
Newport AFC	42	23	8	11	73	58	77
Bedworth United	42	22	8	12	72	55	74
Stourbridge	42	17	9	16	93	79	60
Sutton Coldfield Town	42	17	9	16	82	78	60
Redditch United	42	18	6	18	75	79	60
Tamworth	42	16	11	15	65	51	59
Weston-super-Mare	42	17	7	18	79	86	58
Leicester United	42	16	9	17	67	67	57
Grantham Town	42	16	9	17	60	73	57
Bilston Town	42	15	10	17	74	69	55
Evesham United	42	15	8	19	67	83	53
Bridgnorth Town	42	15	7	20	61	68	52
Dudley Town	42	14	8	20	60	75	50
Yate Town	42	15	5	22	63	81	50
Forest Green Rovers	42	12	6	24	61	97	42
Hinckley Athletic	42	9	11	22	56	89	37
King's Lynn	42	10	6	26	45	90	36
Racing Club Warwick	42	3	7	32	40	88	16

Southern Division

Hastings Town	42	28	7	7	80	37	91
Weymouth	42	22	12	8	64	35	78
Havant Town	42	21	12	9	67	46	75
Braintree Town	42	21	8	13	77	58	71
Buckingham Town	42	19	15	8	57	26	69
Andover	42	18	10	14	73	68	64
Ashford Town	42	17	12	13	66	57	63
Sudbury Town	42	18	9	15	70	66	63
Sittingbourne	42	19	10	13	63	41	61
Burnham	42	15	14	13	57	55	59
Baldock Town	42	16	10	16	62	67	58
Salisbury	42	13	16	13	67	51	55
Hythe Town	42	15	10	17	61	62	55
Margate	42	13	16	13	49	56	55
Newport IOW	42	13	10	19	58	63	49
Dunstable	42	12	12	18	55	67	48
Bury Town	42	14	4	24	52	94	46
Witney Town	42	11	12	19	55	76	45
Fareham Town	42	12	8	22	45	71	44
Erith & Belvedere	42	11	10	21	44	67	43
Canterbury City	42	8	14	20	43	69	38
Gosport Borough	42	6	9	27	32	65	27

Southern Division

Sittingbourne	42	26	12	4	102	43	90
Salisbury	42	27	7	8	87	50	88
Witney Town	42	25	9	8	77	37	84
Gravesend & Northfleet	42	25	4	13	99	63	79
Havant Town	42	23	6	13	78	55	75
Sudbury Town	42	20	11	11	89	54	71
Erith & Belvedere	42	22	5	15	73	66	71
Ashford Town	42	20	8	14	91	66	68
Braintree Town	42	20	6	16	95	65	66
Margate	42	19	7	16	65	58	64
Wealdstone	42	18	7	17	75	69	61
Buckingham Town	42	16	11	15	61	58	59
Baldock Town	42	15	9	18	59	63	54
Poole Town	42	15	7	20	61	69	52
Fareham Town	42	14	8	20	60	65	50
Burnham	42	14	8	20	53	77	50
Canterbury City	42	12	10	20	54	76	46
Newport IOW	42	9	16	17	44	56	43
Fisher Athletic	42	8	9	25	38	98	33
Andover	42	7	9	26	42	99	30
Dunstable	42	5	14	23	42	92	29
Bury Town	42	8	5	29	46	119	29

1993-94

Premier Division

	P	W	D	L	F	A	Pts
Farnborough Town	42	25	7	10	74	44	82
Cheltenham Town	42	21	12	9	67	38	75
Halesowen Town	42	21	11	10	69	46	74
Atherstone United	42	22	7	13	57	43	73
Crawley Town	42	21	10	11	56	42	73
Chelmsford City	42	21	7	14	74	59	70
Trowbridge Town	42	16	17	9	52	41	65
Sittingbourne	42	17	13	12	65	48	64
Corby Town	42	17	8	17	52	56	59
Gloucester City	42	17	6	19	55	60	57
Burton Albion	42	15	11	10	57	49	56
Hastings Town	42	16	7	19	51	60	55
Hednesford Town	42	15	9	18	67	66	54
Gresley Rovers	42	14	11	17	61	72	53
Worcester City	42	14	9	19	61	70	51
Solihull Borough	42	13	11	18	52	57	50
Cambridge City	42	13	11	18	50	60	50
Dorchester Town	42	12	11	19	38	51	47
Moor Green	42	11	10	21	49	66	43
Waterlooville	42	11	10	21	47	69	43
Bashley	42	11	10	21	47	80	43
Nuneaton Borough	42	11	8	23	42	66	41

Midland Division

	P	W	D	L	F	A	Pts
Rushden & Diamonds	42	29	11	2	109	37	98
VS Rugby	42	28	8	6	98	41	92
Weston-super-Mare	42	27	10	5	94	39	91
Newport AFC	42	26	9	7	84	37	87
Clevedon Town	42	24	10	8	75	46	82
Redditch United	42	19	11	12	79	62	68
Tamworth	42	19	7	16	82	68	64
Bilston Town	42	16	10	16	65	73	58
Stourbridge	42	17	6	19	71	75	57
Evesham United	42	16	8	18	50	60	56
Grantham Town	42	16	6	20	77	73	54
Bridgnorth Town	42	15	6	21	56	68	51
Racing Club Warwick	42	13	12	17	53	66	51
Dudley Town	42	13	10	19	64	61	49
Forest Green Rangers	42	12	12	18	61	84	48
Sutton Coldfield Town	42	12	8	22	53	75	44
Bedworth United	42	12	7	23	62	81	43
Hinckley Town	42	11	10	21	44	71	43
Leicester United	42	11	9	22	34	73	42
King's Lynn	42	9	11	22	47	72	38
Yate Town	42	10	6	26	48	86	36
Armitage	42	8	11	23	45	103	35

Southern Division

	P	W	D	L	F	A	Pts
Gravesend & Northfleet	42	27	11	4	87	24	92
Sudbury Town	42	27	8	7	98	47	89
Witney Town	42	27	8	7	69	36	89
Salisbury City	42	26	10	6	90	39	88
Havant Town	42	27	4	11	101	41	85
Ashford Town	42	24	13	5	93	46	85
Baldock Town	42	26	7	9	76	40	85
Newport IOW	42	22	8	12	74	51	74
Margate	42	20	8	14	76	58	68
Weymouth	42	18	9	15	71	65	63
Tonbridge	42	19	5	18	59	62	62
Buckingham Town	42	14	14	14	43	42	56
Braintree Town	42	16	7	19	72	84	55
Fareham Town	42	12	12	18	54	75	48
Poole Town	42	13	6	23	54	86	45
Burnham	42	10	9	23	53	92	39
Fisher 93	42	9	10	23	52	81	37
Dunstable	42	9	7	26	50	91	34
Erith & Belvedere	42	9	5	28	40	72	32
Canterbury City	42	8	7	27	35	80	31
Wealdstone	42	6	7	29	45	95	25
Bury Town	42	3	5	34	36	121	14

1994-95

Premier Division

	P	W	D	L	F	A	Pts
Hednesford Town	42	28	9	5	99	49	93
Cheltenham Town	42	25	11	6	87	39	86
Burton Albion	42	20	15	7	55	39	75
Gloucester City	42	22	8	12	76	48	74
Rushden & Diamonds	42	19	11	12	99	65	68
Dorchester Town	42	19	10	13	84	61	67
Leek Town	42	19	10	13	72	60	67
Gresley Rovers	42	17	12	13	70	63	63
Cambridge City	42	18	8	16	60	55	62
Worcester City	42	14	15	13	46	34	57
Crawley Town	42	15	10	17	64	71	55
Hastings Town	42	13	14	15	55	57	53
Halesowen Town	42	14	10	18	81	80	52
Gravesend & Northfleet	42	16	13	16	38	55	52
Chelmsford City	42	14	6	22	56	60	48
Atherstone United	42	12	12	18	51	67	48
VS Rugby	42	11	14	17	49	61	47
Sudbury Town	42	12	10	20	50	77	46
Solihull Borough	42	10	15	17	39	65	45
Sittingbourne	42	11	10	21	51	73	43
Trowbridge Town	42	9	13	20	43	69	40
Corby Town	42	4	10	28	36	113	21

Corby Town had 1 point deducted for fielding ineligible players

Midland Division

	P	W	D	L	F	A	Pts
Newport AFC	42	29	8	5	106	39	95
Ilkeston Town	42	25	6	11	101	75	81
Tamworth	42	24	8	10	98	70	80
Moor Green	42	23	8	11	105	63	77
Bridgnorth Town	42	22	10	10	75	49	76
Buckingham Town	42	20	14	8	55	37	74
Nuneaton Borough	42	19	11	12	76	55	68
Rothwell Town	42	19	7	16	71	71	64
King's Lynn	42	18	8	16	76	64	62
Racing Club Warwick	42	17	11	14	68	63	62
Dudley Town	42	17	10	15	65	69	61
Bilston Town	42	17	8	17	73	64	59
Bedworth United	42	17	7	18	64	68	58
Evesham United	42	14	14	14	58	56	52
Hinckley Town	42	14	0	18	61	76	52
Stourbridge	42	15	7	20	59	77	52
Sutton Coldfield Town	42	12	10	20	62	72	46
Forest Green Rovers	42	11	13	18	56	76	46
Redditch United	42	8	14	20	47	64	38
Leicester United	42	10	8	24	51	99	38
Grantham Town	42	8	9	25	55	93	33
Armitage	42	2	5	35	35	116	11

Southern Division

	P	W	D	L	F	A	Pts
Salisbury City	42	30	7	5	88	37	97
Baldock Town	42	28	10	4	92	44	94
Havant Town	42	25	10	7	81	34	85
Waterlooville	42	24	8	10	77	36	80
Ashford Town	42	21	12	9	106	72	75
Weston-super-Mare	42	18	13	11	82	54	67
Bashley	42	18	11	13	62	49	65
Weymouth	42	16	13	13	60	55	61
Newporth IOW	42	17	10	15	67	67	61
Witney Town	42	14	14	14	57	57	56
Clevedon Town	42	14	13	15	73	64	55
Tonbridge Angels	42	14	12	16	74	87	54
Margate	42	15	7	20	60	72	52
Braintree Town	42	12	13	17	64	71	49
Wealdstone	42	13	8	21	76	94	47
Yate Town	42	11	13	18	57	75	46
Fisher 93	42	9	16	17	54	70	43
Bury Town	42	11	8	23	59	86	41
Erith & Belvedere	42	10	9	23	49	94	39
Poole Town	42	10	8	24	53	79	38
Fareham Town	42	10	8	24	46	91	38
Burnham	42	7	7	28	40	89	28

1995-96

Premier Division

Rushden & Diamonds	42	29	7	6	99	41	94
Halesowen Town	42	27	11	4	70	36	92
Cheltenham Town	42	21	11	10	76	57	74
Gloucester City	42	21	8	13	65	47	71
Gresley Rovers	42	20	10	12	70	58	70
Worcester City	42	19	12	11	61	43	69
Merthyr Tydfil	42	19	6	17	67	59	63
Hastings Town	42	16	13	13	68	56	61
Crawley Town	42	15	13	14	57	56	58
Sudbury Town	42	15	10	17	69	71	55
Gravesend & Northfleet	42	15	10	17	60	62	55
Chelmsford City	42	13	16	13	46	53	55
Dorchester Town	42	15	8	19	62	57	53
Newport AFC	42	13	13	16	53	59	52
Salisbury City	42	14	10	18	57	69	52
Burton Albion	42	13	12	17	55	56	51
Atherstone United	42	12	12	18	58	75	48
Baldock Town	42	11	14	17	51	56	47
Cambridge City	42	12	10	20	56	68	46
Ilkeston Town	42	11	10	21	53	87	43
Stafford Rangers	42	11	4	27	58	90	37
VS Rugby	42	5	10	27	37	92	25

Midland Division

Nuneaton Borough	42	30	5	7	82	35	95
King's Lynn	42	27	5	10	85	43	84
Bedworth United	42	24	10	8	76	42	81
Moor Green	42	22	8	12	81	47	74
Paget Rangers	42	21	9	12	70	45	72
Tamworth	42	22	3	17	97	64	69
Solihull Borough	42	19	9	14	77	64	66
Rothwell Town	42	17	14	11	79	62	65
Buckingham Town	42	18	9	15	74	62	63
Dudley Town	42	15	16	11	83	66	61
Stourbridge	42	17	8	17	60	63	59
Bilston Town	42	16	9	17	61	62	57
Sutton Coldfield Town	42	16	9	17	62	67	57
Grantham Town	42	17	5	20	71	83	56
Redditch United	42	14	11	17	57	77	53
Leicester United	42	13	13	16	58	72	52
Hinckley Town	42	14	7	21	62	83	49
Racing Club Warwick	42	10	13	19	67	90	43
Evesham United	42	11	6	25	59	94	39
Corby Town	42	9	7	26	52	95	34
Bury Town	42	8	8	26	57	95	32
Bridgnorth Town	42	7	6	29	53	112	27

Bedworth United 1 point deducted, King's Lynn had 2 points deducted

Southern Division

Sittingbourne	42	28	4	10	102	44	88
Ashford Town	42	25	9	8	75	44	84
Waterlooville	42	24	8	10	87	44	80
Newport IOW	42	24	6	12	75	58	78
Braintree Town	42	24	8	10	93	70	77
Weymouth	42	24	4	14	75	55	76
Havant Town	42	23	11	8	73	42	74
Forest Green Rovers	42	22	8	12	85	55	74
Trowbridge Town	42	18	8	16	86	51	62
Yate Town	42	17	8	17	67	59	59
Margate	42	18	5	19	68	62	59
Witney Town	42	16	11	15	60	54	59
Weston-super-Mare	42	16	9	17	78	68	57
Cinderford Town	42	16	8	18	74	77	56
Fisher 93	42	14	13	15	58	59	55
Bashley	42	14	11	17	63	61	53
Clevedon Town	42	15	6	21	70	80	51
Tonbridge Angels	42	13	10	19	58	79	49
Fleet Town	42	14	5	23	58	79	47
Fareham Town	42	12	5	25	71	97	41
Erith & Belvedere	42	4	4	34	38	111	16
Poole Town	42	0	1	41	17	188	1

Braintree Town 3 points deducted, Havant Town had 6 points deducted

1996-97

Premier Division

Gresley Rovers	42	25	10	7	75	40	85
Cheltenham Town	42	21	11	10	76	44	74
Gloucester City	42	21	10	11	81	56	73
Halesowen Town	42	21	10	11	77	54	73
King's Lynn	42	20	8	14	65	61	68
Burton Albion	42	18	12	12	70	53	66
Nuneaton Borough	42	19	9	14	61	52	66
Sittingbourne	42	19	7	16	76	65	64
Merthyr Tydfil	42	17	9	16	69	61	60
Worcester City	42	15	14	13	52	50	59
Atherstone United	42	15	13	14	46	47	58
Salisbury City	42	15	13	14	57	66	58
Sudbury Town	42	16	7	19	72	72	55
Gravesend & Northfleet	42	16	7	19	63	73	55
Dorchester Town	42	14	9	19	62	66	51
Hastings Town	42	12	15	15	49	60	51
Crawley Town	42	13	8	21	49	67	47
Cambridge City	42	11	13	18	57	65	46
Ashford Town	42	9	18	15	53	79	45
Baldock Town	42	11	8	23	52	90	41
Newport AFC	42	9	13	20	40	60	40
Chelmsford City	42	6	14	22	49	70	32

Midland Division

Tamworth	40	30	7	3	90	28	97
Rothwell Town	40	20	11	9	82	54	71
Ilkeston Town	40	19	13	8	76	50	70
Grantham Town	40	22	4	14	65	46	70
Bedworth United	40	18	11	11	77	41	65
Solihull Borough	40	19	8	13	84	62	65
Bilston Town	40	18	10	12	74	57	64
Moor Green	40	18	7	15	88	68	61
Stafford Rangers	40	17	9	14	68	62	60
Raunds Town	40	16	11	13	61	66	59
Racing Club Warwick	40	16	10	14	70	72	58
Shepshed Dynamo	40	14	12	14	64	65	54
Redditch United	40	15	8	17	56	59	53
Paget Rangers	40	13	9	18	42	55	48
Dudley Town	40	12	10	18	70	89	46
Hinckley Town	40	11	11	18	39	63	44
Stourbridge	40	10	9	21	61	81	39
Evesham United	40	9	12	19	55	77	39
VS Rugby	40	9	9	22	49	81	36
Corby Town	40	8	8	24	49	88	32
Sutton Coldfield Town	40	7	9	24	29	85	30

Leicester United FC closed down and their record was expunged from the League table.

Southern Division

Forest Green Rovers	42	27	10	5	87	40	91
St Leonards Stamcroft	42	26	9	7	95	48	87
Havant Town	42	23	10	9	81	49	79
Weston-super-Mare	42	21	13	8	82	43	76
Margate	42	21	9	12	70	47	72
Witney Town	42	20	11	11	71	42	71
Weymouth	42	20	10	12	82	51	70
Tonbridge Angels	42	17	15	10	56	44	66
Newport IOW	42	15	15	12	73	58	60
Fisher Athletic (London)	42	18	6	18	77	77	60
Clevedon Town	42	17	9	16	75	76	60
Fareham Town	42	14	12	16	53	70	54
Bashley	42	15	8	19	73	84	53
Dartford	42	14	10	18	59	64	52
Waterlooville	42	14	9	19	58	67	51
Cirencester Town	42	12	12	18	50	68	48
Cinderford Town	42	13	7	22	64	76	46
Trowbridge Town	42	11	11	20	50	61	44
Yate Town	42	12	8	22	55	87	44
Fleet Town	42	12	6	24	47	91	42
Erith & Belvedere	42	9	10	23	60	95	37
Buckingham Town	42	2	8	32	27	107	14

1997-98

Premier Division

Forest Green Rovers	42	27	8	7	93	55	89
Merthyr Tydfil	42	24	12	6	80	42	84
Burton Albion	42	21	8	13	64	43	71
Dorchester Town	42	19	13	10	63	38	70
Halesowen Town	42	18	15	9	70	38	69
Bath City	42	19	12	11	72	51	69
Worcester City	42	19	12	11	54	44	69
King's Lynn	42	18	11	13	64	65	65
Atherstone United	42	17	12	13	55	49	63
Crawley Town	42	17	8	17	63	60	59
Gloucester City	42	16	11	15	57	57	59
Nuneaton Borough	42	17	6	19	68	61	57
Cambridge City	42	16	8	18	62	70	56
Hastings Town	42	14	12	16	67	70	54
Tamworth	42	14	11	17	68	65	53
Rothwell Town	42	11	16	15	55	73	49
Gresley Rovers	42	14	6	22	59	77	48
Salisbury City	42	12	12	18	53	72	48
Bromsgrove Rovers	42	13	6	23	67	85	45
Sittingbourne	42	12	8	22	47	66	44
Ashford Town	42	8	5	29	34	85	29
St Leonards Stamcroft	42	5	10	27	48	97	25

Midland Division

Grantham Town	40	30	4	6	87	39	94
Ilkeston Town	40	29	6	5	123	39	93
Solihull Borough	40	22	9	9	81	48	75
Raunds Town	40	20	8	12	73	44	68
Wisbech Town	40	20	7	13	79	57	67
Moor Green	40	20	7	13	72	55	67
Bilston Town	40	20	5	15	69	57	65
Blakenall	40	17	13	10	66	55	64
Stafford Rangers	40	18	6	16	57	56	60
Redditch United	40	16	11	13	59	41	59
Stourbridge	40	16	9	15	57	55	57
Hinckley United	40	15	11	14	59	56	56
Brackley Town	40	15	7	18	45	57	52
Bedworth United	40	15	5	20	50	73	50
Racing Club Warwick	40	11	9	20	49	56	42
Shepshed Dynamo	40	9	14	17	55	74	41
Sutton Coldfield Town	40	9	12	19	42	68	39
Paget Rangers	40	9	12	19	40	75	39
VS Rugby	40	8	12	20	53	93	36
Evesham United	40	7	9	24	47	94	30
Corby Town	40	2	8	30	41	112	14

Southern Division

Weymouth	42	32	2	8	107	48	98
Chelmsford City	42	29	8	5	86	39	95
Bashley	42	29	4	9	101	59	91
Newport IOW	42	25	9	8	72	34	84
Fisher Athletic (London)	42	25	5	12	87	50	80
Margate	42	23	8	11	71	42	77
Newport AFC	42	21	6	15	83	65	69
Witney Town	42	20	9	13	74	58	69
Clevedon Town	42	20	7	15	57	55	67
Waterlooville	42	17	7	18	69	64	58
Dartford	42	17	7	18	60	60	58
Havant Town	42	13	14	16	65	70	53
Fleet Town	42	16	5	21	63	83	53
Tonbridge Angels	42	14	10	18	49	55	52
Trowbridge Town	42	14	6	22	55	69	48
Erith & Belvedere	42	11	13	18	47	68	46
Fareham Town	42	12	9	21	75	87	45
Cirencester Town	42	12	7	23	63	88	43
Weston-super-Mare	42	12	5	25	49	86	41
Baldock Town	42	10	5	27	53	81	35
Cinderford Town	42	6	5	31	40	112	23
Yate Town	42	5	7	30	44	97	22

1998-99

Premier Division

Nuneaton Borough	42	27	9	6	91	33	90
Boston United	42	17	16	9	69	51	67
Ilkeston Town	42	18	13	11	72	59	67
Bath City	42	18	11	13	70	44	65
Hastings Town	42	18	11	13	57	49	65
Gloucester City	42	18	11	13	57	52	65
Worcester City	42	18	9	15	58	54	63
Halesowen Town	42	17	11	14	72	60	62
Tamworth	42	19	5	18	62	67	62
King's Lynn	42	17	10	15	53	46	61
Crawley Town	42	17	10	15	57	58	61
Salisbury City	42	16	12	14	56	61	60
Burton Albion	42	17	7	18	58	52	58
Weymouth	42	14	14	14	56	55	56
Merthyr Tydfil	42	15	8	19	52	62	53
Atherstone United	42	12	14	16	47	52	50
Grantham Town	42	14	8	20	51	58	50
Dorchester Town	42	11	15	16	49	63	48
Rothwell Town	42	13	9	20	47	67	48
Cambridge City	42	11	12	19	47	68	45
Gresley Rovers	42	12	8	22	49	73	44
Bromsgrove Rovers	42	8	7	27	38	84	31

Hastings Town resigned from the League

Midland Division

Clevedon Town	42	28	8	6	83	35	92
Newport AFC	42	26	7	9	92	51	85
Redditch United	42	22	12	8	81	45	75
Hinckley United	42	20	12	10	58	40	72
Stafford Rangers	42	21	8	13	92	60	71
Bilston Town	42	20	11	11	79	69	71
Solihull Borough	42	19	12	11	76	53	69
Moor Green	42	20	7	15	71	61	67
Blakenall	42	17	14	11	65	54	65
Shepshed Dynamo	42	17	12	13	62	54	63
Sutton Coldfield Town	42	17	8	17	46	57	59
Stourbridge	42	16	10	16	60	55	58
Evesham United	42	16	9	17	63	63	57
Wisbech Town	42	16	9	17	59	66	57
Weston-super-Mare	42	15	10	17	59	56	55
Bedworth United	42	15	9	18	63	52	54
Cinderford Town	42	13	8	21	61	74	47
Stamford AFC	42	13	7	22	60	75	46
Paget Rangers	42	11	12	19	49	58	45
VS Rugby	42	12	9	21	53	74	45
Racing Club Warwick	42	5	8	29	38	93	23
Bloxwich Town	42	1	2	39	26	151	5

Southern Division

Havant & Waterlooville	42	29	7	6	86	32	94
Margate	42	27	8	7	84	33	89
Folkestone Invicta	42	26	8	8	92	47	86
Newport IOW	42	23	7	12	68	40	76
Chelmsford City	42	20	12	10	91	51	72
Raunds Town	42	19	13	10	87	50	70
Ashford Town	42	17	12	13	59	54	63
Baldock Town	42	17	9	16	60	59	60
Fisher Athletic (London)	42	16	11	15	54	59	59
Bashley	42	17	7	18	74	77	58
Witney Town	42	15	12	15	56	48	57
Cirencester Town	42	16	8	18	61	66	56
Sittingbourne	42	11	18	12	53	56	54
Dartford	42	14	10	18	48	53	52
Erith & Belvedere	42	15	7	20	48	64	52
Tonbridge Angels	42	12	15	15	48	59	51
St Leonards	42	14	8	20	57	72	50
Fleet Town	42	11	11	19	54	72	47
Corby Town	42	10	10	22	48	73	40
Yate Town	42	10	7	25	37	79	37
Andover	42	6	10	26	50	115	28
Brackley Town	42	6	8	28	41	105	26

1999-2000

Premier Division

	P	W	D	L	F	A	Pts
Boston United	42	27	11	4	102	39	92
Burton Albion	42	23	9	10	73	43	78
Margate	42	23	8	11	64	43	77
Bath City	42	19	15	8	70	49	72
King's Lynn	42	19	14	9	59	43	71
Tamworth	42	20	10	12	80	51	70
Newport County	42	16	18	8	67	50	66
Clevedon Town	42	18	9	15	52	52	63
Ilkeston Town	42	16	12	14	77	69	60
Weymouth	42	14	16	12	60	51	58
Halesowen Town	42	14	14	14	52	54	56
Crawley Town	42	15	8	19	68	82	53
Havant & Waterlooville	42	13	13	16	63	68	52
Cambridge City	42	14	10	18	52	66	52
Worcester City	42	13	11	18	60	66	50
Salisbury City	42	14	8	20	70	84	50
Merthyr Tydfil	42	13	9	20	51	63	48
Dorchester Town	42	10	17	15	56	65	47
Grantham Town	42	14	5	23	63	76	47
Gloucester City	42	8	14	20	40	82	38
Rothwell Town	42	5	14	23	48	85	29
Atherstone United	42	5	13	24	30	76	28

Eastern Division

	P	W	D	L	F	A	Pts
Fisher Athletic (London)	42	31	5	6	107	42	98
Folkestone Invicta	42	30	7	5	101	39	97
Newport IOW	42	25	7	10	74	40	82
Chelmsford City	42	24	8	10	74	38	80
Hastings Town	42	22	9	11	76	56	75
Ashford Town	42	21	9	12	70	49	72
Tonbridge Angels	42	20	10	12	82	60	70
Dartford	42	17	6	19	52	58	57
Burnham	42	15	9	18	55	64	54
Baldock Town	42	14	10	18	57	69	52
Erith & Belvedere	42	14	9	19	62	68	51
Witney Town	42	13	11	18	48	60	50
VS Rugby	42	13	11	18	58	79	50
Wisbech Town	42	14	7	21	58	66	49
Spalding United	42	14	6	22	52	71	48
Sittingbourne	42	13	7	22	48	75	46
Stamford	42	9	18	15	50	62	45
St Leonards	42	11	12	19	67	81	45
Raunds Town	42	11	12	19	44	63	45
Bashley	42	12	7	23	56	95	43
Corby Town	42	11	12	19	56	62	42
Fleet Town	42	8	8	26	54	104	32

Corby Town had 3 points deducted for fielding an ineligible player
Raunds Town gave notice to withdraw and take the place of the 2nd
relegated Club. They then unsuccessfully sought re-election

Western Division

	P	W	D	L	F	A	Pts
Stafford Rangers	42	29	6	7	107	47	93
Moor Green	42	26	12	4	85	33	90
Hinckley United	42	25	12	5	89	47	87
Tiverton Town	42	26	7	9	91	44	85
Solihull Borough	42	20	11	11	85	66	71
Blakenall	42	19	12	11	70	46	69
Cirencester Town	42	20	8	14	72	64	68
Bilston Town	42	16	18	8	66	52	66
Cinderford Town	42	17	11	14	62	64	62
Redditch United	42	17	10	15	73	65	61
Gresley Rovers	42	14	15	13	54	49	57
Weston-super-Mare	42	16	9	17	55	55	57
Sutton Coldfield Town	42	13	17	12	49	52	56
Evesham United	42	13	12	17	69	61	51
Bedworth Town	42	13	10	19	52	71	49
Rocester	42	12	12	18	63	78	48
Bromsgrove Rovers	42	13	7	22	59	72	46
Shepshed Dynamo	42	12	7	23	46	66	43
Paget Rangers	42	11	4	27	44	82	37
Racing Club Warwick	42	7	14	21	41	82	35
Stourbridge	42	10	3	29	45	101	33
Yate Town	42	3	3	36	28	108	12

2000-2001

Premier Division

	P	W	D	L	F	A	Pts
Margate	42	28	7	7	75	27	91
Burton Albion	42	25	13	4	76	36	88
King's Lynn	42	18	11	13	67	58	65
Welling United	42	17	13	12	59	55	64
Weymouth	42	17	12	13	69	51	63
Havant & Waterlooville	42	18	9	15	65	53	63
Stafford Rangers	42	18	9	15	70	59	63
Worcester City	42	18	8	16	52	53	62
Moor Green	42	18	8	16	49	53	62
Newport County	42	17	10	15	70	61	61
Crawley Town	42	17	10	15	61	54	61
Tamworth	42	17	8	17	58	55	59
Salisbury City	42	17	8	17	64	69	59
Ilkeston Town	42	16	11	15	51	61	59
Bath City	42	15	13	14	67	68	55
Cambridge City	42	13	11	18	56	59	50
Folkestone Invicta	42	14	6	22	49	74	48
Merthyr Tydfil	42	11	13	18	49	62	46
Clevedon Town	42	11	7	24	61	74	40
Fisher Athletic (London)	42	12	6	24	51	85	39
Dorchester Town	42	10	8	24	40	70	38
Halesowen Town	42	8	13	21	47	69	37

Bath City and Fisher Athletic (London) both had 3 points deducted

Eastern Division

	P	W	D	L	F	A	Pts
Newport IOW	42	28	10	4	91	30	94
Chelmsford City	42	27	9	6	102	45	90
Grantham Town	42	25	11	6	100	47	86
Histon	42	23	11	8	84	53	80
Baldock Town	42	23	10	9	81	44	79
Hastings Town	42	22	10	10	72	50	76
Stamford	42	20	11	11	69	59	71
Tonbridge Angels	42	18	11	13	79	58	65
Langney Sports	42	19	8	15	75	55	65
Rothwell Town	42	20	5	17	86	74	62
Corby Town	42	14	10	18	64	92	52
Ashford Town	42	15	4	23	53	83	49
Banbury United	42	12	11	19	57	54	47
Witney Town	42	12	11	19	55	71	47
Bashley	42	10	14	18	57	71	44
Dartford	42	11	11	20	49	67	44
Burnham	42	10	14	18	39	65	43
Wisbech Town	42	10	9	23	45	89	39
St Leonards	42	9	10	23	55	87	37
Erith & Belvedere	42	10	7	25	49	92	37
Sittingbourne	42	8	9	25	41	79	33
Spalding United	42	7	12	23	35	73	33

Burnham had 1 point deducted, Rothwell Town had 3 points deducted

Western Division

	P	W	D	L	F	A	Pts
Hinckley United	42	30	8	4	102	38	98
Tiverton Town	42	28	7	7	97	36	91
Bilston Town	42	27	9	6	88	48	90
Evesham United	42	27	5	10	86	46	86
Mangotsfield United	42	25	9	8	91	45	84
Solihull Borough	42	22	12	8	73	43	78
Redditch United	42	17	13	12	76	69	64
Weston-super-Mare	42	17	10	15	68	58	61
Atherstone United	42	16	11	15	64	58	59
Rochester	42	18	5	19	57	77	59
Cirencester Town	42	14	15	13	65	74	57
Rugby United	42	13	10	19	51	68	49
Gloucester City	42	12	11	19	76	86	47
Blakenall	42	13	10	19	54	64	46
Shepshed Dynamo	42	12	9	21	56	73	45
Bedworth United	42	12	9	21	38	60	45
Racing Club Warwick	42	13	6	23	46	77	45
Gresley Rovers	42	11	8	23	46	65	41
Cinderford Town	42	11	8	23	56	84	41
Sutton Coldfield Town	42	7	14	21	45	66	35
Paget Rovers	42	9	4	29	38	93	31
Bromsgrove Rovers	42	7	9	26	47	92	30

Blakenall had 3 points deducted

2001-2002

Premier Division

Kettering Town	42	27	6	9	80	41	87
Tamworth	42	24	13	5	81	41	85
Havant & Waterlooville	42	22	9	11	74	50	75
Crawley Town	42	21	10	11	67	48	73
Newport County	42	19	9	14	61	48	66
Tiverton Town	42	17	10	15	70	63	61
Moor Green	42	18	7	17	64	62	61
Worcester City	42	16	12	14	65	54	60
Stafford Rangers	42	17	9	16	70	62	60
Ilkeston Town	42	14	16	12	58	61	58
Weymouth United	42	15	11	16	59	67	56
Hinckley Town	42	14	13	15	64	62	55
Folkestone Invicta	42	14	12	16	51	61	54
Cambridge City	42	12	16	14	60	70	52
Welling United	42	13	12	17	69	66	51
Hednesford Town	42	15	6	21	59	70	51
Bath City	42	13	11	18	56	65	50
Chelmsford City	42	13	11	18	63	75	50
Newport IOW	42	12	12	18	38	61	48
King's Lynn	42	11	13	18	44	57	46
Merthyr Tydfil	42	12	8	22	53	71	44
Salisbury City	42	6	8	28	36	87	26

Eastern Division

Hastings Town	42	29	8	5	85	38	95
Grantham Town	42	29	6	7	99	43	93
Dorchester Town	42	26	10	6	81	36	88
Histon	42	23	8	11	83	49	77
Stamford	42	24	4	14	76	61	76
Fisher Athletic (London)	42	20	10	12	83	56	70
Eastbourne Borough	42	21	6	15	63	46	69
Dartford	42	18	5	19	62	66	59
Erith & Belvedere	42	18	3	21	75	79	57
Bashley	42	15	11	16	71	63	56
Burnham	42	15	10	17	52	54	55
Rugby United	42	16	6	20	55	67	54
Rothwell Town	42	14	8	20	46	66	50
Ashford Town	42	14	6	22	58	78	48
Banbury United	42	13	9	20	53	66	47
Chatham Town	42	13	8	21	56	87	47
Sittingbourne	42	14	4	24	46	69	46
Spalding	42	13	6	23	72	84	45
Tonbridge Angels	42	13	6	23	65	80	45
St Leonards	42	14	3	25	52	88	45
Corby Town	42	10	13	19	54	82	43
Wisbech Town	42	11	8	23	56	84	41

Western Division

Halesowen Town	40	27	9	4	85	24	90
Chippenham Town	40	26	9	5	81	28	87
Weston-super-Mare	40	22	10	8	70	38	76
Solihull Borough	40	20	11	9	75	42	71
Gresley Rovers	40	19	9	12	59	50	66
Sutton Coldfield Town	40	17	11	12	53	46	62
Mangotsfield United	40	17	10	13	74	54	61
Stourport Swifts	40	18	6	16	59	59	60
Atherstone United	40	16	8	16	61	59	56
Clevedon Town	40	15	11	14	57	58	56
Bedworth United	40	16	7	17	59	63	55
Evesham United	40	16	7	17	54	70	55
Cirencester Town	40	17	3	20	64	69	54
Gloucester City	40	14	10	16	48	63	52
Cinderford Town	40	14	9	17	54	67	51
Shepshed Dynamo	40	10	10	20	64	84	40
Bilston Town	40	11	7	22	50	72	40
Redditch United	40	11	6	23	47	77	39
Swindon Supermarine	40	11	4	25	52	76	37
Racing Club Warwick	40	8	11	21	38	63	35
Rocester	40	5	12	23	33	75	27

2002-2003

Premier Division

Tamworth	42	26	10	6	73	32	88
Stafford Rangers	42	21	12	9	76	40	75
Dover Athletic	42	19	14	9	42	35	71
Tiverton Town	42	19	12	11	60	43	69
Chippenham Town	42	17	17	8	59	37	68
Worcester City	42	18	13	11	60	39	67
Crawley Town	42	17	13	12	64	51	64
Havant & Waterlooville	42	15	15	12	67	64	60
Chelmsford City	42	15	12	15	65	63	57
Newport County	42	15	11	16	53	52	56
Hednesford Town	42	14	13	15	59	60	55
Moor Green	42	13	14	15	49	58	53
Hinckley Town	42	12	16	14	61	64	52
Bath City	42	13	13	16	50	61	52
Welling United	42	13	12	17	55	58	51
Grantham Town	42	14	9	19	59	65	51
Weymouth	42	12	15	15	44	62	51
Cambridge City	42	13	10	19	54	56	49
Halesowen Town	42	12	13	17	52	63	49
Hastings United	42	10	13	19	44	57	43
Ilkeston Town	42	10	10	22	54	92	40
Folkestone Invicta	42	7	7	28	57	105	28

Eastern Division

Dorchester Town	42	28	9	5	114	40	93
Eastbourne Borough	42	29	6	7	92	33	93
Stamford	42	27	6	9	80	39	87
Salisbury City	42	27	8	7	81	42	86
Bashley	42	23	12	7	90	44	81
King's Lynn	42	24	7	11	98	62	79
Rothwell Town	42	22	10	10	77	52	76
Banbury United	42	21	11	10	75	50	74
Tonbridge Angels	42	20	11	11	71	55	71
Histon	42	20	7	15	99	62	67
Ashford Town	42	18	9	15	63	57	63
Sittingbourne	42	15	8	19	57	69	53
Burnham	42	15	7	20	62	79	52
Fisher Athletic	42	15	5	22	57	80	50
Chatham Town	42	14	5	23	54	84	47
Newport IOW	42	12	6	24	53	87	42
Dartford	42	11	8	23	48	78	41
Erith & Belvedere	42	11	6	25	65	96	39
Corby Town	42	9	11	22	49	84	38
Fleet Town	42	8	8	26	34	80	32
Spalding United	42	4	6	32	40	108	18
St. Leonards	42	4	4	34	38	116	16

Western Division

Merthyr Tydfil	42	28	8	6	78	32	92
Weston-super-Mare	42	26	7	9	77	42	85
Bromsgrove Rovers	42	23	7	12	73	41	76
Solihull Borough	42	21	13	8	77	48	76
Gloucester City	42	22	9	11	87	58	75
Mangotsfield United	42	21	10	11	106	53	73
Redditch United	42	22	6	14	76	42	72
Rugby United	42	20	9	13	58	43	69
Gresley Rovers	42	19	10	13	63	54	67
Taunton Town	42	20	7	15	76	78	67
Sutton Coldfield Town	42	18	10	14	63	53	64
Evesham United	42	19	6	17	76	72	63
Clevedon Town	42	14	13	15	54	60	55
Cirencester Town	42	15	7	20	62	82	52
Cinderford Town	42	13	12	17	50	67	51
Shepshed Dynamo	42	12	6	24	48	76	42
Stourport Swifts	42	10	11	21	48	66	41
Bedworth United	42	11	7	24	46	74	40
Swindon Supermarine	42	11	5	26	52	85	38
Atherstone United	42	9	10	23	45	78	37
Rocester	42	9	10	23	34	74	37
Racing Club Warwick	42	3	9	30	33	104	18

FOOTBALL CONFERENCE

1979-80

Altrincham	38	24	8	6	79	35	56
Weymouth	38	22	10	6	73	37	54
Worcester City	38	19	11	8	53	36	49
Boston United	38	16	13	9	52	43	45
Gravesend & Northfleet	38	17	10	11	49	44	44
Maidstone United	38	16	11	11	54	37	43
Kettering Town	38	15	13	10	55	50	43
Northwich Victoria	38	16	10	12	50	38	42
Bangor City	38	14	14	10	41	46	42
Nuneaton Borough	38	13	13	12	58	44	39
Scarborough	38	12	15	11	47	38	39
Yeovil Town	38	13	10	15	46	49	36
Telford United	38	13	8	17	52	60	34
Barrow	38	14	6	18	47	55	34
Wealdstone	38	9	15	14	42	54	33
Bath City	38	10	12	16	43	69	32
Barnet	38	10	10	18	32	48	30
AP Leamington	38	7	11	20	32	63	25
Stafford Rangers	38	6	10	22	41	57	22
Redditch United	38	5	8	25	26	69	18

1980-81

Altrincham	38	23	8	7	72	41	54
Kettering Town	38	21	9	8	66	37	51
Scarborough	38	17	13	8	49	29	47
Northwich Victoria	38	17	11	10	53	40	45
Weymouth	38	19	6	13	54	40	44
Bath City	38	16	10	12	51	32	42
Maidstone United	38	16	9	13	64	53	41
Boston United	38	16	9	13	63	58	41
Barrow	38	15	8	15	50	49	38
Frickley Athletic	38	15	8	15	61	62	38
Stafford Rangers	38	11	15	12	56	56	37
Worcester City	38	14	7	17	47	54	35
Telford United	38	13	9	16	47	59	35
Yeovil Town	38	14	6	18	60	64	34
Gravesend & Northfleet	38	13	8	17	48	55	34
AP Leamington	38	10	11	17	47	66	31
Barnet	38	12	7	19	39	64	31
Nuneaton Borough	38	10	9	19	49	65	29
Wealdstone	38	9	11	18	37	56	29
Bangor City	38	6	12	20	35	68	24

1981-82

Runcorn	42	28	9	5	75	37	93
Enfield	42	26	8	8	90	46	86
Telford United	42	23	8	11	70	51	77
Worcester City	42	21	8	13	70	60	71
Dagenham	42	19	12	11	69	51	69
Northwich Victoria	42	20	9	13	56	46	69
Scarborough	42	19	11	12	65	52	68
Barrow	42	18	11	13	59	50	65
Weymouth	42	18	9	15	56	47	63
Boston United	42	17	11	14	61	57	62
Altrincham	42	14	13	15	66	56	55
Bath City	42	15	10	17	50	57	55
Yeovil Town	42	14	11	17	56	68	53
Stafford Rangers	42	12	16	14	48	47	52
Frickley Athletic	42	14	10	18	47	60	52
Maidstone United	42	11	15	16	55	59	48
Trowbridge Town	42	12	11	19	38	54	47
Barnet	42	9	14	19	36	52	41
Kettering Town	42	9	13	20	64	76	40
Gravesend & Northfleet	42	10	10	22	51	69	40
Dartford	42	10	9	23	47	69	39
AP Leamington	42	4	10	28	40	105	22

1982-83

Enfield	42	25	9	8	95	48	84
Maidstone United	42	25	8	9	83	34	83
Wealdstone	42	22	13	7	80	41	79
Runcorn	42	22	8	12	73	53	74
Boston United	42	20	12	10	77	57	72
Telford United	42	20	11	11	69	48	71
Weymouth	42	20	10	12	63	48	70
Northwich Victoria	42	18	10	14	68	63	64
Scarborough	42	17	12	13	71	58	63
Bath City	42	17	9	16	58	55	60
Nuneaton Borough	42	15	13	14	57	60	58
Altrincham	42	15	10	17	62	56	55
Bangor City	42	14	13	15	71	77	55
Dagenham	42	12	15	15	60	65	51
Barnet	42	16	3	23	55	78	51
Frickley Athletic	42	12	13	17	66	77	49
Worcester City	42	12	10	20	58	87	46
Trowbridge Town	42	12	7	23	56	88	43
Kettering Town	42	11	7	24	69	99	40
Yeovil Town	42	11	7	24	63	99	40
Barrow	42	8	12	22	46	74	36
Stafford Rangers	42	5	14	23	40	75	29

1983-84

Maidstone United	42	23	13	6	71	34	70
Nuneaton Borough	42	24	11	7	70	40	69
Altrincham	42	23	9	10	64	39	65
Wealdstone	42	21	14	7	75	36	62
Runcorn	42	20	13	9	61	45	62
Bath City	42	17	12	13	60	48	53
Northwich Victoria	42	16	14	12	54	47	51
Worcester City	42	15	13	14	64	55	49
Barnet	42	16	10	16	55	58	49
Kidderminster Harriers	42	14	14	14	54	61	49
Telford United	42	17	11	14	50	58	49
Frickley Athletic	42	17	10	15	68	56	48
Scarborough	42	14	16	12	52	55	48
Enfield	42	14	9	19	61	58	43
Weymouth	42	13	8	21	54	65	42
Gateshead	42	13	13	17	59	73	42
Boston United	42	13	12	17	66	80	41
Dagenham	42	14	8	20	57	69	40
Kettering Town	42	12	9	21	53	67	37
Yeovil Town	42	12	8	22	55	77	35
Bangor City	42	10	6	26	54	82	29
Trowbridge Town	42	5	7	30	33	87	19

2 points awarded for a Home win, 3 points awarded for an Away win, 1 point awarded for any Draw

1984-85

Wealdstone	42	20	10	12	64	54	62
Nuneaton Borough	42	19	14	9	85	53	58
Dartford	42	17	13	12	57	48	57
Bath City	42	21	9	12	52	49	57
Altrincham	42	21	6	15	63	47	56
Scarborough	42	17	13	12	69	62	54
Enfield	42	17	13	12	84	61	53
Kidderminster Harriers	42	17	8	17	79	77	51
Northwich Victoria	42	16	11	15	50	46	50
Telford United	42	15	14	13	59	54	49
Frickley Athletic	42	18	7	17	65	71	49
Kettering Town	42	15	12	15	68	59	48
Maidstone United	42	15	13	14	58	51	48
Runcorn	42	13	15	14	48	47	48
Barnet	42	15	11	16	59	52	47
Weymouth	42	15	13	14	70	66	45
Boston United	42	15	10	17	69	69	45
Barrow	42	11	16	15	47	57	43
Dagenham	42	13	10	19	47	67	41
Worcester City	42	12	9	21	55	84	38
Gateshead	42	9	12	21	51	82	33
Yeovil Town	42	6	11	25	44	87	25

2 points awarded for a Home win, 3 points awarded for an Away win, 1 point awarded for any Draw.   Gateshead had 1 point deducted

1985-86

Enfield	42	27	10	5	94	47	76
Frickley Athletic	42	25	10	7	78	50	69
Kidderminster Harriers	42	24	7	11	99	62	67
Altrincham	42	22	11	9	70	49	63
Weymouth	42	19	15	8	75	60	61
Runcorn	42	19	14	9	70	44	60
Stafford Rangers	42	19	13	10	61	54	60
Telford United	42	18	10	14	68	66	51
Kettering Town	42	15	15	12	55	53	49
Wealdstone	42	16	9	17	57	56	47
Cheltenham Town	42	16	11	15	69	69	46
Bath City	42	13	11	18	53	54	45
Boston United	42	16	7	19	66	76	44
Barnet	42	13	11	18	56	60	41
Scarborough	42	13	11	18	54	66	40
Northwich Victoria	42	10	12	20	42	54	37
Maidstone United	42	9	16	17	57	66	36
Nuneaton Borough	42	13	5	24	58	73	36
Dagenham	42	10	12	20	48	66	36
Wycombe Wanderers	42	10	13	19	55	84	36
Dartford	42	8	9	25	51	82	26
Barrow	42	7	8	27	41	86	24

2 points awarded for a Home win; 3 points awarded for an Away win;
1 point awarded for any Draw

1986-87

Scarborough	42	27	10	5	64	33	91
Barnet	42	25	10	7	86	39	85
Maidstone United	42	21	10	11	71	48	73
Enfield	42	21	7	14	66	47	70
Altrincham	42	18	15	9	66	53	69
Boston United	42	21	6	15	82	74	69
Sutton United	42	19	11	12	81	51	68
Runcorn	42	18	13	11	71	58	67
Telford United	42	18	10	14	69	59	64
Bath City	42	17	12	13	63	62	63
Cheltenham Town	42	16	13	13	64	50	61
Kidderminster Harriers	42	17	4	21	77	81	55
Stafford Rangers	42	14	11	17	58	60	53
Weymouth	42	13	12	17	68	77	51
Dagenham	42	14	7	21	56	72	49
Kettering Town	42	12	11	19	54	66	47
Northwich Victoria	42	10	14	18	53	69	44
Nuneaton Borough	42	10	14	18	48	73	44
Wealdstone	42	11	10	21	50	70	43
Welling United	42	10	10	22	61	84	40
Frickley Athletic	42	7	11	24	47	82	32
Gateshead	42	6	13	23	48	95	31

1987-88

Lincoln City	42	24	10	8	86	48	82
Barnet	42	23	11	8	93	45	80
Kettering Town	42	22	9	11	68	48	75
Runcorn	42	21	11	10	68	47	74
Telford United	42	20	10	12	65	50	70
Stafford Rangers	42	20	9	13	79	58	69
Kidderminster Harriers	42	18	15	9	75	66	69
Sutton United	42	18	16	8	77	54	66
Maidstone United	42	18	9	15	79	64	63
Weymouth	42	18	9	15	53	43	63
Macclesfield Town	42	18	9	15	64	62	63
Enfield	42	15	10	17	68	78	55
Cheltenham Town	42	11	20	11	64	67	53
Altrincham	42	14	10	18	59	59	52
Fisher Athletic	42	13	13	16	58	61	52
Boston United	42	14	7	21	60	75	49
Northwich Victoria	42	10	17	15	46	57	47
Wycombe Wanderers	42	11	13	18	50	76	46
Welling United	42	11	9	22	50	72	42
Bath City	42	9	10	23	48	76	37
Wealdstone	42	5	17	20	39	76	32
Dagenham	42	5	6	31	37	104	21

1988-89

Maidstone United	40	25	9	6	92	46	84
Kettering Town	40	23	7	10	56	39	76
Boston United	40	22	8	10	61	51	74
Wycombe Wanderers	40	20	11	9	68	52	71
Kidderminster Harriers	40	21	6	13	68	57	69
Runcorn	40	19	8	13	77	53	65
Macclesfield Town	40	17	10	13	63	57	61
Barnet	40	18	7	15	64	69	61
Yeovil Town	40	15	11	14	68	67	56
Northwich Victoria	40	14	11	15	64	65	53
Welling United	40	14	11	15	45	46	53
Sutton United	40	12	15	13	64	54	51
Enfield	40	14	8	18	62	67	50
Altrincham	40	13	10	17	51	61	49
Cheltenham Town	40	12	12	16	55	58	48
Telford United	40	13	9	18	37	43	48
Chorley	40	13	6	21	57	71	45
Fisher Athletic	40	10	11	19	55	65	41
Stafford Rangers	40	11	7	22	49	74	40
Aylesbury United	40	9	9	22	43	71	36
Weymouth	40	7	10	23	37	70	31
Newport County	29	4	7	18	31	62	19

Newport County expelled from League – their record was deleted.

1989-90

Darlington	42	26	9	7	76	25	87
Barnet	42	26	7	9	81	41	85
Runcorn	42	19	13	10	79	62	70
Macclesfield Town	42	17	15	10	56	41	66
Kettering Town	42	18	12	12	66	53	66
Welling United	42	18	10	14	62	50	64
Yeovil Town	42	17	12	13	62	54	63
Sutton United	42	19	6	17	68	64	63
Merthyr Tydfil	42	16	14	12	67	63	62
Wycombe Wanderers	42	17	10	15	64	56	61
Cheltenham Town	42	16	11	15	58	60	59
Telford United	42	15	13	14	56	63	58
Kidderminster Harriers	42	15	9	18	64	67	54
Barrow	42	12	16	14	51	67	52
Northwich Victoria	42	15	5	22	51	67	50
Altrincham	42	12	13	17	49	48	49
Stafford Rangers	42	12	12	18	50	62	48
Boston United	42	13	8	21	48	67	47
Fisher Athletic	42	13	7	22	55	78	46
Chorley	42	13	6	23	42	67	45
Farnborough Town	42	10	12	20	60	73	42
Enfield	42	10	6	26	52	89	36

1990-91

Barnet	42	26	9	7	103	52	87
Colchester United	42	25	10	7	68	35	85
Altrincham	42	23	13	6	87	46	82
Kettering Town	42	23	11	8	67	45	80
Wycombe Wanderers	42	21	11	10	75	46	74
Telford United	42	20	7	15	62	52	67
Macclesfield Town	42	17	12	13	63	52	63
Runcorn	42	16	10	16	69	67	58
Merthyr Tydfil	42	16	9	17	62	61	57
Barrow	42	12	15	15	59	65	57
Welling United	42	13	15	14	55	57	54
Northwich Victoria	42	13	13	16	65	75	52
Kidderminster Harrier	42	14	10	18	56	67	52
Yeovil Town	42	13	11	18	58	58	50
Stafford Rangers	42	12	14	16	48	51	50
Cheltenham Town	42	12	12	18	54	72	48
Gateshead	42	14	6	22	52	92	48
Boston United	42	12	11	19	55	69	47
Slough Town	42	13	6	23	51	80	45
Bath City	42	10	12	20	55	61	42
Sutton United	42	10	9	23	62	82	39
Fisher Athletic	42	5	15	22	38	79	30

1991-92

Team	P	W	D	L	F	A	Pts
Colchester United	42	28	10	4	98	40	94
Wycombe Wanderers	42	30	4	8	84	35	94
Kettering Town	42	20	13	9	72	50	73
Merthyr Tydfil	42	18	14	10	59	56	68
Farnborough Town	42	18	13	12	68	53	66
Telford United	42	19	7	16	62	66	64
Redbridge Forest	42	18	9	15	69	56	63
Boston United	42	18	9	15	71	66	63
Bath City	42	16	12	14	54	51	60
Witton Albion	42	16	10	16	63	60	58
Northwich Victoria	42	16	6	20	63	58	54
Welling United	42	14	12	16	69	79	54
Macclesfield Town	42	13	13	16	50	50	52
Gateshead	42	12	13	18	49	57	48
Yeovil Town	42	11	14	17	40	49	47
Runcorn	42	11	13	18	50	63	46
Stafford Rangers	42	10	16	16	41	59	46
Altrincham	42	11	12	19	61	82	45
Kidderminster Harriers	42	12	9	21	56	77	45
Slough Town	42	13	6	23	56	82	45
Cheltenham Town	42	10	13	19	56	83	43
Barrow	42	8	14	20	52	72	38

1992-93

Team	P	W	D	L	F	A	Pts
Wycombe Wanderers	42	24	11	7	84	37	83
Bromsgrove Rovers	42	18	14	10	67	49	68
Dagenham & Redbridge	42	19	11	12	75	47	67
Yeovil Town	42	18	12	12	59	49	66
Slough Town	42	18	11	13	60	55	65
Stafford Rangers	42	18	10	14	55	47	64
Bath City	42	15	14	13	53	46	59
Woking	42	17	8	17	58	62	59
Kidderminster Harriers	42	14	16	12	60	60	58
Altrincham	42	15	13	14	49	52	58
Northwich Victoria	42	16	8	18	68	55	56
Stalybridge Celtic	42	13	17	12	48	55	56
Kettering Town	42	14	13	15	61	63	55
Gateshead	42	14	10	18	53	56	52
Telford United	42	14	10	18	55	60	52
Merthyr Tydfil	42	14	10	18	51	79	52
Witton Albion	42	11	17	14	62	65	50
Macclesfield	42	12	13	17	40	50	49
Runcorn	42	13	10	19	58	76	49
Welling United	42	12	12	18	57	72	48
Farnborough Town	42	12	11	19	68	87	47
Boston United	42	9	13	20	50	69	40

Dagenham & Redbridge had 1 point deducted

1993-94

Team	P	W	D	L	F	A	Pts
Kidderminster Harriers	42	22	9	11	63	35	75
Kettering Town	42	18	15	8	46	24	72
Woking	42	18	13	11	58	58	67
Southport	42	18	12	12	57	51	66
Runcorn	42	14	19	9	63	57	61
Dagenham & Redbridge	42	15	14	13	62	54	59
Macclesfield Town	42	16	11	15	48	49	59
Dover Athletic	42	17	7	18	48	49	58
Stafford Rangers	42	14	15	13	56	52	57
Altrincham	42	16	9	17	41	42	57
Gateshead	42	15	12	15	45	53	57
Bath City	42	13	17	12	47	38	56
Halifax Town	42	13	16	13	55	49	55
Stalybridge Celtic	42	14	12	16	54	55	54
Northwich Victoria	42	11	19	12	44	45	52
Welling United	42	13	12	17	47	49	51
Telford United	42	13	12	17	41	49	51
Bromsgrove Rovers	42	12	15	15	54	66	51
Yeovil Town	42	14	9	19	49	62	51
Merthyr Tydfil	42	12	15	15	60	61	49
Slough Town	42	11	14	17	44	58	47
Witton Albion	42	7	13	22	37	63	44

Merthyr Tydfil had 2 points deducted

1994-95

Team	P	W	D	L	F	A	Pts
Macclesfield Town	42	24	8	10	70	40	80
Woking	42	21	12	9	76	54	75
Southport	42	21	9	12	68	50	72
Altrincham Town	42	20	8	14	77	60	68
Stevenage Borough	42	20	7	15	68	49	67
Kettering Town	42	19	10	13	73	56	67
Gateshead	42	19	10	13	61	53	67
Halifax Town	42	17	12	13	68	54	63
Runcorn	42	16	10	16	59	71	58
Northwich Victoria	42	14	15	13	77	66	57
Kidderminster Harriers	42	16	9	17	63	61	57
Bath City	42	15	12	15	55	56	57
Bromsgrove Rovers	42	14	3	15	66	69	55
Farnborough Town	42	15	10	17	45	64	55
Dagenham & Redbridge	42	13	13	16	56	69	52
Dover Athletic	42	11	16	15	48	55	49
Welling United	42	13	10	19	57	74	49
Stalybridge Celtic	42	11	14	17	52	72	47
Telford United	42	10	16	16	53	62	46
Merthyr Tydfil	42	11	11	20	53	63	44
Stafford Rangers	42	9	11	22	53	79	38
Yeovil Town	42	8	14	20	50	71	37

Yeovil Town had 1 point deducted for fielding an ineligible player

1995-96

Team	P	W	D	L	F	A	Pts
Stevenage Borough	42	27	10	5	101	44	91
Woking	42	25	8	9	83	54	83
Hednesford Town	42	23	7	12	71	46	76
Macclesfield Town	42	22	9	11	66	49	75
Gateshead	42	18	13	11	58	46	67
Southport	42	18	12	12	77	64	66
Kidderminster Harriers	42	18	10	14	78	66	64
Northwich Victoria	42	16	12	14	72	64	60
Morecambe	42	17	8	17	78	72	59
Farnborough Town	42	15	14	13	63	58	59
Bromsgrove Rovers	42	15	14	13	59	57	59
Altrincham	42	15	13	14	59	64	58
Telford United	42	15	10	17	51	56	55
Stalybridge Celtic	42	16	7	19	59	68	55
Halifax Town	42	13	13	16	49	63	52
Kettering Town	42	13	9	20	68	84	48
Slough Town	42	13	8	21	63	76	47
Bath City	42	13	7	22	45	66	46
Welling United	42	10	15	17	42	53	45
Dover Athletic	42	11	7	24	51	74	40
Runcorn	42	9	8	25	48	87	35
Dagenham & Redbridge	42	7	12	23	43	73	33

1996-97

Team	P	W	D	L	F	A	Pts
Macclesfield Town	42	27	9	6	80	30	90
Kidderminster Harriers	42	26	7	9	84	42	85
Stevenage Borough	42	24	10	8	87	53	82
Morecambe	42	19	9	14	69	56	66
Woking	42	18	10	14	71	63	64
Northwich Victoria	42	17	12	13	61	54	63
Farnborough Town	42	16	13	13	58	53	61
Hednesford Town	42	16	12	14	52	50	60
Telford United	42	16	10	16	46	56	58
Gateshead	42	15	11	16	59	63	56
Southport	42	15	10	17	51	61	55
Rushden & Diamonds	42	14	11	17	61	63	53
Stalybridge Celtic	42	14	10	18	53	58	52
Kettering Town	42	14	9	19	53	62	51
Hayes	42	12	14	16	54	55	50
Slough Town	42	12	14	16	62	65	50
Dover Athletic	42	12	14	16	57	68	50
Welling United	42	13	9	20	50	60	48
Halifax Town	42	12	12	18	55	74	48
Bath City	42	12	11	19	53	80	47
Bromsgrove Rovers	42	12	5	25	41	67	41
Altrincham	42	9	12	21	49	73	39

1997-98

Halifax Town	42	25	12	5	74	43	87
Cheltenham Town	42	23	9	10	63	43	78
Woking	42	22	8	12	72	46	74
Rushden & Diamonds	42	23	5	14	79	57	74
Morecambe	42	21	10	11	77	64	73
Hereford United	42	18	13	11	56	49	67
Hednesford Town	42	18	12	12	59	50	66
Slough Town	42	18	10	14	58	49	64
Northwich Victoria	42	15	15	12	63	59	60
Welling United	42	17	9	16	64	62	60
Yeovil Town	42	17	8	17	73	63	59
Hayes	42	16	10	16	62	52	58
Dover Athletic	42	15	10	17	60	70	55
Kettering Town	42	13	13	16	53	60	52
Stevenage Borough	42	13	12	17	59	63	51
Southport	42	13	11	18	56	58	50
Kidderminster Harriers	42	11	14	17	56	63	49
Farnborough Town	42	12	8	22	56	70	44
Leek Town	42	10	14	18	52	67	44
Telford United	42	10	12	20	53	76	42
Gateshead	42	8	11	23	51	87	35
Stalybridge Celtic	42	7	8	27	48	93	29

2000-2001

Rushden & Diamonds	42	25	11	6	78	36	86
Yeovil Town	42	24	8	10	73	50	80
Dagenham & Redbridge	42	23	8	11	71	54	77
Southport	42	20	9	13	58	46	69
Leigh RMI	42	19	11	12	63	57	68
Telford United	42	19	8	15	51	51	65
Stevenage Borough	42	15	18	9	71	61	63
Chester City	42	16	14	12	49	43	62
Doncaster Rovers	42	15	13	14	47	43	58
Scarborough	42	14	16	12	56	54	58
Hereford United	42	14	15	13	60	46	57
Boston United	42	13	17	12	74	63	56
Nuneaton Borough	42	13	15	14	60	60	54
Woking	42	13	15	14	52	57	54
Dover Athletic	42	14	11	17	54	56	53
Forest Green Rovers	42	11	15	16	43	54	48
Northwich Victoria	42	11	13	18	49	67	46
Hayes	42	12	10	20	44	71	46
Morecambe	42	11	12	19	64	66	45
Kettering Town	42	11	10	21	46	62	43
Kingstonian	42	8	10	24	47	73	34
Hednesford Town	42	5	13	24	46	86	28

1998-99

Cheltenham Town	42	22	14	6	71	36	80
Kettering Town	42	22	10	10	58	37	76
Hayes	42	22	8	12	63	50	74
Rushden & Diamonds	42	20	12	10	71	42	72
Yeovil Town	42	20	11	11	68	54	71
Stevenage Borough	42	17	17	8	62	45	68
Northwich Victoria	42	19	9	14	60	51	66
Kingstonian	42	17	13	12	50	49	64
Woking	42	18	9	15	51	45	62
Hednesford Town	42	15	16	11	49	44	61
Dover Athletic	42	15	13	14	54	48	58
Forest Green Rovers	42	15	13	14	55	50	58
Hereford United	42	15	10	17	49	46	55
Morecambe	42	15	8	19	60	76	53
Kidderminster Harriers	42	14	9	19	56	52	51
Doncaster Rovers	42	12	12	18	51	55	48
Telford United	42	10	16	16	44	60	46
Southport	42	10	15	17	47	59	45
Barrow	42	11	10	21	40	63	43
Welling United	42	9	14	19	44	65	41
Leek Town	42	8	8	26	48	76	32
Farnborough United	42	7	11	24	41	89	32

2001-2002

Boston United	42	25	9	8	84	42	84
Dagenham & Redbridge	42	24	12	6	70	47	84
Yeovil Town	42	19	13	10	66	53	70
Doncaster Rovers	42	18	13	11	68	46	67
Barnet	42	19	10	13	64	48	67
Morecambe	42	17	11	14	63	67	62
Farnborough Town	42	18	7	17	66	54	61
Margate	42	14	16	12	59	53	58
Telford United	42	14	15	13	63	58	57
Nuneaton Borough	42	16	9	17	57	57	57
Stevenage Borough	42	15	10	17	57	60	55
Scarborough	42	14	14	14	55	63	55
Northwich Victoria	42	16	7	19	57	70	55
Chester City	42	15	9	18	54	51	54
Southport	42	13	14	15	53	49	53
Leigh RMI	42	15	8	19	56	58	53
Hereford United	42	14	10	18	50	53	52
Forest Green Rovers	42	12	15	15	54	76	51
Woking	42	13	9	20	59	70	48
Hayes	42	13	5	24	53	80	44
Stalybridge Celtic	42	11	10	21	40	69	43
Dover Athletic	42	11	6	25	41	65	39

1999-2000

Kidderminster Harriers	42	26	7	9	75	40	85
Rushden & Diamonds	42	21	13	8	71	42	76
Morecambe	42	18	16	8	70	48	70
Scarborough	42	19	12	11	60	35	69
Kingstonian	42	20	7	15	58	44	67
Dover Athletic	42	18	12	12	65	56	66
Yeovil Town	42	18	10	14	60	63	64
Hereford United	42	15	14	13	61	52	59
Southport	42	15	13	14	55	56	58
Stevenage Borough	42	16	9	17	60	54	57
Hayes	42	16	8	18	57	58	56
Doncaster Rovers	42	15	9	18	46	48	54
Kettering Town	42	12	16	14	44	50	52
Woking	42	13	13	16	45	53	52
Nuneaton Borough	42	12	15	15	49	53	51
Telford United	42	14	9	19	56	66	51
Hednesford Town	42	15	6	21	45	68	51
Northwich Victoria	42	13	12	17	53	78	51
Forest Green Rovers	42	13	8	21	54	63	47
Welling United	42	13	8	21	54	66	47
Altrincham	42	9	19	14	51	60	46
Sutton United	42	8	10	24	39	75	34

2002-2003

Yeovil Town	42	28	11	3	100	37	95
Morecambe	42	23	9	10	86	42	78
Doncaster Rovers	42	22	12	8	73	47	78
Chester City	42	21	12	9	59	31	75
Dagenham & Redbridge	42	21	9	12	71	59	72
Hereford United	42	19	7	16	64	51	64
Scarborough	42	18	10	14	63	54	64
Halifax Town	42	18	10	14	50	51	64
Forest Green Rovers	42	17	8	17	61	62	59
Margate	42	15	11	16	60	66	56
Barnet	42	13	14	15	65	68	53
Stevenage Borough	42	14	10	18	61	55	52
Farnborough Town	42	13	12	17	57	56	51
Northwich Victoria	42	13	12	17	66	72	51
Telford United	42	14	7	21	54	69	49
Burton Albion	42	13	10	19	52	77	49
Gravesend & Northfleet	42	12	12	18	62	73	48
Leigh RMI	42	14	6	22	44	71	48
Woking	42	11	14	17	52	81	47
Nuneaton Borough	42	13	7	22	51	78	46
Southport	42	11	12	19	54	69	45
Kettering Town	42	8	7	27	37	73	31

ISTHMIAN LEAGUE

1905-06

London Caledonians	10	7	1	2	25	8	15
Clapton	10	6	1	3	11	13	13
Casuals	10	3	4	3	14	14	10
Civil Service	10	4	1	5	16	20	9
Ealing Association	10	3	2	5	15	19	8
Ilford	10	1	3	6	5	12	5

1906-07

Ilford	10	8	2	0	26	9	18
London Caledonians	10	6	0	4	19	14	12
Clapton	10	4	3	3	18	11	11
Civil Service	10	3	1	6	11	19	7
Ealing Association	10	3	1	6	12	22	7
Casuals	10	2	1	7	15	26	5

1907-08

London Caledonians	10	5	2	3	20	15	12
Clapton	10	4	3	3	24	14	11
Ilford	10	5	1	4	28	22	11
Oxford City	10	5	1	4	20	20	11
Dulwich Hamlet	10	3	2	5	15	18	8
West Norwood	10	3	1	6	13	31	7

1908-09

Bromley	18	11	1	6	42	29	23
Leytonstone	18	9	4	5	43	31	22
Ilford	18	9	4	5	37	36	22
Dulwich Hamlet	18	9	2	7	39	30	20
Clapton	18	8	4	6	34	32	20
Oxford City	18	6	4	8	29	32	16
Nunhead	18	7	2	9	31	35	16
Shepherd's Bush	18	6	3	9	26	44	15
London Caledonians	18	4	6	8	25	34	14
West Norwood	18	5	2	11	40	43	12

1909-10

Bromley	18	11	4	3	32	10	26
Clapton	18	10	4	4	56	19	24
Nunhead	18	10	4	4	49	26	24
Ilford	18	10	3	5	31	17	23
Dulwich Hamlet	18	8	4	6	26	26	20
Leytonstone	18	7	3	8	44	46	17
Oxford City	18	5	4	9	28	45	14
London Caledonians	18	5	3	10	19	40	13
West Norwood	18	5	2	11	28	54	12
Shepherd's Bush	18	2	3	13	23	55	7

1910-11

Clapton	18	11	4	3	39	19	26
Leytonstone	18	12	1	5	47	30	25
Dulwich Hamlet	18	8	5	5	28	22	21
Oxford City	18	7	4	7	32	43	18
Ilford	18	8	1	9	41	32	17
Shepherd's Bush	18	7	3	8	31	27	17
Bromley	18	8	4	6	32	27	16
Nunhead	18	5	4	9	32	36	14
West Norwood	18	4	5	9	24	43	13
London Caledonians	18	3	3	12	18	45	9
Bromley had 4 points deducted							

1911-12

London Caledonians	20	11	7	2	39	25	29
Ilford	20	11	3	6	37	24	25
Nunhead	20	10	5	5	36	30	25
Dulwich Hamlet	20	8	5	7	33	23	21
West Norwood	20	9	3	8	38	38	21
Clapton	20	7	5	8	37	37	19
Woking	20	7	5	8	38	41	19
Shepherd's Bush	20	5	6	9	39	49	16
Leytonstone	20	5	6	9	28	38	16
Oxford City	20	5	5	10	33	36	15
Tunbridge Wells	20	5	4	11	23	40	14

1912-13

London Caledonians	20	14	5	1	38	12	33
Leytonstone	20	12	3	5	45	20	27
Nunhead	20	12	3	5	36	23	27
Clapton	20	7	7	6	23	20	21
Dulwich Hamlet	20	8	4	8	34	28	20
Woking	20	7	5	8	33	40	19
Oxford City	20	6	6	8	23	39	18
Ilford	20	6	5	9	27	37	17
Shepherd's Bush	20	5	5	10	26	38	15
Tunbridge Wells	20	5	4	11	22	36	14
West Norwood	20	3	3	14	23	37	9

1913-14

London Caledonians	20	12	6	2	55	23	30
Nunhead	20	11	6	3	49	27	28
Ilford	20	11	4	5	52	35	26
Dulwich Hamlet	20	10	4	6	34	22	24
New Crusaders	20	10	3	7	40	30	23
Oxford City	20	10	0	10	42	42	20
Leytonstone	20	8	4	8	29	32	20
Clapton	20	8	3	9	29	27	19
Shepherd's Bush	20	7	2	11	24	46	16
West Norwood	20	4	3	13	27	47	11
Woking	20	1	1	18	11	61	3

1919

Leytonstone	8	5	1	2	21	7	11
Ilford	8	4	2	2	22	16	10
Dulwich Hamlet	8	3	2	3	19	17	8
Nunhead	8	3	2	3	18	19	8
Clapton	8	0	3	5	14	35	3

1919-20

Dulwich Hamlet	22	15	3	4	58	16	33
Nunhead	22	14	5	3	48	26	33
Tufnell Park	22	12	4	6	45	32	28
Ilford	22	13	1	8	63	42	27
Oxford City	22	12	3	7	63	51	27
London Caledonians	22	10	3	9	32	30	23
Leytonstone	22	8	3	11	50	43	19
Clapton	22	8	3	11	38	44	19
Civil Service	22	7	4	11	35	40	18
Woking	22	6	3	13	36	42	15
West Norwood	22	5	4	13	19	53	14
Casuals	22	3	2	17	20	88	8

1920-21

Ilford	22	16	4	2	70	24	36
London Caledonians	22	13	5	4	45	17	31
Tufnell Park	22	14	3	5	43	24	31
Nunhead	22	12	5	5	53	33	29
Dulwich Hamlet	22	11	6	5	60	30	28
Oxford City	22	12	3	7	56	38	27
Leytonstone	22	8	6	8	36	29	22
Clapton	22	7	7	8	33	52	21
Civil Service	22	3	7	12	28	45	13
Woking	22	3	5	14	16	43	11
Casuals	22	3	3	16	31	87	9
West Norwood	22	2	2	18	18	67	6

1921-22

Ilford	26	17	4	5	66	34	38
Dulwich Hamlet	26	14	8	4	65	24	36
London Caledonians	26	16	4	6	41	21	36
Nunhead	26	12	5	9	65	41	29
Clapton	26	13	3	10	51	46	29
Tufnell Park	26	10	7	9	44	39	27
Oxford City	26	18	2	12	48	47	26
Wycombe Wanderers	26	18	2	12	61	64	26
Civil Service	26	9	8	9	60	48	26
Woking	26	10	6	10	39	49	26
Leytonstone	26	9	6	11	41	48	24
West Norwood	26	8	5	13	43	57	21
Wimbledon	26	7	4	15	52	56	18
Casuals	26	0	2	24	25	107	2

1922-23

Clapton	26	15	7	4	51	33	37
Nunhead	26	15	5	6	52	32	35
London Caledonians	26	13	7	6	43	26	33
Ilford	26	11	7	8	57	38	29
Casuals	26	12	5	9	68	51	29
Civil Service	26	9	10	7	39	36	28
Wycombe Wanderers	26	11	4	11	61	61	26
Dulwich Hamlet	26	9	7	10	60	44	25
Leytonstone	26	9	7	10	45	56	25
Tufnell Park	26	9	5	12	41	45	23
Wimbledon	26	10	2	14	49	50	22
Woking	26	7	6	13	42	67	20
Oxford City	26	6	5	15	45	68	17
West Norwood	26	5	5	16	25	71	15

1923-24

St Albans City	26	17	5	4	72	38	39
Dulwich Hamlet	26	15	6	5	49	28	36
Clapton	26	14	5	7	73	50	33
Wycombe Wanderers	26	14	5	7	88	65	33
London Caledonians	26	14	3	9	53	49	31
Civil Service	26	12	5	9	52	47	29
Casuals	26	13	1	12	65	54	27
Ilford	26	9	6	11	56	59	24
Nunhead	26	8	8	10	41	46	24
Wimbledon	26	8	4	14	43	62	20
Tufnell Park	26	8	2	16	38	53	18
Woking	26	5	8	13	31	62	18
Oxford City	26	7	2	17	53	74	16
Leytonstone	26	6	4	16	41	68	16

1924-25

London Caledonians	26	18	5	3	76	36	41
Clapton	26	19	1	6	64	34	39
St Albans City	26	16	2	8	69	39	34
Tufnell Park	26	11	4	11	47	41	26
Ilford	26	11	4	11	46	42	26
Leytonstone	26	12	2	12	55	63	26
The Casuals	26	12	1	13	55	58	25
Wycombe Wanderers	26	11	2	13	58	61	24
Civil Service	26	10	4	12	52	64	24
Nunhead	26	9	5	12	45	43	23
Wimbledon	26	10	2	14	50	54	22
Dulwich Hamlet	26	8	5	13	42	57	21
Oxford City	26	9	2	15	38	71	20
Woking	26	5	3	18	33	67	13

1925-26

Dulwich Hamlet	26	20	1	5	80	49	41
London Caledonians	26	18	1	7	81	44	37
Clapton	26	14	4	8	64	50	32
Wycombe Wanderers	26	14	3	9	97	83	31
St Albans City	26	12	6	8	76	54	30
Nunhead	26	13	4	9	49	43	30
Ilford	26	13	2	11	81	70	28
Leytonstone	26	12	1	13	75	63	25
Woking	26	8	6	12	56	73	22
Tufnell Park	26	8	5	13	36	53	21
The Casuals	26	8	4	14	48	61	20
Wimbledon	26	9	1	16	61	77	19
Oxford City	26	8	1	17	48	76	17
Civil Service	26	5	1	20	43	99	11

1926-27

St Albans City	26	20	1	5	96	34	41
Ilford	26	18	0	9	76	57	34
Wimbledon	26	15	3	8	72	45	33
Nunhead	26	11	8	7	51	33	30
Woking	26	12	6	8	68	60	30
London Caledonians	26	11	7	8	58	47	29
Clapton	26	11	4	11	58	60	26
Leytonstone	26	11	1	14	54	78	23
Dulwich Hamlet	26	9	4	13	60	58	22
Wycombe Wanderers	26	10	2	14	59	86	22
Tufnell Park	26	8	4	14	45	55	20
Oxford City	26	7	5	14	46	72	19
The Casuals	26	8	3	15	37	78	19
Civil Service	26	6	4	16	48	65	16

1927-28

St Albans City	26	15	5	6	86	50	35
London Caledonians	26	12	9	5	63	38	33
Ilford	26	14	4	8	72	54	32
Woking	26	13	5	8	72	56	31
Nunhead	26	13	2	11	57	54	28
Wimbledon	26	12	3	11	57	48	27
Leytonstone	26	13	1	12	53	56	27
Clapton	26	8	10	8	52	47	26
Dulwich Hamlet	26	8	9	9	56	49	25
The Casuals	26	8	8	10	54	58	24
Wycombe Wanderers	26	9	5	12	60	69	23
Oxford City	26	7	7	12	36	57	21
Civil Service	26	8	4	14	38	76	20
Tufnell Park	26	4	4	18	38	82	12

1928-29

Nunhead	26	15	6	5	47	35	36
London Caledonians	26	15	4	7	65	33	34
Dulwich Hamlet	26	14	6	6	65	34	34
Wimbledon	26	9	10	7	66	54	28
Ilford	26	12	3	11	67	52	27
Clapton	26	11	5	10	60	55	27
Tufnell Park	26	11	5	10	58	55	27
St Albans City	26	12	3	11	63	69	27
Leytonstone	26	11	3	12	56	79	25
Wycombe Wanderers	26	10	3	13	58	60	23
Oxford City	26	10	3	13	61	71	23
The Casuals	26	8	5	13	49	60	21
Woking	26	8	3	15	39	65	19
Civil Service	26	4	5	17	39	71	13

1929-30

Nunhead	26	19	3	4	69	36	41
Dulwich Hamlet	26	15	6	5	74	39	36
Kingstonian	26	15	4	7	57	37	34
Ilford	26	16	1	9	84	60	33
Woking	26	11	5	10	66	65	27
Wimbledon	26	11	2	13	64	66	24
Wycombe Wanderers	26	10	4	12	49	52	24
The Casuals	26	8	7	11	50	51	23
Oxford City	26	10	3	13	45	60	23
St Albans City	26	9	4	13	54	77	22
Clapton	26	8	4	14	47	57	20
London Caledonians	26	8	3	15	49	69	19
Leytonstone	26	8	3	15	48	68	19
Tufnell Park	26	6	7	13	35	54	19

1930-31

Wimbledon	26	18	6	2	69	37	42
Dulwich Hamlet	26	12	9	5	51	39	33
Wycombe Wanderers	26	12	6	8	67	45	30
The Casuals	26	12	6	8	71	56	30
St Albans City	26	11	7	8	67	66	29
Ilford	26	10	6	10	70	62	26
Oxford City	26	10	5	11	43	48	25
London Caledonians	26	8	8	10	43	53	24
Kingstonian	26	10	4	12	49	64	24
Tufnell Park	26	9	5	12	45	61	23
Nunhead	26	9	4	13	49	54	22
Woking	26	9	4	13	56	63	22
Clapton	26	7	4	15	62	75	18
Leytonstone	26	6	4	16	46	65	16

1931-32

Wimbledon	26	17	2	7	60	35	36
Ilford	26	13	9	4	71	45	35
Dulwich Hamlet	26	15	3	8	69	43	33
Wycombe Wanderers	26	14	5	7	72	50	33
Oxford City	26	15	2	9	63	49	32
Kingstonian	26	13	3	10	71	50	29
Tufnell Park	26	9	7	10	50	48	25
Nunhead	26	9	7	10	54	61	25
The Casuals	26	10	4	12	59	65	24
Clapton	26	9	5	12	50	57	23
Leytonstone	26	9	3	14	36	61	21
St Albans City	26	8	4	14	57	78	20
Woking	26	6	5	15	44	64	17
London Caledonians	26	2	7	17	24	74	11

1932-33

Dulwich Hamlet	26	15	6	5	71	45	36
Leytonstone	26	16	4	6	66	43	36
Kingstonian	26	15	2	9	77	49	32
Ilford	26	14	0	12	60	58	28
The Casuals	26	12	2	12	48	36	26
Tufnell Park	26	11	3	12	51	51	25
St Albans City	26	12	1	13	57	63	25
Clapton	26	10	5	11	51	65	25
Oxford City	26	9	6	11	49	54	24
Woking	26	10	4	12	53	61	24
Wycombe Wanderers	26	10	4	12	47	56	24
Nunhead	26	8	6	12	42	50	22
Wimbledon	26	8	5	13	55	67	21
London Caledonians	26	5	6	15	35	64	16

1933-34

Kingstonian	26	15	7	4	80	42	37
Dulwich Hamlet	26	15	5	6	68	36	35
Wimbledon	26	13	7	6	62	35	33
Tufnell Park	26	14	5	7	55	50	33
Ilford	26	15	2	9	60	56	32
The Casuals	26	13	5	8	47	32	31
Leytonstone	26	13	3	10	55	48	29
Nunhead	26	10	5	11	48	44	25
London Caledonians	26	7	8	11	51	53	22
Wycombe Wanderers	26	9	2	15	57	60	20
St Albans City	26	8	4	14	44	75	20
Oxford City	26	7	4	15	45	57	18
Clapton	26	5	6	15	35	62	16
Woking	26	6	1	19	43	81	13

1934-35

Wimbledon	26	14	7	5	63	30	35
Oxford City	26	14	4	8	69	50	32
Leytonstone	26	15	2	9	49	36	32
Dulwich Hamlet	26	11	7	8	66	45	29
Tufnell Park	26	11	7	8	53	44	29
Kingstonian	26	11	6	9	44	40	28
Nunhead	26	10	7	9	35	34	27
London Caledonians	26	9	7	10	40	41	25
St Albans City	26	9	6	11	61	80	24
Ilford	26	9	6	11	40	56	24
Clapton	26	7	7	12	46	48	21
Woking	26	9	3	14	44	68	21
Wycombe Wanderers	26	7	6	13	51	69	20
The Casuals	26	6	5	15	37	57	17

1935-36

Wimbledon	26	19	2	5	82	29	40
The Casuals	26	14	5	7	60	45	33
Ilford	26	13	3	10	67	47	29
Dulwich Hamlet	26	10	8	8	64	47	28
Nunhead	26	11	6	9	51	40	28
Wycombe Wanderers	26	13	2	11	60	68	28
Clapton	26	11	5	10	42	46	27
Oxford City	26	11	4	11	60	58	26
St Albans City	26	11	2	13	59	64	24
Woking	26	9	4	13	43	62	22
Tufnell Park	26	9	3	14	42	61	21
London Caledonians	26	9	3	14	35	52	21
Kingstonian	26	9	2	15	43	56	20
Leytonstone	26	7	3	16	34	67	17

1936-37

Kingstonian	26	18	3	5	63	43	39
Nunhead	26	17	3	6	77	32	37
Leytonstone	26	16	4	6	71	42	36
Ilford	26	14	5	7	86	39	33
Dulwich Hamlet	26	12	6	8	64	48	30
Wycombe Wanderers	26	10	5	11	55	52	25
Wimbledon	26	9	7	10	52	53	25
Clapton	26	10	5	11	42	51	25
The Casuals	26	10	3	13	46	58	23
Woking	26	9	4	13	53	69	22
Oxford City	26	8	5	13	56	89	21
St Albans City	26	7	5	14	44	62	19
Tufnell Park	26	4	7	15	43	74	15
London Caledonians	26	5	4	17	26	66	14

1946-47

Leytonstone	26	19	2	5	92	36	40
Dulwich Hamlet	26	17	3	6	78	46	37
Romford	26	13	8	5	76	52	34
Walthamstow Avenue	26	13	4	9	64	37	30
Oxford City	26	12	6	8	70	51	30
Kingstonian	26	12	4	10	54	57	28
Wycombe Wanderers	26	9	8	9	62	62	26
Wimbledon	26	10	5	11	68	64	25
Ilford	26	7	7	12	66	78	21
Tufnell Park	26	8	5	13	45	69	21
Woking	26	7	7	12	34	62	21
Clapton	26	6	8	12	41	59	20
St Albans City	26	7	5	14	47	79	19
Corinthian Casuals	26	4	4	18	36	80	12

1937-38

Leytonstone	26	17	6	3	72	34	40
Ilford	26	17	3	6	70	39	37
Tufnell Park	26	15	2	9	62	47	32
Nunhead	26	14	3	9	52	44	31
Wycombe Wanderers	26	12	5	9	69	55	29
Dulwich Hamlet	26	13	3	10	57	46	29
Kingstonian	26	12	4	10	51	48	28
Clapton	26	9	6	11	49	53	24
Wimbledon	26	10	3	13	62	49	23
London Caledonians	26	9	4	13	44	55	22
Oxford City	26	7	7	12	35	71	21
The Casuals	26	8	3	15	51	74	19
Woking	26	7	2	17	41	72	16
St Albans City	26	4	5	17	31	60	13

1947-48

Leytonstone	26	19	1	6	87	38	39
Kingstonian	26	16	6	4	74	39	38
Walthamstow Avenue	26	17	3	6	61	37	37
Dulwich Hamlet	26	17	2	7	71	39	36
Wimbledon	26	13	6	7	66	40	32
Romford	26	14	1	11	53	47	29
Oxford City	26	10	5	11	50	68	25
Woking	26	10	3	13	63	55	23
Ilford	26	7	7	12	51	59	22
St Albans City	26	9	2	15	43	56	20
Wycombe Wanderers	26	7	5	14	51	65	19
Tufnell Park	26	7	4	15	38	83	18
Clapton	26	5	4	17	35	69	14
Corinthian Casuals	26	5	2	19	33	81	12

1938-39

Leytonstone	26	18	4	4	68	32	40
Ilford	26	17	4	5	68	32	38
Kingstonian	26	17	3	6	62	39	37
Dulwich Hamlet	26	15	5	6	60	32	35
Wimbledon	26	14	3	9	88	56	31
Nunhead	26	11	6	9	54	44	28
The Casuals	26	11	6	9	54	51	28
Clapton	26	12	2	12	69	61	26
Wycombe Wanderers	26	10	6	10	62	62	26
St Albans City	26	8	5	13	44	50	21
Woking	26	9	2	15	35	56	20
Oxford City	26	4	4	18	44	84	12
Tufnell Park	26	4	4	18	33	87	12
London Caledonians	26	3	4	19	26	81	10

1948-49

Dulwich Hamlet	26	15	6	5	60	31	36
Walthamstow Avenue	26	16	4	6	65	38	36
Wimbledon	26	15	4	7	64	41	34
Ilford	26	14	3	9	56	36	31
Oxford City	26	13	5	8	48	34	31
Leytonstone	26	12	6	8	49	41	30
Woking	26	14	1	11	64	59	29
Romford	26	11	3	12	47	54	25
Kingstonian	26	10	4	12	43	47	24
Corinthian Casuals	26	11	2	13	47	59	24
Wycombe Wanderers	26	11	2	13	49	61	24
St Albans City	26	6	6	14	40	60	16
Clapton	26	5	5	16	32	61	15
Tufnell Park	26	1	5	20	28	70	7

St Albans City had 2 points deducted

1945-46

Walthamstow Avenue	26	21	0	5	100	31	42
Oxford City	26	17	6	3	91	40	40
Romford	26	15	3	8	83	59	33
Dulwich Hamlet	26	14	2	10	63	59	30
Tufnell Park	26	12	4	10	70	55	28
Woking	26	10	7	9	56	54	27
Ilford	26	12	2	12	56	71	26
Leytonstone	26	11	3	12	61	75	25
Wycombe Wanderers	26	9	3	14	80	88	21
Wimbledon	26	7	6	13	52	72	20
Corinthian Casuals	26	8	4	14	58	83	20
Clapton	26	8	3	15	51	62	19
St Albans City	26	6	6	14	48	85	18
Kingstonian	26	6	3	17	48	86	15

1949-50

Leytonstone	26	17	5	4	77	31	39
Wimbledon	26	18	2	6	72	51	38
Kingstonian	26	16	3	7	59	39	35
Walthamstow Avenue	26	14	6	6	73	42	34
Dulwich Hamlet	26	14	3	9	60	47	31
St Albans City	26	12	3	11	59	45	27
Woking	26	10	6	10	60	71	26
Wycombe Wanderers	26	9	7	10	51	52	25
Romford	26	10	4	12	45	49	24
Ilford	26	10	4	12	46	53	24
Clapton	26	8	6	12	51	59	22
Oxford City	26	6	6	14	35	54	18
Corinthian Casuals	26	4	5	17	41	69	13
Tufnell Park	26	3	2	21	24	91	8

1950-51

Leytonstone	26	20	3	3	72	26	43
Walthamstow Avenue	26	15	4	7	57	37	34
Romford	26	15	3	8	58	49	33
Wimbledon	26	13	5	8	58	39	31
Dulwich Hamlet	26	14	2	10	54	43	30
Woking	26	11	6	9	65	55	28
Ilford	26	12	4	10	44	45	28
Corinthian Casuals	26	13	0	13	62	60	26
St Albans City	26	11	4	11	32	36	26
Kingstonian	26	9	4	13	46	54	22
Wycombe Wanderers	26	8	3	15	46	64	19
Oxford City	26	7	4	15	47	65	18
Clapton	26	6	5	15	29	50	17
Tufnell Park Edmonton	26	4	1	21	24	73	9

1951-52

Leytonstone	26	13	9	4	63	36	35
Wimbledon	26	16	3	7	65	44	35
Walthamstow Avenue	26	15	4	7	71	43	34
Romford	26	14	4	8	64	42	32
Kingstonian	26	11	7	8	62	48	29
Wycombe Wanderers	26	12	5	9	64	59	29
Woking	26	11	5	10	60	71	27
Dulwich Hamlet	26	11	4	11	60	53	26
Corinthian Casuals	26	11	4	11	55	66	26
St Albans City	26	9	7	10	48	53	25
Ilford	26	8	5	13	32	47	21
Clapton	26	9	2	15	50	59	20
Oxford City	26	6	3	17	50	72	15
Tufnell Park Edmonton	26	2	6	18	25	73	10

1952-53

Walthamstow Avenue	28	19	6	3	53	25	44
Bromley	28	17	4	7	71	35	38
Leytonstone	28	14	6	8	60	38	34
Wimbledon	28	14	5	9	68	37	33
Kingstonian	28	13	6	9	62	50	32
Dulwich Hamlet	28	15	2	11	62	52	32
Romford	28	12	8	8	62	52	32
Wycombe Wanderers	28	14	2	12	54	62	30
St Albans City	28	11	6	11	43	57	28
Barking	28	9	7	12	42	51	25
Ilford	28	10	4	14	59	57	24
Woking	28	10	4	14	57	72	24
Corinthian Casuals	28	7	9	12	45	56	23
Oxford City	28	5	2	21	37	87	12
Clapton	28	2	5	21	27	71	9

1953-54

Bromley	28	18	3	7	76	45	39
Walthamstow Avenue	28	13	7	8	55	30	33
Wycombe Wanderers	28	15	3	10	65	44	33
Ilford	28	11	10	7	48	44	32
Corinthian Casuals	28	12	7	9	59	44	31
Woking	28	13	4	11	54	58	30
Leytonstone	28	12	5	11	58	48	29
St Albans City	28	11	6	11	54	55	28
Dulwich Hamlet	28	11	6	11	55	57	28
Romford	28	11	5	12	57	54	27
Clapton	28	11	5	12	42	56	27
Barking	28	11	2	15	59	84	24
Kingstonian	28	8	7	13	59	71	23
Wimbledon	28	7	8	13	43	59	22
Oxford City	28	4	6	18	49	84	14

1954-55

Walthamstow Avenue	28	21	1	6	80	38	43
St Albans City	28	18	3	7	61	41	39
Bromley	28	18	2	8	66	34	38
Wycombe Wanderers	28	16	3	9	68	43	35
Ilford	28	13	5	10	64	46	31
Barking	28	15	1	12	55	51	31
Woking	28	12	3	13	75	79	27
Kingstonian	28	10	7	11	47	57	27
Leytonstone	28	10	4	14	35	51	24
Oxford City	28	10	3	15	43	74	23
Clapton	28	9	4	15	41	50	22
Wimbledon	28	10	2	16	48	62	22
Corinthian Casuals	28	9	3	16	50	65	21
Dulwich Hamlet	28	7	5	16	48	60	19
Romford	28	4	10	14	43	73	18

1955-56

Wycombe Wanderers	28	19	5	4	82	36	43
Bromley	28	12	7	9	54	43	31
Leytonstone	28	12	7	9	50	44	31
Woking	28	14	3	11	62	60	31
Barking	28	12	7	9	41	45	31
Kingstonian	28	12	6	10	67	64	30
Walthamstow Avenue	28	13	3	12	61	45	29
Ilford	28	10	8	10	44	52	28
Oxford City	28	10	7	11	48	55	27
Clapton	28	9	8	11	45	48	26
Wimbledon	28	12	2	14	51	62	26
Corinthian Casuals	28	9	7	12	56	56	25
Dulwich Hamlet	28	9	6	13	55	67	24
Romford	28	9	6	13	42	55	24
St Albans City	28	2	10	16	36	62	14

1956-57

Wycombe Wanderers	30	18	6	6	86	53	42
Woking	30	20	1	9	104	47	41
Bromley	30	16	5	9	78	60	37
Oxford City	30	16	3	11	65	57	35
Ilford	30	12	8	10	59	65	32
Tooting & Mitcham United	30	10	11	9	53	48	31
Kingstonian	30	11	9	10	72	77	31
Walthamstow Avenue	30	11	8	11	48	46	30
Dulwich Hamlet	30	13	3	14	65	54	29
St Albans City	30	13	3	14	62	71	29
Leytonstone	30	11	6	13	50	50	28
Clapton	30	9	9	12	48	59	27
Wimbledon	30	10	5	15	47	66	25
Romford	30	10	5	15	53	81	25
Barking	30	7	6	17	48	72	20
Corinthian Casuals	30	7	4	19	46	78	18

1957-58

Tooting & Mitcham United	30	20	6	4	79	33	46
Wycombe Wanderers	30	19	4	7	78	42	42
Walthamstow Avenue	30	17	5	8	63	35	39
Bromley	30	13	9	8	66	51	35
Oxford City	30	13	6	11	59	48	32
Leytonstone	30	13	6	11	49	48	32
Wimbledon	30	15	2	13	64	66	32
Corinthian Casuals	30	12	8	10	62	68	32
Woking	30	12	7	11	70	58	31
Barking	30	10	6	14	49	61	26
St Albans City	30	11	3	16	56	76	25
Clapton	30	8	9	13	42	65	25
Kingstonian	30	7	8	15	45	66	22
Dulwich Hamlet	30	7	7	16	49	64	21
Ilford	30	8	4	18	46	70	20
Romford	30	6	8	16	45	71	20

1958-59

Wimbledon	30	22	3	5	91	38	47
Dulwich Hamlet	30	18	5	7	68	44	41
Wycombe Wanderers	30	18	4	8	93	50	40
Oxford City	30	17	4	9	87	58	38
Walthamstow Avenue	30	16	5	9	59	40	37
Tooting & Mitcham United	30	15	4	11	84	55	34
Barking	30	14	2	14	59	53	30
Woking	30	12	6	12	66	66	30
Bromley	30	11	7	12	56	55	29
Clapton	30	10	6	14	55	67	26
Ilford	30	10	6	14	46	67	26
Kingstonian	30	9	4	17	54	72	22
St Albans City	30	8	6	16	53	89	22
Leytonstone	30	7	6	17	40	87	20
Romford	30	7	5	18	54	76	19
Corinthian Casuals	30	7	5	18	44	92	19

1959-60

Tooting & Mitcham United	30	17	8	5	75	43	42
Wycombe Wanderers	30	19	3	8	84	46	41
Wimbledon	30	18	3	9	66	36	39
Kingstonian	30	18	3	9	76	51	39
Corinthian Casuals	30	18	1	11	69	61	37
Bromley	30	15	6	9	75	46	36
Dulwich Hamlet	30	14	6	10	65	47	34
Walthamstow Avenue	30	11	11	8	48	38	33
Oxford City	30	10	10	10	57	57	30
Leytonstone	30	10	8	12	43	46	28
Woking	30	10	6	14	54	61	26
St Albans City	30	10	6	14	50	65	26
Maidstone United	30	10	5	15	53	60	25
Barking	30	7	4	19	30	75	18
Ilford	30	5	6	19	34	86	16
Clapton	30	3	4	23	32	92	10

1960-61

Bromley	30	20	6	4	89	42	46
Walthamstow Avenue	30	20	5	5	87	38	45
Wimbledon	30	18	6	6	72	43	42
Dulwich Hamlet	30	17	4	9	71	59	35
Maidstone United	30	14	8	8	63	39	36
Leytonstone	30	15	6	9	46	34	36
Tooting & Mitcham United	30	14	3	13	69	51	31
Wycombe Wanderers	30	12	5	13	63	61	29
St Albans City	30	12	4	14	45	72	28
Oxford City	30	10	7	13	59	59	27
Corinthian Casuals	30	9	9	12	49	59	27
Kingstonian	30	10	6	14	55	61	26
Woking	30	10	6	14	58	71	26
Ilford	30	5	8	17	30	69	18
Barking	30	3	8	19	30	76	14
Clapton	30	3	5	22	25	77	11

1961-62

Wimbledon	30	19	6	5	68	24	44
Leytonstone	30	17	7	6	61	44	41
Walthamstow Avenue	30	14	8	8	51	31	36
Kingstonian	30	15	5	10	65	48	35
Tooting & Mitcham United	30	12	10	8	62	47	34
Oxford City	30	12	9	9	56	49	33
Wycombe Wanderers	30	12	7	11	57	51	31
Corinthian Casuals	30	12	7	11	45	51	31
St Albans City	30	10	9	11	55	55	29
Woking	30	9	9	12	51	60	27
Dulwich Hamlet	30	11	4	15	55	66	26
Barking	30	9	8	13	40	64	26
Ilford	30	7	10	13	50	59	24
Bromley	30	10	4	16	49	69	24
Clapton	30	6	8	16	45	67	20
Maidstone United	30	6	7	17	34	59	19

1962-63

Wimbledon	30	19	8	3	84	33	46
Kingstonian	30	18	8	4	79	37	44
Tooting & Mitcham United	30	17	8	5	65	37	42
Ilford	30	19	3	8	70	44	41
Walthamstow Avenue	30	14	7	9	51	44	35
Maidstone United	30	13	8	9	56	45	34
Bromley	30	12	10	8	57	51	34
Leytonstone	30	12	7	11	48	50	31
Wycombe Wanderers	30	10	10	10	56	61	30
St Albans City	30	11	5	14	54	49	27
Barking	30	8	10	12	39	50	26
Oxford City	30	8	9	13	55	64	25
Woking	30	8	6	16	42	66	22
Clapton	30	7	4	19	30	71	18
Dulwich Hamlet	30	4	5	21	30	71	13
Corinthian Casuals	30	4	4	22	28	71	12

1963-64

Wimbledon	38	27	6	5	87	44	60
Hendon	38	25	4	9	124	38	54
Kingstonian	38	24	4	10	100	62	52
Sutton United	38	23	5	10	99	64	51
Enfield	38	20	10	8	96	56	50
Oxford City	38	20	8	10	90	55	48
Tooting & Mitcham United	38	19	8	11	78	51	46
St Albans City	38	14	12	12	62	63	40
Ilford	38	16	8	14	75	79	40
Maidstone United	38	15	8	15	65	71	38
Walthamstow Avenue	38	15	6	17	70	66	36
Leytonstone	38	14	8	16	66	71	36
Wycombe Wanderers	38	13	6	19	74	80	32
Hitchin Town	38	14	4	20	67	100	32
Bromley	38	11	8	19	64	75	30
Barking	38	10	9	19	46	69	29
Woking	38	10	9	19	48	88	29
Corinthian Casuals	38	10	4	24	52	92	24
Dulwich Hamlet	38	6	12	20	47	97	24
Clapton	38	2	5	31	31	120	9

1964-65

Hendon	38	28	7	3	123	49	63
Enfield	38	29	5	4	98	35	63
Kingstonian	38	24	8	6	86	44	56
Leytonstone	38	24	5	9	115	62	53
Oxford City	38	20	7	11	76	51	47
St Albans City	38	18	9	11	63	43	45
Sutton United	38	17	11	10	74	57	45
Wealdstone	38	19	6	13	93	68	44
Bromley	38	14	11	13	71	80	39
Tooting & Mitcham United	38	15	7	16	71	66	37
Hitchin Town	38	13	9	16	61	66	35
Walthamstow Avenue	38	15	5	18	63	82	35
Wycombe Wanderers	38	13	7	18	70	85	33
Corinthian Casuals	38	13	7	18	56	77	33
Barking	38	10	8	20	58	80	28
Ilford	38	8	8	22	43	89	24
Maidstone United	38	8	6	24	49	86	22
Dulwich Hamlet	38	8	5	25	45	79	21
Clapton	38	8	3	27	43	91	19
Woking	38	7	4	27	45	113	18

Hendon beat Enfield in a play-off to decide the Championship

1965-66

Leytonstone	38	27	7	4	98	33	63
Hendon	38	27	5	6	111	55	59
Enfield	38	24	8	6	104	54	56
Wycombe Wanderers	38	25	6	7	100	65	56
Kingstonian	38	24	5	9	94	55	53
Wealdstone	38	20	6	12	90	64	46
Maidstone United	38	19	6	13	74	61	44
St Albans City	38	19	5	14	57	56	43
Sutton United	38	17	7	14	83	72	41
Tooting & Mitcham United	38	16	7	15	65	58	39
Corinthian Casuals	38	17	5	16	74	67	39
Woking	38	12	10	16	60	83	34
Walthamstow Avenue	38	12	9	17	81	75	33
Oxford City	38	10	9	19	49	72	29
Barking	38	10	7	21	51	72	27
Bromley	38	10	5	23	69	101	25
Ilford	38	7	10	21	50	84	24
Hitchin Town	38	6	8	24	57	118	20
Clapton	38	5	6	27	46	103	16
Dulwich Hamlet	38	5	5	28	30	95	15

1966-67

Sutton United	38	26	7	5	89	33	59
Walthamstow Avenue	38	22	12	4	89	47	56
Wycombe Wanderers	38	23	8	7	92	54	54
Enfield	38	25	2	11	87	33	52
Hendon	38	20	9	9	64	37	49
Tooting & Mitcham United	38	19	10	9	76	60	48
Leytonstone	38	19	9	10	67	38	47
St Albans City	38	16	12	10	59	45	44
Kingstonian	38	18	8	12	60	49	44
Oxford City	38	15	9	14	74	61	39
Woking	38	13	10	15	65	71	36
Wealdstone	38	13	8	17	72	73	34
Barking	38	11	12	15	56	61	34
Bromley	38	12	7	19	50	67	31
Clapton	38	10	8	20	49	92	28
Ilford	38	8	10	20	43	77	26
Corinthian Casuals	38	9	7	22	45	68	25
Maidstone United	38	6	10	22	43	90	22
Hitchin Town	38	8	6	24	39	89	22
Dulwich Hamlet	38	3	4	31	33	107	10

1967-68

Enfield	38	28	8	2	85	22	64
Sutton United	38	22	11	5	89	27	55
Hendon	38	23	6	9	90	36	52
Leytonstone	38	21	10	7	78	41	52
St Albans City	38	20	8	10	78	41	48
Walthamstow Avenue	38	19	9	10	81	64	47
Wealdstone	38	19	8	11	80	45	46
Tooting & Mitcham United	38	19	5	14	57	45	43
Barking	38	17	8	13	75	57	42
Oxford City	38	17	4	17	59	58	38
Kingstonian	38	14	10	14	56	61	38
Hitchin Town	38	14	9	15	61	73	37
Bromley	38	12	10	16	58	80	34
Wycombe Wanderers	38	13	5	20	73	85	31
Dulwich Hamlet	38	10	7	21	39	66	27
Clapton	38	10	7	21	51	88	27
Woking	38	8	8	22	50	90	24
Corinthian Casuals	38	7	10	21	40	80	24
Ilford	38	7	7	24	41	77	21
Maidstone United	38	3	4	31	26	131	10

1968-69

Enfield	38	27	7	4	103	28	61
Hitchin Town	38	23	10	5	67	41	56
Sutton United	38	22	9	7	83	29	53
Wycombe Wanderers	38	23	6	9	70	37	52
Wealdstone	38	20	11	7	73	48	51
Hendon	38	22	5	11	69	47	49
St Albans City	38	17	13	8	75	44	47
Barking	38	20	7	11	69	46	47
Oxford City	38	18	8	12	76	64	44
Tooting & Mitcham United	38	16	10	12	68	55	42
Leytonstone	38	18	4	16	71	53	40
Kingstonian	38	15	8	15	62	56	38
Walthamstow Avenue	38	10	10	18	47	71	30
Maidstone United	38	10	8	20	47	75	28
Clapton	38	10	7	21	52	76	27
Woking	38	8	7	23	45	77	23
Bromley	38	8	7	23	52	95	23
Dulwich Hamlet	38	6	9	23	31	77	21
Ilford	38	6	8	24	33	77	20
Corinthian Casuals	38	2	4	32	23	120	8

1969-70

Enfield	38	27	8	3	91	26	62
Wycombe Wanderers	38	25	11	2	85	24	61
Sutton United	38	24	9	5	75	35	57
Barking	38	21	9	8	93	47	51
Hendon	38	19	12	7	77	44	50
St Albans City	38	21	8	9	69	40	50
Hitchin Town	38	19	10	9	71	40	48
Tooting & Mitcham United	38	19	5	14	88	62	43
Leytonstone	38	17	7	14	57	41	41
Wealdstone	38	15	10	13	53	48	40
Oxford City	38	15	7	16	61	78	37
Kingstonian	38	13	9	16	55	57	35
Ilford	38	8	15	15	42	73	31
Dulwich Hamlet	38	8	12	18	46	66	28
Woking	38	10	7	21	46	69	27
Walthamstow Avenue	38	11	5	22	52	81	27
Clapton	38	9	7	22	45	87	25
Maidstone United	38	7	8	23	48	84	22
Corinthian Casuals	38	6	3	29	30	99	15
Bromley	38	3	4	31	28	111	10

1970-71

Wycombe Wanderers	38	28	6	4	93	32	62
Sutton United	38	29	3	6	76	35	61
St Albans City	38	23	10	5	87	26	56
Enfield	38	24	7	7	67	24	55
Ilford	38	21	7	10	74	51	49
Hendon	38	18	11	9	81	37	47
Barking	38	20	4	14	89	59	44
Leytonstone	38	17	10	11	68	50	44
Woking	38	18	6	14	57	50	42
Walthamstow Avenue	38	14	11	13	63	52	39
Oxford City	38	13	10	15	51	48	36
Hitchin Town	38	12	9	17	46	60	33
Wealdstone	38	12	8	18	45	64	32
Tooting & Mitcham United	38	11	9	18	44	66	31
Kingstonian	38	11	8	19	53	71	30
Bromley	38	10	6	22	34	77	26
Dulwich Hamlet	38	7	10	21	30	66	24
Maidstone United	38	7	6	25	42	84	20
Clapton	38	5	7	26	33	101	17
Corinthian Casuals	38	2	8	28	23	103	12

1971-72

Wycombe Wanderers	40	31	3	6	102	20	65
Enfield	40	26	8	6	90	41	60
Walton & Hersham	40	24	8	8	69	25	56
Hendon	40	23	10	7	79	35	56
Bishop's Stortford	40	24	5	11	61	37	53
Sutton United	40	21	10	9	77	43	52
St Albans City	40	23	4	13	74	47	50
Ilford	40	17	11	12	62	52	45
Barking	40	20	4	16	65	61	44
Hitchin Town	40	17	10	13	68	66	44
Bromley	40	16	10	14	67	64	42
Hayes	40	14	12	14	50	48	40
Oxford City	40	13	9	18	67	74	35
Woking	40	11	10	19	52	58	32
Kingstonian	40	10	12	18	49	59	32
Walthamstow Avenue	40	12	8	20	58	71	32
Leytonstone	40	11	8	21	48	68	30
Tooting & Mitcham United	40	6	9	25	38	93	21
Clapton	40	7	7	26	45	118	21
Dulwich Hamlet	40	4	12	24	35	81	20
Corinthian Casuals	40	3	4	33	21	116	10

Second Division

Dagenham	30	22	4	4	68	23	70
Slough Town	30	18	6	6	46	23	60
Hertford Town	30	17	5	8	46	29	56
Chesham Town	30	16	6	8	61	43	54
Aveley	30	16	5	9	50	28	53
Tilbury	30	14	5	11	47	36	47
Maidenhead United	30	12	11	7	36	30	47
Horsham	30	12	9	9	47	35	45
Harwich & Parkeston	30	11	9	10	46	41	42
Staines Town	30	10	8	12	34	41	38
Carshalton Athletic	30	8	8	14	34	51	32
Hampton	30	6	10	14	33	51	28
Harlow Town	30	6	9	15	33	48	27
Finchley	30	6	7	17	29	52	25
Southall	30	3	10	17	17	52	19
Wokingham Town	30	3	8	19	30	74	17

1972-73

Hendon	42	34	6	2	88	18	74
Walton & Hersham	42	25	11	6	60	25	61
Leatherhead	42	23	10	9	76	32	56
Wycombe Wanderers	42	25	6	11	66	32	56
Walthamstow Avenue	42	20	12	10	66	48	52
Tooting & Mitcham United	42	20	11	11	73	39	51
Sutton United	42	21	9	12	69	48	51
Kingstonian	42	20	10	12	60	49	50
Enfield	42	20	8	14	90	54	48
Bishop's Stortford	42	18	12	12	58	51	48
Hayes	42	19	8	15	69	42	46
Dulwich Hamlet	42	18	9	15	59	52	45
Ilford	42	18	9	15	61	59	45
Leytonstone	42	17	11	14	55	54	45
Woking	42	18	8	16	61	56	44
Hitchin Town	42	15	9	18	52	64	39
Barking	42	8	7	27	45	88	23
St Albans City	42	5	12	25	34	76	22
Oxford City	42	6	7	29	30	101	19
Bromley	42	4	10	28	31	70	18
Clapton	42	3	11	28	31	100	17
Corinthian Casuals	42	3	8	31	30	106	14

1973-74

First Division

Wycombe Wanderers	42	27	9	6	96	34	90
Hendon	42	25	13	4	63	20	88
Bishop's Stortford	42	26	9	7	78	26	87
Dulwich Hamlet	42	22	11	9	71	38	77
Leatherhead	42	23	6	13	81	44	75
Walton & Hersham	42	20	12	10	68	50	72
Woking	42	22	6	14	63	55	72
Leytonstone	42	20	9	13	63	44	69
Ilford	42	20	8	14	60	44	68
Hayes	42	17	14	11	65	43	65
Oxford City	42	15	16	11	45	47	61
Sutton United	42	13	16	13	51	52	55
Hitchin Town	42	15	10	17	68	73	55
Barking	42	14	12	16	57	58	54
Kingstonian	42	12	15	15	47	46	51
Tooting & Mitcham United	42	14	9	19	57	62	51
Enfield	42	13	11	18	50	57	50
Walthamstow Avenue	42	11	13	18	46	62	46
Bromley	42	7	9	26	37	81	30
Clapton	42	8	3	31	36	128	27
St Albans City	42	4	7	31	30	92	19
Corinthian Casuals	42	3	4	35	31	107	13

1974-75

First Division

Wycombe Wanderers	42	28	11	3	93	30	95
Enfield	42	29	8	5	78	26	95
Dagenham	42	28	5	9	95	44	89
Tooting & Mitcham United	42	25	9	8	78	46	84
Dulwich Hamlet	42	24	10	8	75	38	82
Leatherhead	42	23	10	9	83	42	79
Ilford	42	23	10	9	98	51	79
Oxford City	42	17	9	16	63	56	60
Slough Town	42	17	6	19	68	52	57
Sutton United	42	17	6	19	68	63	57
Bishop's Stortford	42	17	6	19	56	64	57
Hitchin Town	42	15	10	17	57	71	55
Hendon	42	15	7	20	59	74	52
Walthamstow Avenue	42	13	9	20	56	62	48
Woking	42	12	10	20	53	73	46
Hayes	42	10	14	18	52	66	44
Barking	42	12	8	22	57	81	44
Leytonstone	42	12	7	23	42	61	43
Kingstonian	42	13	4	25	48	73	43
Clapton	42	12	4	26	46	96	40
Walton & Hersham	42	9	4	29	37	108	31
Bromley	42	6	3	33	25	110	21

Second Division

Staines Town	34	23	2	9	65	23	71
Southall	34	20	3	11	55	41	63
Tilbury	34	19	5	10	64	36	60
Harwich & Parkeston	34	18	4	12	52	44	58
Chesham United	34	17	6	11	59	39	57
St Albans City	34	15	11	8	42	37	56
Harlow Town	34	16	6	12	53	47	54
Horsham	34	16	5	13	59	49	53
Maidenhead United	34	13	7	14	38	40	46
Hampton	34	12	7	15	44	42	43
Croydon	34	11	10	13	48	55	43
Hertford Town	34	10	7	17	35	52	37
Boreham Wood	34	7	15	12	41	49	36
Wokingham Town	34	10	6	18	32	43	36
Finchley	34	9	9	16	36	53	36
Carshalton Athletic	34	9	9	16	38	58	36
Aveley	34	9	7	18	34	63	34
Corinthian Casuals	34	8	9	17	35	59	33

Tilbury had 2 points deducted

1975-76

First Division

Enfield	42	26	9	7	83	38	87
Wycombe Wanderers	42	24	10	8	71	41	82
Dagenham	42	25	6	11	89	55	81
Ilford	42	22	10	10	58	39	76
Dulwich Hamlet	42	22	5	15	67	41	71
Hendon	42	20	11	11	60	41	71
Tooting & Mitcham United	42	19	11	12	73	49	68
Leatherhead	42	19	10	13	63	53	67
Staines Town	42	19	9	14	46	37	66
Slough Town	42	17	12	13	58	45	63
Sutton United	42	17	11	14	71	60	62
Bishop's Stortford	42	15	12	15	51	47	57
Walthamstow Avenue	42	14	11	17	47	60	53
Woking	42	14	9	19	58	62	51
Barking	42	15	6	21	57	70	51
Hitchin Town	42	13	11	18	45	57	50
Hayes	42	10	19	13	44	48	49
Kingstonian	42	13	8	21	53	87	47
Southall & Ealing Borough	42	11	9	22	56	69	42
Leytonstone	42	10	10	22	41	63	40
Oxford City	42	9	8	25	29	65	35
Clapton	42	3	3	36	19	112	12

Second Division

Tilbury	42	32	6	4	97	30	102
Croydon	42	28	14	0	81	27	98
Carshalton Athletic	42	28	6	8	75	37	90
Chesham United	42	21	12	9	91	51	75
Harwich & Parkeston	42	21	11	10	78	56	74
Hampton	42	21	9	12	72	52	72
St Albans City	42	18	12	12	59	48	66
Boreham Wood	42	17	12	13	68	50	63
Harrow Borough	42	15	12	15	71	74	57
Hornchurch	42	15	11	16	61	61	56
Horsham	42	14	13	15	60	55	55
Wembley	42	14	13	15	51	54	55
Wokingham Town	42	13	16	13	45	52	55
Walton & Hersham	42	14	12	16	61	56	54
Finchley	42	14	11	17	52	53	53
Bromley	42	11	11	20	64	86	44
Aveley	42	11	9	22	34	51	42
Harlow Town	42	11	9	22	50	73	42
Maidenhead United	42	6	17	19	32	65	35
Ware	42	7	12	23	50	95	33
Hertford Town	42	5	9	28	32	87	24
Corinthian Casuals	42	4	7	31	42	113	19

1976-77

First Division

Enfield	42	24	12	6	63	34	84
Wycombe Wanderers	42	25	8	9	71	34	83
Dagenham	42	23	10	9	80	39	79
Hendon	42	19	10	13	60	48	67
Tilbury	42	18	13	11	57	49	67
Tooting & Mitcham	42	18	10	14	85	72	64
Walthamstow Avenue	42	19	7	16	61	55	64
Slough Town	42	18	9	15	51	46	63
Hitchin Town	42	19	6	17	60	66	63
Leatherhead	42	18	7	17	61	47	61
Staines Town	42	16	13	13	52	48	61
Leytonstone	42	16	11	15	59	57	59
Barking	42	16	9	17	63	61	57
Southall & Ealing Borough	42	15	8	19	52	64	53
Croydon	42	13	10	19	38	52	49
Sutton United	42	14	7	21	40	55	49
Kingstonian	42	13	7	22	45	60	46
Hayes	42	12	10	20	49	69	46
Woking	42	11	12	19	47	61	45
Bishop's Stortford	42	11	11	20	51	71	44
Dulwich Hamlet	42	11	8	23	52	68	41
Ilford	42	10	8	24	32	73	38

Second Division

Boreham Wood	42	35	4	5	80	26	103
Carshalton Athletic	42	25	12	5	80	33	87
Harwich & Parkeston	42	23	8	11	93	61	77
Wembley	42	23	8	11	82	58	77
Harrow Borough	42	21	12	9	78	44	75
Horsham	42	23	5	14	67	56	74
Bromley	42	20	10	12	71	46	70
Oxford City	42	20	8	14	73	55	68
Hampton	42	20	8	14	62	45	68
Wokingham Town	42	16	14	12	60	44	62
Hornchurch	42	18	7	17	62	53	61
Chesham United	42	17	10	15	63	66	61
St Albans City	42	16	12	14	59	53	60
Walton & Hersham	42	17	9	16	57	56	60
Aveley	42	14	8	20	49	62	50
Corinthian Casuals	42	13	6	23	52	75	45
Harlow Town	42	11	8	23	39	77	41
Hertford Town	42	9	9	24	45	80	36
Maidenhead United	42	8	8	26	36	73	32
Clapton	42	7	9	28	43	87	30
Finchley	42	5	13	24	36	82	28
Ware	42	5	8	29	43	98	23

1977-78

Premier Division

Enfield	42	35	5	2	96	27	110
Dagenham	42	24	7	11	78	55	79
Wycombe Wanderers	42	22	9	11	66	41	75
Tooting & Mitcham United	42	22	8	12	64	49	74
Hitchin Town	42	20	9	13	69	53	69
Sutton United	42	18	12	12	66	57	66
Leatherhead	42	18	11	13	62	48	65
Croydon	42	18	10	14	61	52	64
Walthamstow Avenue	42	17	12	13	64	61	63
Barking	42	17	7	18	76	66	58
Carshalton Athletic	42	15	11	16	60	62	56
Hayes	42	15	11	16	46	53	56
Hendon	42	16	7	19	57	55	55
Woking	42	14	11	17	62	62	53
Boreham Wood	42	15	8	19	48	65	53
Slough Town	42	14	8	20	52	69	0
Staines Town	42	12	13	17	46	60	49
Tilbury	42	11	12	19	57	68	45
Kingstonian	42	8	13	21	43	65	37
Leytonstone	42	7	15	20	44	71	36
Southall & Ealing Borough	42	6	15	21	43	74	33
Bishop's Stortford	42	7	8	27	36	83	29

First Division

Dulwich Hamlet	42	28	9	5	91	25	93
Oxford City	42	26	5	11	85	44	83
Bromley	42	23	13	6	74	41	82
Walton & Hersham	42	22	11	9	69	41	77
Ilford	42	21	14	7	57	47	77
St Albans City	42	22	10	10	83	46	76
Wokingham Town	42	19	12	11	69	48	69
Harlow Town	42	19	8	15	63	49	65
Harrow Borough	42	17	10	15	59	54	61
Maidenhead United	42	16	13	13	55	54	61
Hertford Town	42	15	14	13	57	51	59
Chesham United	42	14	13	15	69	70	55
Hampton	42	13	13	16	49	53	52
Harwich & Parkeston	42	12	13	17	68	79	49
Wembley	42	15	3	24	56	82	48
Horsham	42	12	10	20	41	57	46
Finchley	42	11	13	18	41	68	46
Aveley	42	13	7	22	47	75	46
Ware	42	8	13	21	61	95	37
Clapton	42	10	6	26	46	78	36
Hornchurch	42	8	10	24	47	81	34
Corinthian Casuals	42	3	10	29	40	88	19

Second Division

Epsom & Ewell	32	21	5	6	65	34	68
Metropolitan Police	32	19	6	7	53	30	63
Farnborough Town	32	19	4	9	68	40	61
Molesey	32	17	8	7	47	27	59
Egham Town	32	15	9	8	52	34	54
Tring Town	32	14	11	7	62	32	53
Letchworth Garden City	32	14	11	7	67	48	53
Lewes	32	13	7	12	52	51	46
Rainham Town	32	13	6	13	42	50	45
Worthing	32	11	9	12	40	45	42
Eastbourne United	32	10	8	14	40	50	38
Cheshunt	32	9	6	17	43	60	33
Feltham	32	7	9	16	30	49	30
Camberley Town	32	6	11	15	32	49	29
Hemel Hempstead	32	6	9	17	33	50	27
Epping Town	32	7	6	19	37	64	27
Willesden	32	7	3	22	38	88	24

Second Division

Farnborough Town	34	26	3	5	77	34	81
Camberley Town	34	21	8	5	71	32	71
Molesey	34	19	11	4	55	33	68
Lewes	34	19	6	9	66	50	63
Feltham	34	16	7	11	47	36	55
Letchworth Garden City	34	14	10	10	56	48	52
Eastbourne United	34	16	4	14	47	45	52
Hemel Hempstead	34	13	11	10	46	37	50
Epping Town	34	14	7	13	49	44	49
Rainham Town	34	13	10	11	42	41	49
Cheshunt	34	11	8	15	43	49	41
Hungerford Town	34	11	8	15	48	58	41
Worthing	34	9	8	17	40	50	35
Hornchurch	34	9	8	17	39	62	35
Egham Town	34	7	12	15	48	54	33
Tring Town	34	6	8	20	33	56	26
Willesden	34	6	8	20	41	77	26
Corinthian Casuals	34	4	7	23	23	65	19

1978-79

Premier Division

Barking	42	28	9	5	92	50	93
Dagenham	42	25	6	11	83	63	81
Enfield	42	22	11	9	69	37	77
Dulwich Hamlet	42	21	13	8	69	39	76
Slough Town	42	20	12	10	61	44	72
Wycombe Wanderers	42	20	9	13	59	44	69
Woking	42	18	14	10	79	59	68
Croydon	42	19	9	14	61	51	66
Hendon	42	16	14	12	55	48	62
Leatherhead	42	17	9	16	57	45	60
Sutton United	42	17	9	16	62	51	60
Tooting & Mitcham United	42	15	14	13	52	52	59
Walthamstow Avenue	42	15	6	21	61	69	51
Tilbury	42	13	1	18	60	76	50
Boreham Wood	42	13	10	19	50	67	49
Hitchin Town	42	12	11	19	59	71	47
Carshalton Athletic	42	10	16	16	49	69	46
Hayes	42	9	18	15	45	58	45
Oxford City	42	12	7	23	50	80	43
Staines Town	42	6	16	20	40	64	34
Leytonstone	42	8	7	27	36	75	31
Kingstonian	42	3	15	24	35	72	24

1979-80

Premier Division

Enfield	42	25	9	8	74	32	84
Walthamstow Avenue	42	24	9	9	87	48	81
Dulwich Hamlet	42	21	16	5	66	37	79
Sutton United	42	20	13	9	67	40	73
Dagenham	42	20	13	9	82	56	73
Tooting & Mitcham United	42	21	6	15	62	59	69
Barking	42	19	10	13	72	51	67
Harrow Borough	42	17	15	10	64	51	66
Woking	42	17	13	12	78	59	64
Wycombe Wanderers	42	17	13	12	72	53	64
Harlow Town	42	14	12	16	55	61	54
Hitchin Town	42	13	15	14	55	69	54
Hendon	42	12	13	17	50	57	49
Slough Town	42	13	10	19	54	71	49
Boreham Wood	42	13	10	19	50	69	49
Staines Town	42	14	6	22	46	67	48
Hayes	42	12	9	21	48	68	45
Leatherhead	42	11	11	20	51	60	44
Carshalton Athletic	42	12	7	23	48	78	43
Croydon	42	10	10	22	51	59	40
Oxford City	42	10	9	23	49	87	39
Tilbury	42	7	11	24	41	90	30

Tilbury had 2 points deducted

First Division

Harlow Town	42	31	7	4	93	32	100
Harrow Borough	42	26	8	8	85	49	86
Maidenhead United	42	25	6	11	77	50	81
Bishop's Stortford	42	22	11	9	68	40	77
Horsham	42	23	7	12	63	47	76
Hertford Town	42	21	11	10	62	41	74
Harwich & Parkeston	42	22	5	15	90	57	71
Bromley	42	18	12	12	76	50	66
Hampton	42	17	11	14	59	47	62
Epsom & Ewell	42	18	7	17	69	41	61
Wembley	42	15	14	13	57	57	59
Aveley	42	17	6	19	57	67	57
Wokingham Town	42	17	8	17	64	68	56
Clapton	42	15	8	19	67	80	53
Metropolitan Police	42	12	13	17	58	55	49
Walton & Hersham	42	12	9	21	47	71	45
Ilford	42	13	5	24	48	80	44
Ware	42	11	10	21	46	69	43
Chesham United	42	11	9	22	46	66	42
Finchley	42	7	15	20	43	75	36
St Albans City	42	7	7	28	43	90	28
Southall & Ealing Borough	42	5	5	32	41	114	20

Wokingham Town had 3 points deducted

First Division

Leytonstone & Ilford	42	31	6	5	83	35	99
Bromley	42	24	10	8	93	44	82
Maidenhead United	42	24	8	10	81	46	80
Bishop's Stortford	42	24	8	10	74	47	80
Kingstonian	42	22	8	12	59	44	74
Chesham United	42	18	13	11	68	56	67
St Albans City	42	17	13	12	65	47	64
Farnborough Town	42	19	7	16	70	57	64
Epsom & Ewell	42	18	7	17	62	57	61
Camberley Town	42	16	10	16	43	38	58
Walton & Hersham	42	15	12	15	61	50	57
Wembley	42	16	8	18	46	52	56
Wokingham Town	42	14	11	17	45	49	53
Hertford Town	42	13	11	18	71	74	50
Aveley	42	12	13	17	45	55	49
Hampton	42	14	7	21	57	74	49
Finchley	42	13	9	20	44	59	48
Metropolitan Police	42	13	8	21	46	67	47
Ware	42	11	12	19	45	61	45
Clapton	42	14	3	25	48	77	45
Harwich & Parkeston	42	11	6	25	51	84	38
Horsham	42	6	4	32	29	113	22

Harwich & Parkeston had 1 point deducted

Second Division

Billericay Town	36	31	3	2	100	18	96
Lewes	36	24	7	5	82	33	79
Hungerford Town	36	21	8	7	78	36	71
Eastbourne United	36	21	6	9	77	45	69
Letchworth Garden City	36	21	6	9	63	32	69
Hornchurch	36	21	6	9	66	39	69
Molesey	36	15	9	12	67	60	54
Barton Rovers	36	15	7	14	49	49	52
Worthing	36	14	9	13	58	54	51
Cheshunt	36	13	7	16	47	52	46
Rainham Town	36	12	7	17	54	65	43
Egham Town	36	11	9	16	47	53	42
Southall & Ealing Borough	36	11	6	19	43	69	39
Feltham	36	8	11	17	23	49	35
Tring Town	36	7	13	16	38	55	34
Epping Town	36	10	4	22	44	69	34
Willesden	36	9	6	21	32	83	33
Hemel Hempstead	36	4	9	23	33	72	21
Corinthian Casuals	36	6	3	27	24	92	21

Second Division

Feltham	38	24	10	4	65	30	82
Hornchurch	38	25	6	7	74	35	81
Hungerford Town	38	23	10	5	84	29	79
Barton Rovers	38	19	11	8	61	25	68
Worthing	38	19	11	8	74	43	68
Cheshunt	38	19	11	8	57	33	68
Letchworth Garden City	38	18	7	13	49	40	61
Southall	38	14	11	13	48	52	53
Dorking Town	38	13	12	13	47	45	51
Horsham	38	16	3	19	47	47	51
Hemel Hempstead	38	14	7	17	47	54	49
Egham Town	38	13	9	16	45	62	48
Harwich & Parkeston	38	12	11	15	57	58	47
Rainham Town	38	11	13	14	44	45	46
Epping Town	38	12	7	19	37	50	43
Eastbourne United	38	11	10	17	59	75	43
Willesden	38	11	8	19	57	68	41
Tring Town	38	11	6	21	40	71	39
Molesey	38	4	9	25	31	83	21
Corinthian Casuals	38	1	8	29	17	95	11

1980-81

Premier Division

Slough Town	42	23	13	6	73	34	82
Enfield	42	23	11	8	81	43	80
Wycombe Wanderers	42	22	9	11	76	49	75
Leytonstone & Ilford	42	19	12	11	78	57	69
Sutton United	42	19	12	11	82	65	69
Hendon	42	18	10	14	66	58	64
Dagenham	42	17	11	14	79	66	62
Hayes	42	18	8	16	45	50	62
Harrow Borough	42	16	11	15	57	52	59
Bromley	42	16	9	17	63	69	57
Staines Town	42	15	9	18	60	61	54
Tooting & Mitcham United	42	15	8	19	49	53	53
Hitchin Town	42	14	10	18	64	62	52
Croydon	42	12	15	15	51	51	51
Dulwich Hamlet	42	13	12	17	62	67	51
Leatherhead	42	12	14	16	36	50	50
Carshalton Athletic	42	14	8	20	57	82	50
Barking	42	13	12	17	58	72	49
Harlow Town	42	11	15	16	53	66	48
Walthamstow Avenue	42	13	7	22	50	81	46
Boreham Wood	42	10	13	19	46	69	43
Woking	42	11	7	24	40	69	37

Barking had 1 point deducted
Woking had 3 points deducted

First Division

Bishop's Stortford	42	30	6	6	84	28	96
Billericay Town	42	29	6	7	67	34	93
Epsom & Ewell	42	24	12	6	80	36	84
Farnborough Town	42	23	11	8	75	39	80
St Albans City	42	24	5	13	85	61	77
Kingstonian	42	20	9	13	63	52	66
Oxford City	42	18	9	15	71	48	63
Wokingham Town	42	16	15	11	70	56	63
Metropolitan Police	42	18	7	17	61	58	61
Chesham United	42	17	7	18	64	64	58
Lewes	42	17	7	18	72	83	58
Maidenhead United	42	16	7	19	58	62	55
Walton & Hersham	42	12	15	15	46	53	51
Hertford Town	42	13	11	18	46	65	50
Hampton	42	12	13	17	46	53	49
Aveley	42	13	9	20	54	55	48
Wembley	42	13	8	21	47	61	47
Clapton	42	12	8	22	53	86	44
Ware	42	9	13	20	50	69	40
Tilbury	42	10	8	24	42	84	35
Camberley Town	42	8	7	27	42	88	31
Finchley	42	6	11	25	36	77	29

Kingstonian and Tilbury both had 3 points deducted

1981-82

Premier Division

Leytonstone & Ilford	42	26	5	11	91	52	83
Sutton United	42	22	9	11	72	49	75
Wycombe Wanderers	42	21	10	11	63	48	73
Staines Town	42	21	9	12	58	45	72
Walthamstow Avenue	42	21	7	14	81	62	70
Harrow Borough	42	18	13	11	77	55	67
Tooting & Mitcham United	42	19	10	13	58	47	67
Slough Town	42	17	13	12	64	54	64
Leatherhead	42	16	12	14	57	52	60
Hayes	42	16	10	16	58	52	58
Croydon	42	16	9	17	59	57	57
Barking	42	14	14	14	53	51	56
Hendon	42	13	13	16	56	65	52
Dulwich Hamlet	42	14	10	18	47	59	52
Bishop's Stortford	42	15	5	22	50	70	50
Carshalton Athletic	42	14	8	20	58	86	50
Billericay Town	42	11	16	15	41	50	49
Hitchin Town	42	12	11	19	56	77	47
Bromley	42	13	7	22	63	79	46
Woking	42	11	13	18	57	75	46
Harlow Town	42	10	11	21	50	73	41
Boreham Wood	42	8	13	21	47	58	37

First Division

Wokingham Town	40	29	5	6	86	30	92
Bognor Regis Town	40	23	10	7	65	34	79
Metropolitan Police	40	22	11	7	75	48	77
Oxford City	40	21	11	8	82	47	74
Feltham	40	20	8	12	65	49	68
Lewes	40	19	7	14	73	66	64
Hertford Town	40	16	10	14	62	54	58
Wembley	40	14	15	11	69	55	57
Farnborough Town	40	15	11	14	71	57	56
Epsom & Ewell	40	16	8	16	52	44	56
Kingstonian	40	16	7	17	57	56	55
Hampton	40	15	9	16	52	52	54
Hornchurch	40	13	15	12	42	50	54
Aveley	40	14	10	16	46	58	54
St Albans City	40	14	9	17	55	55	51
Maidenhead United	40	11	10	19	49	70	43
Tilbury	40	9	15	16	49	66	42
Walton & Hersham	40	10	11	19	43	65	41
Chesham United	40	9	9	22	41	71	36
Clapton	40	9	7	24	44	75	34
Ware	40	5	2	33	29	105	17

Second Division

Worthing	40	29	6	5	95	25	93
Cheshunt	40	25	7	8	79	33	82
Hungerford Town	40	22	10	8	89	42	74
Barton Rovers	40	22	8	10	65	32	74
Windsor & Eton	40	22	6	12	69	49	72
Corinthian Casuals	40	19	12	9	67	50	69
Harwich & Parkeston	40	19	12	9	64	47	69
Letchworth Garden City	40	15	11	14	67	55	56
Dorking Town	40	13	17	10	52	44	56
Hemel Hempstead	40	15	9	16	54	49	54
Basildon United	40	16	5	19	64	51	53
Finchley	40	14	9	17	57	68	51
Southall	40	12	14	14	36	42	50
Epping Town	40	12	11	17	48	62	47
Molesey	40	13	7	20	61	73	46
Egham Town	40	11	9	20	56	64	42
Rainham Town	40	11	9	20	53	83	42
Tring Town	40	9	13	18	49	78	40
Eastbourne United	40	9	12	19	51	73	39
Horsham	40	10	9	21	42	79	39
Camberley Town	40	3	2	35	21	140	11

Hungerford Town had 2 points deducted

Second Division

Clapton	42	30	4	8	96	46	94
Windsor & Eton	42	27	7	8	98	43	88
Barton Rovers	42	26	6	10	86	48	84
Leyton Wingate	42	25	8	9	111	41	83
Basildon United	42	23	13	6	92	42	82
Uxbridge	42	22	12	8	80	42	78
Hungerford Town	42	22	10	10	82	39	76
Corinthian Casuals	42	23	6	13	95	48	75
Egham Town	42	21	8	13	77	67	71
Tring Town	42	20	10	12	86	59	70
Letchworth Garden City	42	18	13	11	68	53	66
Southall	42	18	7	17	81	80	61
Molesey	42	17	9	16	73	56	60
Dorking Town	42	15	9	18	56	75	54
Hemel Hempstead	42	12	14	16	53	59	50
Rainham Town	42	14	4	24	57	94	46
Eastbourne United	42	10	6	26	54	104	36
Epping Town	42	6	8	28	29	89	26
Ware	42	6	6	30	34	97	24
Finchley	42	4	12	26	28	92	24
Horsham	42	5	7	30	32	106	22
Harwich & Parkeston	42	5	7	30	42	130	22

Letchworth Garden City had 1 point deducted

1982-83

Premier Division

Wycombe Wanderers	42	26	7	9	79	47	85
Leytonstone & Ilford	42	24	9	9	71	39	81
Harrow Borough	42	24	7	11	91	58	79
Hayes	42	23	9	10	63	41	78
Sutton United	42	20	8	14	96	71	68
Dulwich Hamlet	42	18	14	10	59	52	68
Slough Town	42	18	13	11	73	36	67
Bognor Regis Town	42	19	8	15	53	48	65
Tooting & Mitcham United	42	18	9	15	65	62	63
Billericay Town	42	17	10	15	54	51	61
Croydon	42	17	9	16	68	58	60
Hendon	42	18	6	18	68	61	60
Bishop's Stortford	42	17	9	16	61	58	60
Barking	42	14	14	14	47	55	56
Bromley	42	14	12	16	51	50	54
Carshalton Athletic	42	15	9	18	58	60	54
Wokingham Town	42	13	9	20	37	51	48
Walthamstow Avenue	42	12	11	19	48	64	47
Staines Town	42	12	11	19	62	79	47
Hitchin Town	42	11	9	22	49	77	42
Woking	42	6	6	30	30	79	24
Leatherhead	42	4	5	33	35	121	17

1983-84

Premier Division

Harrow Borough	42	25	13	4	73	42	88
Worthing	42	20	11	11	89	72	71
Slough Town	42	20	9	13	73	56	69
Sutton United	42	18	12	12	67	45	66
Hayes	42	17	13	12	56	41	64
Hitchin Town	42	16	15	11	58	57	63
Wycombe Wanderers	42	16	14	12	63	52	62
Wokingham Town	42	18	10	14	78	55	61
Hendon	42	17	10	15	62	51	61
Dulwich Hamlet	42	16	11	15	61	64	59
Bishop's Stortford	42	15	13	14	56	57	58
Harlow Town	42	15	11	16	64	70	56
Bognor Regis Town	42	14	13	15	62	69	55
Staines Town	42	15	9	18	63	72	54
Billericay Town	42	15	8	19	53	73	53
Barking	42	13	13	16	60	64	52
Croydon	42	14	10	18	52	58	52
Walthamstow Avenue	42	13	10	19	53	67	49
Leytonstone & Ilford	42	13	9	20	54	67	48
Carshalton Athletic	42	11	10	21	59	72	43
Tooting & Mitcham United	42	10	13	19	50	63	43
Bromley	42	7	11	24	33	72	32

Wokingham Town had 3 points deducted

First Division

Worthing	40	25	6	9	76	39	81
Harlow Town	40	21	11	8	84	55	74
Farnborough Town	40	20	13	7	69	39	73
Hertford Town	40	20	11	9	70	61	71
Oxford City	40	19	13	8	70	49	70
Boreham Wood	40	21	6	13	62	42	69
Metropolitan Police	40	19	9	12	77	57	66
Walton & Hersham	40	17	6	17	65	59	57
Hampton	40	15	10	15	62	60	55
Wembley	40	14	10	16	62	61	52
Aveley	40	15	7	18	52	62	52
Kingstonian	40	13	12	15	53	53	51
Tilbury	40	12	10	18	41	47	46
Feltham	40	11	12	17	45	54	45
Chesham United	40	13	6	21	43	70	45
Epsom & Ewell	40	10	14	16	44	49	44
Lewes	40	12	8	20	47	71	44
Cheshunt	40	10	13	17	41	49	43
Hornchurch	40	11	8	21	45	74	41
Maidenhead United	40	10	10	20	57	87	40
St Albans City	40	10	9	21	52	79	37

St Albans City had 2 points deducted

First Division

Windsor & Eton	42	26	7	9	89	44	85
Epsom & Ewell	42	23	9	10	73	51	78
Wembley	42	21	11	10	65	32	74
Maidenhead United	42	22	8	12	67	42	74
Boreham Wood	42	22	7	13	74	43	73
Farnborough Town	42	18	12	12	78	60	66
Hampton	42	18	12	12	65	49	66
Metropolitan Police	42	20	5	17	79	64	65
Chesham United	42	18	8	16	64	57	62
Tilbury	42	17	10	15	54	64	61
Leatherhead	42	15	10	17	67	56	55
Aveley	42	15	10	17	49	53	55
Woking	42	16	7	19	66	73	55
Hertford Town	42	15	9	18	56	73	54
Oxford City	42	14	9	19	57	56	51
Lewes	42	13	12	17	49	65	51
Walton & Hersham	42	13	10	19	52	70	49
Hornchurch	42	13	10	19	43	65	49
Kingstonian	42	13	9	20	47	67	48
Clapton	42	12	11	19	49	67	47
Cheshunt	42	12	8	22	45	64	44
Feltham	42	7	4	31	31	106	25

Second Division

Basildon United	42	30	7	5	88	27	97
St Albans City	42	29	9	5	100	46	96
Leyton Wingate	42	29	4	9	97	41	91
Tring Town	42	23	11	8	89	44	80
Corinthian Casuals	42	23	11	8	75	47	80
Hungerford Town	42	21	12	9	94	47	75
Uxbridge	42	18	15	9	61	36	69
Grays Athletic	42	20	9	13	72	57	69
Dorking	42	21	5	16	66	54	68
Southall	42	20	8	14	79	60	65
Egham Town	42	16	15	11	59	49	63
Epping Town	42	15	16	11	61	50	61
Molesey	42	13	14	15	59	68	53
Barton Rovers	42	15	8	19	54	64	53
Letchworth Garden City	42	15	7	20	48	66	52
Newbury Town	42	14	5	23	60	82	47
Hemel Hempstead	42	12	9	21	63	69	45
Rainham Town	42	7	5	30	38	114	26
Finchley	42	5	9	28	28	78	24
Eastbourne United	42	7	3	32	36	98	24
Ware	42	6	6	30	48	114	24
Horsham	42	7	4	31	40	104	23

Southall had 2 points deducted
Horsham had 3 points deducted

1984-85

Premier Division

Sutton United	42	23	15	4	115	55	84
Worthing	42	24	8	10	89	59	80
Wycombe Wanderers	42	24	6	12	68	46	78
Wokingham Town	42	20	13	9	74	54	73
Windsor & Eton	42	19	10	13	65	55	67
Bognor Regis Town	42	20	6	16	67	58	66
Dulwich Hamlet	42	16	17	9	82	57	65
Harrow Borough	42	18	8	16	70	56	62
Hayes	42	17	8	17	60	56	59
Tooting & Mitcham United	42	16	11	15	64	66	59
Walthamstow Avenue	42	15	11	16	64	65	56
Croydon	42	15	12	15	62	63	54
Epsom & Ewell	42	13	14	15	65	62	53
Slough Town	42	13	12	17	69	74	51
Carshalton Athletic	42	14	8	20	55	68	50
Bishop's Stortford	42	12	12	18	48	67	48
Hendon	42	9	19	14	62	65	46
Billericay Town	42	11	14	17	53	74	46
Barking	42	13	7	22	43	75	46
Hitchin Town	42	10	15	17	55	70	45
Leytonstone & Ilford	42	11	10	21	37	72	43
Harlow Town	42	5	12	25	45	95	27

Billercay Town had 1 point deducted
Croydon had 3 points deducted

First Division

Farnborough Town	42	26	8	8	101	45	86
Kingstonian	42	23	10	9	67	39	79
Leatherhead	42	23	10	9	109	61	76
Chesham United	42	22	8	12	78	46	74
Wembley	42	20	10	12	59	40	70
St Albans City	42	19	10	13	79	60	67
Tilbury	42	18	13	11	86	68	67
Bromley	42	18	9	15	71	64	63
Hampton	42	17	11	14	75	62	62
Staines Town	42	16	11	15	59	53	59
Maidenhead United	42	17	8	17	65	64	59
Walton & Hersham	42	16	8	18	60	69	55
Aveley	42	16	7	19	62	78	55
Oxford City	42	14	12	16	62	53	54
Lewes	42	15	9	18	70	72	54
Basildon United	42	15	8	19	55	61	53
Boreham Wood	42	15	7	20	72	83	52
Hornchurch	42	15	6	21	55	74	51
Woking	42	15	6	21	60	91	51
Metropolitan Police	42	10	12	20	65	92	42
Clapton	42	5	11	26	50	124	26
Hertford Town	42	5	10	27	36	97	25

Walton & Hersham had 1 point deducted
Leatherhead had 3 points deducted

Second Division North

Leyton Wingate	38	24	9	5	98	50	81
Finchley	38	24	8	6	66	31	79
Heybridge Swifts	38	22	9	7	71	33	75
Stevenage Borough	38	23	6	9	79	49	75
Saffron Walden Town	38	22	8	8	73	31	74
Tring Town	38	19	11	8	76	41	68
Chalfont St Peter	38	17	10	11	72	41	61
Flackwell Heath	38	16	11	11	54	40	59
Berkhamsted Town	38	15	12	11	50	42	57
Letchworth Garden City	38	17	6	15	66	69	57
Royston Town	38	13	9	16	47	77	48
Cheshunt	38	14	5	19	52	57	47
Marlow	38	13	6	19	64	81	45
Hemel Hempstead	38	11	7	20	49	65	40
Barton Rovers	38	9	8	21	40	62	35
Wolverton Town	38	9	8	21	38	77	35
Kingsbury Town	38	9	7	22	53	72	34
Harefield United	38	7	9	22	51	81	30
Haringey Borough	38	6	12	20	38	79	30
Ware	38	7	5	26	40	100	26

Finchley had 1 point deducted
The record of Epping Town was expunged

Second Division South

Grays Athletic	36	24	9	3	84	25	81
Uxbridge	36	22	10	4	81	20	76
Molesey	36	20	5	11	62	42	65
Hungerford Town	36	18	9	9	71	49	63
Whyteleafe	36	17	10	9	66	34	61
Egham Town	36	17	7	12	54	42	58
Southall	36	18	3	15	54	57	57
Bracknell Town	36	15	7	14	54	48	52
Banstead Athletic	36	14	8	14	63	70	50
Horsham	36	13	10	13	44	39	49
Ruislip Manor	36	13	10	13	48	49	49
Dorking	36	12	11	13	45	50	47
Rainham Town	36	12	8	16	58	61	44
Feltham	36	10	13	13	44	58	43
Camberley Town	36	10	12	14	44	54	42
Eastbourne United	36	10	9	17	66	72	39
Petersfield Town	36	9	5	22	41	80	32
Newbury Town	36	8	7	21	35	69	16
Chertsey Town	36	2	3	31	23	118	6

Chertsey Town had 3 points deducted
Newbury Town had 15 points deducted

1985-86

Premier Division

Sutton United	42	29	8	5	109	39	95
Yeovil Town	42	28	7	7	92	48	91
Farnborough Town	42	23	8	11	90	50	77
Croydon	42	23	7	12	70	50	76
Harrow Borough	42	21	8	13	76	66	71
Slough Town	42	18	8	16	66	68	62
Bishop's Stortford	42	17	10	15	55	61	61
Kingstonian	42	15	15	12	57	56	60
Dulwich Hamlet	42	17	9	16	64	79	60
Wokingham Town	42	16	10	16	67	64	58
Windsor & Eton	42	17	7	18	58	75	58
Tooting & Mitcham United	42	14	11	17	65	76	53
Walthamstow Avenue	42	12	14	16	69	70	50
Worthing	42	13	10	19	72	82	49
Bognor Regis Town	42	15	6	21	63	70	48
Hayes	42	10	17	15	55	61	47
Hitchin Town	42	11	14	17	53	69	47
Barking	42	11	13	18	45	55	46
Hendon	42	10	10	19	59	77	43
Carshalton Athletic	42	9	13	20	56	79	40
Billericay Town	42	9	12	21	59	78	39
Epsom & Ewell	42	8	12	22	63	90	36

Bognor Regis Town had 3 points deducted

First Division

St Albans City	42	23	11	8	92	61	80
Bromley	42	24	8	10	68	41	80
Wembley	42	22	12	8	59	30	78
Oxford City	42	22	11	9	75	51	77
Hampton	42	21	11	10	63	45	74
Leyton Wingate	42	21	10	11	77	56	73
Uxbridge	42	20	8	14	64	49	68
Staines Town	42	18	10	14	69	66	64
Boreham Wood	42	15	16	11	62	54	61
Walton & Hersham	42	16	10	16	68	71	58
Lewes	42	16	8	18	61	75	56
Leytonstone & Ilford	42	13	15	14	57	67	54
Finchley	42	12	17	13	61	59	53
Grays Athletic	42	13	11	18	69	75	50
Leatherhead	42	14	8	20	62	68	50
Tilbury	42	13	11	18	60	66	50
Maidenhead United	42	13	7	22	61	67	46
Basildon United	42	12	9	21	52	72	45
Hornchurch	42	11	11	20	44	59	44
Chesham United	42	12	6	24	51	87	42
Harlow Town	42	8	14	20	53	70	38
Aveley	42	8	6	28	59	98	30

Second Division North

Stevenage Borough	38	26	6	6	71	24	84
Kingsbury Town	38	25	8	5	84	35	83
Heybridge Swifts	38	20	8	10	65	46	68
Cheshunt	38	18	10	10	60	40	64
Hertford Town	38	17	7	14	60	50	58
Chalfont St Peter	38	15	11	12	53	50	56
Tring Town	38	14	13	11	58	46	55
Royston Town	38	13	13	12	59	57	52
Saffron Walden Town	38	13	12	13	61	65	51
Berkhamsted Town	38	14	8	16	45	52	50
Haringey Borough	38	14	7	17	49	51	49
Letchworth Garden City	38	13	8	17	46	52	47
Rainham Town	38	14	4	20	54	91	46
Hemel Hempstead	38	12	9	17	50	66	45
Ware	38	11	11	16	56	61	44
Vauxhall Motors	38	11	10	17	58	62	43
Barton Rovers	38	12	7	19	50	60	43
Harefield United	38	9	12	17	56	72	39
Clapton	38	10	7	21	51	90	37
Wolverton Town	38	8	11	19	42	58	35

Second Division South

Southwick	38	25	8	5	86	34	83
Bracknell Town	38	24	9	5	80	23	81
Woking	38	23	9	6	94	45	78
Newbury Town	38	22	7	9	86	53	73
Whyteleafe	38	21	10	7	61	41	73
Molesey	38	21	8	9	59	39	71
Metropolitan Police	38	20	6	12	72	48	66
Southall	38	19	7	12	76	58	64
Dorking	38	18	10	10	70	57	64
Feltham	38	16	7	15	65	60	55
Banstead Athletic	38	15	8	15	60	66	53
Petersfield United	38	12	9	17	61	71	45
Hungerford Town	38	11	6	21	57	78	39
Flackwell Heath	38	11	6	21	46	72	39
Eastbourne United	38	9	8	21	51	81	35
Camberley Town	38	9	7	22	53	64	34
Egham Town	38	7	8	23	41	83	29
Horsham	38	6	10	22	33	74	28
Ruislip Manor	38	5	12	21	44	87	27
Marlow	38	6	5	27	47	108	23

1986-87

Premier Division

Wycombe Wanderers	42	32	5	5	103	32	101
Yeovil Town	42	28	8	6	71	27	92
Slough Town	42	23	8	11	70	44	77
Hendon	42	22	7	13	67	53	73
Bognor Regis Town	42	20	10	12	85	61	70
Harrow Borough	42	20	10	12	68	44	70
Croydon	42	18	10	14	51	48	64
Barking	42	16	14	12	76	56	62
Farnborough Town	42	17	11	14	66	72	62
Bishop's Stortford	42	15	15	12	62	57	60
Bromley	42	16	11	15	63	72	59
Kingstonian	42	16	9	17	58	50	57
Windsor & Eton	42	13	15	14	47	52	54
St Albans City	42	14	9	19	61	70	51
Carshalton Athletic	42	13	9	20	55	68	48
Wokingham Town	42	14	6	22	47	61	48
Hayes	42	12	12	18	45	68	48
Dulwich Hamlet	42	12	10	20	62	71	46
Tooting & Mitcham United	42	12	9	21	51	53	45
Hitchin Town	42	13	5	24	56	69	44
Worthing	42	8	9	25	58	107	33
Walthamstow Avenue	42	4	6	32	36	113	18

First Division

Leytonstone & Ilford	42	30	5	7	78	29	95
Leyton Wingate	42	23	13	6	68	31	82
Bracknell Town	42	24	9	9	92	48	81
Southwick	42	23	7	12	80	66	76
Wembley	42	21	9	12	61	47	72
Grays Athletic	42	19	10	13	76	64	67
Kingsbury Town	42	20	7	15	69	67	67
Boreham Wood	42	20	6	16	59	52	66
Uxbridge	42	18	9	15	60	59	63
Leatherhead	42	17	11	14	45	48	62
Hampton	42	18	5	19	57	55	59
Basildon United	42	16	10	16	58	60	58
Billericay Town	42	14	12	16	57	52	54
Staines Town	42	13	13	16	40	51	52
Lewes	42	15	6	21	55	65	51
Stevenage Borough	42	12	11	19	61	67	47
Oxford City	42	11	10	21	64	72	43
Walton & Hersham	42	11	10	21	53	74	43
Tilbury	42	12	7	23	46	70	43
Epsom & Ewell	42	12	7	23	44	68	43
Maidenhead United	42	11	4	27	44	76	37
Finchley	42	6	11	25	44	90	29

Second Division North

Chesham United	42	28	6	8	81	48	90
Wolverton Town	42	23	14	5	74	32	83
Haringey Borough	42	22	13	7	86	40	79
Heybridge Swifts	42	21	11	10	81	54	74
Aveley	42	19	13	10	68	50	70
Letchworth Garden City	42	19	11	12	77	62	68
Barton Rovers	42	18	11	13	49	39	65
Tring Town	42	19	7	16	69	49	64
Collier Row	42	19	5	18	67	65	62
Ware	42	17	8	17	51	50	59
Saffron Walden Town	42	14	14	14	56	54	56
Wivenhoe Town	42	15	11	16	61	61	56
Vauxhall Motors	42	15	10	17	61	57	55
Hornchurch	42	13	16	13	60	60	55
Hertford Town	42	14	13	15	52	53	55
Berkhamsted Town	42	12	16	14	62	64	52
Harlow Town	42	13	11	18	45	55	50
Rainham Town	42	12	11	19	53	70	47
Clapton	42	10	11	21	45	63	41
Hemel Hempstead	42	9	12	21	48	77	39
Royston Town	42	4	12	26	37	109	24
Cheshunt	42	5	6	31	43	114	21

Second Division South

Woking	40	27	7	6	110	32	88
Marlow	40	28	4	8	78	36	88
Dorking	40	24	12	4	78	30	84
Feltham	40	25	3	12	79	34	78
Ruislip Manor	40	22	10	8	85	47	76
Chertsey Town	40	18	11	11	56	44	65
Metropolitan Police	40	16	13	11	70	61	61
Chalfont St Peter	40	17	10	13	60	55	61
Hungerford Town	40	14	14	12	55	48	56
Harefield United	40	14	14	12	53	47	56
Eastbourne United	40	15	10	15	72	59	55
Whyteleafe	40	12	15	13	52	63	51
Horsham	40	14	8	18	54	61	50
Egham Town	40	14	6	20	45	77	48
Camberley Town	40	13	3	24	62	89	42
Flackwell Heath	40	9	11	20	34	63	38
Banstead Athletic	40	7	15	18	44	61	36
Petersfield United	40	9	8	23	45	84	34
Molesey	40	7	12	21	37	89	33
Newbury Town	40	6	14	20	51	83	32
Southall	40	6	6	28	28	85	24

1987-88

Premier Division

Yeovil Town	42	24	9	9	66	34	81
Bromley	42	23	7	12	68	40	76
Slough Town	42	21	9	12	67	41	72
Leytonstone & Ilford	42	20	11	11	59	43	71
Wokingham Town	42	21	7	14	62	52	70
Hayes	42	20	9	13	62	48	69
Windsor & Eton	42	16	17	9	59	43	65
Farnborough Town	42	17	11	14	63	60	62
Carshalton Athletic	42	16	13	13	49	41	61
Hendon	42	16	12	14	62	58	60
Tooting & Mitcham United	42	15	14	13	57	59	59
Harrow Borough	42	15	11	16	53	58	56
Bishop's Stortford	42	15	10	17	55	58	55
Kingstonian	42	14	12	16	47	53	54
St Albans City	42	15	6	21	60	69	51
Bognor Regis Town	42	14	9	19	41	57	51
Leyton Wingate	42	14	8	20	58	64	50
Croydon	42	11	13	18	40	52	46
Barking	42	11	12	19	44	57	45
Dulwich Hamlet	42	10	11	21	46	64	41
Hitchin Town	42	10	8	24	46	79	38
Basingstoke Town	42	6	17	19	37	71	35

First Division

Marlow	42	32	5	5	100	44	101
Grays Athletic	42	30	10	2	74	25	100
Woking	42	25	7	10	91	52	82
Boreham Wood	42	21	9	12	65	45	72
Staines Town	42	19	11	12	71	48	68
Wembley	42	18	11	13	54	46	65
Basildon United	42	18	9	15	65	58	63
Walton & Hersham	42	15	16	11	53	44	61
Hampton	42	17	10	15	59	54	61
Leatherhead	42	16	11	15	64	53	59
Southwick	42	13	12	17	59	63	51
Oxford City	42	13	12	17	70	77	51
Worthing	42	14	8	20	67	73	50
Kingsbury Town	42	11	17	14	62	69	50
Walthamstow Avenue	42	13	11	18	53	63	50
Lewes	42	12	13	17	83	77	49
Uxbridge	42	11	16	15	41	47	49
Chesham United	42	12	10	20	69	77	46
Bracknell Town	42	12	9	21	54	80	45
Billericay Town	42	11	11	20	58	88	44
Stevenage Borough	42	11	9	22	36	64	42
Wolverton Town	42	3	3	36	23	124	12

Second Division North

Wivenhoe Town	42	26	10	6	105	42	88
Collier Row	42	22	13	7	71	39	79
Tilbury	42	18	15	9	61	40	69
Berkhamsted Town	42	19	12	11	71	53	69
Harlow Town	42	17	16	9	67	36	67
Ware	42	17	15	10	63	58	66
Witham Town	42	17	14	11	69	47	65
Vauxhall Motors	42	16	17	9	56	42	65
Heybridge Swifts	42	17	13	12	56	50	64
Tring Town	42	18	6	18	69	67	60
Letchworth Garden City	42	18	5	19	59	64	59
Finchley	42	16	10	16	67	54	58
Clapton	42	14	15	13	50	62	57
Hornchurch	42	13	15	14	56	65	54
Barton Rovers	42	13	10	19	43	60	49
Rainham Town	42	12	12	18	63	66	48
Royston Town	42	13	8	21	49	70	47
Saffron Walden Town	42	13	7	22	34	67	46
Hemel Hempstead	42	11	12	19	38	71	45
Haringey Borough	42	11	8	23	54	78	41
Aveley	42	8	13	21	42	65	37
Hertford Town	42	8	4	30	45	92	28

Second Division South

Chalfont St Peter	42	26	9	7	81	35	87
Metropolitan Police	42	23	17	2	80	32	86
Dorking	42	25	11	6	86	39	86
Feltham	42	21	12	9	74	41	75
Epsom & Ewell	42	21	11	10	71	49	74
Chertsey Town	42	22	7	13	63	47	73
Whyteleafe	42	20	11	11	84	55	71
Hungerford Town	42	21	7	14	66	54	70
Ruislip Manor	42	21	5	16	74	57	68
Yeading	42	19	10	13	83	56	67
Maidenhead United	42	18	12	12	69	54	66
Eastbourne United	42	18	10	14	67	57	64
Harefield United	42	18	6	18	59	60	60
Egham Town	42	12	12	18	45	55	48
Horsham	42	12	10	20	45	66	46
Southall	42	13	7	22	45	72	46
Molesey	42	11	11	20	42	63	44
Newbury Town	42	8	13	21	40	81	37
Camberley Town	42	9	9	24	51	94	36
Flackwell Heath	42	6	8	28	42	96	26
Banstead Athletic	42	6	7	29	34	81	25
Petersfield United	42	6	7	29	45	102	25

1988-89

Premier Division

Leytonstone & Ilford	42	26	11	5	76	36	89
Farnborough Town	42	24	9	9	85	61	81
Slough Town	42	24	6	12	72	42	78
Carshalton Athletic	42	19	15	8	59	36	72
Grays Athletic	42	19	13	10	62	47	70
Kingstonian	42	19	11	12	54	37	68
Bishop's Stortford	42	20	6	16	70	56	66
Hayes	42	18	12	12	6	47	66
Bognor Regis Town	42	17	11	14	38	49	62
Barking	42	16	13	13	49	45	61
Wokingham Town	42	15	11	16	60	54	56
Hendon	42	13	17	12	51	68	56
Windsor & Eton	42	14	13	15	52	50	55
Bromley	42	13	15	14	61	48	54
Leyton Wingate	42	13	15	14	55	56	54
Dulwich Hamlet	42	12	12	18	58	57	48
St Albans City	42	12	9	21	51	59	45
Dagenham	42	11	12	19	53	68	45
Harrow Borough	42	9	13	20	53	75	40
Marlow	42	9	11	22	48	83	38
Tooting & Mitcham United	42	10	6	26	41	81	36
Croydon	42	4	9	29	27	81	21

First Division

Staines Town	40	26	9	5	79	29	87
Basingstoke Town	40	25	8	7	85	36	83
Woking	40	24	10	6	72	30	82
Hitchin Town	40	21	11	8	60	32	74
Wivenhoe Town	40	22	6	12	62	44	72
Lewes	40	21	8	11	72	54	71
Walton & Hersham	40	21	7	12	56	36	70
Kingsbury Town	40	20	7	13	65	41	67
Uxbridge	40	19	7	14	60	54	64
Wembley	40	18	6	16	45	58	60
Boreham Wood	40	16	9	15	57	52	57
Leatherhead	40	14	8	18	56	58	50
Metropolitan Police	40	13	9	18	52	68	48
Chesham United	40	12	9	19	54	67	45
Southwick	40	9	15	16	44	58	42
Chalfont St Peter	40	11	9	20	56	82	42
Hampton	40	7	14	19	37	62	35
Worthing	40	8	10	22	49	80	32
Collier Row	40	8	7	25	37	82	31
Bracknell Town	40	8	6	26	38	70	30
Basildon Town	40	6	7	27	34	77	25

Worthing had 2 points deducted.

Second Division North

Harlow Town	42	27	9	6	83	38	90
Purfleet	42	22	12	8	60	42	78
Tring Town	42	22	10	10	65	44	76
Stevenage Borough	42	20	13	9	84	55	73
Heybridge Swifts	42	21	9	12	64	43	72
Billericay Town	42	19	11	12	65	52	68
Clapton	42	18	11	13	65	56	65
Barton Rovers	42	18	11	13	58	50	65
Aveley	42	18	10	14	54	52	64
Hertford Town	42	16	13	13	62	49	59
Ware	42	17	8	17	60	65	59
Hemel Hempstead	42	16	10	16	55	58	58
Witham Town	42	16	7	19	69	67	55
Vauxhall Motors	42	15	9	18	53	57	54
Berkhamsted Town	42	14	10	18	57	70	52
Hornchurch	42	11	16	15	59	61	49
Tilbury	42	13	10	19	53	60	49
Royston Town	42	12	7	23	46	72	43
Rainham Town	42	9	15	18	49	62	42
Saffron Walden Town	42	8	16	18	54	72	40
Letchworth Garden City	42	4	18	20	34	71	30
Wolverton Town	42	5	7	30	42	95	13

Hertford Town 2 points deducted, Wolverton Town 9 points deducted.

Second Division South

Dorking	40	32	4	4	109	35	100
Whyteleafe	40	25	9	6	86	41	84
Finchley	40	21	9	10	70	45	72
Molesey	40	19	13	8	58	42	70
Harefield United	40	19	7	14	56	45	64
Hungerford Town	40	17	13	10	55	45	64
Ruislip Manor	40	16	9	15	56	43	57
Feltham	40	16	9	15	58	53	57
Epsom & Ewell	40	16	8	16	55	55	56
Egham Town	40	16	7	17	54	58	55
Eastbourne United	40	15	9	16	68	61	54
Chertsey Town	40	13	14	13	55	58	53
Flackwell Heath	40	13	11	16	51	49	50
Camberley Town	40	15	5	20	51	71	50
Yeading	40	13	9	18	47	63	46
Banstead Athletic	40	12	8	20	50	65	44
Maidenhead United	40	10	13	17	44	61	43
Southall	40	11	10	19	41	73	43
Newbury Town	40	11	8	21	47	65	41
Horsham	40	7	14	19	36	68	35
Petersfield United	40	5	7	28	36	87	22

Yeading had 2 points deducted.

1989-90

Premier Division

Slough Town	42	27	11	4	85	38	92
Wokingham Town	42	26	11	5	67	34	89
Aylesbury United	42	25	9	8	86	30	84
Kingstonian	42	24	9	9	87	51	81
Grays Athletic	42	19	13	10	59	44	70
Dagenham	42	17	15	10	54	43	66
Leyton Wingate	42	20	6	16	54	48	66
Basingstoke Town	42	18	9	15	65	55	63
Bishop's Stortford	42	19	6	17	60	59	63
Carshalton Athletic	42	19	5	18	63	59	59
Redbridge Forest	42	16	11	15	65	62	59
Hendon	42	15	10	17	54	63	55
Windsor & Eton	42	13	15	14	51	47	54
Hayes	42	14	11	17	61	59	53
St Albans City	42	13	10	19	49	59	49
Staines Town	42	14	6	22	53	69	48
Marlow	42	11	13	18	42	59	46
Harrow Borough	42	11	10	21	51	79	43
Bognor Regis Town	42	9	14	19	37	67	41
Barking	42	7	11	24	53	86	32
Bromley	42	7	11	24	32	69	32
Dulwich Hamlet	42	6	8	28	32	80	26

Carshalton Athletic had 3 points deducted.

First Division

Wivenhoe Town	42	31	7	4	94	36	100
Woking	42	30	8	4	102	29	98
Southwick	42	23	15	4	68	30	84
Hitchin Town	42	22	13	7	60	30	79
Walton & Hersham	42	20	10	12	68	50	70
Dorking	42	19	12	11	66	41	69
Boreham Wood	42	17	13	12	60	59	64
Harlow Town	42	16	13	13	60	53	61
Metropolitan Police	42	16	11	15	54	59	59
Chesham United	42	15	12	15	46	49	57
Chalfont St Peter	42	14	13	15	50	59	55
Tooting & Mitcham United	42	14	13	15	42	51	55
Worthing	42	15	8	19	56	63	53
Whyteleafe	42	11	16	15	50	65	49
Lewes	42	12	11	19	55	65	47
Wembley	42	11	10	21	57	68	43
Croydon	42	9	16	17	43	57	43
Uxbridge	42	11	10	21	52	75	43
Hampton	42	8	13	21	28	51	37
Leatherhead	42	7	10	25	34	77	31
Purfleet	42	7	8	27	33	78	29
Kingsbury Town	42	8	10	24	45	78	25

Kingsbury Town had 9 points deducted

Second Division North

Heybridge Swifts	42	26	9	7	79	29	87
Aveley	42	23	16	3	68	24	85
Hertford Town	42	24	11	7	92	51	83
Stevenage Borough	42	21	16	5	70	31	79
Barton Rovers	42	22	6	14	60	45	72
Tilbury	42	20	9	13	68	54	69
Basildon United	42	13	20	9	50	44	59
Collier Row	42	15	13	14	43	45	58
Royston Town	42	15	11	16	63	72	56
Saffron Walden Town	42	15	11	16	60	73	56
Vauxhall Motors	42	14	13	15	55	54	55
Clapton	42	13	16	13	50	46	54
Ware	42	14	11	17	53	59	53
Hemel Hempstead	42	14	9	19	58	70	51
Billericay Town	42	13	11	18	49	58	50
Hornchurch	42	12	12	18	49	64	48
Berkhamsted Town	42	9	16	17	44	68	43
Finchley	42	11	10	21	50	75	43
Tring Town	42	10	9	23	48	70	39
Witham Town	42	8	14	20	44	56	38
Rainham Town	42	9	11	22	48	75	38
Letchworth Garden City	42	7	12	23	30	68	33

Clapton had 1 point deducted.

Second Division South

Yeading	40	29	4	7	86	37	91
Molesey	40	24	11	5	76	30	83
Abingdon Town	40	22	9	9	64	39	75
Ruislip Manor	40	20	12	8	60	32	72
Maidenhead United	40	20	12	8	66	39	72
Southall	40	22	5	13	56	33	71
Newbury Town	40	21	7	12	50	36	70
Flackwell Heath	40	16	11	13	69	65	59
Hungerford Town	40	14	16	10	54	51	58
Egham Town	40	12	14	14	39	38	50
Banstead Athletic	40	14	8	18	46	47	50
Harefield United	40	13	9	18	44	46	48
Chertsey Town	40	13	9	18	53	58	48
Epsom & Ewell	40	13	9	18	49	54	48
Malden Vale	40	13	7	20	36	67	46
Eastbourne United	40	11	10	19	47	65	43
Camberley Town	40	11	9	20	44	66	42
Feltham	40	11	7	22	47	80	40
Bracknell Town	40	10	9	21	40	57	39
Petersfield United	40	10	8	22	48	93	38
Horsham	40	4	8	28	29	70	20

Second Division North

Stevenage Borough	42	34	5	3	122	29	107
Vauxhall Motors	42	24	10	8	82	50	82
Billericay Town	42	22	8	12	70	41	74
Ware	42	22	8	12	78	51	74
Berkhamsted Town	42	19	11	12	60	51	68
Witham Town	42	19	10	13	70	59	67
Purfleet	42	17	14	11	68	57	65
Rainham Town	42	19	7	16	57	46	64
Hemel Hempstead	42	16	14	12	62	56	62
Barton Rovers	42	17	10	15	61	58	61
Saffron Walden Town	42	16	13	13	72	77	61
Collier Row	42	16	11	15	63	63	59
Kingsbury Town	42	17	8	17	64	72	59
Edgware Town	42	17	7	18	73	65	58
Hertford Town	42	16	10	16	69	70	58
Royston Town	42	14	15	13	78	62	57
Tilbury	42	14	6	22	70	79	48
Basildon United	42	11	10	21	61	90	43
Hornchurch	42	10	9	23	53	87	39
Clapton	42	9	10	23	54	93	34
Finchley	42	6	7	29	50	112	24
Tring Town	42	1	9	32	30	99	12

Finchley had 1 point deducted
Clapton had 3 points deducted

1990-91

Premier Division

Redbridge Forest	42	29	6	7	74	43	93
Enfield	42	26	11	5	83	30	89
Aylesbury United	42	24	11	7	90	47	83
Woking	42	24	10	8	84	39	82
Kingstonian	42	21	12	9	86	57	75
Grays Athletic	42	20	8	14	66	53	68
Marlow	42	18	13	11	72	49	67
Hayes	42	20	5	17	60	57	65
Carshalton Athletic	42	19	7	16	80	67	64
Wivenhoe Town	42	16	11	15	69	66	59
Wokingham Town	42	15	13	14	58	54	58
Windsor & Eton	42	15	10	17	48	63	55
Bishop's Stortford	42	14	12	16	54	49	54
Dagenham	42	13	11	18	62	68	50
Hendon	42	12	10	20	48	62	46
St Albans City	42	11	12	19	60	74	45
Bognor Regis Town	42	12	8	22	44	71	44
Basingstoke Town	42	12	7	23	57	95	43
Staines Town	42	10	10	22	46	79	39
Harrow Borough	42	10	8	24	57	84	38
Barking	42	8	10	24	41	85	34
Leyton Wingate	42	7	7	28	44	91	28

Staines Town had 1 point deducted

Second Division South

Abingdon Town	42	29	7	6	95	28	94
Maidenhead United	42	28	8	6	85	33	92
Egham Town	42	27	6	9	100	46	87
Malden Vale	42	26	5	11	72	44	83
Ruislip Manor	42	25	5	12	93	44	80
Southall	42	23	10	9	84	43	79
Harefield United	42	23	10	9	81	56	79
Newbury Town	42	23	8	11	71	45	77
Hungerford Town	42	16	13	13	84	69	61
Leatherhead	42	17	9	16	82	55	60
Banstead Athletic	42	15	13	14	58	62	58
Hampton	42	14	15	13	62	43	57
Epsom & Ewell	42	15	12	15	49	50	57
Chertsey Town	42	15	9	18	76	72	54
Horsham	42	14	7	21	58	67	49
Flackwell Heath	42	11	11	20	56	78	44
Bracknell Town	42	11	7	24	60	97	40
Feltham	42	10	8	24	45	80	38
Cove	42	10	7	25	51	94	37
Eastbourne United	42	10	7	25	53	109	37
Petersfield United	42	6	3	33	35	119	21
Camberley Town	42	1	6	35	27	143	9

1991-92

Premier Division

Woking	42	30	7	5	96	25	97
Enfield	42	24	7	11	59	45	79
Sutton United	42	19	13	10	88	51	70
Chesham United	42	20	10	12	67	48	70
Wokingham Town	42	19	10	13	73	58	67
Marlow	42	20	7	15	56	50	67
Aylesbury United	42	16	17	9	69	46	65
Carshalton Athletic	42	18	8	16	64	67	62
Dagenham	42	15	16	11	70	59	61
Kingstonian	42	17	8	17	71	65	59
Windsor & Eton	42	15	11	16	56	56	56
Bromley	42	14	12	16	51	57	54
St Albans City	42	14	11	17	66	70	53
Basingstoke Town	42	14	11	17	56	65	53
Grays Athletic	42	14	11	17	53	68	53
Wivenhoe Town	42	16	4	22	56	81	52
Hendon	42	13	9	20	59	73	48
Harrow Borough	42	11	13	18	58	78	46
Hayes	42	10	14	18	52	63	44
Staines Town	42	11	10	21	43	73	43
Bognor Regis Town	42	9	11	22	51	89	38
Bishop's Stortford	42	7	12	23	41	68	33

First Division

Chesham United	42	27	8	7	102	37	89
Bromley	42	22	14	6	62	37	80
Yeading	42	23	8	11	75	45	77
Aveley	42	21	9	12	76	43	72
Hitchin Town	42	21	9	12	78	50	72
Tooting & Mitcham United	42	20	12	10	71	48	72
Walton & Hersham	42	21	8	13	73	48	71
Molesey	42	22	5	15	65	46	71
Whyteleafe	42	21	6	15	62	53	69
Dorking	42	20	5	17	78	67	65
Chalfont St Peter	42	19	5	18	56	63	62
Dulwich Hamlet	42	16	11	15	67	54	59
Harlow Town	42	17	8	17	73	64	59
Boreham Wood	42	15	8	19	46	53	53
Wembley	42	13	12	17	62	59	51
Uxbridge	42	15	5	22	45	61	50
Croydon	42	15	5	22	44	85	50
Heybridge Swifts	42	13	10	19	46	59	49
Southwick	42	13	8	21	49	75	47
Lewes	42	10	8	24	49	82	38
Metropolitan Police	42	9	6	27	55	76	33
Worthing	42	2	4	36	28	157	10

First Division

Stevenage Borough	40	30	6	4	95	37	96
Yeading	40	24	10	6	83	34	82
Dulwich Hamlet	40	22	9	9	71	40	75
Boreham Wood	40	22	7	11	65	40	73
Wembley	40	21	6	13	54	43	69
Abingdon Town	40	19	8	13	60	47	65
Tooting & Mitcham United	40	16	13	11	57	45	61
Hitchin Town	40	17	10	13	55	45	61
Walton & Hersham	40	15	13	12	62	50	58
Molesey	40	16	9	15	55	61	57
Dorking	40	16	7	17	68	65	55
Barking	40	14	11	15	51	54	53
Chalfont St Peter	40	15	6	19	62	70	51
Leyton Wingate	40	13	11	16	53	56	50
Uxbridge	40	13	8	19	47	62	47
Maidenhead United	40	13	7	20	52	61	46
Harlow Town	40	11	9	20	50	70	42
Croydon	40	11	6	23	44	68	39
Heybridge Swifts	40	8	9	23	33	71	33
Whyteleafe	40	7	10	23	42	78	31
Aveley	40	8	3	29	33	95	27

Second Division

Purfleet	42	27	8	7	97	48	89
Lewes	42	23	14	5	74	36	83
Billericay Town	42	24	8	10	75	44	80
Leatherhead	42	23	6	13	68	40	75
Ruislip Manor	42	20	9	13	74	51	69
Egham Town	42	19	12	11	81	62	69
Metropolitan Police	42	20	9	13	76	58	69
Saffron Walden Town	42	19	11	12	86	67	68
Hemel Hempstead	42	18	10	14	63	50	64
Hungerford Town	42	18	7	17	53	58	61
Barton Rovers	42	17	8	17	61	64	59
Worthing	42	17	8	17	67	72	59
Witham Town	42	16	11	15	56	61	59
Banstead Athletic	42	16	10	16	69	58	58
Malden Vale	42	15	12	15	63	48	57
Rainham Town	42	14	13	15	53	48	55
Ware	42	14	9	19	58	62	51
Berkhamsted Town	42	13	11	18	56	57	50
Harefield United	42	11	7	24	47	66	40
Southall	42	8	7	27	39	93	31
Southwick	42	6	2	34	29	115	20
Newbury Town	42	4	8	30	30	117	20

Third Division

Edgware Town	40	30	3	7	106	44	93
Chertsey Town	40	29	4	7	115	44	91
Tilbury	40	26	9	5	84	40	87
Hampton	40	26	5	9	93	35	83
Horsham	40	23	8	9	92	51	77
Cove	40	21	9	10	74	49	72
Flackwell Heath	40	19	12	9	78	50	69
Thame United	40	19	7	14	73	46	64
Epsom & Ewell	40	17	11	12	55	50	62
Collier Row	40	17	9	14	67	59	60
Royston Town	40	17	7	16	59	58	58
Kingsbury Town	40	12	10	18	54	61	46
Hertford Town	40	12	10	18	55	73	46
Petersfield United	40	12	9	19	45	67	45
Camberley Town	40	11	8	21	52	69	41
Feltham & Hounslow	40	11	2	22	53	78	40
Bracknell Town	40	10	7	23	48	90	37
Hornchurch	40	8	7	25	40	87	31
Tring Town	40	9	4	27	35	94	31
Clapton	40	9	3	28	47	92	30
Eastbourne United	40	5	5	30	34	121	20

1992-93

Premier Division

Chesham United	42	30	8	4	104	34	98
St Albans City	42	28	9	5	103	50	93
Enfield	42	25	6	11	94	48	81
Carshalton Athletic	42	22	10	10	96	56	76
Sutton United	42	18	14	10	74	57	68
Grays Athletic	42	18	11	13	61	64	65
Stevenage Borough	42	8	8	16	62	60	62
Harrow Borough	42	16	14	12	59	60	62
Hayes	42	16	13	13	64	59	61
Aylesbury United	42	18	6	18	70	77	60
Hendon	42	12	18	12	52	54	54
Basingstoke Town	42	12	17	13	49	45	53
Kingstonian	42	14	10	18	59	58	52
Dulwich Hamlet	42	12	14	16	52	66	50
Marlow	42	12	11	19	72	73	47
Wokingham Town	42	11	13	18	62	81	46
Bromley	42	11	13	18	51	72	46
Wivenhoe Town	42	13	7	22	41	75	46
Yeading	42	11	12	19	58	66	45
Staines Town	42	10	13	19	59	77	43
Windsor & Eton	42	8	7	27	40	90	31
Bognor Regis Town	42	5	10	27	46	106	25

First Division

Hitchin Town	40	25	7	8	67	29	82
Molesey	40	23	11	6	81	38	80
Dorking	40	23	9	8	73	40	78
Purfleet	40	19	12	9	67	42	69
Bishop's Stortford	40	19	10	11	63	42	67
Abingdon Town	40	17	13	10	65	47	64
Tooting & Mitcham United	40	17	12	11	68	46	63
Billericay Town	40	18	6	16	67	61	60
Wembley	40	14	15	11	44	34	57
Walton & Hersham	40	14	12	14	58	54	54
Boreham Wood	40	12	14	14	44	43	50
Maidenhead United	40	10	18	12	45	50	48
Leyton	40	11	14	15	56	61	47
Whyteleafe	40	12	10	18	63	71	46
Uxbridge	40	11	13	16	50	59	46
Heybridge Swifts	40	11	9	20	47	65	42
Croydon	40	11	9	20	54	82	42
Chalfont St Peter	40	7	17	16	48	70	38
Barking	40	10	8	22	42	80	38
Lewes	40	9	10	21	34	80	37
Aveley	40	9	7	24	45	87	34

Second Division

Worthing	42	28	7	7	105	50	91
Ruislip Manor	42	25	12	5	78	33	87
Berkhamsted Town	42	24	8	10	77	55	80
Hemel Hempstead	42	22	12	8	84	52	78
Metropolitan Police	42	22	6	14	84	51	72
Malden Vale	42	20	9	13	78	54	69
Chertsey Town	42	20	7	15	84	60	67
Saffron Walden Town	42	19	10	13	63	49	67
Newbury Town	42	14	18	10	53	51	60
Hampton	42	16	11	15	59	59	59
Edgware Town	42	16	10	16	84	75	58
Egham Town	42	16	9	17	60	71	57
Banstead Athletic	42	14	13	15	67	52	55
Leatherhead	42	14	11	17	66	61	53
Ware	42	12	11	19	68	76	47
Witham Town	42	10	16	16	54	65	46
Tilbury	42	12	8	22	55	101	44
Barton Rovers	42	9	14	19	40	66	41
Hungerford Town	42	11	8	23	37	93	41
Rainham Town	42	9	10	23	56	80	37
Harefield United	42	10	7	25	37	72	37
Southall	42	7	7	28	43	106	28

Third Division

Team	P	W	D	L	F	A	Pts
Aldershot Town	38	28	8	2	90	35	92
Thame United	38	21	11	6	84	38	74
Collier Row	38	21	11	6	68	30	74
Leighton Town	38	21	10	7	89	47	73
Cove	38	21	8	9	69	42	71
Northwood	38	19	11	8	84	68	68
Royston Town	38	17	8	13	59	42	59
East Thurrock United	38	17	7	14	69	58	58
Kingsbury Town	38	15	9	14	62	59	54
Hertford Town	38	14	10	14	61	64	52
Flackwell Heath	38	15	6	17	82	76	51
Tring Town	38	12	11	15	59	63	47
Hornchurch	38	11	13	14	53	52	46
Horsham	38	12	7	19	63	72	43
Epsom & Ewell	38	10	11	17	52	67	41
Bracknell Town	38	7	13	18	52	94	34
Clapton	38	8	7	23	46	74	31
Camberley Town	38	8	7	23	37	72	31
Petersfield United	38	6	12	20	36	90	30
Feltham & Hounslow	38	5	4	29	47	119	19

Second Division

Team	P	W	D	L	F	A	Pts
Newbury Town	42	32	7	3	115	36	103
Chertsey Town	42	33	3	6	121	48	102
Aldershot Town	42	30	7	5	78	27	97
Barton Rovers	42	25	8	9	68	37	83
Witham Town	42	21	10	11	68	51	73
Malden Vale	42	20	10	12	70	49	70
Thame United	42	19	12	11	87	51	69
Metropolitan Police	42	20	9	13	75	54	69
Banstead Athletic	42	19	9	14	56	53	66
Aveley	42	19	5	18	60	66	62
Edgware Town	42	16	10	16	88	75	58
Saffron Walden Town	42	17	7	18	61	62	58
Hemel Hempstead	42	14	11	17	47	43	53
Egham Town	42	14	8	20	48	65	50
Ware	42	14	7	21	48	76	49
Hungerford Town	42	13	7	22	56	66	46
Tilbury	42	13	3	26	59	81	42
Hampton	42	12	5	25	42	70	41
Leatherhead	42	10	6	26	46	92	36
Lewes	42	8	11	24	38	85	34
Collier Row	42	7	8	27	37	88	29
Rainham Town	42	4	2	36	24	116	14

Third Division

Team	P	W	D	L	F	A	Pts
Bracknell Town	40	25	8	7	78	29	83
Cheshunt	40	23	12	5	62	34	81
Oxford City	40	24	6	10	94	55	78
Harlow Town	40	22	11	7	61	36	77
Southall	40	17	12	11	66	53	63
Camberley Town	40	18	7	15	56	50	61
Hertford Town	40	18	6	16	67	65	60
Royston Town	40	15	11	14	44	41	56
Northwood	40	15	11	14	78	77	56
Epsom & Ewell	40	15	9	16	63	62	54
Harefield United	40	12	15	13	45	55	51
Cove	40	15	6	19	59	74	51
Kingsbury Town	40	12	14	14	57	54	50
Feltham & Hounslow	40	14	7	19	60	63	49
Leighton Town	40	12	11	17	51	64	47
East Thurrock Town	40	10	15	15	65	64	45
Clapton	40	12	9	19	51	65	45
Hornchurch	40	12	8	20	42	60	44
Tring Town	40	10	11	19	48	64	41
Flackwell Heath	40	9	11	20	44	83	38
Horsham	40	6	8	26	43	86	26

1993-94

Premier Division

Team	P	W	D	L	F	A	Pts
Stevenage Borough	42	31	4	7	88	39	97
Enfield	42	28	8	6	80	28	92
Marlow	42	25	7	10	90	67	82
Chesham United	42	24	8	10	73	45	80
Sutton United	42	23	10	9	77	31	79
Carshalton Athletic	42	22	7	13	81	53	73
St Albans City	42	21	10	11	81	54	73
Hitchin Town	42	21	7	14	81	56	70
Harrow Borough	42	18	11	13	54	56	65
Kingstonian	42	18	9	15	101	64	63
Hendon	42	18	9	15	61	51	63
Aylesbury United	42	17	7	18	64	67	58
Hayes	42	15	8	19	63	72	53
Grays Athletic	42	15	5	22	56	69	50
Bromley	42	14	7	21	56	69	49
Dulwich Hamlet	42	13	8	21	52	74	47
Yeading	42	11	13	18	58	66	46
Molesey	42	11	11	20	44	62	44
Wokingham Town	42	11	6	25	38	67	39
Dorking	42	9	4	29	58	104	31
Basingstoke Town	42	5	12	25	38	86	27
Wivenhoe Town	42	5	3	34	38	152	18

First Division

Team	P	W	D	L	F	A	Pts
Bishop's Stortford	42	24	13	5	83	31	85
Purfleet	42	22	12	8	70	44	78
Walton & Hersham	42	22	11	9	81	53	77
Tooting & Mitcham United	42	21	12	9	66	37	75
Heybridge Swifts	42	20	11	11	72	45	71
Billericay Town	42	20	11	11	70	51	71
Abingdon Town	42	20	10	12	61	50	70
Worthing	42	19	11	12	79	46	68
Leyton	42	20	8	14	88	66	68
Boreham Wood	42	17	15	10	69	50	66
Staines Town	42	18	9	15	85	56	63
Bognor Regis Town	42	15	14	13	57	48	59
Wembley	42	16	10	16	66	52	58
Barking	42	15	11	16	63	69	56
Uxbridge	42	15	8	19	57	58	53
Whyteleafe	42	15	6	21	71	90	51
Maidenhead United	42	12	13	17	52	48	49
Berkhamsted Town	42	12	9	21	65	77	45
Ruislip Manor	42	10	8	24	42	79	38
Chalfont St Peter	42	7	10	25	40	79	31
Windsor & Eton	42	8	7	27	47	94	31
Croydon	42	3	3	36	37	198	12

1994-95

Premier Division

Team	P	W	D	L	F	A	Pts
Enfield	42	26	9	5	106	43	93
Slough Town	42	22	13	7	82	56	79
Hayes	42	20	14	8	66	47	74
Aylesbury United	42	21	6	15	86	59	69
Hitchin Town	42	18	12	12	68	59	66
Bromley	42	18	11	13	76	67	65
St Albans City	42	17	13	12	96	81	64
Molesey	42	18	8	16	65	61	62
Yeading	42	14	15	13	60	59	57
Harrow Borough	42	17	6	19	64	67	57
Dulwich Hamlet	42	16	9	17	70	82	57
Carshalton Athletic	42	16	9	17	69	84	57
Kingstonian	42	16	8	18	62	57	56
Walton & Hersham	42	14	11	17	75	73	53
Sutton United	42	13	12	17	74	69	51
Purfleet	42	13	12	17	76	90	51
Hendon	42	12	14	16	57	65	50
Grays Athletic	42	11	16	15	57	61	49
Bishop's Stortford	42	12	11	19	53	76	47
Chesham United	42	12	9	21	60	87	45
Marlow	42	10	9	23	52	84	39
Wokingham Town	42	6	9	27	39	86	27

First Division

Boreham Wood	42	31	5	6	90	38	98
Worthing	42	21	13	8	93	49	76
Chertsey Town	42	21	11	10	109	57	74
Aldershot Town	42	23	5	14	80	53	74
Billericay Town	42	20	9	13	68	52	69
Staines Town	42	17	12	13	83	65	63
Basingstoke Town	42	17	10	15	81	71	61
Tooting & Mitcham United	42	15	14	13	58	48	59
Wembley	42	16	11	15	70	61	59
Abingdon Town	42	16	11	15	67	69	59
Whyteleafe	42	17	7	18	70	78	58
Maidenhead United	42	15	12	15	73	76	57
Uxbridge	42	15	11	16	54	62	56
Leyton	42	15	10	17	67	66	55
Barking	42	16	7	19	74	77	55
Heybridge Swifts	42	16	6	20	73	78	54
Ruislip Manor	42	14	11	17	70	75	53
Bognor Regis Town	42	13	14	15	57	63	53
Berkhamsted Town	42	14	10	18	54	70	52
Newbury Town	42	12	15	15	58	71	51
Wivenhoe Town	42	8	7	27	47	94	31
Dorking	42	3	3	36	40	163	12

Second Division

Thame United	42	30	3	9	97	49	93
Barton Rovers	42	25	7	10	93	51	82
Oxford City	42	24	8	10	86	47	80
Bracknell Town	42	23	9	10	86	47	78
Metropolitan Police	42	19	12	11	81	65	69
Hampton	42	20	9	13	79	74	69
Croydon	42	20	5	17	85	65	65
Banstead Athletic	42	18	10	14	73	59	64
Saffron Walden Town	42	17	13	12	64	59	64
Chalfont St Peter	42	17	12	13	67	54	63
Witham Town	42	18	9	15	75	64	63
Leatherhead	42	16	12	14	71	75	60
Edgware Town	42	16	10	16	70	66	58
Tilbury	42	15	9	18	62	82	54
Cheshunt	42	13	13	16	66	81	52
Ware	42	14	7	21	61	81	49
Egham Town	42	11	14	17	60	65	47
Hemel Hempstead	42	10	11	21	45	76	41
Hungerford Town	42	11	7	24	55	81	40
Windsor & Eton	42	10	8	24	58	84	38
Aveley	42	9	5	28	48	95	32
Malden Vale	42	5	9	28	46	108	24

Third Division

Collier Row	40	30	5	5	86	23	95
Canvey Island	40	28	4	8	88	42	88
Bedford Town	40	22	11	7	90	50	77
Northwood	40	22	8	10	80	47	74
Horsham	40	22	6	12	84	61	72
Southall	40	21	8	11	87	59	71
Leighton Town	40	20	8	12	66	43	68
Camberley Town	40	19	8	13	59	39	65
Kingsbury Town	40	18	11	1	72	54	65
Hornchurch	40	17	8	15	64	63	59
Clapton	40	14	11	15	69	61	53
Tring Town	40	13	12	15	68	69	51
East Thurrock United	40	14	8	18	60	79	50
Epsom & Ewell	40	13	10	17	58	62	49
Harlow Town	40	13	8	19	53	83	47
Harefield United	40	12	8	20	51	79	44
Hertford Town	40	11	10	19	56	78	43
Feltham & Hounslow	40	13	4	23	64	87	43
Flackwell Heath	40	8	4	28	50	99	28
Lewes	40	6	5	29	34	104	23
Cove	40	3	5	32	37	94	14

1995-96

Premier Division

Hayes	42	24	14	4	76	32	86
Enfield	42	26	8	8	78	35	86
Boreham Wood	42	24	1	7	69	29	83
Yeovil Town	42	23	11	8	83	51	80
Dulwich Hamlet	42	23	11	8	85	59	80
Carshalton Athletic	42	22	8	12	68	49	74
St Albans City	42	20	12	10	70	41	72
Kingstonian	42	20	11	11	62	38	71
Harrow Borough	42	19	10	13	70	56	67
Sutton United	42	17	14	11	71	56	65
Aylesbury United	42	17	12	13	71	58	63
Bishop's Stortford	42	16	9	17	61	62	57
Yeading	42	11	14	17	48	60	47
Hendon	42	12	10	20	52	65	46
Chertsey Town	42	13	6	23	45	71	45
Purfleet	42	12	8	22	48	67	44
Grays Athletic	42	11	11	20	43	63	44
Hitchin Town	42	10	10	22	41	74	40
Bromley	42	10	7	25	52	91	37
Molesey	42	9	9	24	46	81	36
Walton & Hersham	42	9	7	26	42	79	34
Worthing	42	4	7	31	42	106	19

First Division

Oxford City	42	28	7	7	98	60	91
Heybridge Swifts	42	27	7	8	97	43	88
Staines Town	42	23	11	8	82	59	80
Leyton Pennant	42	22	7	13	77	57	73
Aldershot Town	42	21	9	12	81	46	72
Billericay Town	42	19	9	14	58	58	66
Bognor Regis Town	42	18	11	13	71	53	65
Marlow	42	19	5	18	72	75	62
Basingstoke Town	42	16	13	13	70	60	61
Uxbridge	42	16	12	14	46	49	60
Wokingham Town	42	16	10	16	62	65	58
Chesham United	42	15	12	15	51	44	57
Thame United	42	14	13	15	64	73	55
Maidenhead United	42	12	14	16	50	63	50
Whyteleafe	42	12	13	17	71	81	49
Abingdon Town	42	13	9	20	63	80	48
Barton Rovers	42	12	10	20	69	87	46
Berkhamsted Town	42	11	11	20	52	68	44
Tooting & Mitcham United	42	11	10	21	45	64	43
Ruislip Manor	42	11	9	22	55	77	42
Wembley	42	11	8	23	49	66	41
Barking	42	4	12	26	35	90	24

Second Division

Canvey Island	40	25	12	3	91	36	87
Croydon	40	25	6	9	78	42	81
Hampton	40	23	10	7	74	44	79
Banstead Athletic	40	21	11	8	72	36	74
Collier Row	40	21	11	8	73	41	74
Wivenhoe Town	40	21	8	11	82	57	71
Metropolitan Police	40	18	10	12	57	45	64
Bedford Town	40	18	10	12	69	59	64
Bracknell Town	40	18	8	14	69	50	62
Edgware Town	40	16	9	15	72	67	57
Tilbury	40	12	11	17	52	62	47
Ware	40	13	8	19	55	80	47
Chalfont St Peter	40	11	13	16	58	63	46
Leatherhead	40	12	10	18	71	77	46
Saffron Walden Town	40	11	12	17	56	58	45
Cheshunt	40	10	12	18	56	90	42
Hemel Hempstead	40	10	10	20	46	62	40
Egham Town	40	12	3	25	42	74	39
Witham Town	40	8	10	22	35	68	34
Hungerford Town	40	9	7	24	44	79	34
Dorking	40	8	5	27	44	104	29

Third Division

	P	W	D	L	F	A	Pts
Horsham	40	29	5	6	95	40	92
Leighton Town	40	28	5	7	95	34	89
Windsor & Eton	40	27	6	7	117	46	87
Wealdstone	40	23	8	9	104	39	77
Harlow Town	40	22	10	8	85	62	76
Northwood	40	20	9	11	76	56	69
Epsom & Ewell	40	18	14	8	95	57	68
Kingsbury Town	40	15	16	9	61	48	61
East Thurrock United	40	17	8	15	61	50	59
Aveley	40	16	10	14	62	53	58
Wingate & Finchley	40	16	7	17	74	70	55
Lewes	40	14	7	19	56	72	49
Flackwell Heath	40	14	5	21	60	84	47
Hornchurch	40	11	8	21	55	77	41
Harefield United	40	11	7	22	49	89	40
Tring Town	40	10	8	22	40	78	38
Camberley Town	40	9	9	22	45	81	36
Hertford Town	40	10	5	25	72	103	35
Cove	40	8	10	22	37	89	34
Clapton	40	9	6	25	48	89	33
Southall	40	9	5	26	34	104	32

Second Division

	P	W	D	L	F	A	Pts
Collier Row & Romford	42	28	12	2	93	33	96
Leatherhead	42	30	5	7	116	45	95
Wembley	42	23	11	8	92	45	80
Barking	42	22	13	7	69	40	79
Horsham	42	22	11	9	78	48	77
Edgware Town	42	20	14	8	74	50	74
Bedford Town	42	21	8	13	77	43	71
Banstead Athletic	42	21	5	16	75	52	68
Windsor & Eton	42	17	13	12	65	62	64
Leighton Town	42	17	12	13	64	52	63
Bracknell Town	42	17	9	16	78	71	60
Wivenhoe Town	42	17	9	16	69	62	60
Chalfont St Peter	42	14	13	15	53	61	55
Hungerford Town	42	14	13	15	68	77	55
Metropolitan Police	42	14	7	21	72	75	49
Tilbury	42	14	7	21	68	77	49
Witham Town	42	11	10	21	39	67	43
Egham Town	42	10	9	23	47	86	39
Cheshunt	42	9	3	30	37	101	30
Ware	42	7	8	27	44	80	29
Dorking	42	7	6	29	40	100	27
Hemel Hempstead	42	5	6	31	34	125	21

Third Division

	P	W	D	L	F	A	Pts
Wealdstone	32	24	3	5	72	24	75
Braintree Town	32	23	5	4	99	29	74
Northwood	32	18	10	4	60	31	64
Harlow Town	32	19	4	9	60	41	61
Aveley	32	17	6	9	64	39	57
East Thurrock United	32	16	6	10	58	51	54
Camberley Town	32	15	6	11	55	44	51
Wingate & Finchley	32	11	7	14	52	63	40
Hornchurch	32	11	6	15	35	51	39
Clapton	32	11	6	15	31	49	39
Lewes	32	10	8	14	45	53	38
Kingsbury Town	32	11	4	17	41	54	37
Hertford Town	32	10	6	16	55	65	36
Epsom & Ewell	32	8	5	19	62	78	29
Flackwell Heath	32	8	5	19	36	71	29
Tring Town	32	7	3	22	33	74	24
Southall	32	6	4	22	28	69	22

1996-97

Premier Division

	P	W	D	L	F	A	Pts
Yeovil Town	42	31	8	3	83	34	101
Enfield	42	28	11	3	91	29	98
Sutton United	42	18	13	11	87	70	67
Dagenham & Redbridge	42	18	11	13	57	43	65
Yeading	42	17	14	11	58	47	65
St Albans City	42	18	11	13	65	55	65
Aylesbury United	42	18	11	13	64	54	65
Purfleet	42	17	11	14	67	63	62
Heybridge Swifts	42	16	14	12	62	62	62
Boreham Wood	42	15	13	14	56	52	58
Kingstonian	42	16	8	18	79	79	56
Dulwich Hamlet	42	14	13	15	57	57	55
Carshalton Athletic	42	14	11	17	51	56	53
Hitchin Town	42	15	7	20	67	73	52
Oxford City	42	14	10	18	67	83	52
Hendon	42	13	12	17	53	59	51
Harrow Borough	42	12	14	16	58	62	50
Bromley	42	13	9	20	67	72	48
Bishop's Stortford	42	10	13	19	43	64	43
Staines Town	42	10	8	24	46	71	38
Grays Athletic	42	8	9	25	43	78	33
Chertsey Town	42	8	7	27	40	98	31

First Division

	P	W	D	L	F	A	Pts
Chesham United	42	27	6	9	80	46	87
Basingstoke Town	42	22	13	7	81	38	79
Walton & Hersham	42	21	13	8	67	41	76
Hampton	42	21	12	9	62	39	75
Billericay Town	42	21	12	9	69	49	75
Bognor Regis Town	42	21	9	12	63	44	72
Aldershot Town	42	19	14	9	67	45	71
Uxbridge	42	15	17	10	65	48	62
Whyteleafe	42	18	7	17	71	68	61
Molesey	42	17	9	16	50	53	60
Abingdon Town	42	15	11	16	44	42	56
Leyton Pennant	42	14	12	16	71	72	54
Maidenhead United	42	15	10	17	57	57	52
Wokingham Town	42	14	10	18	41	45	52
Thame United	42	13	10	19	57	69	49
Worthing	42	11	11	20	58	77	44
Barton Rovers	42	11	11	20	61	58	44
Croydon	42	11	10	21	40	57	43
Berkhamsted Town	42	11	9	22	47	66	42
Canvey Island	42	9	14	19	52	71	41
Marlow	42	11	6	25	41	84	39
Tooting & Mitcham United	42	8	8	26	40	85	32

Maidenhead United had 3 points deducted

1997-98

Premier Division

	P	W	D	L	F	A	Pts
Kingstonian	42	25	12	5	84	35	87
Boreham Wood	42	23	11	8	81	42	80
Sutton United	42	22	12	8	83	56	78
Dagenham & Redbridge	42	21	10	11	73	50	73
Hendon	42	21	10	11	69	50	73
Heybridge Swifts	42	18	11	13	74	62	65
Enfield	42	18	8	16	66	58	62
Basingstoke Town	42	17	11	14	56	60	62
Walton & Hersham	42	18	6	18	70	60	60
Purfleet	42	15	13	14	57	58	58
St Albans City	42	17	7	18	54	59	58
Harrow Borough	42	15	10	17	60	67	55
Gravesend & Northfleet	42	15	8	19	65	67	53
Chesham United	42	14	10	18	71	70	52
Bromley	42	13	13	16	53	53	52
Dulwich Hamlet	42	13	11	18	56	67	50
Carshalton Athletic	42	13	9	20	54	77	48
Aylesbury United	42	13	8	21	55	70	47
Bishop's Stortford	42	14	5	23	53	69	47
Yeading	42	12	11	19	49	65	47
Hitchin Town	42	8	15	19	45	62	39
Oxford City	42	7	9	26	35	76	30

First Division

Aldershot Town	42	28	8	6	89	36	92
Billericay Town	42	25	6	11	78	44	81
Hampton	42	22	15	5	75	47	81
Maidenhead United	42	25	5	12	76	37	80
Uxbridge	42	23	6	13	66	59	75
Grays Athletic	42	21	10	11	79	49	73
Romford	42	21	8	13	92	59	71
Bognor Regis Town	42	20	9	13	77	45	69
Leatherhead	42	18	11	13	70	51	65
Leyton Pennant	42	17	11	14	66	58	62
Chertsey Town	42	16	13	13	83	70	61
Worthing	42	17	6	19	64	71	57
Berkhamsted Town	42	15	8	19	59	69	53
Staines Town	42	13	10	19	54	74	49
Croydon	42	13	10	19	47	64	49
Barton Rovers	42	11	13	18	53	72	46
Wembley	42	10	15	17	38	61	45
Molesey	42	10	11	21	47	65	41
Whyteleafe	42	10	10	22	48	83	40
Wokingham Town	42	7	10	25	41	74	31
Abingdon Town	42	9	4	29	47	101	31
Thame United	42	7	9	25	33	96	30

Second Division

Canvey Island	42	30	8	4	116	41	98
Braintree Town	42	29	11	2	117	45	98
Wealdstone	42	24	11	7	81	46	83
Bedford Town	42	22	12	8	55	25	78
Metropolitan Police	42	21	8	13	80	65	71
Wivenhoe Town	42	18	12	12	84	66	66
Edgware Town	42	18	10	14	81	65	64
Chalfont St Peter	42	17	13	12	63	60	64
Northwood	42	17	11	14	65	69	62
Windsor & Eton	42	17	7	18	75	72	58
Tooting & Mitcham United	42	16	9	17	58	56	57
Barking	42	15	12	15	62	75	57
Banstead Athletic	42	15	9	18	60	63	54
Marlow	42	16	5	21	64	78	53
Horsham	42	13	9	20	67	75	48
Bracknell Town	42	13	8	21	68	93	47
Leighton Town	42	13	6	23	45	78	45
Hungerford Town	42	11	11	20	66	77	44
Witham Town	42	9	13	20	55	68	40
Tilbury	42	9	12	21	57	88	39
Egham Town	42	9	5	28	47	101	32
Cheshunt	42	4	10	28	31	90	32

Third Division

Hemel Hempstead	38	27	6	5	86	28	87
Hertford Town	38	26	5	7	77	31	83
Harlow Town	38	24	11	3	81	43	83
Camberley Town	38	24	7	7	93	43	79
Ford United	38	23	9	6	90	34	78
East Thurrock United	38	23	7	8	70	40	76
Epsom & Ewell	38	17	6	15	69	57	57
Ware	38	17	6	15	69	57	57
Aveley	38	16	7	15	65	57	55
Corinthian Casuals	38	16	6	16	59	57	54
Hornchurch	38	12	9	17	55	68	45
Clapton	38	13	6	19	46	61	45
Flackwell Heath	38	12	9	17	50	76	45
Croydon Athletic	38	12	7	19	58	63	43
Tring Town	38	12	7	19	51	69	43
Southall	38	10	6	22	41	85	36
Dorking	38	9	6	23	49	94	33
Wingate & Finchley	38	7	8	23	46	80	29
Lewes	38	7	5	26	34	88	26
Kingsbury Town	38	5	3	30	35	93	18

1998-99

Premier Division

Sutton United	42	27	7	8	89	39	88
Aylesbury United	42	23	8	11	67	38	77
Dagenham & Redbridge	42	20	13	9	71	44	73
Purfleet	42	22	7	13	71	54	73
Enfield	42	21	9	12	73	49	72
St Albans City	42	17	17	8	71	52	68
Aldershot Town	42	16	14	12	83	48	62
Basingstoke Town	42	17	10	15	63	53	61
Harrow Borough	42	17	9	16	72	66	60
Gravesend & Northfleet	42	18	6	18	54	53	60
Slough Town	42	16	11	15	60	53	59
Billericay Town	42	15	13	14	54	56	58
Hendon	42	16	9	17	70	71	57
Boreham Wood	42	14	15	13	59	63	57
Chesham United	42	15	9	18	58	79	54
Dulwich Hamlet	42	14	8	20	53	63	50
Heybridge Swifts	42	13	9	20	51	85	48
Walton & Hersham	42	12	7	23	50	77	43
Hampton	42	10	12	20	41	71	42
Carshalton Athletic	42	10	10	22	47	82	40
Bishops Stortford	42	9	10	23	49	90	37
Bromley	42	8	11	23	50	72	35

First Division

Canvey Island	42	28	6	8	76	41	90
Hitchin Town	42	25	10	7	75	38	85
Wealdstone	42	26	6	10	75	48	84
Braintree Town	42	20	10	12	75	48	70
Bognor Regis Town	42	20	8	14	63	44	68
Grays Athletic	42	19	11	12	56	42	68
Oxford City	42	16	14	12	58	51	62
Croydon	42	16	13	13	53	53	61
Chertsey Town	42	14	16	12	57	57	58
Romford	42	14	15	13	58	63	57
Maidenhead United	42	13	15	14	50	46	54
Worthing	42	13	13	16	47	61	52
Leyton Pennant	42	13	12	17	62	70	51
Uxbridge	42	13	11	18	54	51	50
Barton Rovers	42	11	15	16	43	49	48
Yeading	42	12	10	20	51	55	46
Leatherhead	42	12	9	21	48	59	45
Whyteleafe	42	13	6	23	51	72	45
Staines Town	42	10	15	17	33	57	45
Molesey	42	8	20	14	35	52	44
Wembley	42	10	10	22	36	71	40
Berkhamsted Town	42	10	7	25	53	81	37

Second Division

Bedford Town	42	29	7	6	89	31	94
Harlow Town	42	27	8	7	100	47	89
Thame United	42	26	8	8	89	50	86
Hemel Hempstead	42	21	12	9	90	50	75
Windsor & Eton	42	22	6	14	87	55	72
Banstead Athletic	42	21	8	13	83	62	71
Northwood	42	20	7	15	67	68	67
Tooting & Mitcham United	42	19	9	14	63	62	66
Chalfont St Peter	42	16	12	14	70	71	60
Metropolitan Police	42	17	8	17	61	58	59
Leighton Town	42	16	10	16	60	64	58
Horsham	42	17	6	19	74	67	57
Marlow	42	16	9	17	72	68	57
Edgware Town	42	14	10	18	65	68	52
Witham Town	42	12	15	15	64	64	51
Hungerford Town	42	13	12	17	59	61	51
Wivenhoe Town	42	14	8	20	71	83	50
Wokingham Town	42	14	4	24	44	79	46
Barking	42	10	11	21	50	75	41
Hertford Town	42	11	2	29	44	96	35
Bracknell Town	42	7	10	25	48	92	31
Abingdon Town	42	6	6	30	48	124	24

Third Division

Ford United	38	27	5	6	110	42	86
Wingate & Finchley	38	25	5	8	79	38	80
Cheshunt	38	23	10	5	70	41	79
Lewes	38	25	3	10	86	45	78
Epsom & Ewell	38	19	5	14	61	51	62
Ware	38	19	4	15	79	60	61
Tilbury	38	17	8	13	74	52	59
Croydon Athletic	38	16	10	12	82	59	58
East Thurrock United	38	15	13	10	74	56	58
Egham Town	38	16	8	14	65	58	56
Corinthian Casuals	38	16	7	15	70	71	55
Southall	38	14	9	15	68	66	51
Camberley Town	38	14	8	16	66	77	50
Aveley	38	12	7	19	50	67	43
Flackwell Heath	38	11	9	18	59	70	42
Hornchurch	38	10	9	19	48	73	39
Clapton	38	11	6	21	48	89	39
Dorking	38	8	7	23	52	98	31
Kingsbury Town	38	6	3	29	40	98	21
Tring Town	38	5	6	27	38	108	21

Second Division

Hemel Hempstead	42	31	8	3	98	27	101
Northwood	42	29	9	4	109	40	96
Ford United	42	28	8	6	108	41	92
Berkhamsted Town	42	22	8	12	75	52	74
Windsor & Eton	42	20	13	9	73	53	73
Wivenhoe Town	42	20	9	13	61	47	69
Barking	42	18	13	11	70	51	67
Marlow	42	20	4	18	86	66	64
Metropolitan Police	42	18	7	17	75	71	61
Banstead Athletic	42	16	11	15	55	56	59
Tooting & Mitcham United	42	16	7	19	72	74	55
Wokingham Town	42	15	9	18	58	80	54
Wembley	42	14	11	17	47	53	53
Edgware Town	42	13	11	18	72	71	50
Hungerford Town	42	13	10	19	61	78	49
Cheshunt	42	12	12	18	53	65	48
Horsham	42	13	8	21	66	81	47
Leighton Town	42	13	8	21	65	84	47
Molesey	42	10	12	20	54	69	42
Wingate & Finchley	42	11	7	24	54	97	40
Witham Town	42	7	9	26	39	110	30
Chalfont St Peter	42	2	8	32	39	124	14

Third Division

East Thurrock United	40	26	7	7	89	42	85
Great Wakering Rovers	40	25	7	8	81	41	82
Tilbury	40	21	12	7	67	39	75
Hornchurch	40	19	12	9	72	57	69
Croydon Athletic	40	19	11	10	85	52	68
Epsom & Ewell	40	18	12	10	67	46	66
Lewes	40	18	10	12	73	51	64
Bracknell Town	40	15	16	9	81	64	61
Aveley	40	17	10	13	73	64	61
Corinthian Casuals	40	16	10	14	59	51	58
Flackwell Heath	40	17	6	17	74	76	57
Ware	40	16	8	16	74	62	56
Egham Town	40	14	13	13	48	43	55
Hertford Town	40	15	10	15	63	60	55
Abingdon Town	40	10	12	18	48	64	42
Kingsbury Town	40	11	8	21	55	86	41
Camberley Town	40	11	7	22	44	79	40
Tring Town	40	10	9	21	37	64	39
Dorking	40	9	10	21	53	69	37
Clapton	40	9	7	24	50	93	34
Southall	40	3	5	32	33	123	14

1999-2000

Premier Division

Dagenham & Redbridge	42	32	5	5	97	35	101
Aldershot Town	42	24	5	13	71	51	77
Chesham United	42	20	10	12	64	50	70
Purfleet	42	18	15	9	70	48	69
Canvey Island	42	21	6	15	70	53	69
St Albans City	42	19	10	13	75	55	67
Billericay Town	42	18	12	12	62	62	66
Hendon	42	18	8	16	61	64	62
Slough Town	42	17	9	16	61	59	60
Dulwich Hamlet	42	17	5	20	62	68	56
Gravesend & Northfleet	42	15	10	17	66	67	55
Farnborough Town	42	14	11	17	52	55	53
Hampton & Richmond Borough	42	13	13	16	49	57	52
Enfield	42	13	11	18	64	68	50
Heybridge Swifts	42	13	11	18	57	65	50
Hitchin Town	42	13	11	18	59	72	50
Carshalton Athletic	42	12	12	18	55	65	48
Basingstoke Town	42	13	9	20	56	71	48
Harrow Borough	42	14	6	22	54	70	48
Aylesbury United	42	13	9	20	64	81	48
Boreham Wood	42	11	10	21	44	71	43
Walton & Hersham	42	11	8	23	44	70	41

First Division

Croydon	42	25	9	8	85	47	84
Grays Athletic	42	21	12	9	80	44	75
Maidenhead United	42	20	15	7	72	45	75
Thame United	42	20	13	9	61	38	73
Worthing	42	19	12	11	80	60	69
Staines Town	42	19	12	11	63	52	69
Whyteleafe	42	20	9	13	60	49	69
Bedford Town	42	17	12	13	59	52	63
Bromley	42	17	9	16	63	65	60
Uxbridge	42	15	13	14	60	44	58
Bishop's Stortford	42	16	10	16	57	62	58
Barton Rovers	42	16	8	18	64	83	56
Oxford City	42	17	4	21	57	55	55
Braintree Town	42	15	10	17	65	74	55
Yeading	42	12	18	12	53	54	54
Wealdstone	42	13	12	17	51	58	51
Bognor Regis Town	42	12	13	17	47	53	49
Harlow Town	42	11	13	18	62	76	46
Romford	42	12	9	21	51	70	45
Leatherhead	42	9	13	20	47	70	40
Chertsey Town	42	9	5	28	50	84	32
Leyton Pennant	42	7	9	26	34	85	30

2000-2001

Premier Division

Farnborough Town	42	31	6	5	86	27	99
Canvey Island	42	27	8	7	79	41	89
Basingstoke Town	42	22	13	7	73	40	79
Aldershot Town	41	21	11	9	73	39	74
Chesham United	42	22	6	14	78	52	72
Gravesend & Northfleet	42	22	5	15	62	45	71
Heybridge Swifts	42	18	13	11	74	60	67
Billericay Town	41	18	13	10	62	54	67
Hampton & Richmond Borough	42	18	12	12	73	60	66
Hitchin Town	42	18	5	19	72	69	59
Purfleet	42	14	13	15	55	55	55
Hendon	42	16	6	18	62	62	54
Sutton United	41	14	11	16	74	70	53
St Albans City	42	15	5	22	50	69	50
Grays Athletic	42	14	8	20	49	68	50
Maidenhead United	42	15	2	25	47	63	47
Croydon	42	12	10	20	55	77	46
Enfield	42	12	9	21	48	74	45
Harrow Borough	41	10	11	20	61	90	41
Slough Town	42	10	9	23	40	62	39
Carshalton Athletic	42	10	6	26	40	85	36
Dulwich Hamlet	42	4	10	28	33	84	22

First Division

	P	W	D	L	F	A	Pts
Boreham Wood	42	26	7	9	82	49	85
Bedford Town	42	22	16	4	81	40	82
Braintree Town	42	25	6	11	112	60	81
Bishop's Stortford	42	24	6	12	103	76	78
Thame United	42	22	8	12	86	54	74
Ford United	42	19	12	11	70	58	69
Uxbridge	42	21	5	16	73	55	68
Northwood	42	20	8	14	89	81	68
Whyteleafe	42	20	6	16	62	69	66
Oxford City	42	16	13	13	64	49	61
Harlow Town	42	15	16	11	70	66	61
Worthing	42	16	9	17	69	69	57
Staines Town	42	16	8	18	60	66	56
Aylesbury United	42	17	4	21	65	55	55
Yeading	42	15	9	18	72	74	54
Bognor Regis Town	42	13	11	18	71	71	50
Walton & Hersham	42	14	8	20	59	80	50
Bromley	42	14	6	22	63	86	48
Wealdstone	42	12	9	21	54	73	45
Leatherhead	42	12	4	26	37	87	40
Romford	42	9	4	29	53	113	31
Barton Rovers	42	2	9	31	30	94	15

Second Division

	P	W	D	L	F	A	Pts
Tooting & Mitcham United	42	26	11	5	92	35	89
Windsor	42	24	10	8	70	40	82
Barking	42	23	13	6	82	54	82
Berkhamsted Town	42	24	8	10	99	49	80
Wivenhoe Town	42	23	11	8	78	52	80
Hemel Hempstead	42	22	10	10	74	44	76
Horsham	42	19	9	14	84	61	66
Chertsey Town	42	18	9	15	59	59	63
Great Wakering Rovers	42	16	13	13	69	59	61
Tilbury	42	18	6	18	61	67	60
Banstead Athletic	42	17	8	17	69	58	59
East Thurrock United	42	16	11	15	72	64	59
Metropolitan Police	42	18	4	20	64	77	58
Marlow	42	15	11	16	62	61	56
Molesey	42	14	9	19	53	61	51
Wembley	42	12	10	20	39	63	46
Hungerford Town	42	11	9	22	40	73	42
Leyton Pennant	42	10	11	21	47	74	41
Cheshunt	42	11	6	25	48	77	39
Edgware Town	42	9	9	24	41	77	36
Leighton Town	42	8	10	24	44	87	34
Wokingham Town	42	3	12	27	39	94	20

Wokingham Town had 1 point deducted

Third Division

	P	W	D	L	F	A	Pts
Arlesey Town	42	34	6	2	138	37	108
Lewes	41	25	11	5	104	34	86
Ashford Town	42	26	7	9	102	49	85
Flackwell Heath	42	24	10	8	93	51	82
Corinthian Casuals	42	24	10	8	83	50	82
Aveley	42	24	3	15	85	61	75
Epsom & Ewell	42	23	4	15	76	52	73
Witham Town	42	21	9	12	76	57	72
Bracknell Town	41	19	10	12	90	70	67
Croydon Athletic	41	15	12	14	78	63	57
Ware	42	17	6	19	75	76	57
Tring Town	42	16	9	17	60	71	57
Egham Town	42	15	11	16	60	60	56
Hornchurch	42	14	13	15	73	60	55
Wingate & Finchley	42	15	7	20	75	75	52
Kingsbury Town	42	11	8	23	74	100	41
Abingdon Town	42	12	7	23	53	102	40
Dorking	42	10	9	23	59	99	39
Hertford Town	41	9	8	24	57	97	35
Camberley Town	42	8	8	26	53	107	32
Clapton	42	5	9	28	48	121	24
Chalfont St Peter	42	4	1	37	30	150	13

Abingdon Town had 3 points deducted

2001-2002

Premier Division

	P	W	D	L	F	A	Pts
Gravesend & Northfleet	42	31	6	5	90	33	99
Canvey Island	42	30	5	7	107	41	95
Aldershot Town	42	22	7	13	76	51	73
Braintree Town	42	23	4	15	66	61	73
Purfleet	42	19	15	8	67	44	72
Grays Athletic	42	20	10	12	65	55	70
Chesham United	42	19	10	13	69	53	67
Hendon Town	42	19	5	18	66	54	62
Billericay Town	42	16	13	13	59	60	61
St Albans City	42	16	9	17	71	60	57
Hitchin Town	42	15	10	17	73	81	55
Sutton Albion	42	13	15	14	62	62	54
Heybridge Swifts	42	15	9	18	68	85	54
Kingstonian	42	13	13	16	50	56	52
Boreham Wood	42	15	6	21	49	62	51
Maidenhead United	42	15	5	22	51	63	50
Bedford Town	42	12	12	18	64	69	48
Basingstoke Town	42	11	15	16	50	68	48
Enfield	42	11	9	22	48	77	42
Hampton & Richmond Borough	42	9	13	20	51	71	40
Harrow Borough	42	8	10	24	50	89	34
Croydon	42	7	5	30	36	93	26

First Division

	P	W	D	L	F	A	Pts
Ford United	42	27	7	8	92	56	88
Bishop's Stortford	42	26	9	7	104	51	87
Aylesbury United	42	23	10	9	96	64	79
Bognor Regis Town	42	20	13	9	74	55	73
Northwood	42	19	11	12	92	64	68
Carshalton Athletic	42	17	16	9	64	53	67
Harlow Town	42	19	9	14	77	65	66
Slough Town	42	17	11	14	68	51	62
Uxbridge	42	18	6	18	68	65	60
Oxford City	42	17	9	16	59	60	60
Thame United	42	15	14	13	75	61	59
Tooting & Mitcham United	42	16	11	15	70	70	59
Walton & Hersham	42	16	10	16	75	70	58
Yeading	42	16	10	16	84	90	58
Worthing	42	15	8	19	69	65	53
Staines Town	42	12	11	19	45	60	47
Dulwich Hamlet	42	11	13	18	64	76	46
Wealdstone	42	11	12	19	60	82	45
Bromley	42	10	11	21	44	74	41
Whyteleafe	42	10	11	21	46	86	41
Barking & East Ham United	42	8	7	27	61	123	31
Windsor & Eton	42	7	5	30	53	93	26

Second Division

	P	W	D	L	F	A	Pts
Lewes	42	29	9	4	108	31	96
Horsham	42	27	9	6	104	44	90
Berkhamstead Town	42	23	10	9	82	51	79
Arlesey Town	42	23	6	13	89	55	75
Banstead Athletic	42	22	8	12	83	54	74
Leyton Pennant	42	22	8	12	84	60	74
Great Wakering Rovers	42	21	8	13	64	37	71
East Thurrock United	42	21	8	13	67	59	71
Marlow	42	18	13	11	73	63	67
Hemel Hempstead Town	42	18	10	14	82	66	64
Leatherhead	42	17	6	19	72	62	57
Ashford Town	42	15	11	16	58	71	56
Metropolitan Police	42	16	7	19	84	84	55
Barton Rovers	42	15	9	18	54	60	54
Hungerford Town	42	14	9	19	56	75	51
Tilbury	42	15	6	21	55	74	51
Chertsey Town	42	10	14	18	79	112	44
Wembley	42	9	10	23	51	82	37
Molesey	42	10	6	26	40	93	36
Cheshunt	42	7	13	22	51	84	34
Wivenhoe Town	42	8	9	25	55	111	33
Romford	42	4	7	31	42	105	19

Third Division

Croydon Athletic	42	30	5	7	138	41	95
Hornchurch	42	25	11	6	96	46	86
Aveley	42	26	6	10	109	55	84
Bracknell Town	42	25	8	9	96	54	83
Epsom & Ewell	42	20	15	7	79	51	75
Egham Town	42	21	11	10	72	59	74
Wingate & Finchley	42	20	9	13	80	60	69
Dorking	42	18	14	10	77	66	68
Tring Town	42	19	11	12	64	62	68
Corinthian-Casuals	42	18	13	11	69	44	67
Hertford Town	42	20	7	15	88	74	67
Witham Town	42	15	10	17	66	72	55
Ware	42	14	10	18	74	76	52
Chalfont St Peter	42	15	4	23	69	92	49
Wokingham Town	42	14	6	22	79	105	48
Abingdon Town	42	13	7	22	61	75	46
Leighton Town	42	8	12	22	56	95	36
Kingsbury Town	42	8	11	23	58	91	35
Edgware Town	42	9	7	26	65	101	34
Flackwell Heath	42	9	8	25	53	99	32
Clapton	42	9	4	29	45	118	31
Camberley Town	42	7	9	26	37	95	30

Division One (South)

Carshalton Athletic	46	28	8	10	73	44	92
Bognor Regis Town	46	26	10	10	92	34	88
Lewes	46	24	16	6	106	50	88
Dulwich Hamlet	46	23	12	11	73	49	81
Whyteleafe	46	21	13	12	74	51	76
Bromley	46	21	13	12	70	53	76
Walton & Hersham	46	20	13	13	87	63	73
Horsham	46	21	9	16	80	58	72
Epsom & Ewell	46	19	12	15	67	66	69
Egham Town	46	19	10	17	62	71	67
Tooting & Mitcham United	46	18	9	19	83	78	63
Worthing	46	17	12	17	78	75	63
Windsor & Eton	46	18	9	19	66	65	63
Leatherhead	46	16	13	17	71	66	61
Staines Town	46	14	16	16	57	63	58
Banstead Athletic	46	14	15	17	58	59	57
Ashford Town (Middlesex)	46	14	11	21	47	70	53
Croydon	46	15	8	23	56	87	53
Croydon Athletic	46	13	13	20	52	66	52
Bracknell Town	46	12	16	18	57	74	52
Corinthian Casuals	46	12	14	20	50	68	50
Molesey	46	13	9	24	52	79	48
Metropolitan Police	46	12	10	24	50	76	46
Chertsey Town	46	3	7	36	43	139	16

2002-2003

Premier Division

Aldershot Town	46	33	6	7	81	36	105
Canvey Island	46	28	8	10	112	56	92
Hendon	46	22	13	11	70	56	79
St. Albans City	46	23	8	15	73	65	77
Basingstoke Town	46	23	7	16	80	60	76
Sutton United	46	22	9	15	77	62	75
Hayes	46	20	13	13	67	54	73
Purfleet	46	19	15	12	68	48	72
Bedford Town	46	21	9	16	66	58	72
Maidenhead United	46	16	17	13	75	63	65
Kingstonian	46	16	17	13	71	64	65
Billericay Town	46	17	11	18	46	44	62
Bishopis Stortford	46	16	11	19	74	72	59
Hitchin Town	46	15	13	18	69	67	58
Ford United	46	15	12	19	78	84	57
Braintree Town	46	14	12	20	59	71	54
Aylesbury United	46	13	15	18	62	75	54
Harrow Borough	46	15	9	22	54	75	54
Grays Athletic	46	14	11	21	53	59	53
Heybridge Swifts	46	13	14	19	52	80	53
Chesham United	46	14	10	22	56	81	52
Boreham Wood	46	11	15	20	50	58	48
Enfield	46	9	11	26	47	101	38
Hampton & Richmond Borough	46	3	14	29	35	86	23

Division Two

Cheshunt	30	25	3	2	91	29	78
Leyton	30	21	5	4	77	22	68
Flackwell Heath	30	17	3	10	52	44	54
Abingdon Town	30	14	11	5	65	42	53
Hungerford Town	30	12	12	6	49	36	48
Leighton Town	30	14	3	13	61	43	45
Witham Town	30	12	8	10	40	43	44
Ware	30	12	5	13	47	53	41
Clapton	30	12	5	13	40	47	41
Tring Town	30	11	5	14	49	58	38
Kingsbury Town	30	9	11	10	38	48	38
Edgware Town	30	10	3	17	49	65	33
Wokingham Town	30	7	7	16	34	81	28
Dorking	30	6	6	18	49	63	24
Chalfont St. Peter	30	6	5	19	34	63	23
Camberley Town	30	4	4	22	23	61	16

Division One (North)

Northwood	46	28	7	11	109	56	91
Hornchurch	46	25	15	6	85	48	90
Hemel Hempstead Town	46	26	7	13	70	55	85
Slough Town	46	22	14	10	86	59	80
Uxbridge	46	23	10	13	62	41	79
Aveley	46	21	14	11	66	48	77
Berkhamsted Town	46	21	13	12	92	68	76
Thame United	46	20	12	14	84	51	72
Wealdstone	46	21	9	16	85	69	72
Harlow Town	46	20	12	14	66	53	72
Marlow	46	19	10	17	74	63	67
Barking & East Ham United	46	19	9	18	73	76	66
Yeading	46	18	11	17	77	69	65
Great Wakering Rovers	46	17	14	15	64	70	65
Oxford City	46	17	13	16	55	51	64
Arlesey Town	46	17	12	17	69	71	63
East Thurrock United	46	17	10	19	75	79	61
Wingate & Finchley	46	15	11	20	70	74	56
Barton Rovers	46	15	7	24	53	65	52
Tilbury	46	14	7	25	55	96	49
Wivenhoe Town	46	9	11	26	56	94	38
Leyton Pennant	46	9	7	30	38	81	34
Wembley	46	7	11	28	57	111	32
Hertford Town	46	6	6	34	46	119	24

NORTHERN PREMIER LEAGUE

1968-69

Macclesfield Town	38	27	6	5	82	38	60
Wigan Athletic	38	18	12	8	59	41	48
Morecambe	38	16	14	8	64	37	46
Gainsborough Trinity	38	19	8	11	64	43	46
South Shields	38	19	8	11	78	56	46
Bangor City	38	18	9	11	102	64	45
Hyde United	38	16	10	12	71	65	42
Goole Town	38	15	10	13	80	78	40
Altrincham	38	14	10	14	69	52	38
Fleetwood	38	16	6	16	58	58	38
Gateshead	38	14	9	15	42	48	37
South Liverpool	38	12	13	13	56	66	37
Northwich Victoria	38	16	5	17	59	82	37
Boston United	38	14	8	16	59	65	36
Runcorn	38	12	11	15	59	63	35
Netherfield	38	12	4	22	51	69	28
Scarborough	38	9	10	19	49	68	28
Ashington	38	10	8	20	48	74	28
Chorley	38	8	9	21	46	75	25
Worksop Town	38	6	8	24	34	88	20

1969-70

Macclesfield Town	38	22	8	8	72	41	52
Wigan Athletic	38	20	12	6	56	32	52
Boston United	38	21	8	9	65	33	50
Scarborough	38	20	10	8	74	39	50
South Shields	38	19	7	12	66	43	45
Gainsborough Trinity	38	16	11	11	64	49	43
Stafford Rangers	38	16	7	15	59	52	39
Bangor City	38	15	9	14	68	63	39
Northwich Victoria	38	15	8	15	60	66	38
Netherfield	38	14	9	15	56	54	37
Hyde United	38	15	7	16	59	59	37
Altincham	38	14	8	16	62	65	36
Fleetwood	38	13	10	15	53	60	36
Runcorn	38	11	13	14	57	72	35
Morecambe	38	10	13	15	41	51	33
South Liverpool	38	11	11	16	44	55	33
Great Harwood	38	10	9	19	63	92	29
Matlock Town	38	8	12	18	52	67	28
Goole Town	38	10	6	22	50	71	26
Gateshead	38	5	12	21	37	94	22

1970-71

Wigan Athletic	42	27	13	2	91	32	67
Stafford Rangers	42	27	7	8	87	51	61
Scarborough	42	23	12	7	83	40	58
Boston United	42	22	12	8	69	31	56
Macclesfield Town	42	23	10	9	84	45	56
Northwich Victoria	42	22	5	15	71	55	49
Bangor City	42	19	10	13	72	61	48
Altrincham	42	19	10	13	80	76	48
South Liverpool	42	15	15	12	67	57	45
Chorley	42	14	14	14	58	61	42
Gainsborough Trinity	42	15	11	16	65	63	41
Morecambe	42	14	11	17	67	79	39
South Shields	42	12	14	16	67	66	38
Bradford Park Avenue	42	15	8	19	54	73	38
Lancaster City	42	12	12	18	53	76	36
Netherfield	42	13	9	20	59	57	35
Matlock Town	42	10	13	19	58	80	33
Fleetwood	42	10	11	21	56	90	31
Great Harwood	42	8	13	21	66	98	29
Runcorn	42	10	5	27	58	84	25
Kirkby Town	42	6	13	23	57	93	25
Goole Town	42	10	4	28	44	98	24

1971-72

Stafford Rangers	46	30	11	5	91	32	71
Boston United	46	28	13	5	87	37	69
Wigan Athletic	46	27	10	9	70	43	64
Scarborough	46	21	15	10	75	46	57
Northwich Victoria	46	20	14	12	65	59	54
Macclesfield Town	46	18	15	13	61	50	51
Gainsborough Trinity	46	21	9	16	93	79	51
South Shields	46	18	14	14	75	57	50
Bangor City	46	20	8	18	93	74	48
Altrincham	46	18	11	17	72	58	47
Skelmersdale United	46	19	9	18	61	58	47
Matlock Town	46	20	7	19	67	75	47
Chorley	46	17	12	17	66	59	46
Lancaster City	46	15	14	17	84	84	44
Great Harwood	46	15	14	17	60	74	44
Ellesmere Port Town	46	17	9	20	67	71	43
Morecambe	46	15	10	21	51	64	40
Bradford Park Avenue	46	13	13	20	54	71	39
Netherfield	46	16	5	25	51	73	37
Fleetwood	46	11	15	20	43	67	37
South Liverpool	46	12	12	22	61	73	36
Runcorn	46	8	14	24	48	80	30
Goole Town	46	9	10	27	51	97	28
Kirkby Town	46	6	12	28	38	104	24

1972-73

Boston United	46	27	16	3	88	34	70
Scarborough	46	26	9	11	72	39	61
Wigan Athletic	46	23	14	9	69	38	60
Altrincham	46	22	16	8	75	55	60
Bradford Park Avenue	46	19	17	10	63	50	55
Stafford Rangers	46	20	11	15	63	46	51
Gainsborough Trinity	46	18	13	15	70	50	49
Northwich Victoria	46	17	15	14	74	62	49
Netherfield	46	20	9	17	68	65	49
Macclesfield Town	46	16	16	14	58	47	48
Ellesmere Port Town	46	18	11	17	72	56	47
Skelmersdale United	46	15	16	15	58	59	46
Bangor City	46	16	13	17	70	60	45
Mossley	46	17	11	18	70	73	45
Morecambe	46	17	11	18	62	70	45
Great Harwood	46	14	15	17	63	74	43
South Liverpool	46	12	19	15	47	57	43
Runcorn	46	15	12	19	75	78	42
Goole Town	46	13	13	20	64	73	39
South Shields	46	17	4	25	64	81	38
Matlock Town	46	11	11	24	42	80	33
Lancaster City	46	10	11	25	53	78	31
Barrow	46	12	6	28	52	101	30
Fleetwood	46	5	15	26	31	77	25

1973-74

Boston United	46	27	11	8	69	32	65
Wigan Athletic	46	28	8	10	96	39	64
Altrincham	46	26	11	9	77	34	63
Stafford Rangers	46	27	9	10	101	45	63
Scarborough	46	22	14	10	62	43	58
South Shields	46	25	6	15	87	48	56
Runcorn	46	21	14	11	72	47	56
Macclesfield Town	46	18	15	13	48	47	51
Bangor City	46	19	11	16	65	56	49
Gainsborough Trinity	46	18	11	17	77	64	47
South Liverpool	46	16	15	15	55	47	47
Skelmersdale United	46	16	13	17	50	59	45
Goole Town	46	14	15	17	60	69	43
Fleetwood	46	14	15	17	48	68	43
Mossley	46	15	11	20	53	65	41
Northwich Victoria	46	14	13	19	68	75	41
Morecambe	46	13	13	20	62	84	39
Buxton	46	14	10	22	45	71	38
Matlock Town	46	11	14	21	50	79	36
Great Harwood	46	10	14	22	52	74	34
Bradford Park Avenue	46	9	15	22	42	84	33
Barrow	46	13	7	26	46	94	33
Lancaster City	46	10	12	24	52	67	32
Netherfield	46	11	5	30	42	88	27

1974-75

Wigan Athletic	46	33	6	7	94	38	72
Runcorn	46	30	8	8	102	42	68
Altrincham	46	26	12	8	87	43	64
Stafford Rangers	46	25	13	8	81	39	63
Scarborough	46	24	12	10	73	45	60
Mossley	46	23	11	12	78	52	57
Gateshead United	46	22	12	12	74	48	56
Goole Town	46	19	12	15	75	71	50
Northwich Victoria	46	18	12	16	83	71	48
Great Harwood	46	17	14	15	69	66	48
Matlock Town	46	19	8	19	87	79	46
Boston United	46	16	14	16	64	63	46
Morecambe	46	14	15	17	71	87	43
Worksop Town	46	14	14	18	69	66	42
South Liverpool	46	14	14	18	59	71	42
Buxton	46	11	17	18	50	77	39
Macclesfield Town	46	11	14	21	46	62	36
Lancaster City	46	13	10	23	53	76	36
Bangor City	46	13	9	24	56	67	35
Gainsborough Trinity	46	10	15	21	46	79	35
Skelmersdale United	46	13	7	26	63	93	33
Barrow	46	9	15	22	45	72	33
Netherfield	46	12	8	26	42	91	32
Fleetwood	46	5	10	31	26	97	20

1975-76

Runcorn	46	29	10	7	95	42	68
Stafford Rangers	46	26	15	5	81	41	67
Scarborough	46	26	10	10	84	43	62
Matlock Town	46	26	9	11	96	63	61
Boston United	46	27	6	13	95	58	60
Wigan Athletic	46	21	15	10	81	42	57
Altrincham	46	20	14	12	77	57	54
Bangor City	46	21	12	13	80	70	54
Mossley	46	21	11	14	70	58	53
Goole Town	46	20	13	13	58	49	53
Northwich Victoria	46	17	17	12	79	59	51
Lancaster City	46	18	9	19	61	70	45
Worksop Town	46	17	10	19	63	56	44
Gainsborough Trinity	46	13	17	16	58	69	43
Macclesfield Town	46	15	12	19	50	64	42
Gateshead United	46	17	7	22	64	63	41
Buxton	46	11	13	22	37	62	35
Skelmersdale United	46	12	10	24	45	74	34
Netherfield	46	11	11	24	55	76	33
Morecambe	46	11	11	24	47	67	33
Great Harwood	46	13	7	26	58	86	33
South Liverpool	46	12	9	25	45	78	33
Barrow	46	12	9	25	47	84	33
Fleetwood	46	3	9	34	36	131	15

1976-77

Boston United	44	27	11	6	82	35	65
Northwich Victoria	44	27	11	6	85	43	65
Matlock Town	44	26	11	7	108	57	63
Bangor City	44	22	11	11	87	52	55
Scarborough	44	21	12	11	77	66	54
Goole Town	44	23	6	15	64	50	52
Lancaster City	44	21	9	14	71	58	51
Gateshead United	44	18	12	14	80	64	48
Mossley	44	17	14	13	74	59	48
Altrincham	44	19	9	16	60	53	47
Stafford Rangers	44	16	14	14	60	55	46
Runcorn	44	15	14	15	57	49	44
Worksop Town	44	16	12	16	50	58	44
Wigan Athletic	44	14	15	15	62	54	43
Morecambe	44	13	11	20	59	75	37
Gainsborough Trinity	44	13	10	21	58	74	36
Great Harwood	44	11	14	19	63	84	36
Buxton	44	11	13	20	48	63	35
Macclesfield Town	44	8	15	21	41	68	31
Frickley Athletic	44	11	8	25	53	93	30
Barrow	44	11	6	27	56	87	28
South Liverpool	44	10	8	26	51	104	28
Netherfield	44	9	8	27	47	92	26

1977-78

Boston United	46	31	9	6	85	35	71
Wigan Athletic	46	25	15	6	83	45	65
Bangor City	46	26	10	10	92	50	62
Scarborough	46	26	10	10	80	39	62
Altrincham	46	22	15	9	84	49	59
Northwich Victoria	46	22	14	10	83	55	50
Stafford Rangers	46	22	13	11	71	41	57
Runcorn	46	19	18	9	70	44	56
Mossley	46	22	11	13	85	73	55
Matlock Town	46	21	12	13	79	60	54
Lancaster City	46	15	14	17	66	82	44
Frickley Athletic	46	15	12	19	77	81	42
Barrow	46	14	12	20	50	61	40
Goole Town	46	15	9	22	60	68	39
Great Harwood	46	13	13	20	66	83	39
Gainsborough Trinity	46	14	10	22	61	74	38
Gateshead	46	16	5	25	65	74	37
Netherfield	46	11	13	22	50	80	35
Workington	46	13	8	25	48	80	34
Worksop Town	46	12	10	24	45	84	34
Morecambe	46	11	11	24	67	92	33
Macclesfield Town	46	12	9	25	60	92	33
Buxton	46	13	6	27	60	95	32
South Liverpool	46	9	7	30	53	111	25

1978-79

Mossley	44	32	5	7	117	48	69
Altrincham	44	25	11	8	93	39	61
Matlock Town	44	24	8	12	100	59	56
Scarborough	44	19	14	11	61	44	52
Southport	44	19	14	11	62	49	52
Boston United	44	17	18	9	40	33	52
Runcorn	44	21	9	14	79	54	51
Stafford Rangers	44	18	14	12	67	41	50
Goole Town	44	17	15	12	56	61	49
Northwich Victoria	44	18	11	15	64	52	47
Lancaster City	44	17	12	15	62	54	46
Bangor City	44	15	14	15	65	66	44
Worksop Town	44	13	14	17	55	67	40
Workington	44	16	7	21	62	74	39
Netherfield	44	13	11	20	39	69	37
Barrow	44	14	9	21	47	78	37
Gainsborough Trinity	44	12	12	20	52	67	36
Morecambe	44	11	13	20	55	65	35
Frickley Athletic	44	13	9	22	58	70	35
South Liverpool	44	12	10	22	48	85	34
Gateshead	44	11	11	22	42	63	33
Buxton	44	11	9	24	50	84	31
Macclesfield Town	44	8	10	26	40	92	26

1979-80

Mossley	42	28	9	5	96	41	65
Witton Albion	42	28	8	6	89	30	64
Frickley Athletic	42	24	13	5	93	48	61
Burton Albion	42	25	6	11	83	42	56
Matlock Town	42	18	17	7	87	53	53
Buxton	42	21	9	12	61	48	51
Worksop Town	42	20	10	12	65	52	50
Macclesfield Town	42	18	11	13	67	53	47
Grantham	42	18	8	16	71	65	44
Marine	42	16	10	16	65	57	42
Goole Town	42	14	13	15	61	63	41
Lancaster City	42	13	13	16	74	77	39
Oswestry Town	42	12	14	16	44	60	38
Gainsborough Trinity	42	14	8	20	64	75	36
Runcorn	42	11	11	20	46	63	33
Gateshead	42	11	11	20	50	77	33
Morecambe	42	10	12	20	40	59	32
Netherfield	42	7	15	20	37	66	29
Southport	42	8	13	21	30	75	29
South Liverpool	42	7	14	21	51	84	28
Workington	42	8	12	22	50	85	28
Tamworth	42	8	9	25	26	77	25

1980-81

Runcorn	42	32	7	3	99	22	71
Mossley	42	24	7	11	95	55	55
Marine	42	22	10	10	60	41	54
Buxton	42	21	7	14	64	50	49
Gainsborough Trinity	42	17	13	12	50	57	47
Burton Albion	42	19	8	15	63	54	46
Witton Albion	42	19	8	15	70	62	46
Goole Town	42	14	16	12	56	50	44
South Liverpool	42	19	6	17	59	64	44
Workington	42	15	13	14	57	48	43
Gateshead	42	12	18	12	65	61	42
Worksop Town	42	15	11	16	66	61	41
Macclesfield Town	42	13	13	16	52	69	39
Grantham	42	14	9	19	57	74	37
Matlock Town	42	12	12	18	57	80	36
Lancaster City	42	13	9	20	48	70	35
Netherfield	42	11	12	19	73	81	34
Oswestry Town	42	13	8	21	54	67	34
King's Lynn	42	8	18	16	46	65	34
Southport	42	11	11	26	42	68	33
Morecambe	42	11	8	23	42	74	30
Tamworth	42	9	12	21	38	76	30

1981-82

Bangor City	42	27	8	7	108	60	62
Mossley	42	24	11	7	76	43	59
Witton Albion	42	22	10	10	75	44	54
Gateshead	42	19	14	9	65	49	52
King's Lynn	42	19	12	11	61	36	50
Grantham	42	18	13	11	65	53	49
Burton Albion	42	19	9	14	71	62	47
Southport	42	16	14	12	63	55	46
Marine	42	17	12	13	64	57	46
Macclesfield Town	42	17	9	16	67	58	43
Workington	42	18	7	17	62	60	43
Worksop Town	42	15	13	14	52	60	43
South Liverpool	42	13	13	16	55	57	39
Goole Town	42	13	13	16	56	60	39
Oswestry Town	42	14	11	17	55	59	39
Buxton	42	14	11	17	48	56	39
Lancaster City	42	13	12	17	47	50	38
Gainsborough Trinity	42	10	13	19	60	69	33
Tamworth	42	10	9	23	31	56	29
Morecambe	42	9	11	22	43	86	29
Matlock Town	42	7	12	23	38	72	26
Netherfield	42	5	9	28	31	91	19

1982-83

Gateshead	42	32	4	6	114	43	100
Mossley	42	25	9	8	77	42	84
Burton Albion	42	24	9	9	81	53	81
Chorley	42	23	11	8	77	49	80
Macclesfield Town	42	24	8	10	71	49	80
Marine	42	17	17	8	81	57	68
Workington	42	19	10	13	71	55	67
Hyde United	42	18	12	12	91	63	66
King's Lynn	42	17	13	12	62	44	64
Matlock Town	42	18	10	14	70	65	64
Witton Albion	42	17	12	13	82	52	63
Buxton	42	17	9	16	60	62	60
Morecambe	42	16	11	15	75	66	59
Grantham	42	15	13	14	49	50	58
Southport	42	11	14	17	58	65	47
Goole Town	42	13	7	22	52	66	46
Gainsborough Trinity	42	11	9	22	60	71	42
Oswestry Town	42	10	8	24	56	99	38
South Liverpool	42	7	15	20	57	91	36
Tamworth	42	7	8	27	44	97	29
Worksop Town	42	5	10	27	50	98	25
Netherfield	42	2	9	31	28	129	15

1983-84

Barrow	42	29	10	3	92	38	97
Matlock Town	42	23	8	11	72	48	77
South Liverpool	42	22	11	9	55	44	77
Grantham	42	20	8	14	64	51	68
Burton Albion	42	17	13	12	61	47	64
Macclesfield Town	42	18	10	14	65	55	64
Rhyl	42	19	6	17	64	55	63
Horwich	42	18	9	15	64	59	63
Gainsborough Trinity	42	17	11	14	82	66	62
Stafford Rangers	42	15	17	10	65	52	62
Hyde United	42	17	8	17	61	63	59
Marine	42	16	10	16	63	68	58
Witton Albion	42	14	14	14	64	57	56
Chorley	42	14	11	17	68	65	53
Workington	42	14	9	19	53	57	51
Southport	42	14	14	14	64	57	50
Worksop Town	42	13	8	21	57	74	47
Goole Town	42	12	10	20	59	80	46
Morecambe	42	11	12	19	59	75	45
Oswestry Town	42	11	8	23	66	97	41
Buxton	42	11	6	25	52	91	39
Mossley	42	9	9	24	47	74	33

Mossley had 3 points deducted

1984-85

Stafford Rangers	42	26	8	8	81	40	86
Macclesfield Town	42	23	13	6	67	39	82
Witton Albion	42	22	8	12	57	39	74
Hyde United	42	21	8	13	68	52	71
Marine	42	18	15	9	59	34	69
Burton Albion	42	18	15	9	70	49	69
Worksop Town	42	19	10	13	68	56	67
Workington	42	18	9	15	59	53	53
Horwich	42	16	14	12	67	50	62
Bangor City	42	17	9	16	70	61	60
Gainsborough Trinity	42	14	14	14	72	73	56
Southport	42	15	9	18	65	66	54
Matlock Town	42	14	9	19	56	66	51
Oswestry Town	42	14	9	19	59	75	51
Mossley	42	14	9	19	45	65	51
Goole Town	42	13	11	18	60	65	50
Rhyl	42	11	14	17	52	63	47
Morecambe	42	11	14	17	51	67	47
Chorley	42	12	10	20	47	63	46
South Liverpool	42	9	15	18	43	71	42
Grantham	42	8	13	21	41	69	36
Buxton	42	8	6	28	38	79	30

Grantham had 1 point deducted

1985-86

Gateshead	42	24	10	8	85	51	82
Marine	42	23	11	8	63	35	80
Morecambe	42	17	17	8	59	39	68
Gainsborough Trinity	42	18	14	10	66	52	68
Burton Albion	42	18	12	12	64	47	66
Southport	42	17	11	14	70	66	62
Worksop Town	42	17	10	15	51	48	61
Workington	42	14	18	10	54	46	59
Macclesfield Town	42	17	8	17	67	65	59
Hyde United	42	14	15	13	63	62	57
Witton Albion	42	15	13	14	56	59	57
Mossley	42	13	16	13	56	60	55
Bangor City	42	13	15	14	51	51	54
Rhyl	42	14	10	18	65	71	52
South Liverpool	42	11	17	14	43	44	50
Horwich	42	15	6	21	53	63	50
Caernarfon Town	42	11	17	14	51	63	50
Oswestry Town	42	12	13	17	51	60	49
Buxton	42	11	12	19	55	76	45
Chorley	42	9	15	18	56	64	42
Matlock Town	42	9	15	18	59	75	42
Goole Town	42	7	11	24	37	78	31

Workington, Witton Albion, Horwich and Goole Town all had 1 point deducted.

1986-87

Macclesfield Town	42	26	10	6	80	47	88
Bangor City	42	25	12	5	74	35	87
Caernarfon Town	42	20	16	6	67	40	76
Marine	42	21	10	11	70	43	73
South Liverpool	42	21	10	11	58	40	73
Morecambe	42	20	12	10	68	49	72
Matlock Town	42	20	10	12	81	67	70
Southport	42	19	11	12	67	49	68
Chorley	42	16	12	14	58	59	60
Mossley	42	15	12	15	57	52	57
Hyde United	42	15	10	17	81	70	55
Burton Albion	42	16	6	20	56	68	54
Buxton	42	13	14	15	71	68	53
Witton Albion	42	15	8	19	68	79	53
Barrow	42	15	7	20	42	57	52
Goole Town	42	13	12	17	58	62	51
Oswestry Town	42	14	8	20	55	83	50
Rhyl	42	10	15	17	56	74	45
Worksop Town	42	9	13	20	56	74	40
Gainsborough Trinity	42	9	10	23	53	77	37
Workington	42	5	14	23	38	70	28
Horwich RMI	42	3	12	27	36	85	20

Workington and Horwich RMI both had 1 point deducted.

1987-88

Premier Division

Chorley	42	26	10	6	78	35	88
Hyde United	42	25	10	7	91	52	85
Caernarfon Town	42	22	10	10	56	34	76
Morecambe	42	19	15	8	61	41	72
Barrow	42	21	8	13	70	41	71
Worksop Town	42	20	11	11	74	55	71
Bangor City	42	20	10	12	71	55	70
Rhyl	42	18	13	11	70	42	67
Marine	42	19	10	13	67	45	67
Frickley Athletic	42	18	11	13	61	55	65
Witton Albion	42	16	12	14	61	47	60
Goole Town	42	17	9	16	71	61	60
Horwich	42	17	9	16	46	42	60
Southport	42	15	12	15	43	48	57
South Liverpool	42	10	19	13	56	64	49
Buxton	42	11	14	17	72	76	47
Mossley	42	11	11	20	54	75	44
Gateshead	42	11	7	24	52	71	40
Matlock Town	42	10	8	24	58	89	38
Gainsborough Trinity	42	8	10	24	38	81	34
Oswestry Town	42	6	10	26	44	101	28
Workington	42	6	3	33	28	113	21

First Division

Fleetwood Town	36	22	7	7	85	45	73
Stalybridge Celtic	36	22	6	8	72	42	72
Leek Town	36	20	10	6	63	38	70
Accrington Stanley	36	21	6	9	71	39	69
Farsley Celtic	36	18	9	9	64	48	60
Droylsden	36	16	10	10	63	48	58
Eastwood Hanley	36	14	12	10	50	37	54
Winsford United	36	15	6	15	59	47	51
Congleton Town	36	12	16	8	43	39	51
Harrogate Town	36	13	9	14	51	50	48
Alfreton Town	36	13	8	15	53	54	47
Radcliffe Borough	36	11	13	12	66	62	46
Irlam Town	36	12	10	14	39	45	46
Penrith	36	11	11	14	46	51	44
Sutton Town	36	11	5	20	51	96	38
Lancaster City	36	10	6	20	45	72	36
Eastwood Town	36	8	10	18	45	65	34
Curzon Ashton	36	8	4	24	43	73	28
Netherfield	36	4	4	28	35	93	16

Congleton Town had 1 point deducted
Farsley Celtic had 3 points deducted

1988-89

Premier Division

Barrow	42	26	9	7	89	35	87
Hyde United	42	24	8	10	77	44	80
Witton Albion	42	22	13	7	67	39	79
Bangor City	42	22	10	10	77	48	76
Marine	42	23	7	12	69	48	76
Goole Town	42	22	7	13	75	60	73
Fleetwood Town	42	19	16	7	53	44	73
Rhyl	42	18	10	14	75	65	64
Frickley Athletic	42	17	10	15	64	53	61
Mossley	42	17	9	16	56	58	60
South Liverpool	42	15	13	14	65	57	58
Caernarfon Town	42	15	10	17	49	53	55
Matlock Town	42	16	5	21	65	73	53
Southport	42	13	12	17	66	52	51
Buxton	42	12	14	16	61	63	50
Morecambe	42	13	9	20	55	60	47
Gainsborough Trinity	42	12	11	19	56	73	47
Shepshed Charterhouse	42	14	8	20	19	80	44
Stalybridge Celtic	42	9	13	20	16	81	40
Horwich	42	7	14	21	12	70	35
Gateshead	42	7	13	22	36	70	34
Worksop Town	42	6	5	31	42	103	23

Morecambe had 1 point deducted
Shepshed Charterhouse had 6 points deducted

First Division

Colne Dynamo	42	30	11	1	102	21	98
Bishop Auckland	42	28	5	9	78	28	89
Leek Town	42	25	11	6	74	41	85
Droylsden	42	25	9	8	84	48	84
Whitley Bay	42	23	6	13	77	49	75
Accrington Stanley	42	21	10	11	81	60	73
Lancaster City	42	21	8	13	76	54	71
Harrogate Town	42	19	7	16	68	61	64
Newtown	42	15	12	15	65	59	57
Congleton Town	42	15	11	16	62	66	56
Workington	42	17	3	22	59	74	54
Eastwood Town	42	14	10	13	55	61	52
Curzon Ashton	42	13	11	18	74	72	50
Farsley Celtic	42	12	13	17	52	73	49
Irlam Town	42	11	14	17	53	63	47
Penrith	42	14	5	23	61	91	47
Radcliffe Borough	42	12	10	20	62	86	46
Eastwood Hanley	42	11	12	10	46	67	45
Winsford United	42	13	6	23	58	93	35
Alfreton Town	42	8	11	23	44	92	35
Netherfield	42	8	9	25	57	90	32
Sutton Town	42	7	6	29	70	109	23

Leek Town and Netherfield both had 1 point deducted
Colne Dynamo had 3 points deducted
Sutton Town had 4 points deducted

1989-90

Premier Division

Colne Dynamoes	42	32	6	4	86	40	102
Gateshead	42	22	10	10	78	58	76
Witton Albion	42	22	7	13	67	39	73
Hyde United	42	21	8	13	73	50	71
South Liverpool	42	20	9	13	89	79	69
Matlock Town	42	18	12	12	61	42	66
Southport	42	17	14	11	54	48	65
Fleetwood Town	42	17	12	13	73	66	63
Marine	42	16	14	12	59	55	62
Bangor City	42	15	15	12	64	58	60
Bishop Auckland	42	17	8	17	72	64	59
Frickley Athletic	42	16	8	18	56	61	56
Horwich	42	15	13	14	66	69	55
Morecambe	42	15	9	18	58	70	54
Gainsborough Trinity	42	16	8	18	59	55	53
Buxton	42	15	8	19	59	72	53
Stalybridge Celtic	42	12	9	21	48	61	45
Mossley	42	11	10	21	61	82	43
Goole Town	42	12	5	25	54	77	41
Shepshed	42	11	7	24	55	82	40
Caernarfon Town	42	10	8	24	56	86	38
Rhyl	42	7	10	25	43	77	30

Rhyl had 1 point deducted
Horwich and Gainsborough Trinity both had 3 points deducted

First Division

Leek Town	42	26	8	8	70	31	86
Droylsden	42	27	6	9	81	46	80
Accrington Stanley	42	22	10	10	80	53	76
Whitley Bay	42	21	11	10	93	59	74
Emley	42	20	9	13	70	42	69
Congleton Town	42	20	12	10	65	53	69
Winsford United	42	18	10	14	65	53	64
Curzon Ashton	42	17	11	14	66	60	62
Harrogate Town	42	17	9	16	68	62	60
Lancaster City	42	15	14	13	73	54	59
Eastwood Town	42	16	11	15	61	64	59
Farsley Celtic	42	17	6	19	71	75	57
Rossendale United	42	15	9	18	73	69	54
Newtown	42	14	12	16	49	62	54
Irlam Town	42	14	11	17	61	66	53
Workington	42	14	8	20	56	64	50
Radcliffe Borough	42	14	7	21	47	63	49
Alfreton Town	42	13	8	21	59	85	47
Worksop Town	42	13	5	24	56	95	44
Netherfield	42	11	6	25	56	89	39
Eastwood Hanley	42	10	6	26	45	76	36
Penrith	42	9	9	24	44	88	36

Congleton Town 3 points deducted. Droylsden 7 points deducted.

1990-91

Premier Division

Witton Albion	40	28	9	3	81	31	93
Stalybridge Celtic	40	22	11	7	44	26	77
Morecambe	40	19	16	5	72	44	73
Fleetwood Town	40	20	9	11	69	44	69
Southport	40	18	14	8	66	48	68
Marine	40	18	11	11	56	39	65
Bishop Auckland	40	17	10	13	62	56	61
Buxton	40	17	11	12	66	61	59
Leek Town	40	15	11	14	48	44	56
Frickley Athletic	40	16	6	18	64	62	54
Hyde United	40	14	11	15	73	63	53
Goole Town	40	14	10	16	68	74	52
Droylsden	40	12	11	17	67	70	47
Chorley	40	12	10	18	55	55	46
Mossley	40	13	10	17	55	68	45
Horwich	40	13	6	21	62	81	45
Matlock Town	40	12	7	21	52	70	43
Bangor City	40	9	12	19	52	70	39
South Liverpool	40	10	9	21	58	92	39
Gainsborough Trinity	40	9	11	20	57	84	38
Shepshed Charterhouse	40	6	7	27	38	83	25

First Division

Whitley Bay	42	25	10	7	95	38	85
Emley	42	24	12	6	78	37	84
Worksop Town	42	25	7	10	85	56	82
Accrington Stanley	42	21	13	8	83	57	76
Rhyl	42	21	7	14	62	63	70
Eastwood Town	42	17	11	14	70	60	62
Warrington Town	42	17	10	15	68	52	61
Lancaster City	42	19	8	15	58	56	61
Bridlington Town	42	15	15	12	72	52	60
Curzon Ashton	42	14	14	14	49	57	56
Congleton Town	42	14	12	16	57	71	54
Netherfield	42	14	11	17	67	66	53
Newtown	42	13	12	17	68	75	51
Caernarfon Town	42	13	10	19	51	64	49
Rossendale United	42	12	13	17	66	67	48
Radcliffe Borough	42	12	12	18	50	69	48
Irlam Town	42	12	11	19	55	76	47
Winsford United	42	11	13	18	51	66	46
Harrogate Town	42	11	13	18	55	73	46
Workington	42	11	11	20	54	67	41
Farsley Celtic	42	11	9	22	49	78	39
Alfreton Town	42	7	12	23	41	84	33

1991-92

Premier Division

Stalybridge Celtic	42	26	14	2	84	33	92
Marine	42	23	9	10	64	32	78
Morecambe	42	21	13	8	70	44	76
Leek Town	42	21	10	11	62	49	73
Buxton	42	21	9	12	65	47	72
Emley	42	18	11	13	69	47	65
Southport	42	16	17	9	57	48	65
Accrington Stanley	42	17	12	13	78	62	63
Hyde United	42	17	9	16	69	67	60
Fleetwood United	42	17	8	17	67	64	59
Bishop Auckland	42	16	9	17	48	58	57
Goole Town	42	15	9	18	60	72	54
Horwich	42	13	14	15	44	52	53
Frickley Athletic	42	12	16	14	61	57	52
Droylsden	42	12	14	16	62	72	50
Mossley	42	15	4	23	51	73	49
Whitley Bay	42	13	9	20	53	79	48
Gainsborough Trinity	42	11	13	18	48	63	46
Matlock Town	42	12	9	21	59	87	45
Bangor City	42	11	10	21	46	57	43
Chorley	42	11	9	22	61	82	42
Shepshed Albion	42	6	8	28	46	79	26

First Division

Colwyn Bay	42	30	4	8	99	49	94
Winsford United	42	29	6	7	96	41	93
Worksop Town	42	25	5	12	101	54	80
Guiseley	42	22	12	8	93	56	78
Caernarfon Town	42	23	9	10	78	47	78
Bridlington Town	42	22	9	11	86	46	75
Warrington Town	42	20	8	14	79	64	68
Knowsley United	42	18	10	14	69	52	64
Netherfield	42	18	7	17	54	61	61
Harrogate Town	42	14	16	12	73	69	58
Curzon Ashton	42	15	9	18	71	83	54
Farsley Celtic	42	15	9	18	79	101	53
Radcliffe Borough	42	15	9	18	67	72	51
Newtown	42	15	6	21	60	95	51
Eastwood Town	42	13	11	18	59	70	50
Lancaster City	42	10	19	13	55	62	49
Congleton Town	42	14	5	23	59	81	47
Rhyl	42	11	10	21	59	69	43
Rossendale United	42	9	11	22	61	90	38
Alfreton Town	42	12	2	28	63	98	38
Irlam Town	42	9	7	26	45	95	33
Workington	42	7	8	27	45	99	28

Farsley Celtic 1 point deducted. Radcliffe Borough 3 points deducted.

1992-93

Premier Division

Southport	42	29	9	4	103	31	96
Winsford United	42	27	9	6	91	43	90
Morecambe	42	25	11	6	93	51	86
Marine	42	26	8	8	83	47	86
Leek Town	42	21	11	10	86	51	74
Accrington Stanley	42	20	13	9	79	45	73
Frickley Athletic	42	21	6	15	62	52	69
Barrow	42	18	11	13	71	55	65
Hyde United	42	17	13	12	87	71	64
Bishop Auckland	42	17	11	14	63	52	62
Gainsborough Trinity	42	17	8	17	63	66	59
Colwyn Bay	42	16	6	20	80	79	54
Horwich	42	14	10	18	72	79	52
Buxton	42	13	10	19	60	75	49
Matlock Town	42	13	11	18	56	79	47
Emley	42	13	6	23	62	91	45
Whitley Bay	42	11	8	23	57	96	41
Chorley	42	10	10	22	52	93	40
Fleetwood Town	42	10	7	25	50	77	37
Droylsden	42	10	7	25	47	84	37
Mossley	42	7	8	27	53	95	29
Goole Town	42	6	9	27	47	105	27

Matlock Town had 3 points deducted

First Division

Bridlington Town	40	25	11	4	84	35	86
Knowsley United	40	23	7	10	86	48	76
Ashton United	40	22	8	10	81	54	74
Guiseley	40	20	10	10	90	64	70
Warrington Town	40	19	10	11	85	57	67
Gretna	40	17	12	11	64	47	63
Curzon Ashton	40	16	15	9	69	63	63
Great Harwood Town	40	17	9	14	66	57	60
Alfreton Town	40	15	9	16	80	80	54
Harrogate Town	40	14	12	14	77	81	54
Worksop Town	40	15	9	16	66	70	54
Radcliffe Borough	40	13	14	13	66	69	53
Workington	40	13	13	14	51	61	52
Eastwood Town	40	3	11	16	49	52	50
Netherfield	40	11	14	15	68	63	47
Caernarfon Town	40	13	8	19	66	74	47
Farsley Celtic	40	12	8	20	64	77	44
Lancaster City	40	10	12	18	49	76	42
Shepshed Albion	40	9	12	19	46	66	39
Congleton Town	40	10	7	23	58	95	37
Rossendale United	40	5	5	30	50	126	20

1993-94

Premier Division

Marine	42	27	9	6	106	62	90
Leek Town	42	27	8	7	79	50	89
Boston United	42	23	9	10	90	43	78
Bishop Auckland	42	23	9	10	73	58	78
Frickley Athletic	42	21	12	9	90	51	75
Colwyn Bay	42	18	14	10	74	51	68
Morecambe	42	20	7	15	90	56	67
Barrow	42	18	10	14	59	51	64
Hyde United	42	17	10	15	80	71	61
Chorley	42	17	10	15	70	67	61
Whitley Bay	42	17	9	16	61	72	60
Gainsborough Trinity	42	15	11	16	64	66	56
Emley	42	12	16	14	63	71	52
Matlock Town	42	13	12	17	71	76	51
Buxton	42	13	10	19	67	73	49
Accrington Stanley	42	14	7	21	63	85	49
Droylsden	42	11	14	17	57	82	47
Knowsley United	42	11	11	20	52	66	44
Winsford United	42	9	11	22	50	74	38
Horwich RMI	42	8	12	22	50	75	35
Bridlington Town	42	7	10	25	41	91	28
Fleetwood Town	42	7	7	28	55	114	28

Horwich RMI 1 point deducted. Bridlington Town 3 points deducted

First Division

Guiseley	40	29	6	5	87	37	93
Spennymoor United	40	25	6	9	95	50	81
Ashton United	40	24	7	9	85	41	79
Lancaster City	40	20	10	10	74	46	70
Netherfield	40	20	6	14	68	60	66
Alfreton Town	40	18	10	12	83	70	64
Warrington Town	40	17	11	12	52	48	62
Goole Town	40	16	11	13	72	58	59
Great Harwood Town	40	15	14	11	56	60	59
Gretna	40	16	7	17	64	65	55
Workington	40	14	10	16	70	74	52
Worksop Town	40	14	9	17	79	87	51
Bamber Bridge	40	13	11	16	62	59	50
Curzon Ashton	40	13	8	19	62	71	47
Congleton Town	40	12	9	19	53	68	45
Radcliffe Borough	40	10	14	16	62	75	44
Mossley	40	10	12	18	44	68	39
Caernarfon Town	40	9	11	20	54	88	38
Farsley Celtic	40	6	16	18	42	77	34
Harrogate Town	40	8	9	23	40	86	33
Eastwood Town	40	7	11	22	47	63	32

Mossley had 3 points deducted

1994-95

Premier Division

Marine	42	29	11	2	83	27	98
Morecambe	42	28	10	4	99	34	94
Guiseley	42	28	9	5	96	50	93
Hyde United	42	22	10	10	89	59	76
Boston United	42	20	11	11	80	43	71
Spennymoor United	42	20	11	11	66	52	71
Buxton	42	18	9	15	65	62	63
Gainsborough Trinity	42	16	13	13	69	61	61
Bishop Auckland	42	16	12	14	68	55	57
Witton Albion	42	14	14	14	54	56	56
Barrow	42	17	5	20	68	71	56
Colwyn Bay	42	16	8	18	71	80	56
Emley	42	14	13	15	62	68	55
Matlock Town	42	15	5	22	62	72	50
Accrington Stanley	42	12	13	17	55	77	49
Knowsley United	42	11	14	17	64	83	47
Winsford United	42	10	11	21	56	75	41
Chorley	42	11	7	24	64	87	40
Frickley Athletic	42	10	10	22	53	79	40
Droylsden	42	10	8	24	56	93	38
Whitley Bay	42	8	8	26	46	97	32
Horwich RMI	42	9	4	29	49	94	31

Bishop Auckland had 3 points deducted

First Division

Blyth Spartans	42	26	9	7	95	55	87
Bamber Bridge	42	25	10	7	101	51	85
Warrington Town	42	25	9	8	74	40	84
Alfreton Town	42	25	7	10	94	49	82
Lancaster City	42	23	10	9	81	44	79
Worksop Town	42	19	14	9	95	68	71
Radcliffe Borough	42	18	10	14	76	70	64
Ashton United	42	18	10	14	80	70	64
Netherfield	42	17	7	118	54	56	58
Eastwood Town	42	14	13	15	67	61	55
Gretna	42	14	13	15	64	66	55
Atherton Laburnum Rovers	42	14	8	20	60	67	50
Harrogate Town	42	14	8	20	57	78	50
Caernarfon Town	42	13	10	19	59	62	49
Curzon Ashton	42	10	16	16	64	80	46
Great Harwood Town	42	11	13	18	66	87	46
Congleton Town	42	11	13	18	52	75	46
Fleetwood	42	12	11	19	51	74	44
Farsley Celtic	42	12	7	23	66	100	43
Workington	42	12	6	24	61	91	42
Goole Town	42	11	7	24	46	81	40
Mossley	42	11	5	26	52	90	37

Mossley had 1 point deducted. Fleetwood had 3 points deducted

1995-96

Premier Division

Bamber Bridge	42	20	16	6	81	49	76
Boston United	42	23	6	13	86	59	75
Hyde United	42	21	11	10	86	51	74
Barrow	42	20	13	9	69	42	73
Gainsborough Trinity	42	20	13	9	60	41	73
Blyth Spartans	42	17	13	12	75	61	64
Accrington Stanley	42	17	14	11	62	54	62
Emley	42	17	10	15	57	53	61
Spennymoor United	42	14	18	10	67	61	60
Guiseley	42	15	14	13	62	57	59
Bishop Auckland	42	16	11	15	60	55	59
Marine	42	15	14	13	59	54	59
Witton Albion	42	17	8	17	60	62	59
Chorley	42	14	9	19	67	74	48
Knowsley United	42	14	6	22	61	89	48
Winsford United	42	10	16	16	56	79	46
Leek Town	42	10	15	17	52	55	45
Colwyn Bay	42	8	21	13	43	57	45
Frickley Athletic	42	11	14	17	63	87	44
Buxton	42	9	11	22	43	72	38
Droylsden	42	10	8	24	58	100	38
Matlock Town	42	8	11	23	71	86	35

Accrington Stanley, Chorley & Frickley Town all had 3 points deducted

First Division

Lancaster City	40	24	11	5	79	38	83
Alfreton Town	40	23	9	8	79	47	78
Lincoln United	40	22	7	11	80	56	73
Curzon Ashton	40	20	7	13	73	53	67
Farsley Celtic	40	19	9	12	66	61	66
Radcliffe Borough	40	17	13	10	70	48	64
Eastwood Town	40	18	9	13	60	47	63
Whitley Bay	40	18	8	14	72	62	62
Ashton United	40	19	7	14	73	65	60
Atherton Laburnum Rovers	40	15	12	13	60	61	57
Worksop Town	40	16	8	16	84	90	56
Gretna	40	13	13	14	75	65	52
Warrington Town	40	13	10	17	75	72	49
Leigh	40	14	7	19	53	59	49
Netherfield	40	13	10	17	64	73	49
Workington	40	11	12	17	50	62	45
Bradford Park Avenue	40	9	14	17	57	72	41
Congleton Town	40	11	11	18	36	59	41
Great Harwood Town	40	9	7	24	44	78	33
Fleetwood	40	7	10	23	41	81	31
Harrogate Town	40	7	10	23	54	96	31

Great Harwood Town had 1 point deducted, Congleton Town had 3 points deducted and Ashton United had 4 points deducted

1996-97

Premier Division

Leek Town	44	28	9	7	71	35	93
Bishop Auckland	44	23	14	7	88	43	83
Hyde United	44	22	16	6	93	46	82
Emley	44	23	12	9	89	54	81
Barrow	44	23	11	10	71	45	80
Boston United	44	22	13	9	74	47	79
Blyth Spartans	44	22	11	11	74	49	77
Marine	44	20	15	9	53	37	75
Guiseley	44	20	11	13	63	54	71
Gainsborough Trinity	44	18	12	14	65	46	66
Accrington Stanley	44	18	12	14	77	70	66
Runcorn	44	15	15	14	63	62	60
Chorley	44	16	9	19	69	66	57
Winsford United	44	13	14	17	50	56	53
Knowsley United	44	12	14	18	58	79	49
Colwyn Bay	44	11	13	20	60	76	46
Lancaster City	44	12	9	23	48	75	45
Frickley Athletic	44	12	8	24	62	91	44
Spennymoor United	44	10	10	24	52	68	40
Bamber Bridge	44	11	7	26	59	99	40
Alfreton Town	44	8	13	23	45	83	37
Witton Albion	44	5	14	25	41	91	39
Buxton	44	5	12	27	33	86	27

Knowsley United had 1 point deducted

First Division

Radcliffe Borough	42	26	7	9	77	33	85
Leigh	42	24	11	7	65	33	83
Lincoln United	42	25	8	9	78	47	83
Farsley Celtic	42	23	8	11	75	48	77
Worksop Town	42	20	12	10	68	38	69
Stocksbridge Park Steels	42	19	11	12	66	54	68
Bradford Park Avenue	42	20	8	14	58	50	68
Ashton United	42	17	14	11	73	52	65
Great Harwood Town	42	16	12	14	56	46	60
Droylsden	42	15	14	13	69	67	59
Matlock Town	42	16	10	16	61	69	58
Whitley Bay	42	14	12	16	47	54	54
Flixton	42	15	7	20	57	72	52
Netherfield	42	12	14	16	54	56	50
Eastwood Town	42	12	14	16	42	50	50
Gretna	42	10	18	14	55	68	48
Harrogate Town	42	13	8	21	55	76	47
Congleton Town	42	12	9	21	47	64	45
Workington	42	10	12	20	45	63	42
Curzon Ashton	42	8	10	24	48	79	34
Warrington Town	42	5	18	19	42	79	33
Atherton Laburnum Rovers	42	7	9	26	45	85	30

Worksop Town had 3 points deducted

1997-98

Premier Division

Barrow	42	25	8	9	61	29	83
Boston United	42	22	12	8	55	40	78
Leigh RMI	42	21	13	8	63	41	76
Runcorn	42	22	9	11	80	50	75
Gainsborough Trinity	42	22	9	11	60	39	75
Emley	42	22	8	12	81	61	74
Winsford United	42	19	12	11	54	43	69
Altrincham	42	18	11	13	76	44	65
Guiseley	42	16	16	10	61	53	64
Bishop Auckland	42	17	12	13	78	60	63
Marine	42	15	11	16	56	59	56
Hyde United	42	13	16	13	60	55	55
Colwyn Bay	42	15	9	18	53	57	54
Spennymoor United	42	14	11	17	58	72	52
Chorley	42	14	7	21	51	70	49
Frickley Athletic	42	12	12	18	45	62	48
Lancaster City	42	13	8	21	55	74	47
Blyth Spartans	42	12	13	17	52	63	39
Bamber Bridge	42	9	12	21	51	74	39
Accrington Stanley	42	8	14	20	49	68	38
Radcliffe Borough	42	6	12	24	39	70	30
Alfreton Town	42	3	13	26	32	86	22

Spennymoor United had 1 point deducted
Blyth Spartans had 10 points deducted

First Division

Whitby Town	42	30	8	4	99	48	98
Worksop Town	42	28	7	7	93	44	91
Ashton Town	42	26	9	7	93	43	87
Droylsden	42	24	8	10	70	49	80
Lincoln United	42	20	11	11	76	62	71
Farsley Celtic	42	20	10	12	72	66	70
Witton Albion	42	19	9	14	77	55	66
Eastwood Town	42	18	12	12	68	51	66
Bradford Park Avenue	42	18	11	13	62	46	65
Belper Town	42	18	7	17	68	66	61
Stocksbridge Park Steels	42	17	9	16	68	63	60
Trafford	42	16	6	20	59	61	54
Whitley Bay	42	14	12	16	60	63	54
Matlock Town	42	14	11	17	68	65	53
Gretna	42	13	9	20	58	64	48
Netherfield	42	12	11	19	55	75	47
Flixton	42	10	12	20	45	73	42
Congleton Town	42	11	8	23	65	101	41
Harrogate Town	42	8	14	20	57	80	38
Great Harwood Town	42	8	12	22	42	88	36
Workington	42	8	7	27	38	84	31
Buxton	42	7	3	32	41	87	24

1998-99

Premier Division

Altrincham	42	23	11	8	67	33	80
Worksop Town	42	22	10	10	66	48	76
Guiseley	42	21	9	12	64	47	72
Bamber Bridge	42	18	15	9	63	48	69
Gateshead	42	18	11	13	69	58	65
Gainsborough Trinity	42	19	8	15	65	59	65
Whitby Town	42	17	13	12	77	62	64
Leigh	42	16	15	11	63	54	63
Hyde United	42	16	11	15	61	48	59
Stalybridge Celtic	42	16	11	15	71	63	59
Winsford United	42	14	15	13	56	52	57
Runcorn	42	12	19	11	46	49	55
Emley	42	12	17	13	47	49	53
Blyth Spartans	42	14	9	19	56	64	51
Colwyn Bay	42	12	13	17	60	71	49
Frickley Athletic	42	11	15	16	55	71	48
Marine	42	10	17	15	61	69	47
Spennymoor United	42	12	11	19	52	71	47
Lancaster City	42	11	13	18	50	62	46
Bishop Auckland	42	10	15	17	49	67	45
Chorley	42	8	15	19	45	68	39
Accrington Stanley	42	9	9	24	47	77	36

First Division

Droylsden	42	26	8	8	97	55	86
Hucknall Town	42	26	11	5	80	38	86
Ashton United	42	22	12	8	79	46	78
Lincoln United	42	20	12	10	94	65	72
Eastwood Town	42	20	8	14	65	69	68
Radcliffe Borough	42	19	8	15	78	62	65
Burscough	42	19	8	15	67	61	65
Witton Albion	42	18	9	15	70	63	63
Bradford Park Avenue	42	17	11	14	64	55	62
Stocksbridge Park Steels	42	16	13	13	64	60	61
Harrogate Town	42	17	7	18	75	77	58
Gretna	42	16	10	16	73	80	58
Belper Town	42	15	11	16	58	57	56
Trafford	42	14	11	17	50	58	53
Netherfield Kendal	42	13	10	19	51	64	49
Flixton	42	12	12	18	50	64	48
Matlock Town	42	14	6	22	53	72	48
Farsley Celtic	42	11	13	18	56	73	46
Whitley Bay	42	10	9	23	53	77	39
Congleton Town	42	8	15	19	65	91	39
Great Harwood Town	42	10	8	24	51	73	38
Alfreton Town	42	9	8	25	53	86	35

Hucknall Town had 3 points deducted

1999-2000

Premier Division

Leigh	44	28	8	8	91	45	92
Hyde United	44	24	13	7	77	44	85
Gateshead	44	23	13	8	79	41	82
Marine	44	21	16	7	78	46	79
Emley	44	20	12	12	54	41	72
Lancaster City	44	20	11	13	65	55	71
Stalybridge Celtic	44	18	12	14	64	54	66
Bishop Auckland	44	18	11	15	63	61	65
Runcorn	44	18	10	16	64	55	64
Worksop Town	44	19	6	19	78	65	63
Gainsborough Trinity	44	16	15	13	59	49	63
Whitby Town	44	15	13	16	66	66	58
Barrow	44	14	15	15	65	59	57
Blyth Spartans	44	15	9	20	62	67	54
Droylsden	44	14	12	18	53	60	54
Frickley Athletic	44	15	9	20	64	85	54
Bamber Bridge	44	14	11	19	70	67	53
Hucknall Town	44	14	11	19	55	61	53
Leek Town	44	14	10	20	58	79	52
Colwyn Bay	44	12	12	20	46	85	48
Spennymoor United	44	10	13	21	41	71	42
Guiseley	44	8	17	19	52	72	41
Winsford United	44	3	7	34	40	116	16

Spennymoor United had 1 point deducted

First Division

Accrington Stanley	42	25	9	8	96	43	84
Burscough	42	22	18	2	81	35	84
Witton Albion	42	23	15	4	88	46	84
Bradford Park Avenue	42	23	9	10	77	48	78
Radcliffe Borough	42	22	12	8	71	48	78
Farsley Celtic	42	19	11	12	66	52	68
Matlock Town	42	17	16	9	72	55	67
Ossett Town	42	17	8	17	77	55	59
Stocksbridge Park Steels	42	16	8	18	55	70	56
Eastwood Town	42	15	11	16	64	65	55
Harrogate Town	42	14	12	16	65	67	54
Congleton Town	42	14	12	16	63	73	54
Chorley	42	13	15	14	53	64	54
Ashton United	42	12	16	14	65	67	52
Workington	42	13	13	16	49	55	52
Lincoln United	42	13	12	17	52	80	51
Belper Town	42	13	11	18	59	72	50
Trafford	42	11	12	19	55	63	45
Gretna	42	11	7	24	48	78	40
Netherfield Kendal	42	8	9	25	46	82	33
Flixton	42	7	9	26	47	85	30
Whitley Bay	42	7	9	26	41	87	30

Eastwood Town had 1 point deducted

2000-2001

Premier Division

Stalybridge Celtic	44	31	9	4	96	32	102
Emley	44	31	8	5	86	42	101
Bishop Auckland	44	26	7	11	89	53	85
Lancaster City	44	24	9	11	84	60	81
Worksop Town	44	20	13	11	102	60	73
Barrow	44	21	9	14	83	53	72
Altrincham	44	20	10	14	80	59	70
Gainsborough Trinity	44	17	14	13	59	56	65
Accrington Stanley	44	18	10	16	72	65	64
Hucknall Town	44	17	12	15	57	63	63
Gateshead	44	16	12	16	67	61	60
Bamber Bridge	44	17	8	19	63	65	59
Runcorn	44	15	10	19	56	71	55
Blyth Spartans	44	15	9	20	61	64	54
Burscough	44	14	10	20	59	68	52
Hyde United	44	13	12	19	72	79	51
Whitby Town	44	13	11	20	60	76	50
Marine	44	12	13	19	62	78	49
Colwyn Bay	44	12	10	22	68	102	46
Frickley Athletic	44	10	15	19	50	79	45
Droylsden	44	13	6	25	50	80	45
Leek Town	44	12	8	24	45	70	44
Spennymoor United	44	4	5	35	32	108	17

First Division

Bradford Park Avenue	42	28	5	9	83	40	89
Vauxhall Motors	42	23	10	9	95	50	79
Ashton United	42	23	9	10	91	49	78
Stocksbridge Park Steels	42	19	13	10	80	60	70
Trafford	42	20	9	13	70	62	68
Belper Town	42	18	11	13	71	62	65
Witton Albion	42	15	16	11	51	50	61
Ossett Town	42	16	12	14	66	58	60
Radcliffe Borough	42	17	8	17	72	71	59
Chorley	42	15	14	13	71	70	59
Harrogate Town	42	15	10	17	60	70	55
Matlock Town	42	14	10	18	70	74	52
North Ferriby United	42	14	10	18	64	73	52
Workington	42	13	12	17	53	60	51
Lincoln United	42	13	12	17	60	75	51
Gretna	42	12	12	18	72	82	48
Guiseley	42	11	15	16	37	50	48
Kendal Town	42	12	12	18	60	69	47
Farsley Celtic	42	12	11	19	53	71	47
Eastwood Town	42	12	8	21	40	63	47
Winsford United	42	13	11	18	61	70	44
Congleton Town	42	13	6	28	43	94	30

Trafford and Kendal Town both had 1 point deducted
Winsford United had 6 points deducted

2001-2002

Premier Division

Burton Albion	44	31	11	2	106	30	104
Vauxhall Motors	44	27	8	9	86	55	89
Lancaster City	44	23	9	12	80	57	78
Worksop Town	44	23	9	12	74	51	78
Emley	44	22	9	13	69	55	75
Accrington Stanley	44	21	9	14	89	64	72
Runcorn FC Halton	44	21	8	15	76	53	71
Barrow	44	19	10	15	75	59	67
Altrincham	44	19	9	16	66	58	66
Bradford Park Avenue	44	18	5	21	77	76	59
Droylsden	44	17	8	19	65	78	59
Blyth Spartans	44	14	16	14	59	62	58
Frickley Athletic	44	16	11	17	63	69	58
Gateshead	44	14	14	16	58	71	56
Whitby Town	44	15	8	21	61	76	53
Hucknall Town	44	14	9	21	50	68	51
Marine	44	11	17	16	62	71	50
Burscough	44	15	5	24	69	86	50
Gainsborough Trinity	44	13	10	21	61	76	49
Colwyn Bay	44	12	11	21	49	82	47
Bishop Auckland	44	12	8	24	46	68	44
Hyde United	44	10	10	24	61	87	40
Bamber Bridge	44	7	10	27	38	88	30

First Division

Harrogate Town	42	25	11	6	80	35	86
Ossett Town	42	21	13	8	73	44	76
Ashton United	42	21	12	9	90	63	75
Spennymoor United	42	22	6	14	75	73	72
Radcliffe Borough	42	20	8	14	73	51	68
Leek Town	42	20	8	14	67	51	68
Gretna	42	19	7	16	66	66	63
Eastwood Town	42	17	11	14	61	59	62
Rossendale United	42	17	10	15	69	58	61
Witton Albion	42	17	10	15	72	68	61
Guiseley	42	18	7	17	60	67	61
North Ferriby United	42	14	16	12	71	60	58
Chorley	42	16	9	17	59	57	57
Matlock Town	42	15	9	18	49	48	54
Trafford	42	14	9	19	64	80	51
Workington	42	12	12	18	51	57	48
Farsley Celtic	42	12	11	19	64	78	47
Belper Town	42	12	11	19	49	66	47
Lincoln United	42	11	14	17	62	80	47
Stocksbridge Park Steels	42	12	9	21	55	76	45
Kendal Town	42	9	9	24	52	76	36
Ossett Albion	42	8	8	26	43	92	32

Division One

Alfreton Town	42	26	9	7	106	59	87
Spennymoor United	42	27	6	9	81	42	87
Radcliffe Borough	42	25	10	7	90	46	85
North Ferriby United	42	23	9	10	78	45	78
Chorley	42	21	10	11	80	51	73
Belper Town	42	20	13	9	53	42	73
Witton Albion	42	19	15	8	67	50	72
Matlock Town	42	20	10	12	67	48	70
Leek Town	42	20	9	13	63	46	69
Workington	42	19	10	13	73	60	67
Farsley Celtic	42	17	11	14	66	67	62
Kendal Town	42	18	7	17	68	58	61
Bamber Bridge	42	15	9	18	55	59	54
Guiseley	42	14	11	17	68	63	53
Bishop Auckland	42	13	10	19	58	83	49
Lincoln United	42	12	9	21	67	77	45
Stocksbridge PS	42	11	9	22	54	81	42
Rossendale United	42	12	5	25	58	88	41
Kidsgrove Athletic	42	9	11	22	49	71	38
Ossett Town	42	8	9	25	39	80	33
Eastwood Town	42	5	8	29	33	92	23
Trafford	42	5	6	31	34	99	21

2002-2003

Premier Division

Accrington Stanley	44	30	10	4	97	44	100
Barrow	44	24	12	8	84	52	84
Vauxhall Motors	44	22	10	12	81	46	76
Stalybridge Celtic	44	21	13	10	77	51	76
Worksop Town	44	21	9	14	82	67	72
Harrogate Town	44	21	8	15	75	63	71
Bradford Park Avenue	44	20	10	14	73	70	70
Hucknall Town	44	17	15	12	72	62	66
Droylsden	44	18	10	16	62	52	64
Whitby Town	44	17	12	15	80	69	63
Marine	44	17	10	17	63	60	61
Wakefield & Emley	44	14	18	12	46	49	60
Runcorn FC Halton	44	15	15	14	69	74	60
Altrincham	44	17	9	18	58	63	60
Gansborough Trinity	44	16	11	17	67	66	59
Ashton United	44	15	13	16	71	79	58
Lancaster City	44	16	9	19	71	75	57
Burscough	44	14	9	21	44	51	51
Blyth Spartans	44	14	9	21	67	87	51
Frickley Athletic	44	13	8	23	45	78	47
Gateshead	44	10	11	23	60	81	41
Colwyn Bay	44	5	9	30	52	99	24
Hyde United	44	5	8	31	40	98	23

FORMATION — After the closure of The Combination in 1911 and the Manchester League a year later, senior non-League clubs in Cheshire found that there was no suitable league covering the county and so they had little alternative other than to join the more northerly based Lancashire Combination. However after the intervention of the war there was a new opportunity to organise themselves and so the Cheshire League was founded on 23rd April, 1919 at a meeting held at the Moseley Hotel, Manchester. The 13 founder members of the league were Altrincham, Chester, Crewe Alexandra Reserves, Crichton's Athletic, Macclesfield, Monk's Hall, Mossley, Nantwich Town, Northwich Victoria, Runcorn, Tranmere Rovers Reserves, Winsford United and Witton Albion. Dukinfield were one of eight clubs who had attended the initial meeting but were unable to take up their place due to lack of a suitable ground.

Before the war, seven of the 13 founder members – Altrincham, Chester, Crewe Alexandra Reserves, Macclesfield, Nantwich Town, Northwich Victoria and Witton Albion – had played in the Lancashire Combination and Tranmere Rovers Reserves had played in the West Cheshire League. Mossley had played in the Ashton and District League before the war and joined the Manchester Section of the Lancashire Combination in the unofficial 1918-19 season. Monk's Hall also played in the Lancashire Combination's Manchester Section in 1918-19 but their immediate pre-war league and those of Crichton's Athletic and Winsford United have not been found. Runcorn were a recently formed club who had taken part in the Lancashire Combination's Liverpool Section in 1918-19.

SEASONAL NOTES — Changes are noted either against the season in which they occurred or the year concerned if the changes were in the close season.

1919-20   Tranmere Rovers Reserves left during the season and joined the Lancashire Combination. This allowed their first team to move into the Central League to take the place of Port Vale who had moved into the Football League to take over the fixtures of Leeds City who had been disbanded by order of the F.A.. Tranmere Rovers Reserves' record in the Cheshire League was expunged.

1920   The league was increased to 18 clubs by the election of six new clubs. The six were (with their previous league in brackets where known): Ashton National, Congleton Town (North Staffordshire District League), Connah's Quay and Shotton, Sandbach Ramblers (North Staffordshire District League), Stalybridge Celtic Reserves (Lancashire Combination) and Tranmere Rovers Reserves (Lancashire Combination).

1921   The league was increased to 20 clubs by the election of Ellesmere Port Cement from the West Cheshire League and Whitchurch. Crichton's Athletic changed name to Saltney Athletic.

1921-22   Monk's Hall disbanded and resigned and their fixtures were taken over by Stockport County "A".

1922   Stockport County moved their reserves into the Cheshire League from the Lancashire Combination as a replacement for their "A" team. Middlewich joined the league in place of Connah's Quay and Shotton who moved to the Welsh National League (North).

1923   Saltney Athletic resigned but the league was increased to 22 clubs by the election of Hurst from the Lancashire Combination, Port Vale Reserves from the Central League and Wallasey United who were a new club who had been formed following a split between members of New Brighton FC. Stalybridge Celtic resigned from the Football League Division Three North and placed their first team in the Cheshire League instead of their reserves.

1924   Wallasey United disbanded and Stockport County Reserves also left. They were replaced by Manchester North End from the Lancashire Combination and Ellesmere Port Town from the Liverpool County Combination.

1925   Ellesmere Port Cement left the league for the West Cheshire League and were replaced by Eccles United from the Lancashire Combination.

1927   Ellesmere Port Town resigned and disbanded. Stockport County Reserves rejoined the league.

1928   Eccles United left and joined the Manchester League and Stockport County Reserves left and joined the Central League. The Cheshire League was thus reduced to 20 clubs.

1929   League once more increased to 22 clubs by the election of Connah's Quay and Shotton who rejoined from the Welsh National League (North) and Manchester Central Reserves from the Manchester League.

1930   Middlewich left the league and were replaced by Hyde United from the Manchester League.

1931   Chester were elected to the Football League Division Three (North) and placed their reserves in the Cheshire League instead of their first team. Manchester Central moved their first team from the Lancashire Combination into the Cheshire League to replace their reserves who moved into the Manchester League.

1931-32   Connah's Quay and Shotton withdrew in about November 1931 due to financial difficulties. They disbanded and their record was deleted.

1932   Manchester Central resigned from the league and disbanded. They and Connah's Quay were replaced by Buxton from the Manchester League, and a new club called Wigan Athletic who had been formed to replace the former Football League club Wigan Borough who had disbanded during the 1931-32 season.

1933   Whitchurch left the league and Port Vale Reserves moved to the Birmingham League. Prescot Cables joined the league from the Lancashire Combination and Stockport County Reserves returned from the Central League.

1934   Sandbach Ramblers left the league and were replaced by Port Vale Reserves who returned from the Birmingham League.

1936   Prescot Cables returned to the Lancashire Combination. Rhyl joined from the Birmingham League.

1938   Nantwich Town left the league and were replaced by Wellington Town from the Birmingham League.

1939   Manchester North End resigned and disbanded due to financial difficulties. Their place was taken by Wrexham Reserves from the Midland Mid-Week League.

1939-40. The planned 1939-40 season started on 26th August 1939 but was suspended when war was declared on 3rd September. It is believed that all 22 clubs played their opening two games but not all of the results have been traced.

Instead of the planned peace-time competition, the Cheshire League organised a scaled down competition of 16 clubs playing in two geographically based sections, east and west. There were two competitions in each section, the first ran from the end of September 1939 until the end of December, and the second ran from January until May, 1940. The clubs who finished top of the table in the two east competitions then met in a play-off and the overall championship was decided by another play-off between the east section play-off winners and Runcorn, who had won both west section competitions.

Seven of the 22 members of the league did not compete, probably because of war-time difficulties such as travel. The seven were Congleton Town, Crewe Alexandra Reserves, Port Vale Reserves, Rhyl, Tranmere Rovers Reserves, Wellington Town and Wrexham Reserves. The number of clubs competing was made up to 16 by the inclusion of Droylsden who had started the 1939-40 peace-time season in the Lancashire Combination. Stockport County Reserves only played 11 of their planned 14 games in the 1939 east section and withdrew from the 1940 series of games. Buxton also withdrew from the 1940 east section series but this was made up to seven clubs by transferring Macclesfield from the west section. The west section 1940 series was maintained at eight clubs by the replacement of Macclesfield with South Liverpool who like Droylsden, had started the 1939-40 peace-time season in the Lancashire Combination.

1940-45   The Cheshire League did not operate.

1945   When the war ended, the Cheshire League restarted operations in the 1945-46 season. Of the 22 members who had started the 1939-40 peace-time season, 17 rejoined the league but five did not. The five were Altrincham, Ashton National, Congleton Town, Macclesfield and Winsford United. Of these five, Ashton National joined the Manchester League instead while Altrincham, Congleton Town and Macclesfield rejoined the league for the 1946-47 season and Winsford United for the 1947-48 season.

The membership for the 1945-46 season was made up to 20 by the inclusion of three additional clubs. These were Droylsden and South Liverpool, who had both played in the Lancashire Combination before the war but had joined the Cheshire League's unofficial war-time competition in 1939, and Oldham Athletic Reserves who had also played in the Lancashire Combination before the war.

1946   Oldham Athletic Reserves left to rejoin the Lancashire Combination while the Cheshire League was increased to 22 clubs as three pre-war members – Altrincham, Congleton Town and Macclesfield – rejoined, Macclesfield having now changed name to Macclesfield Town. Winsford United also applied to rejoin but were refused as it was considered that their ground needed further renewal work.

1946-47   Hurst changed their name to Ashton United on 1st February, 1947.

1947   Wigan Athletic were not re-elected and moved to the Lancashire Combination, being replaced by Winsford United who rejoined following ground improvements.

1948   Ashton United left and joined the Lancashire Combination. They were replaced by Ellesmere Port Town from the Liverpool County Combination.

1950.   Droylsden left to join the Manchester League. Bangor City joined from the Lancashire Combination.

1952   South Liverpool joined the Lancs. Combination. Stafford Rangers joined from the Birmingham Combination.

1958   Wellington Town left to join the Southern League. Stockport County Reserves also left and joined the North Regional League, a new league formed for reserve sides of northern Football League clubs. The Cheshire League was thus reduced to 20 clubs.

1959   Crewe Alexandra Reserves and Port Vale Reserves both left to join the North Regional League. They were replaced by Oswestry Town from the Birmingham League and Wigan Rovers who were a new club.

1960   League membership increased to 22 by the election of Frickley Colliery from the Midland League and Sankeys (Wellington) from the Shropshire County League.

1961   Wigan Rovers left joined the Lancashire Combination. Wigan Athletic joined from the Lancs. Combination.

1965   Congleton Town joined the Manchester League, Sankeys (Wellington) returned to the Shropshire County League. These two were replaced by New Brighton from the Lancashire Combination and Stockport County Reserves.

1968   The first step in the establishment of the non-League pyramid for the northern half of the country was taken with the formation of the Northern Premier League (NPL) and seven of the Cheshire League's strongest clubs left to help to form the new league. The seven clubs were Altrincham, Bangor City, Hyde United, Macclesfield Town, Northwich Victoria, Runcorn and Wigan Athletic. Stockport County Reserves and Wrexham Reserves also left the Cheshire League. These nine were partially replaced by seven new clubs, five of which came from the Lancashire Combination – Ashton United, Droylsden, Guinness Exports, Horwich RMI and Skelmersdale United – while the other two were Nantwich Town from the Manchester League and Sandbach Ramblers from the Mid-Cheshire League. The Cheshire League was thus reduced to 20 clubs.

1969   Stafford Rangers left to join the NPL and were replaced by Marine from the Lancashire Combination. Chester Reserves also left and were replaced by Port Vale Reserves.

1970   Frickley Colliery returned to the Midland League and Tranmere Rovers Reserves also left. The league was increased to 22 clubs by the election of Burscough and Rossendale United from the Lancashire Combination, Hyde United who returned from the NPL and Oldham Athletic Reserves. Guinness Exports changed name to Ormskirk.

1971   Skelmersdale United and Ellesmere Port Town left for the NPL and Port Vale Reserves also left. These three were replaced by three clubs from the Lancashire Combination – Formby, Prestwich Heys and Radcliffe Borough.

1972   Mossley left for the NPL and were replaced by Chorley who moved down from the NPL.

1973   Buxton left for the NPL and were replaced by Leek Town from the Manchester League.

1974   Ormskirk disbanded and were replaced by New Mills from the Manchester League.

1975   Oswestry Town left and joined the Southern League and Oldham Athletic Reserves and Sandbach Ramblers also left. They were replaced by Darwen and St. Helens Town from the Lancashire Combination and Middlewich Athletic from the Mid-Cheshire League.

1978   The Cheshire League decided to form a second division. All existing members were placed in the new Division One with the exception of Prestwich Heys who were placed in Division Two. Their place in Division One was taken by Fleetwood Town who were a new club formed to replace the former NPL club Fleetwood, who had disbanded in 1976. Division Two was made up to 18 clubs by the election of Accrington Stanley, Ashton Town, Atherton Collieries, Bootle, Ford Motors, Kirkby Town, Maghull and Skelmersdale United who were all from the Lancashire Combination, together with Congleton Town, Prescot Town and Warrington Town from the Mid-Cheshire League; Anson Villa, Curzon Ashton, Glossop and Irlam Town from the Manchester League; Eastwood Hanley from the West Midland League and Prescot BI from the Liverpool County Combination. Goal difference instead of goal average was introduced for teams level on points.

1979   Marine and Witton Albion moved up from Division One to the NPL. Division One was reduced to 20 clubs.

1980   Prescot Town changed their name to Prescot Cables. Accrington Stanley were not promoted due to difficulties with their ground and Kirkby Town were promoted instead. Anson Villa dropped out of Division Two but it was increased to 20 clubs by the election of Atherton Laburnum Rovers from the Bolton Combination, Leyland Motors from the Lancashire Combination and Salford from the Manchester League.

1981   New Brighton left and joined the South Wirral League and were replaced by Ellesmere Port and Neston who joined from the Clwyd League.

1982   The Cheshire League merged with the Lancashire Combination to form the North-West Counties League and 37 of the 40 Cheshire League clubs took their place in the new league. The 3 exceptions were Chorley and Hyde United who moved up from Division One to the NPL and Middlewich Athletic from Division Two who initially applied to join the new league but then withdrew their application and rejoined the Mid-Cheshire League instead. All other Division One clubs moved to Division One of the North-West Counties League with the exceptions of Droylsden, Fleetwood Town and Rossendale United who moved to Division Two. All other Cheshire League Division Two clubs moved into Division Two with the exceptions of Congleton Town, Leyland Motors and Rhyl who moved into Division One and Ashton Town, Atherton Collieries, Maghull, Prestwich Heys and Warrington Town who moved into Division Three. The Cheshire League thus closed down.

TABLE ERRORS

A number of the tables published at the time contained errors. Additional research has resulted in most of these being corrected; those remaining are noted below.

1923-24   Goals for 1 higher than goals against.

1924-25   Goals for 4 higher than goals against.

1926-27   Goals for 1 higher than goals against.

1927-28   Goals for 14 lower than goals against.

1939-40   Goals for 2 lower than goals against in 1940 east section unofficial competition.

CHESHIRE LEAGUE

1919-1920

Subsidiary Competition – Section A

Mossley	10	6	2	2	24	14	14
Altrincham	10	3	5	2	15	13	11
Northwich Victoria	10	3	5	2	14	13	11
Witton Albion	10	3	2	5	15	15	8
Winsford United	10	2	4	4	15	16	8
Macclesfield	10	2	4	4	11	23	8

Subsidiary Competition – Section B

Crewe Alexandra Reserves	10	7	1	2	33	13	15
Runcorn	10	5	4	1	20	15	14
Monk's Hall	10	5	1	4	26	19	11
Crichton's Athletic	10	5	0	5	15	21	10
Chester	10	2	1	7	23	37	5
Nantwich Town	10	2	1	7	14	26	5

Subsidiary Competition – Final

Mossley 2   Crewe Alexandra Reserves 1
Crewe Alexandra Reserves 4   Mossley 0
Crewe Alexandra Reserves won 5-2 on aggregate.

1920-21

Winsford United	34	19	6	9	67	48	44
Congleton Town	34	17	8	9	68	56	42
Runcorn	34	17	7	10	64	42	41
Monk's Hall	34	16	9	9	58	40	41
Crewe Alexandra Reserves	34	15	9	10	80	51	39
Macclesfield	34	16	7	11	67	50	39
Crichton's Athletic	34	16	6	12	72	62	38
Mossley	34	14	8	12	49	48	36
Altrincham	34	14	8	12	59	70	36
Chester	34	15	5	14	72	74	35
Nantwich Town	34	14	6	14	82	72	34
Ashton National	34	14	5	15	69	64	33
Northwich Victoria	34	12	5	17	53	60	29
Tranmere Rovers Reserves	34	13	3	18	52	69	29
Stalybridge Celtic Reserves	34	11	5	18	61	74	27
Sandbach Ramblers	34	8	9	17	42	68	25
Witton Albion	34	10	3	21	48	77	23
Connah's Quay & Shotton	34	6	9	19	44	82	21

1921-22

Chester	38	25	3	10	78	50	53
Congleton Town	38	22	6	10	82	49	50
Ashton National	38	23	2	13	78	63	48
Witton Albion	38	20	7	11	77	54	47
Stalybridge Celtic Reserves	38	18	8	12	71	59	44
Nantwich Town	38	15	13	10	71	57	43
Northwich Victoria	38	15	10	13	62	40	40
Macclesfield	38	13	13	12	60	64	39
Connah's Quay & Shotton	38	13	12	13	51	52	38
Whitchurch	38	16	6	16	65	71	38
Winsford United	38	13	12	13	53	64	38
Altrincham	38	13	9	16	75	70	35
Sandbach Ramblers	38	13	9	16	51	54	35
Ellesmere Port Cement	38	14	6	18	61	63	34
Crewe Alexandra Reserves	38	13	8	17	61	70	34
Saltney Athletic	38	9	15	14	65	75	33
Mossley	38	11	7	20	54	84	29
Stockport County "A"	38	11	6	21	57	102	28
Tranmere Rovers Reserves	38	10	7	21	59	66	27
Runcorn	38	10	7	21	56	80	27

Stockport County "A" took over the fixtures of Monk's Hall
Saltney Athletic were previously known as Crichton's Athletic

1922-23

Crewe Alexandra Reserves	38	27	6	5	102	42	60
Stockport County Reserves	38	20	8	10	89	58	48
Altrincham	38	19	10	9	86	60	48
Macclesfield	38	18	10	10	84	52	46
Ellesmere Port Cement	38	18	7	13	69	48	43
Saltney Athletic	38	20	3	15	75	83	43
Winsford United	38	17	7	14	51	52	41
Tranmere Rovers Reserves	38	16	9	13	69	71	41
Mossley	38	15	10	13	76	62	40
Stalybridge Celtic Reserves	38	15	9	14	56	49	39
Ashton National	38	14	10	14	75	57	38
Whitchurch	38	14	9	15	66	78	37
Congleton Town	38	14	8	16	64	71	36
Nantwich Town	38	15	5	18	61	84	35
Chester	38	13	8	17	59	60	34
Sandbach Ramblers	38	10	10	18	53	81	30
Runcorn	38	11	5	22	56	85	27
Northwich Victoria	38	8	10	20	47	75	26
Witton Albion	38	9	7	22	43	83	25
Middlewich	38	8	7	23	40	70	23

1923-24

Crewe Alexandra Reserves	42	28	5	9	96	62	61
Port Vale Reserves	42	24	10	8	109	60	58
Whitchurch	42	24	8	10	81	52	56
Stalybridge Celtic	42	24	6	12	93	50	54
Stockport County Reserves	42	21	12	9	92	56	54
Northwich Victoria	42	18	10	14	85	77	46
Congleton Town	42	18	9	15	86	59	45
Hurst	42	19	7	16	78	76	45
Macclesfield	42	18	6	18	82	67	42
Altrincham	42	19	4	19	69	75	42
Ashton National	42	15	11	16	59	60	41
Ellesmere Port Cement	42	14	12	16	66	64	40
Mossley	42	16	8	18	77	90	40
Winsford United	42	17	5	20	56	77	39
Wallasey United	42	13	12	17	50	71	38
Chester	42	11	15	16	59	66	37
Witton Albion	42	14	9	19	55	67	37
Tranmere Rovers Reserves	42	13	9	20	78	90	35
Runcorn	42	13	9	20	54	68	35
Middlewich	42	12	8	22	56	101	32
Nantwich Town	42	9	6	27	53	101	24
Sandbach Ramblers	42	7	9	26	41	85	23

1924-25

Port Vale Reserves	42	25	10	7	112	43	60
Northwich Victoria	42	25	6	11	94	58	56
Stalybridge Celtic	42	24	7	11	92	52	55
Ashton National	42	24	6	12	94	50	54
Hurst	42	22	10	10	101	61	54
Macclesfield	42	21	6	15	79	77	48
Tranmere Rovers Reserves	42	21	5	16	106	79	47
Crewe Alexandra Reserves	42	20	5	17	91	68	45
Mossley	42	17	8	17	85	83	42
Winsford United	42	18	6	18	83	87	42
Middlewich	42	18	6	18	67	71	42
Altrincham	42	16	7	19	70	93	39
Manchester North End	42	15	7	20	96	95	37
Congleton Town	42	14	8	20	77	93	36
Whitchurch	42	12	12	18	55	86	36
Sandbach Ramblers	42	12	11	19	57	81	35
Chester	42	14	7	21	59	103	35
Witton Albion	42	13	7	22	59	82	33
Nantwich Town	42	12	9	21	72	102	33
Runcorn	42	14	5	23	62	94	33
Ellesmere Port Cement	42	13	6	23	67	84	32
Ellesmere Port Town	42	12	6	24	56	88	30

1925-26

Team	P	W	D	L	F	A	Pts
Chester	42	29	5	8	110	57	63
Port Vale Reserves	42	26	6	10	115	58	58
Congleton Town	42	25	6	11	125	74	56
Stalybridge Celtic	42	24	4	14	133	77	52
Witton Albion	42	21	8	13	121	85	50
Ashton National	42	20	8	14	98	84	48
Winsford United	42	22	3	17	96	87	47
Nantwich Town	42	19	9	14	90	90	47
Tranmere Rovers Reserves	42	17	11	14	104	97	45
Manchester North End	42	18	7	17	92	111	43
Crewe Alexandra Reserves	42	18	6	18	96	75	42
Runcorn	42	19	4	19	79	92	42
Hurst	42	16	9	17	114	95	41
Mossley	42	14	8	20	80	106	36
Ellesmere Port Town	42	16	4	22	73	107	36
Altrincham	42	15	4	23	85	94	34
Sandbach Ramblers	42	14	6	22	81	92	34
Northwich Victoria	42	14	5	23	75	101	33
Whitchurch	42	14	4	24	85	124	32
Macclesfield	42	12	8	22	88	142	32
Middlewich	42	13	4	25	76	120	30
Eccles United	42	9	5	28	84	132	23

1926-27

Team	P	W	D	L	F	A	Pts
Chester	42	31	3	8	147	67	65
Ashton National	42	29	4	9	119	63	62
Tranmere Rovers Reserves	42	28	4	10	163	72	60
Congleton Town	42	27	5	10	125	59	59
Stalybridge Celtic	42	26	6	10	136	79	58
Crewe Alexandra Reserves	42	26	6	10	118	81	58
Port Vale Reserves	42	24	5	13	119	74	53
Manchester North End	42	24	3	15	156	90	51
Altrincham	42	20	7	15	129	108	47
Runcorn	42	19	7	16	94	101	45
Macclesfield	42	19	5	18	113	112	43
Nantwich Town	42	16	10	16	95	86	42
Winsford United	42	18	5	19	120	97	41
Middlewich	42	15	6	21	99	132	36
Witton Albion	42	13	6	23	79	108	32
Eccles United	42	10	9	23	84	127	29
Mossley	42	11	7	24	88	146	29
Northwich Victoria	42	11	4	27	70	141	26
Whitchurch	42	10	6	26	62	134	26
Hurst	42	8	6	28	65	119	22
Sandbach Ramblers	42	7	7	28	59	124	21
Ellesmere Port Town	42	8	3	31	77	196	19

1927-28

Team	P	W	D	L	F	A	Pts
Port Vale Reserves	42	31	5	6	147	48	67
Stockport County Reserves	42	26	9	7	158	81	61
Ashton National	42	28	5	9	145	78	61
Congleton Town	42	26	7	9	105	60	59
Chester	42	23	6	13	120	73	52
Winsford United	42	21	9	12	122	101	51
Stalybridge Celtic	42	21	6	15	120	93	48
Runcorn	42	19	10	13	86	81	48
Manchester North End	42	20	7	15	133	101	47
Hurst	42	19	7	16	105	101	45
Tranmere Rovers Reserves	42	21	3	18	104	101	45
Crewe Alexandra Reserves	42	17	9	16	112	98	43
Witton Albion	42	18	7	17	89	98	43
Middlewich	42	15	8	19	87	102	38
Sandbach Ramblers	42	13	8	21	89	101	34
Nantwich Town	42	15	3	24	103	133	33
Macclesfield	42	13	5	24	75	117	31
Northwich Victoria	42	10	9	23	88	136	29
Mossley	42	12	5	25	86	138	29
Altrincham	42	10	4	28	77	146	24
Whitchurch	42	8	2	32	77	166	18
Eccles United	42	7	4	31	64	153	18

1928-29

Team	P	W	D	L	F	A	Pts
Port Vale Reserves	38	24	6	8	121	64	54
Ashton National	38	23	5	10	115	70	51
Winsford United	38	22	7	9	109	74	51
Congleton Town	38	21	7	10	97	76	49
Manchester North End	38	20	8	10	122	81	48
Tranmere Rovers Reserves	38	18	8	12	128	88	44
Stalybridge Celtic	38	19	6	13	92	75	44
Chester	38	19	5	14	99	75	43
Crewe Alexandra Reserves	38	18	5	15	92	84	41
Macclesfield	38	17	3	18	94	93	37
Runcorn	38	13	11	14	86	94	37
Hurst	38	14	8	16	126	119	36
Mossley	38	14	8	16	89	93	36
Northwich Victoria	38	13	7	18	85	90	33
Sandbach Ramblers	38	14	2	22	101	116	30
Whitchurch	38	13	4	21	96	115	30
Witton Albion	38	9	12	17	62	82	30
Middlewich	38	11	4	23	51	125	26
Altrincham	38	8	7	23	74	128	23
Nantwich Town	38	8	1	29	62	159	17

1929-30

Team	P	W	D	L	F	A	Pts
Port Vale Reserves	42	29	6	7	146	49	64
Connah's Quay and Shotton	42	30	3	9	148	59	63
Tranmere Rovers Reserves	42	26	6	10	154	90	58
Macclesfield	42	24	7	11	139	109	55
Ashton National	42	24	4	14	118	70	52
Stalybridge Celtic	42	25	2	15	136	109	52
Runcorn	42	23	5	14	123	98	51
Sandbach Ramblers	42	21	5	16	112	108	47
Chester	42	18	5	19	120	109	41
Mossley	42	18	5	19	99	126	41
Crewe Alexandra Reserves	42	15	10	17	99	115	40
Northwich Victoria	42	19	2	21	95	111	40
Witton Albion	42	15	8	19	105	120	38
Winsford United	42	16	5	21	105	128	37
Manchester Central Reserves	42	15	4	23	92	125	34
Manchester North End	42	14	4	24	115	130	32
Congleton Town	42	11	10	21	69	92	32
Whitchurch	42	14	4	24	86	122	32
Hurst	42	14	2	26	96	130	30
Nantwich Town	42	12	5	25	69	112	29
Middlewich	42	12	5	25	70	125	29
Altrincham	42	12	3	27	81	140	27

1930-31

Team	P	W	D	L	F	A	Pts
Port Vale Reserves	42	33	5	4	163	48	71
Chester	42	31	6	5	170	59	68
Hyde United	42	25	6	11	133	84	56
Altrincham	42	22	8	12	123	96	52
Runcorn	42	20	9	13	129	83	49
Stalybridge Celtic	42	21	6	15	122	114	48
Crewe Alexandra Reserves	42	19	8	15	132	104	46
Ashton National	42	18	8	16	114	90	44
Macclesfield	42	20	4	18	112	101	44
Sandbach Ramblers	42	19	4	19	123	124	42
Witton Albion	42	18	6	18	97	103	42
Tranmere Rovers Reserves	42	18	6	18	105	120	42
Manchester North End	42	19	4	19	97	119	42
Hurst	42	18	5	19	132	115	41
Congleton Town	42	14	8	20	68	112	36
Mossley	42	12	10	20	104	124	34
Northwich Victoria	42	15	3	24	105	135	33
Connah's Quay and Shotton	42	15	2	25	96	122	32
Winsford United	42	13	4	25	98	151	30
Whitchurch	42	10	7	25	79	160	27
Nantwich Town	42	9	8	25	83	132	26
Manchester Central Reserves	42	7	5	30	51	140	19

1931-32

	P	W	D	L	F	A	Pts
Macclesfield	40	25	8	7	119	65	58
Port Vale Reserves	40	25	5	10	110	50	55
Stalybridge Celtic	40	25	5	10	124	71	55
Altrincham	40	25	5	10	94	69	55
Manchester Central	40	23	7	10	108	68	53
Hyde United	40	22	7	11	98	66	51
Tranmere Rovers Reserves	40	22	4	14	116	80	48
Congleton Town	40	20	6	14	105	81	46
Chester Reserves	40	17	10	13	82	73	44
Crewe Alexandra Reserves	40	19	6	15	89	107	44
Runcorn	40	18	5	17	104	97	41
Manchester North End	40	18	4	18	106	103	40
Hurst	40	16	6	18	98	108	38
Ashton National	40	16	3	21	110	92	35
Mossley	40	13	7	20	71	104	33
Winsford United	40	12	4	24	70	99	28
Whitchurch	40	10	8	22	74	109	28
Witton Albion	40	10	7	23	73	116	27
Northwich Victoria	40	10	7	23	76	122	27
Sandbach Ramblers	40	8	5	27	68	120	21
Nantwich Town	40	1	11	28	60	155	13

Connah's Quay and Shotton withdrew during the season and their record was deleted.

1932-33

	P	W	D	L	F	A	Pts
Macclesfield	42	29	5	8	121	64	63
Port Vale Reserves	42	26	5	11	112	57	57
Manchester North End	42	24	7	11	124	78	55
Hurst	42	25	4	13	129	98	54
Wigan Athletic	42	21	11	10	121	54	53
Ashton National	42	23	7	12	130	83	53
Congleton Town	42	22	6	14	105	103	50
Hyde United	42	22	5	15	105	93	49
Crewe Alexandra Reserves	42	19	8	15	110	77	46
Stalybridge Celtic	42	19	8	15	132	100	46
Chester Reserves	42	21	2	19	118	109	44
Altrincham	42	17	9	16	108	95	43
Mossley	42	19	4	19	96	101	42
Tranmere Rovers Reserves	42	18	5	19	108	118	41
Northwich Victoria	42	17	6	19	100	123	40
Buxton	42	16	5	21	81	92	37
Runcorn	42	15	6	21	88	109	36
Nantwich Town	42	12	7	23	84	133	31
Witton Albion	42	9	7	26	71	119	25
Winsford United	42	8	6	28	65	143	22
Sandbach Ramblers	42	6	7	29	63	146	19
Whitchurch	42	6	6	30	70	146	18

1933-34

	P	W	D	L	F	A	Pts
Wigan Athletic	42	30	6	6	111	46	66
Macclesfield	42	29	3	10	142	71	61
Witton Albion	42	21	9	12	85	75	51
Stockport County Reserves	42	23	3	16	104	77	49
Prescot Cables	42	21	7	14	93	78	49
Altrincham	42	19	9	14	99	72	47
Tranmere Rovers Reserves	42	22	3	17	110	98	47
Manchester North End	42	21	4	17	132	105	46
Stalybridge Celtic	42	18	9	15	100	84	45
Ashton National	42	21	3	18	89	85	45
Hyde United	42	19	6	17	99	84	44
Mossley	42	15	12	15	91	87	42
Runcorn	42	19	2	21	91	104	40
Chester Reserves	42	16	7	19	84	97	39
Buxton	42	14	11	17	81	95	39
Hurst	42	17	3	22	103	111	37
Nantwich Town	42	15	4	23	77	112	34
Crewe Alexandra Reserves	42	16	2	24	71	111	34
Congleton Town	42	11	8	23	84	97	30
Northwich Victoria	42	14	2	26	63	87	30
Winsford United	42	11	6	25	70	118	28
Sandbach Ramblers	42	8	5	29	57	142	21

1934-35

	P	W	D	L	F	A	Pts
Wigan Athletic	42	27	9	6	153	59	63
Altrincham	42	26	11	5	118	57	63
Stalybridge Celtic	42	28	7	7	136	74	63
Port Vale Reserves	42	23	6	13	113	69	52
Hyde United	42	21	6	15	89	73	48
Stockport County Reserves	42	21	5	16	94	88	47
Chester Reserves	42	22	2	18	116	98	46
Macclesfield	42	19	7	16	137	83	45
Buxton	42	19	5	18	95	95	43
Manchester North End	42	15	9	18	112	110	39
Congleton Town	42	17	5	20	93	113	39
Mossley	42	17	5	20	97	119	39
Ashton National	42	15	7	20	68	86	37
Witton Albion	42	16	5	21	60	106	37
Hurst	42	13	10	19	82	101	36
Northwich Victoria	42	14	7	21	83	95	35
Prescot Cables	42	13	9	20	79	100	35
Winsford United	42	12	9	21	68	104	33
Tranmere Rovers Reserves	42	14	4	24	82	110	32
Runcorn	42	14	3	25	95	147	31
Nantwich Town	42	11	9	22	71	121	31
Crewe Alexandra Reserves	42	12	6	24	72	105	30

1935-36

	P	W	D	L	F	A	Pts
Wigan Athletic	42	31	6	5	136	46	68
Altrincham	42	22	11	9	88	51	55
Stockport County Reserves	42	23	8	11	103	57	54
Chester Reserves	42	22	9	11	104	85	53
Stalybridge Celtic	42	23	6	13	112	64	52
Runcorn	42	21	8	13	129	88	50
Northwich Victoria	42	20	10	12	98	74	50
Crewe Alexandra Reserves	42	21	6	15	113	84	48
Macclesfield	42	21	4	17	105	106	46
Port Vale Reserves	42	17	10	15	69	72	44
Buxton	42	18	7	17	95	90	43
Hurst	42	16	10	16	89	106	42
Tranmere Rovers Reserves	42	16	9	17	113	120	41
Manchester North End	42	17	6	19	94	107	40
Hyde United	42	17	5	20	107	108	39
Mossley	42	16	4	22	90	113	36
Congleton Town	42	15	4	23	95	114	34
Prescot Cables	42	15	4	23	59	94	34
Nantwich Town	42	13	7	22	74	115	33
Witton Albion	42	11	5	26	58	96	27
Ashton National	42	7	8	27	64	114	22
Winsford United	42	4	5	33	44	135	13

1936-37

	P	W	D	L	F	A	Pts
Runcorn	42	30	6	6	156	60	66
Stockport County Reserves	42	23	11	8	105	55	57
Northwich Victoria	42	27	3	12	92	52	57
Witton Albion	42	24	8	10	107	56	56
Port Vale Reserves	42	22	8	12	97	91	52
Buxton	42	22	6	14	107	89	50
Ashton National	42	18	9	15	97	96	45
Wigan Athletic	42	19	6	17	94	73	44
Stalybridge Celtic	42	19	6	17	96	81	44
Rhyl	42	17	9	16	75	71	43
Crewe Alexandra Reserves	42	18	5	19	77	88	41
Chester Reserves	42	14	9	19	79	93	37
Altrincham	42	14	8	20	91	94	36
Congleton Town	42	15	6	21	83	104	36
Winsford United	42	14	8	20	75	94	36
Tranmere Rovers Reserves	42	15	6	21	74	100	36
Mossley	42	11	13	18	84	108	35
Manchester North End	42	15	5	22	85	113	35
Macclesfield	42	14	6	22	74	96	34
Hyde United	42	13	7	22	97	114	33
Nantwich Town	42	11	6	25	78	146	28
Hurst	42	9	5	28	76	125	23

1937-38

Tranmere Rovers Reserves	42	30	6	6	148	45	66
Runcorn	42	30	3	9	123	54	63
Stockport County Reserves	42	29	4	9	104	48	62
Hyde United	42	24	8	10	105	67	56
Crewe Alexandra Reserves	42	21	11	10	99	61	53
Witton Albion	42	20	7	15	104	68	47
Mossley	42	19	9	14	86	76	47
Northwich Victoria	42	19	6	17	86	79	44
Altrincham	42	17	10	15	77	80	44
Stalybridge Celtic	42	18	6	18	96	86	42
Wigan Athletic	42	19	4	19	95	89	42
Port Vale Reserves	42	16	7	19	77	76	39
Chester Reserves	42	17	4	21	84	92	38
Manchester North End	42	18	2	22	112	131	38
Macclesfield	42	14	10	18	96	115	38
Congleton Town	42	16	6	20	74	122	38
Ashton National	42	16	5	21	78	92	37
Buxton	42	14	5	23	87	108	33
Winsford United	42	12	6	24	71	98	30
Rhyl	42	11	7	24	74	117	29
Nantwich Town	42	8	4	30	59	149	20
Hurst	42	7	4	31	63	145	18

1938-39

Runcorn	42	28	6	8	134	60	62
Tranmere Rovers Reserves	42	29	2	11	136	63	60
Ashton National	42	25	7	10	131	90	57
Crewe Alexandra Reserves	42	26	4	12	132	74	56
Wellington Town	42	23	8	11	108	68	54
Chester Reserves	42	22	8	12	111	74	52
Wigan Athletic	42	21	5	16	104	84	47
Northwich Victoria	42	20	7	15	88	87	47
Witton Albion	42	17	9	16	94	78	43
Hyde United	42	20	3	19	84	91	43
Congleton Town	42	16	10	16	80	89	42
Mossley	42	14	12	16	77	78	40
Port Vale Reserves	42	18	4	20	84	86	40
Hurst	42	15	10	17	86	113	40
Stockport County Reserves	42	18	3	21	86	90	39
Buxton	42	12	11	19	71	93	35
Macclesfield	42	14	7	21	55	90	35
Stalybridge Celtic	42	13	8	21	87	108	34
Rhyl	42	12	9	21	94	117	33
Altrincham	42	9	7	26	72	119	25
Winsford United	42	8	6	28	57	134	22
Manchester North End	42	7	4	31	57	142	18

1939-40

Unofficial war-time competition

1939 series, east section

Droylsden	14	9	2	3	52	31	20
Ashton National	13	7	3	3	47	35	17
Hyde United	14	7	3	4	27	24	17
Hurst	13	7	1	5	29	32	15
Buxton	14	5	4	5	29	31	14
Stalybridge Celtic	14	5	1	8	34	38	11
Mossley	13	2	3	8	26	35	7
Stockport County Reserves	11	2	1	8	22	40	5

Three games were not played.

1939 series, west section

Runcorn	14	7	6	1	46	28	20
Altrincham	14	7	3	4	45	29	17
Witton Albion	14	5	5	4	32	28	15
Winsford United	14	6	3	5	25	25	15
Northwich Victoria	13	6	3	4	23	26	15
Chester Reserves	13	5	1	7	32	40	11
Wigan Athletic	14	3	3	8	37	46	9
Macclesfield	14	3	2	9	28	46	8

One game was not played.

1940 series, east section

Hyde United	12	8	2	2	40	21	18
Droylsden	12	7	1	4	35	25	15
Ashton National	12	6	1	5	36	31	13
Mossley	12	5	3	4	24	27	13
Hurst	12	4	3	5	29	33	11
Macclesfield	12	4	0	8	23	42	8
Stalybridge Celtic	12	1	4	7	26	36	6

1940 series, west section

Runcorn	14	9	4	1	49	21	22
Witton Albion	14	8	2	4	31	24	18
Altrincham	14	8	1	5	35	31	17
Chester Reserves	14	6	2	6	31	33	14
South Liverpool	14	4	4	6	34	36	12
Northwich Victoria	14	5	1	8	20	33	11
Wigan Athletic	14	4	3	7	32	46	11
Winsford United	14	2	3	9	16	24	7

East Section play-off

Droylsden 6   Hyde United 5   •   Hyde United 0   Droylsden 1
Droylsden won 7-5 on aggregate

West Section –   Runcorn won both competitions

Championship play-off

Runcorn 4   Droylsden 1   •   Droylsden 2   Runcorn 1
Runcorn won 5-3 on aggregate

1945-46

Wellington Town	38	29	1	8	150	53	59
Droylsden	38	24	3	11	126	65	51
Buxton	38	21	8	9	131	72	50
Witton Albion	38	21	4	13	98	69	46
Chester Reserves	38	20	4	14	118	86	44
Stalybridge Celtic	38	19	6	13	102	99	44
South Liverpool	38	19	5	14	99	94	43
Hyde United	38	17	8	13	83	66	42
Runcorn	38	17	6	15	97	98	40
Hurst	38	17	6	15	95	108	40
Northwich Victoria	38	16	4	18	79	102	36
Stockport County Reserves	38	15	4	19	79	107	34
Oldham Athletic Reserves	38	13	6	19	87	116	32
Crewe Alexandra Reserves	38	11	9	18	74	104	31
Rhyl	38	11	8	19	96	116	30
Wigan Athletic	38	12	6	20	88	117	30
Wrexham Reserves	38	12	6	20	54	76	30
Port Vale Reserves	38	11	5	22	73	91	27
Tranmere Rovers Reserves	38	12	2	24	76	115	26
Mossley	38	11	3	24	85	136	25

1946-47

Wellington Town	42	25	7	10	113	69	57
Buxton	42	24	8	10	117	79	56
South Liverpool	42	23	9	10	92	62	55
Port Vale Reserves	42	24	6	12	100	58	54
Northwich Victoria	42	21	11	10	95	69	53
Stalybridge Celtic	42	24	5	13	108	89	53
Witton Albion	42	20	7	15	96	84	47
Droylsden	42	22	1	19	108	101	45
Mossley	42	17	10	15	94	90	44
Altrincham	42	17	8	17	85	83	42
Hyde United	42	19	3	20	108	100	41
Runcorn	42	13	13	16	80	89	39
Wrexham Reserves	42	17	4	21	81	80	38
Rhyl	42	16	6	20	96	106	38
Macclesfield Town	42	16	6	20	77	89	38
Chester Reserves	42	16	4	22	70	91	36
Congleton Town	42	15	5	22	83	100	35
Tranmere Rovers Reserves	42	14	7	21	70	89	35
Stockport County Reserves	42	14	7	21	79	104	35
Crewe Alexandra Reserves	42	13	6	23	90	120	32
Hurst	42	8	10	24	65	107	26
Wigan Athletic	42	9	7	26	66	114	25

Hurst changed their name to Ashton United on 1st February, 1947.

1947-48

Team	P	W	D	L	F	A	Pts
Rhyl	42	30	8	4	121	54	68
Northwich Victoria	42	24	9	9	109	58	57
Witton Albion	42	24	8	10	104	59	56
Wellington Town	42	23	8	11	111	65	54
Stalybridge Celtic	42	18	11	13	85	87	47
Tranmere Rovers Reserves	42	18	9	15	76	62	45
Winsford United	42	22	1	19	90	83	45
Crewe Alexandra Reserves	42	19	7	16	80	80	45
South Liverpool	42	18	7	17	81	81	43
Chester Reserves	42	18	6	18	83	92	42
Stockport County Reserves	42	16	9	17	87	84	41
Hyde United	42	18	4	20	88	83	40
Wrexham Reserves	42	17	5	20	85	71	39
Runcorn	42	15	9	18	79	88	39
Altrincham	42	17	5	20	100	115	39
Port Vale Reserves	42	16	7	19	53	69	39
Droylsden	42	13	11	18	80	82	37
Macclesfield Town	42	13	11	18	78	83	37
Buxton	42	13	6	23	89	113	32
Mossley	42	14	4	24	66	99	32
Ashton United	42	11	3	28	74	143	25
Congleton Town	42	9	4	29	50	118	22

1948-49

Team	P	W	D	L	F	A	Pts
Witton Albion	42	29	6	7	106	39	64
Rhyl	42	27	7	8	110	53	61
Northwich Victoria	42	26	9	7	118	67	61
Winsford United	42	25	8	9	95	59	58
Mossley	42	21	9	12	97	74	51
Wellington Town	42	20	10	12	91	68	50
South Liverpool	42	18	9	15	94	91	45
Wrexham Reserves	42	17	10	15	81	77	44
Stalybridge Celtic	42	18	7	17	79	90	43
Altrincham	42	18	6	18	91	95	42
Macclesfield Town	42	16	9	17	82	80	41
Runcorn	42	17	7	18	76	79	41
Chester Reserves	42	17	4	21	78	88	38
Hyde United	42	14	9	19	80	87	37
Ellesmere Port Town	42	14	8	20	80	96	36
Port Vale Reserves	42	13	10	19	65	79	36
Buxton	42	15	6	21	77	104	36
Crewe Alexandra Reserves	42	13	7	22	74	88	33
Stockport County Reserves	42	10	12	20	65	81	32
Congleton Town	42	11	7	24	78	113	29
Tranmere Rovers Reserves	42	11	4	27	57	101	26
Droylsden	42	7	6	29	59	124	20

1949-50

Team	P	W	D	L	F	A	Pts
Witton Albion	42	25	13	4	101	42	63
Rhyl	42	28	6	8	116	42	62
Stockport County Reserves	42	21	14	7	78	46	56
Northwich Victoria	42	22	7	13	101	61	51
Winsford United	42	16	18	8	78	56	50
Altrincham	42	20	10	12	79	64	50
Runcorn	42	18	11	13	70	52	47
Macclesfield Town	42	21	5	16	88	76	47
Wellington Town	42	17	13	12	70	67	47
Crewe Alexandra Reserves	42	16	10	16	86	78	42
Hyde United	42	16	10	16	81	83	42
Ellesmere Port Town	42	16	10	16	69	79	42
Buxton	42	11	16	15	78	88	38
Tranmere Rovers Reserves	42	15	8	19	62	80	38
Congleton Town	42	15	5	22	65	99	35
Chester Reserves	42	12	11	19	56	89	35
South Liverpool	42	12	9	21	65	78	33
Port Vale Reserves	42	9	15	18	51	62	33
Mossley	42	8	16	18	53	92	32
Stalybridge Celtic	42	9	11	22	57	85	29
Droylsden	42	9	9	24	69	114	27
Wrexham Reserves	42	9	7	26	54	94	25

1950-51

Team	P	W	D	L	F	A	Pts
Rhyl	42	31	6	5	99	36	68
Witton Albion	42	28	4	10	116	56	60
Northwich Victoria	42	27	5	10	116	58	59
Tranmere Rovers Reserves	42	23	5	14	73	52	51
Macclesfield Town	42	20	11	11	90	67	51
Wellington Town	42	20	9	13	80	55	49
Bangor City	42	20	8	14	85	70	48
Port Vale Reserves	42	19	10	13	71	66	48
Winsford United	42	19	9	14	84	67	47
Altrincham	42	19	8	15	77	63	46
Wrexham Reserves	42	19	6	17	88	68	44
Ellesmere Port Town	42	17	6	19	73	78	40
Stockport County Reserves	42	15	9	18	52	50	39
Runcorn	42	15	8	19	81	89	38
Buxton	42	14	9	19	55	69	37
Crewe Alexandra Reserves	42	15	6	21	88	102	36
South Liverpool	42	13	6	23	65	101	32
Hyde United	42	11	6	25	51	90	28
Stalybridge Celtic	42	12	4	26	55	125	28
Mossley	42	11	5	26	51	91	27
Congleton Town	42	9	9	24	54	102	27
Chester Reserves	42	6	9	27	65	114	21

1951-52

Team	P	W	D	L	F	A	Pts
Wellington Town	42	26	9	7	85	44	61
Rhyl	42	25	8	9	101	58	58
Port Vale Reserves	42	21	11	10	77	41	53
Witton Albion	42	22	7	13	77	46	51
Tranmere Rovers Reserves	42	20	9	13	79	57	49
Northwich Victoria	42	21	6	15	78	70	48
Mossley	42	22	4	16	90	89	48
Altrincham	42	19	9	14	78	72	47
Crewe Alexandra Reserves	42	19	8	15	114	83	46
Stockport County Reserves	42	16	12	14	66	61	44
Bangor City	42	17	9	16	79	68	43
Wrexham Reserves	42	16	10	16	88	83	42
Runcorn	42	16	10	16	75	76	42
Macclesfield Town	42	15	12	15	62	69	42
Winsford United	42	17	6	19	72	84	40
Congleton Town	42	17	5	20	66	93	39
Chester Reserves	42	15	7	20	65	79	37
Stalybridge Celtic	42	13	7	22	56	83	33
Buxton	42	10	11	21	73	84	31
Ellesmere Port Town	42	11	4	27	70	104	26
South Liverpool	42	7	10	25	45	98	24
Hyde United	42	7	6	29	66	120	20

1952-53

Team	P	W	D	L	F	A	Pts
Macclesfield Town	42	27	8	7	103	63	62
Wellington Town	42	25	9	8	89	44	59
Stockport County Reserves	42	24	9	9	85	52	57
Rhyl	42	20	14	8	104	76	54
Bangor City	42	23	7	12	87	68	53
Tranmere Rovers Reserves	42	18	14	10	95	71	50
Port Vale Reserves	42	17	14	11	77	65	48
Witton Albion	42	18	9	15	107	100	45
Buxton	42	17	10	15	76	81	44
Crewe Alexandra Reserves	42	18	5	19	72	75	41
Stalybridge Celtic	42	16	9	17	84	88	41
Runcorn	42	18	3	21	83	97	39
Chester Reserves	42	12	13	17	78	88	37
Wrexham Reserves	42	15	7	20	69	78	37
Ellesmere Port Town	42	16	5	21	70	81	37
Northwich Victoria	42	13	8	21	61	82	34
Winsford United	42	13	7	22	70	82	33
Mossley	42	13	6	23	57	86	32
Hyde United	42	11	10	21	71	108	32
Stafford Rangers	42	11	9	22	67	73	31
Congleton Town	42	11	8	23	64	91	30
Altrincham	42	8	12	22	54	84	28

1953-54

Witton Albion	42	27	7	8	117	62	61
Bangor City	42	23	7	12	104	63	53
Stockport County Reserves	42	22	7	13	93	75	51
Hyde United	42	19	12	11	86	73	50
Macclesfield Town	42	20	9	13	97	78	49
Altrincham	42	21	7	14	75	67	49
Crewe Alexandra Reserves	42	19	10	13	87	65	48
Tranmere Rovers Reserves	42	18	11	13	79	62	47
Wrexham Reserves	42	21	5	16	85	69	47
Wellington Town	42	21	5	16	80	66	47
Rhyl	42	19	9	14	70	61	47
Chester Reserves	42	16	8	18	67	70	40
Port Vale Reserves	42	17	6	19	69	75	40
Winsford United	42	15	8	19	70	76	38
Ellesmere Port Town	42	13	9	20	54	75	35
Stalybridge Celtic	42	14	7	21	62	88	35
Mossley	42	11	12	19	66	89	34
Runcorn	42	13	8	21	63	86	34
Northwich Victoria	42	13	7	22	72	97	33
Stafford Rangers	42	11	10	21	73	89	32
Congleton Town	42	11	5	26	66	109	27
Buxton	42	10	7	25	58	98	27

1954-55

Hyde United	42	25	10	7	125	64	60
Wellington Town	42	24	7	11	91	59	55
Stafford Rangers	42	19	14	9	74	50	52
Wrexham Reserves	42	20	11	11	105	68	51
Stockport County Reserves	42	22	6	14	96	65	50
Stalybridge Celtic	42	21	8	13	73	68	50
Macclesfield Town	42	20	7	15	103	82	47
Ellesmere Port Town	42	18	9	15	62	63	45
Runcorn	42	20	4	18	86	74	44
Tranmere Rovers Reserves	42	19	5	18	82	85	43
Port Vale Reserves	42	17	8	17	71	71	42
Altrincham	42	15	11	16	71	77	41
Witton Albion	42	17	5	20	98	95	39
Chester Reserves	42	13	13	16	76	86	39
Bangor City	42	16	7	19	78	96	39
Rhyl	42	14	9	19	66	75	37
Winsford United	42	16	5	21	68	82	37
Mossley	42	11	13	18	65	75	35
Crewe Alexandra Reserves	42	11	12	19	75	97	34
Congleton Town	42	12	8	22	65	88	32
Northwich Victoria	42	11	6	25	68	117	28
Buxton	42	7	10	25	59	124	24

1955-56

Hyde United	42	27	7	8	138	78	61
Rhyl	42	22	12	8	93	68	56
Wellington Town	42	22	10	10	112	59	54
Northwich Victoria	42	22	10	10	99	70	54
Ellesmere Port Town	42	20	13	9	81	51	53
Port Vale Reserves	42	21	8	13	94	80	50
Witton Albion	42	16	16	10	91	80	48
Wrexham Reserves	42	19	8	15	109	88	46
Chester Reserves	42	16	13	13	90	74	45
Runcorn	42	20	5	17	93	88	45
Buxton	42	19	6	17	94	78	44
Winsford United	42	16	11	15	73	76	43
Stockport County Reserves	42	17	8	17	82	76	42
Altrincham	42	15	8	19	74	78	38
Tranmere Rovers Reserves	42	13	12	17	59	74	38
Stalybridge Celtic	42	13	10	19	64	82	36
Bangor City	42	13	7	22	71	107	33
Stafford Rangers	42	12	9	21	52	80	33
Mossley	42	10	13	19	68	114	33
Congleton Town	42	10	6	26	68	104	26
Macclesfield Town	42	10	6	26	70	115	26
Crewe Alexandra Reserves	42	8	4	30	55	110	20

1956-57

Northwich Victoria	42	25	7	10	139	72	57
Hyde United	42	25	5	12	129	102	55
Wellington Town	42	22	10	10	92	58	54
Witton Albion	42	22	9	11	84	66	53
Rhyl	42	22	6	14	111	71	50
Stockport County Reserves	42	19	12	11	105	73	50
Chester Reserves	42	20	8	14	86	87	48
Winsford United	42	20	6	16	92	77	46
Buxton	42	19	7	16	79	86	45
Macclesfield Town	42	17	10	15	102	73	44
Ellesmere Port Town	42	17	10	15	86	77	44
Wrexham Reserves	42	15	10	17	98	101	40
Stalybridge Celtic	42	15	9	18	86	111	39
Runcorn	42	13	13	16	67	88	39
Tranmere Rovers Reserves	42	16	6	20	99	95	38
Altrincham	42	14	7	21	94	102	35
Port Vale Reserves	42	13	9	20	78	96	35
Mossley	42	10	15	17	62	96	35
Congleton Town	42	12	10	20	79	111	34
Stafford Rangers	42	12	9	21	57	74	33
Bangor City	42	10	8	24	73	115	28
Crewe Alexandra Reserves	42	9	4	29	72	139	22

1957-58

Ellesmere Port Town	42	24	10	8	91	53	58
Hyde United	42	26	6	10	106	68	58
Northwich Victoria	42	22	10	10	91	66	54
Port Vale Reserves	42	22	8	12	80	51	52
Chester Reserves	42	22	7	13	91	63	51
Tranmere Rovers Reserves	42	21	7	14	103	72	49
Buxton	42	20	9	13	86	66	49
Bangor City	42	19	11	12	81	68	49
Rhyl	42	22	4	16	94	76	48
Witton Albion	42	19	8	15	91	84	46
Wrexham Reserves	42	19	8	15	71	67	46
Wellington Town	42	19	8	15	89	88	46
Winsford United	42	17	8	17	87	83	42
Runcorn	42	15	10	17	71	74	40
Altrincham	42	14	10	18	70	78	38
Stafford Rangers	42	14	8	20	68	104	36
Crewe Alexandra Reserves	42	12	11	19	86	95	35
Congleton Town	42	13	8	21	52	76	34
Stockport County Reserves	42	11	10	21	67	84	32
Stalybridge Celtic	42	7	7	28	57	96	21
Macclesfield Town	42	6	9	27	71	136	21
Mossley	42	7	5	30	57	112	19

1958-59

Ellesmere Port Town	38	25	7	6	106	41	57
Bangor City	38	22	5	11	85	61	49
Tranmere Rovers Reserves	38	21	5	12	90	55	47
Port Vale Reserves	38	20	6	12	90	51	46
Chester Reserves	38	20	6	12	73	63	46
Wrexham Reserves	38	20	3	15	85	75	43
Rhyl	38	15	12	11	72	76	42
Hyde United	38	19	3	16	73	69	41
Buxton	38	16	8	14	87	71	40
Northwich Victoria	38	16	7	15	96	74	39
Winsford United	38	15	9	14	80	69	39
Runcorn	38	13	11	14	67	57	37
Altrincham	38	14	6	18	57	64	34
Crewe Alexandra Reserves	38	13	8	17	73	94	34
Mossley	38	13	5	20	78	97	31
Witton Albion	38	12	6	20	71	90	30
Stafford Rangers	38	11	8	19	60	98	30
Macclesfield Town	38	11	5	22	67	99	27
Congleton Town	38	12	3	23	60	104	27
Stalybridge Celtic	38	8	5	25	60	122	21

1959-60

	P	W	D	L	F	A	Pts
Ellesmere Port Town	38	25	6	7	80	46	56
Hyde United	38	22	8	8	100	56	52
Winsford United	38	19	11	8	85	48	49
Buxton	38	21	7	10	85	56	49
Runcorn	38	21	5	12	87	70	47
Northwich Victoria	38	17	11	10	70	44	45
Bangor City	38	18	6	14	86	58	42
Mossley	38	18	6	14	77	70	42
Altrincham	38	14	11	13	65	73	39
Oswestry Town	38	15	8	15	82	84	38
Tranmere Rovers Reserves	38	16	5	17	72	73	37
Rhyl	38	15	7	16	50	58	37
Macclesfield Town	38	15	6	17	83	81	36
Wrexham Reserves	38	14	7	17	70	83	35
Stalybridge Celtic	38	13	6	19	65	86	32
Witton Albion	38	13	4	21	86	96	30
Chester Reserves	38	12	6	20	57	83	30
Congleton Town	38	9	8	21	59	87	26
Stafford Rangers	38	11	4	23	54	83	26
Wigan Rovers	38	4	4	30	41	119	12

1960-61

	P	W	D	L	F	A	Pts
Macclesfield Town	42	26	9	7	133	69	61
Ellesmere Port Town	42	25	6	11	111	61	56
Frickley Colliery	42	24	8	10	103	65	56
Mossley	42	23	7	12	93	66	53
Oswestry Town	42	23	7	12	113	84	53
Bangor City	42	22	8	12	103	65	52
Wrexham Reserves	42	22	6	14	109	83	50
Buxton	42	21	7	14	96	76	49
Hyde United	42	19	10	13	91	60	48
Runcorn	42	18	10	14	89	77	46
Witton Albion	42	16	14	12	89	78	46
Northwich Victoria	42	20	6	16	93	84	46
Tranmere Rovers Reserves	42	19	5	18	93	90	43
Winsford United	42	14	9	19	76	101	37
Chester Reserves	42	14	8	20	67	85	36
Sankeys (Wellington)	42	13	10	19	77	98	36
Congleton Town	42	14	7	21	67	91	35
Rhyl	42	11	7	24	65	85	29
Stalybridge Celtic	42	11	5	26	85	123	27
Stafford Rangers	42	8	10	24	54	84	26
Altrincham	42	8	6	28	68	125	22
Wigan Rovers	42	7	3	32	44	169	17

1961-62

	P	W	D	L	F	A	Pts
Ellesmere Port Town	42	25	13	4	103	52	63
Macclesfield Town	42	25	10	7	109	61	60
Runcorn	42	27	3	12	108	60	57
Northwich Victoria	42	25	5	12	103	56	55
Wigan Athletic	42	24	7	11	86	51	55
Hyde United	42	24	4	14	81	65	52
Buxton	42	21	6	15	98	79	48
Mossley	42	20	7	15	87	78	47
Stalybridge Celtic	42	17	7	18	79	74	41
Bangor City	42	15	11	16	86	86	41
Altrincham	42	15	10	17	58	64	40
Sankeys (Wellington)	42	16	7	19	76	74	39
Stafford Rangers	42	12	13	17	72	84	37
Rhyl	42	12	11	19	52	63	35
Congleton Town	42	12	11	19	57	78	35
Wrexham Reserves	42	12	11	19	53	79	35
Oswestry Town	42	13	8	21	76	103	34
Winsford United	42	12	8	22	73	100	32
Chester Reserves	42	11	10	21	66	106	32
Tranmere Rovers Reserves	42	10	9	23	73	111	29
Frickley Colliery	42	10	9	23	65	108	29
Witton Albion	42	11	6	25	70	99	28

1962-63

	P	W	D	L	F	A	Pts
Runcorn	42	26	13	3	95	43	65
Buxton	42	24	7	11	104	71	55
Tranmere Rovers Reserves	42	19	15	8	88	57	53
Stalybridge Celtic	42	22	9	11	98	71	53
Macclesfield Town	42	20	12	10	87	59	52
Ellesmere Port Town	42	19	14	9	78	57	52
Wigan Athletic	42	22	6	14	70	54	50
Altrincham	42	19	8	15	90	68	46
Northwich Victoria	42	15	15	12	77	68	45
Winsford United	42	16	11	15	69	73	43
Frickley Colliery	42	16	11	15	66	79	43
Hyde United	42	14	14	14	81	74	42
Bangor City	42	13	16	13	71	68	42
Witton Albion	42	16	10	16	84	86	42
Wrexham Reserves	42	18	4	20	72	86	40
Congleton Town	42	16	7	19	73	80	39
Rhyl	42	12	10	20	64	86	34
Sankeys (Wellington)	42	10	13	19	64	76	33
Mossley	42	10	9	23	55	81	29
Stafford Rangers	42	9	10	23	50	90	28
Chester Reserves	42	7	7	28	62	105	21
Oswestry Town	42	6	5	31	53	119	17

1963-64

	P	W	D	L	F	A	Pts
Macclesfield Town	42	30	9	3	112	38	69
Sankeys (Wellington)	42	23	10	9	98	57	56
Altrincham	42	22	8	12	94	68	52
Bangor City	42	21	9	12	75	55	51
Witton Albion	42	22	7	13	64	64	51
Tranmere Rovers Reserves	42	19	10	13	108	71	48
Runcorn	42	19	10	13	81	71	48
Ellesmere Port Town	42	20	8	14	77	76	48
Buxton	42	18	11	13	92	77	47
Hyde United	42	18	11	13	64	60	47
Frickley Colliery	42	18	9	15	65	57	45
Wigan Athletic	42	18	7	17	94	82	43
Mossley	42	16	7	19	66	77	39
Rhyl	42	13	12	17	73	88	38
Oswestry Town	42	13	10	19	85	94	36
Stafford Rangers	42	15	6	21	66	89	36
Chester Reserves	42	15	5	22	70	82	35
Stalybridge Celtic	42	14	6	22	66	80	34
Northwich Victoria	42	13	6	23	64	87	32
Winsford United	42	9	11	22	61	98	29
Congleton Town	42	4	13	25	43	95	21
Wrexham Reserves	42	7	5	30	58	113	19

1964-65

	P	W	D	L	F	A	Pts
Wigan Athletic	42	32	3	7	121	46	67
Macclesfield Town	42	28	6	8	115	45	62
Runcorn	42	27	5	10	121	60	59
Bangor City	42	25	4	13	94	58	54
Tranmere Rovers Reserves	42	22	6	14	93	70	50
Hyde United	42	22	6	14	96	76	50
Frickley Colliery	42	21	8	13	79	74	50
Altrincham	42	18	12	12	74	55	48
Stalybridge Celtic	42	17	11	14	78	74	45
Ellesmere Port Town	42	19	6	17	79	60	44
Northwich Victoria	42	18	6	18	100	87	42
Rhyl	42	17	6	19	69	79	40
Oswestry Town	42	17	5	20	100	100	39
Mossley	42	13	12	17	57	62	38
Buxton	42	15	7	20	77	99	37
Witton Albion	42	14	8	20	79	90	36
Winsford United	42	15	5	22	66	96	35
Wrexham Reserves	42	13	9	20	58	99	35
Sankeys (Wellington)	42	10	13	19	70	87	33
Chester Reserves	42	11	8	23	65	99	30
Stafford Rangers	42	6	5	31	44	120	17
Congleton Town	42	3	7	32	46	145	13

1965-66

Team	P	W	D	L	F	A	Pts
Altrincham	42	33	7	2	132	49	73
Wigan Athletic	42	32	8	2	133	40	72
Macclesfield Town	42	26	8	8	102	48	60
Bangor City	42	24	6	12	91	67	54
Runcorn	42	22	7	13	105	77	51
Stalybridge Celtic	42	21	8	13	98	84	50
Northwich Victoria	42	20	6	16	93	77	46
Hyde United	42	16	11	15	74	72	43
Ellesmere Port Town	42	16	10	16	97	80	42
Stockport County Reserves	42	14	13	15	61	65	41
New Brighton	42	17	6	19	76	86	40
Buxton	42	15	8	19	74	82	38
Tranmere Rovers Reserves	42	13	11	18	85	88	37
Frickley Colliery	42	13	11	18	76	102	37
Mossley	42	13	10	19	66	72	36
Oswestry Town	42	15	6	21	78	102	36
Witton Albion	42	14	7	21	93	107	35
Wrexham Reserves	42	15	5	22	92	107	35
Stafford Rangers	42	9	10	23	60	109	28
Rhyl	42	8	10	24	57	104	26
Chester Reserves	42	9	7	26	52	116	25

1966-67

Team	P	W	D	L	F	A	Pts
Altrincham	42	31	5	6	123	45	67
Wigan Athletic	42	26	8	8	101	61	60
Northwich Victoria	42	22	13	7	91	55	57
Hyde United	42	24	8	10	101	56	56
Macclesfield Town	42	24	8	10	78	47	56
Witton Albion	42	21	9	12	74	56	51
Bangor City	42	20	8	14	90	77	48
Frickley Colliery	42	18	10	14	71	69	46
Runcorn	42	16	11	15	75	75	43
New Brighton	42	16	7	19	69	73	39
Mossley	42	15	9	18	66	71	39
Chester Reserves	42	13	12	17	72	71	38
Oswestry Town	42	15	8	19	64	89	38
Ellesmere Port Town	42	11	15	16	61	70	37
Stafford Rangers	42	12	12	18	59	66	36
Buxton	42	13	10	19	69	78	36
Tranmere Rovers Reserves	42	14	8	20	66	84	36
Stockport County Reserves	42	12	9	21	58	76	33
Rhyl	42	11	9	22	59	86	31
Stalybridge Celtic	42	11	8	23	52	85	30
Wrexham Reserves	42	11	3	28	66	114	25
Winsford United	42	8	6	28	46	107	22

1967-68

Team	P	W	D	L	F	A	Pts
Macclesfield Town	42	28	10	4	96	39	66
Altrincham	42	28	7	7	108	64	63
Bangor City	42	24	9	9	99	61	57
Witton Albion	42	21	12	9	90	65	54
Mossley	42	20	13	9	90	62	53
Tranmere Rovers Reserves	42	22	6	14	71	50	50
Northwich Victoria	42	22	6	14	82	64	50
Wigan Athletic	42	18	12	12	62	48	48
Stafford Rangers	42	18	11	13	88	58	47
Hyde United	42	17	12	13	97	74	46
New Brighton	42	16	10	16	60	69	42
Ellesmere Port Town	42	15	11	16	68	67	41
Runcorn	42	16	8	18	99	95	40
Wrexham Reserves	42	16	8	18	72	77	40
Buxton	42	14	8	20	71	86	36
Rhyl	42	12	10	20	63	78	34
Winsford United	42	13	7	22	50	82	33
Oswestry Town	42	13	6	23	63	106	32
Frickley Colliery	42	10	10	22	61	83	30
Stockport County Reserves	42	10	7	25	55	92	27
Stalybridge Celtic	42	6	14	22	54	93	26
Chester Reserves	42	2	5	35	48	134	9

1968-69

Team	P	W	D	L	F	A	Pts
Skelmersdale United	38	29	6	3	103	34	64
Stafford Rangers	38	26	6	6	98	46	58
Mossley	38	26	5	7	90	45	57
Guinness Exports	38	19	9	10	75	46	47
Stalybridge Celtic	38	19	6	13	88	66	44
Tranmere Rovers Reserves	38	17	8	13	63	46	42
New Brighton	38	18	5	15	51	48	41
Buxton	38	16	8	14	71	53	40
Witton Albion	38	15	9	14	62	60	39
Horwich RMI	38	13	13	12	54	63	39
Frickley Colliery	38	12	12	14	64	65	36
Nantwich Town	38	13	9	16	74	79	35
Droylsden	38	14	7	17	64	89	35
Ellesmere Port Town	38	12	9	17	57	66	33
Oswestry Town	38	12	9	17	67	90	33
Winsford United	38	12	6	20	49	70	30
Rhyl	38	11	6	21	58	78	28
Sandbach Ramblers	38	9	4	25	54	91	22
Chester Reserves	38	8	5	25	47	99	21
Ashton United	38	5	6	27	44	99	16

1969-70

Team	P	W	D	L	F	A	Pts
Skelmersdale United	38	30	6	2	104	18	66
Mossley	38	23	6	9	101	47	52
Stalybridge Celtic	38	20	9	9	81	54	49
Horwich RMI	38	21	6	11	93	59	48
Buxton	38	19	8	11	64	59	46
Guinness Exports	38	20	5	13	76	64	45
Tranmere Rovers Reserves	38	18	7	13	68	52	43
Rhyl	38	16	11	11	70	55	43
Ellesmere Port Town	38	18	6	14	54	49	42
Marine	38	15	8	15	69	68	38
Droylsden	38	16	5	17	72	68	37
Oswestry Town	38	16	5	17	63	66	37
Witton Albion	38	15	6	17	71	80	36
Frickley Colliery	38	15	5	18	60	71	35
Sandbach Ramblers	38	14	6	18	57	80	34
Nantwich Town	38	11	4	23	53	78	26
Winsford United	38	10	5	23	43	79	25
Ashton United	38	10	3	25	56	98	23
Port Vale Reserves	38	7	4	27	46	100	18
New Brighton	38	4	9	25	31	87	17

1970-71

Team	P	W	D	L	F	A	Pts
Rossendale United	42	28	11	3	84	39	67
Burscough	42	24	12	6	106	61	60
Skelmersdale United	42	22	12	8	87	48	56
Mossley	42	24	6	12	81	51	54
Ellesmere Port Town	42	16	17	9	56	38	49
Stalybridge Celtic	42	20	7	15	74	59	47
Horwich RMI	42	16	12	14	67	55	44
Buxton	42	18	8	16	69	72	44
Marine	42	16	11	15	66	59	43
Ormskirk	42	17	8	17	62	64	42
Oswestry Town	42	15	12	15	75	81	42
Witton Albion	42	12	17	13	68	68	41
Ashton United	42	15	9	18	65	72	39
Rhyl	42	13	13	16	49	56	39
Sandbach Ramblers	42	14	10	18	54	67	38
Hyde United	42	12	13	17	69	80	37
Oldham Athletic Reserves	42	13	9	20	64	74	35
Nantwich Town	42	11	13	18	56	70	35
Droylsden	42	9	16	17	59	72	34
Winsford United	42	10	14	18	55	80	34
Port Vale Reserves	42	7	10	25	38	88	24
New Brighton	42	6	29	35	85	20	

Ormskirk were formerly called Guinness Exports

1971-72

Rhyl	42	31	4	7	95	33	66
Rossendale United	42	26	5	11	90	65	57
Marine	42	23	9	10	72	48	55
Buxton	42	21	12	9	81	47	54
Oswestry Town	42	21	7	14	84	66	49
Mossley	42	20	7	15	74	55	47
Burscough	42	19	9	14	71	56	47
Hyde United	42	17	10	15	79	72	44
Droylsden	42	16	11	15	77	70	43
Oldham Athletic Reserves	42	16	9	17	66	63	41
Stalybridge Celtic	42	16	9	17	68	65	41
Prestwich Heys	42	13	14	15	74	94	40
Horwich RMI	42	16	6	20	61	82	38
Witton Albion	42	17	3	22	75	82	37
Winsford United	42	16	5	21	57	82	37
Ormskirk	42	12	11	19	54	54	35
Sandbach Ramblers	42	11	13	18	51	68	35
Ashton United	42	14	7	21	57	79	35
Radcliffe Borough	42	11	10	21	65	82	32
Formby	42	11	10	21	61	92	32
New Brighton	42	11	8	23	58	86	30
Nantwich Town	42	12	5	25	59	88	29

1974-75

Leek Town	42	27	9	6	92	49	63
Winsford United	42	26	9	7	108	58	61
Sandbach Ramblers	42	21	15	6	80	56	57
Oldham Athletic Reserves	42	24	8	10	85	43	56
Marine	42	24	7	11	73	40	55
Chorley	42	19	11	12	86	68	49
Burscough	42	19	10	13	70	49	48
Rossendale United	42	17	13	12	77	64	47
Formby	42	16	13	13	55	55	45
Oswestry Town	42	16	10	16	56	52	42
Horwich RMI	42	17	7	18	60	59	41
New Mills	42	14	11	17	68	82	39
Stalybridge Celtic	42	14	10	18	66	69	38
Rhyl	42	14	10	18	72	78	38
New Brighton	42	12	14	16	53	60	38
Witton Albion	42	10	17	15	59	69	37
Droylsden	42	14	8	20	53	78	36
Nantwich Town	42	9	14	19	63	87	32
Ashton United	42	11	7	24	43	86	29
Hyde United	42	9	8	25	62	80	26
Radcliffe Borough	42	6	12	24	50	97	24
Prestwich Heys	42	8	7	27	48	100	23

1972-73

Buxton	42	28	8	6	89	32	64
Marine	42	27	7	8	73	36	61
Hyde United	42	22	9	11	75	49	53
Stalybridge Celtic	42	17	19	6	83	57	53
Rossendale United	42	21	9	12	62	40	51
Sandbach Ramblers	42	19	10	13	66	55	48
Burscough	42	17	13	12	63	53	47
Formby	42	17	12	13	60	64	46
Chorley	42	18	9	15	69	50	45
Witton Albion	42	16	11	15	63	51	43
Oldham Athletic Reserves	42	16	8	18	60	52	40
New Brighton	42	16	8	18	47	64	40
Oswestry Town	42	12	15	15	75	73	39
Ormskirk	42	12	14	16	53	60	38
Winsford United	42	13	12	17	57	72	38
Rhyl	42	9	16	17	52	73	34
Droylsden	42	11	11	20	62	75	33
Radcliffe Borough	42	11	11	20	60	88	33
Nantwich Town	42	10	12	20	44	69	32
Ashton United	42	12	6	24	61	86	30
Horwich RMI	42	6	16	20	57	83	28
Prestwich Heys	42	9	10	23	47	96	28

1975-76

Marine	42	28	8	6	94	34	64
Chorley	42	29	5	8	88	33	63
Leek Town	42	27	7	8	74	33	61
Winsford United	42	24	10	8	83	44	58
Witton Albion	42	20	14	8	71	37	54
Nantwich Town	42	23	8	11	88	54	54
Middlewich Athletic	42	20	8	14	61	51	48
Stalybridge Celtic	42	20	6	16	67	47	46
Droylsden	42	17	11	14	66	55	45
New Brighton	42	19	7	16	59	57	45
Rossendale United	42	17	9	16	66	62	43
Burscough	42	16	10	16	68	73	42
Hyde United	42	15	11	16	73	75	41
St. Helens Town	42	14	11	17	54	57	39
Formby	42	10	15	17	44	59	35
Ashton United	42	13	8	21	50	63	34
Radcliffe Borough	42	13	5	24	56	94	31
Horwich RMI	42	8	13	21	42	90	29
Rhyl	42	8	10	24	46	83	26
Darwen	42	9	7	26	49	89	25
New Mills	42	8	6	28	47	95	22
Prestwich Heys	42	6	7	29	39	103	19

1973-74

Marine	42	28	8	6	79	26	64
Rossendale United	42	29	6	7	87	39	64
Chorley	42	23	11	8	68	39	57
Leek Town	42	23	11	8	75	49	57
Sandbach Ramblers	42	19	16	7	66	40	54
Burscough	42	19	10	13	70	54	48
Formby	42	17	12	13	62	53	46
Stalybridge Celtic	42	17	12	13	65	63	46
Witton Albion	42	14	17	11	57	48	45
Oldham Athletic Reserves	42	15	11	16	53	49	41
Winsford United	42	12	16	14	51	51	40
Radcliffe Borough	42	12	15	15	57	67	39
Droylsden	42	13	12	17	57	68	38
New Brighton	42	16	6	20	52	63	38
Rhyl	42	14	10	18	67	82	38
Hyde United	42	14	8	20	65	67	36
Oswestry Town	42	12	12	18	61	78	36
Nantwich Town	42	8	13	21	57	82	29
Ashton United	42	11	7	24	59	97	29
Horwich RMI	42	10	7	25	52	74	27
Ormskirk	42	9	9	24	51	88	27
Prestwich Heys	42	7	11	24	54	88	25

1976-77

Winsford United	42	31	8	3	98	41	70
Chorley	42	28	6	8	80	35	62
Witton Albion	42	27	6	9	91	32	60
Leek Town	42	24	10	8	91	37	58
Stalybridge Celtic	42	23	10	9	66	44	56
Nantwich Town	42	22	7	13	72	59	51
Marine	42	18	14	10	62	40	50
Horwich RMI	42	18	10	14	72	58	46
Formby	42	17	9	16	59	56	43
St. Helens Town	42	16	10	16	51	58	42
New Brighton	42	13	14	15	64	60	40
Ashton United	42	15	10	17	65	72	40
Prestwich Heys	42	16	8	18	56	63	40
Burscough	42	12	15	15	60	65	39
Rhyl	42	13	9	20	54	69	35
Droylsden	42	13	8	21	60	78	34
Hyde United	42	12	9	21	57	74	33
New Mills	42	10	10	22	47	67	30
Darwen	42	10	8	24	50	81	28
Rossendale United	42	9	10	23	48	85	28
Middlewich Athletic	42	9	4	29	48	108	22
Radcliffe Borough	42	4	9	29	44	113	17

1977-78

Marine	42	26	10	6	101	48	62
Stalybridge Celtic	42	23	12	7	75	47	58
Witton Albion	42	21	14	7	98	54	56
Hyde United	42	21	13	8	68	37	55
Winsford United	42	24	7	11	80	51	55
Ashton United	42	20	13	9	88	56	53
Horwich RMI	42	19	14	9	62	50	52
Leek Town	42	20	10	12	62	45	50
Chorley	42	19	11	12	69	48	49
Formby	42	18	11	13	71	57	47
Middlewich Athletic	42	15	15	12	67	66	45
St. Helens Town	42	15	15	12	53	55	45
Droylsden	42	15	10	17	54	56	40
Burscough	42	13	12	17	56	63	38
Darwen	42	14	6	22	50	68	34
Nantwich Town	42	9	13	20	56	69	31
Rhyl	42	10	10	22	44	67	30
New Brighton	42	10	10	22	35	69	30
New Mills	42	9	9	24	42	72	27
Rossendale United	42	11	4	27	51	110	26
Prestwich Heys	42	6	9	27	42	88	21
Radcliffe Borough	42	7	6	29	46	94	20

1978-79

Division One

Horwich RMI	42	35	2	5	89	45	72
Witton Albion	42	30	4	8	114	38	64
Marine	42	29	5	8	104	38	63
Stalybridge Celtic	42	25	5	12	93	47	55
Burscough	42	19	15	8	59	31	53
Winsford United	42	21	11	10	74	49	53
Chorley	42	21	8	13	66	43	50
Formby	42	20	9	13	73	57	49
Leek Town	42	19	10	13	62	43	48
Droylsden	42	18	9	15	62	61	45
Nantwich Town	42	18	8	16	76	72	44
Fleetwood Town	42	17	10	15	70	68	44
Hyde United	42	15	12	15	59	57	42
St. Helens Town	42	16	9	17	59	57	41
Darwen	42	15	9	18	52	53	39
Rhyl	42	15	8	19	53	60	38
Ashton United	42	13	5	24	63	94	31
New Mills	42	9	11	22	58	82	29
Rossendale United	42	11	6	25	51	108	28
Radcliffe Borough	42	4	7	31	37	115	15
New Brighton	42	3	5	34	36	115	11
Middlewich Athletic	42	3	4	35	43	120	10

Division Two

Bootle	34	19	9	6	61	35	47
Curzon Ashton	34	18	9	7	57	32	45
Prescot Town	34	20	5	9	68	37	43
Kirkby Town	34	18	6	10	66	42	42
Accrington Stanley	34	18	6	10	65	43	42
Irlam Town	34	16	10	8	47	33	42
Congleton Town	34	14	13	7	52	31	41
Prescot BI	34	15	11	8	55	42	41
Eastwood Hanley	34	15	9	10	60	47	39
Prestwich Heys	34	17	5	12	53	41	37
Maghull	34	11	7	16	41	50	29
Ford Motors	34	9	10	15	38	52	28
Anson Villa	34	10	7	17	39	60	27
Warrington Town	34	11	5	18	45	69	27
Atherton Collieries	34	8	9	17	43	56	25
Skelmersdale United	34	9	6	19	36	53	24
Glossop	34	6	6	22	42	83	18
Ashton Town	34	3	5	26	22	84	11

Prescot Town and Prestwich Heys both had 2 points deducted for fielding ineligible players.

1979-80

Division One

Stalybridge Celtic	38	26	7	5	94	46	59
Winsford United	38	23	6	9	72	41	52
Chorley	38	20	11	7	60	35	51
Ashton United	38	15	15	8	71	65	45
Burscough	38	16	11	11	67	54	43
Hyde United	38	16	10	12	60	48	42
Droylsden	38	15	10	13	63	45	40
Horwich RMI	38	13	12	13	53	52	38
Curzon Ashton	38	11	14	13	48	55	36
Darwen	38	12	12	14	41	52	36
Rossendale United	38	12	12	14	48	73	36
St. Helens Town	38	10	15	13	59	55	35
Bootle	38	14	7	17	50	53	35
Nantwich Town	38	14	7	17	53	62	35
New Mills	38	11	13	14	44	57	35
Formby	38	13	7	18	50	58	33
Fleetwood Town	38	10	11	17	51	63	31
Leek Town	38	10	9	19	45	66	29
Rhyl	38	10	7	21	54	66	27
Radcliffe Borough	38	6	10	22	45	82	22

Division Two

Prescot Town	34	22	7	5	89	25	51
Accrington Stanley	34	20	9	5	67	33	49
Kirkby Town	34	23	3	8	70	40	49
Prescot BI	34	19	7	8	77	54	45
Congleton Town	34	18	8	8	61	42	44
Eastwood Hanley	34	15	10	9	65	44	40
Glossop	34	14	7	13	53	45	35
Maghull	34	12	10	12	49	49	34
Ford Motors	34	13	6	15	48	44	32
New Brighton	34	13	6	15	59	63	32
Atherton Collieries	34	9	14	11	44	48	32
Irlam Town	34	12	7	15	48	49	31
Middlewich Athletic	34	12	6	16	55	64	30
Skelmersdale United	34	9	10	15	46	69	28
Warrington Town	34	9	6	19	48	80	24
Prestwich Heys	34	8	6	20	36	71	22
Ashton Town	34	3	12	19	35	83	18
Anson Villa	34	5	6	23	29	76	16

1980-81

Division One

Nantwich Town	38	26	6	6	87	34	58
Hyde United	38	23	9	6	75	27	55
Winsford United	38	20	10	8	75	38	50
Formby	38	21	7	10	65	39	49
Stalybridge Celtic	38	16	15	7	62	50	47
Chorley	38	17	11	10	65	48	45
Bootle	38	18	7	13	68	53	43
Prescot Cables	38	16	9	13	60	46	41
Horwich RMI	38	15	9	14	53	49	39
Leek Town	38	15	9	14	50	47	39
Ashton United	38	12	12	14	70	73	36
Curzon Ashton	38	14	8	16	48	63	36
St. Helens Town	38	14	7	17	63	82	35
Fleetwood Town	38	9	13	16	33	53	31
Rossendale United	38	9	12	17	49	69	30
Burscough	38	11	6	21	52	62	28
Darwen	38	8	10	20	46	74	26
Droylsden	38	9	8	21	49	82	26
Kirkby Town	38	6	11	21	30	65	23
New Mills	38	8	7	23	34	80	23

Prescot Cables were formerly known as Prescot Town.

Division Two

Accrington Stanley	38	26	3	9	73	20	55
Glossop	38	23	9	6	76	38	55
Leyland Motors	38	20	10	8	68	42	50
Middlewich Athletic	38	20	10	8	56	32	50
Atherton Laburnum Rovers	38	19	11	8	61	39	49
Prescot BI	38	20	5	13	59	40	45
Rhyl	38	20	5	13	69	57	45
Maghull	38	15	12	11	55	41	42
Ford Motors	38	16	9	13	49	52	41
Congleton Town	38	16	8	14	67	55	40
Radcliffe Borough	38	15	10	13	58	48	40
Irlam Town	38	15	6	17	49	51	36
Warrington Town	38	15	5	18	59	78	35
Prestwich Heys	38	15	4	19	66	68	34
Salford	38	9	13	16	50	70	31
Eastwood Hanley	38	12	6	20	47	55	30
Skelmersdale United	38	9	10	19	51	68	28
Atherton Collieries	38	8	5	25	39	83	21
Ashton Town	38	6	5	27	40	93	17
New Brighton	38	6	4	28	31	93	16

1981-82

Division One

Hyde United	38	27	8	3	91	34	62
Chorley	38	23	9	6	70	34	55
Burscough	38	21	10	7	70	39	52
Winsford United	38	21	9	8	68	43	51
Rossendale United	38	18	10	10	62	44	46
Glossop	38	13	19	6	52	30	45
Darwen	38	16	10	12	63	62	40
Curzon Ashton	38	12	15	11	57	50	39
Prescot Cables	38	16	8	14	51	45	38
Stalybridge Celtic	38	14	9	15	71	66	37
Fleetwood Town	38	12	13	13	42	55	37
Formby	38	12	11	15	42	55	35
Accrington Stanley	38	11	11	16	40	57	33
Nantwich Town	38	10	13	15	48	49	31
Leek Town	38	10	11	17	39	45	31
Horwich RMI	38	12	7	19	58	72	31
Bootle	38	11	12	15	49	47	30
St. Helens Town	38	7	11	20	34	71	25
Ashton United	38	8	6	24	38	77	22
Droylsden	38	3	4	31	26	96	10

Darwen, Prescot Cables and Nantwich Town all had 2 points deducted for fielding ineligible players.
Bootle had 4 points deducted for fielding ineligible players.

Division Two

Congleton Town	38	25	9	4	67	20	59
Rhyl	38	24	10	4	84	29	58
Irlam Town	38	23	10	5	67	27	56
Leyland Motors	38	19	14	5	79	45	52
Maghull	38	20	7	11	64	48	47
Radcliffe Borough	38	18	7	13	64	39	43
Kirkby Town	38	17	9	12	53	42	43
Warrington Town	38	17	8	13	52	35	42
Eastwood Hanley	38	16	9	13	62	51	39
Middlewich Athletic	38	15	11	12	42	34	39
Atherton Laburnum Rovers	38	14	11	13	46	46	39
Ford Motors	38	13	10	15	48	59	36
Prescot BI	38	14	7	17	64	70	35
Ellesmere Port & Neston	38	13	6	19	43	55	32
Skelmersdale United	38	13	5	20	32	49	29
Salford	38	9	6	23	34	65	24
Atherton Collieries	38	8	7	23	41	85	23
Ashton Town	38	6	9	23	40	76	21
New Mills	38	6	8	24	31	93	20
Prestwich Heys	38	5	7	26	30	75	15

Eastwood Hanley, Middlewich Athletic, Skelmersdale United and Prestwich Heys all had 2 points deducted for fielding ineligible players.

FORMATION

The success of the new Football League in the 1888-89 season encouraged areas where the game was popular to start their own leagues. Lancashire was in the forefront of the development of the game and discussions regarding the formation of a Lancashire League for the 1889-90 season began even before the 1888-89 season had finished. Peter Cullen's "Official History of Bury F.C." published by Yore Publications records that was the case at Bury where the subject was discussed at a committee meeting on 26th March 1889 and the same thing probably happened at other clubs as well. Eventually a meeting was held at the Saddle Hotel in Bolton and the following 14 clubs became founder members : Blackpool, Blackburn Park Road, Bury, Earlestown, Fleetwood Rangers, Heywood, Heywood Central, Higher Walton, Hyde, Nelson, Oswaldtwistle Rovers, Rossendale, Southport Central and West Manchester.

FORMATION

Changes are noted either against the season in which they occurred or the year concerned if the changes were in the close season.

1889-90   Earlestown were expelled for refusing to fulfil their fixtures and their record was deleted.

1890   Hyde left to join The Combination and Blackburn Park Road also left. Burnley Union Star joined from the North-East Lancashire League. League reduced to 12 clubs.

1890-91   Burnley Union Star did not complete their fixtures and their record was deleted.

1891   Oswaldtwistle Rovers left and joined the North-East Lancashire League. Witton (from Blackburn) joined from The Combination and South Shore (from Blackpool) also joined.

1892   Heywood and Witton both left. Fairfield joined as did two new Liverpool clubs. These were Liverpool Caledonians and Liverpool. The latter had been founded in March 1892 by the landlord of the Anfield Road ground when Everton left the ground over a dispute on how much rent they should pay. League increased to 13 clubs.

1892-93   Liverpool Caledonians went into liquidation during the season and their record was deleted.

1893   Liverpool left and joined the Football League and Higher Walton also left. Accrington decided to join rather than be relegated to Division Two of the Football League and Barrow also joined. League continued with 12 clubs.

1893-94   Barrow resigned on November 20th and Bacup from the North-East Lancashire League took over their fixtures.

1894   Bury left and joined the Football League but the league was increased to 14 clubs by the election of Chorley from the Lancashire Alliance, Clitheroe from the North-East Lancashire League and Stockport County from The Combination.

1895   Accrington left and joined the Lancashire Combination and Heywood Central also left. Ashton North End and Stalybridge Rovers joined from The Combination, Liverpool South End joined from the Liverpool and District League and Halliwell Rovers also joined. League increased to 16 clubs.

1896   Blackpool left and joined the Football League and were replaced by Oldham County from The Combination.

1896-97   Liverpool South End resigned in February 1897 because of financial problems and their record was deleted.

1897   Fleetwood Rangers left and joined the Lancashire Combination, Rossendale disbanded and West Manchester also left. The league was increased to 17 clubs by the election of New Brighton Tower and Wigan County who were both new clubs, Horwich from the Lancashire Alliance, Middleton from The Combination and Rochdale from the Lancashire Combination.

1897-98   Fairfield disbanded in October, Oldham County resigned in November and Bacup resigned in February. All three clubs' records were deleted.

1898   New Brighton Tower left and joined the Football League and Clitheroe also left. They were replaced by Crewe Alexandra and Rock Ferry, both from The Combination so the league continued with 14 clubs.

1898-99   Rock Ferry resigned on 9th February when their record was P14 W6 L8 F29 A33 P12. Haydock from the Lancashire Alliance took over their fixtures. Nelson disbanded in January and their record was deleted when it was P10 W5 D2 L3 F25 A21 P12.

1899   Ashton North End and Halliwell Rovers left but league increased to 16 clubs by the election of Blackpool who were not re-elected to the Football League and Darwen who did not seek re-election, plus Earlestown from the Lancashire Alliance and South Liverpool and White Star Wanderers (of Bootle) who were both from The Combination.

1899-1900   South Shore amalgamated with Blackpool in December 1899 and their record was deleted.

1900   Blackpool and Stockport County were both elected to the Football League and White Star Wanderers returned to The Combination. Wigan County disbanded and Horwich, Middleton and South Liverpool also left. These were replaced by four clubs who were: a re-formed Nelson from the North-East Lancashire League, Wigan United who were a new club and the reserves of Blackburn Rovers and Bolton Wanderers who both joined from the Lancashire Combination. League reduced to 12 clubs.

1900-01   Rochdale disbanded in January 1901 and their record was deleted.

1901   Nelson and the reserves of Blackburn Rovers and Bolton Wanderers all left and joined the Lancashire Combination and Crewe Alexandra left and joined the Birmingham League. League increased to 13 clubs by the election of Barrow, Rochdale Town and St. Helens Town who were all new clubs, Prescot from the Lancashire Alliance, Workington from the Cumberland County League and Bacup.

1902   Prescot and Haydock both left and St. Helens Recreation joined from the Lancashire Combination. League reduced to 12 clubs.

1903   The Lancashire League closed down and 9 of its 12 clubs joined the new Second Division of the Lancashire Combination. The 3 exceptions were Darwen who joined Division One of the Lancashire Combination, Workington who returned to the Cumberland County League and Wigan United who disbanded.

LANCASHIRE LEAGUE

1889-90

Higher Walton	24	14	4	6	68	43	32
Bury	24	14	3	7	65	35	31
Heywood Central	24	14	2	8	64	38	30
Nelson	24	12	4	8	55	44	28
Blackpool	24	10	6	8	61	46	26
Southport Central	24	9	7	8	40	32	25
Heywood	24	10	5	9	54	49	25
Blackburn Park Road	24	8	6	10	44	47	22
West Manchester	24	9	4	11	44	70	22
Hyde	24	8	5	11	46	56	21
Oswaldtwistle Rovers	24	8	4	12	39	62	20
Fleetwood Rangers	24	7	5	12	35	51	19
Rossendale	24	4	3	17	37	79	11

Earlestown were expelled for failure to fulfil fixtures and their record was deleted.

1890-91

Bury	20	15	3	2	74	32	33
Blackpool	20	14	2	4	62	39	30
Heywood Central	20	13	3	4	77	34	29
Nelson	20	10	4	6	68	54	24
Heywood	20	8	4	8	42	54	20
Southport Central	20	8	3	9	43	55	19
Rossendale	20	8	1	11	42	43	17
Fleetwood Rangers	20	6	4	10	39	61	16
Higher Walton	20	6	3	11	45	57	15
West Manchester	20	3	4	13	41	70	10
Oswaldtwistle Rovers	20	1	5	14	25	59	7

Burnley Union Star did not complete their fixtures and their record was deleted.

1891-92

Bury	22	20	0	2	76	21	40
Blackpool	22	16	3	3	77	32	35
Fleetwood Rangers	22	12	5	5	84	44	29
Rossendale	22	12	3	7	64	38	27
Southport Central	22	12	3	7	59	47	27
Nelson	22	10	4	8	82	63	24
Heywood Central	22	10	3	9	67	46	23
South Shore	22	5	7	10	51	69	17
Higher Walton	22	5	7	10	46	64	17
West Manchester	22	4	4	14	40	76	12
Witton	22	3	2	17	31	111	8
Heywood	22	1	3	18	23	89	5

1892-93

Liverpool	22	17	2	3	66	19	36
Blackpool	22	17	2	3	82	31	36
Bury	22	17	1	4	83	24	35
Fleetwood Rangers	22	10	5	7	47	51	25
West Manchester	22	10	4	8	68	55	24
Heywood Central	22	11	1	10	54	60	23
Rossendale	22	8	2	12	46	55	18
Southport Central	22	7	2	13	33	44	16
South Shore	22	5	6	11	46	66	16
Fairfield	22	5	6	11	34	53	16
Nelson	22	4	2	16	54	73	10
Higher Walton	22	3	3	16	28	110	9

Liverpool Caledonians disbanded and their record was deleted.

1893-94

Blackpool	22	15	3	4	73	32	33
Bury	22	13	4	5	85	35	30
Southport Central	22	13	0	9	57	42	26
Accrington	22	11	4	7	51	39	26
Nelson	22	10	6	6	70	55	26
Fleetwood Rangers	22	10	2	10	52	49	22
West Manchester	22	9	3	10	43	52	21
South Shore	22	10	0	12	50	68	20
Fairfield	22	8	2	12	40	61	18
Rossendale	22	7	3	12	57	57	17
Heywood Central	22	7	2	13	38	80	14
Bacup	22	2	5	15	39	85	9

Heywood Central had 2 points deducted for playing an ineligible player. Barrow resigned from the League on November 20th and Bacup took over their fixtures.

1894-95

Fairfield	26	17	3	6	68	32	37
Blackpool	26	16	2	8	89	34	34
Nelson	26	14	5	7	75	48	33
Southport Central	26	14	4	8	68	43	32
Fleetwood Rangers	26	13	6	7	62	49	32
Bacup	26	13	5	8	65	55	31
Chorley	26	11	3	12	69	56	25
West Manchester	26	10	5	11	61	63	25
Stockport County	26	10	5	11	53	69	25
South Shore	26	9	6	11	59	45	24
Rossendale	26	10	3	13	52	51	23
Accrington	26	10	2	14	62	63	22
Clitheroe	26	7	1	18	61	93	15
Heywood Central	26	3	0	23	28	171	6

1895-96

Nelson	30	22	4	4	105	39	48
Halliwell Rovers	30	18	3	9	86	55	39
Fairfield	30	17	5	8	65	42	39
Southport Central	30	17	4	9	72	51	38
Liverpool South End	30	15	3	12	63	53	33
Stalybridge Rovers	30	14	4	12	58	65	32
Bacup	30	11	9	10	79	61	31
Chorley	30	12	7	11	66	53	31
South Shore	30	13	5	12	57	60	31
Ashton North End	30	11	7	12	75	77	29
Rossendale	30	13	3	14	47	55	29
Stockport County	30	13	3	14	56	70	29
Blackpool	30	11	6	13	65	50	28
Fleetwood Rangers	30	8	5	17	53	68	21
West Manchester	30	6	1	23	34	109	13
Clitheroe	30	3	3	24	36	109	9

1896-97

Chorley	28	21	3	4	66	23	45
Fairfield	28	19	3	6	77	35	41
Halliwell Rovers	28	14	7	7	74	47	35
Southport Central	28	16	2	10	84	51	34
Clitheroe	28	15	4	9	54	35	34
Stalybridge Rovers	28	14	6	8	51	34	34
Oldham County	28	14	4	10	60	53	32
Nelson	28	13	5	10	66	38	31
Stockport County	28	15	1	12	52	42	31
Ashton North End	28	10	4	14	43	58	24
Bacup	28	6	6	16	46	67	18
West Manchester	28	7	4	17	40	67	18
Fleetwood Rangers	28	6	4	18	33	92	16
South Shore	28	6	3	19	45	73	15
Rossendale	28	5	2	21	37	113	12

Liverpool South End resigned in February 1897 due to financial problems and their record was deleted.

1897-98

New Brighton Tower	26	20	2	4	48	17	42
Nelson	26	17	3	6	72	33	37
Stockport County	26	15	4	7	60	27	34
Halliwell Rovers	26	15	4	7	71	38	34
Chorley	26	13	6	7	51	27	32
Ashton North End	26	12	6	8	50	47	30
Southport Central	26	13	3	10	51	41	29
Wigan County	26	11	5	10	52	41	27
Stalybridge Rovers	26	11	5	10	55	49	27
Middleton	26	11	4	11	58	75	26
South Shore	26	7	6	13	36	59	20
Rochdale	26	5	3	18	47	77	13
Clitheroe	26	2	3	21	20	84	7
Horwich	26	2	2	22	22	78	6

Fairfield resigned in October, Oldham County in November and Bacup in February and their records were all deleted.

1898-1899

Chorley	24	17	5	2	42	17	39
Southport Central	24	12	8	4	41	18	32
Ashton North End	24	13	5	6	35	29	31
Crewe Alexandra	24	11	5	8	61	34	27
Stalybridge Rovers	24	12	3	9	53	53	27
Stockport County	24	12	2	10	48	42	26
Wigan County	24	8	8	8	57	36	24
Middleton	24	8	8	8	40	41	24
Haydock	24	10	0	14	43	48	20
Halliwell Rovers	24	6	5	13	31	42	17
Horwich	24	8	1	15	27	47	17
Rochdale	24	6	3	15	34	80	15
South Shore	24	5	3	16	28	53	13

Rock Ferry resigned and Haydock took over their fixtures when their record was

	14	6	0	8	29	33	12

Nelson disbanded and their record was deleted. At the time, their record was as follows

	10	5	2	3	25	21	12

1899-1900

Stockport County	28	21	3	4	80	23	45
Stalybridge Rovers	28	16	8	4	61	23	40
Blackpool	28	16	6	6	79	36	38
Crewe Alexandra	28	16	4	8	87	48	36
Darwen	28	13	10	5	56	31	36
Chorley	28	15	6	7	49	28	36
Southport Central	28	14	5	9	49	32	33
White Star Wanderers	28	11	4	13	51	56	26
Rochdale	28	9	7	12	50	53	25
Haydock	28	9	5	14	40	57	23
Earlestown	28	7	5	16	40	64	19
Wigan County	28	5	8	15	26	59	18
South Liverpool	28	5	7	16	32	66	17
Horwich	28	5	6	17	27	70	16
Middleton	28	5	2	21	18	99	12

South Shore amalgamated with Blackpool in December 1899 and their record was deleted.

1900-1901

Stalybridge Rovers	20	15	3	2	55	14	33
Southport Central	20	15	3	2	49	15	33
Crewe Alexandra	20	12	2	6	45	23	26
Darwen	20	10	3	7	40	25	23
Blackburn Rovers Reserves	20	6	8	6	34	31	20
Nelson	20	8	4	8	33	35	20
Chorley	20	9	1	10	31	26	19
Earlestown	20	8	3	9	31	45	19
Bolton Wanderers Reserves	20	4	4	12	26	41	12
Wigan United	20	3	3	14	21	49	9
Haydock	20	2	2	16	12	73	6

Rochdale disbanded in January 1901 and their record was deleted.

1901-1902

Darwen	24	18	6	0	78	16	42
Southport Central	24	16	4	4	56	25	36
Wigan United	24	15	3	6	56	25	33
Earlestown	24	12	5	7	54	37	29
Stalybridge Rovers	24	11	4	9	36	29	26
St. Helens Town	24	11	3	10	42	43	25
Rochdale Town	24	10	3	11	48	46	23
Workington	24	9	4	11	57	50	22
Prescot	24	9	4	11	40	40	22
Barrow	24	8	3	13	52	58	19
Chorley	24	7	4	13	44	57	18
Bacup	24	4	3	17	31	81	11
Haydock	24	2	2	20	17	104	6

1902-1903

Southport Central	22	17	2	3	49	18	36
Darwen	22	15	1	6	68	21	31
Barrow	22	14	3	5	45	24	31
Stalybridge Rovers	22	12	4	6	40	25	28
St. Helens Recreation	22	13	1	8	51	41	27
Workington	22	11	3	8	57	47	25
Rochdale Town	22	9	3	10	54	52	21
St. Helens Town	22	8	2	12	31	42	18
Earlestown	22	8	0	14	43	48	16
Chorley	22	7	2	13	38	50	16
Bacup	22	3	4	15	25	77	10
Wigan United	22	1	3	18	18	74	5

FORMATION

The immediate success of the Football League when it was founded in 1888 soon led to many other leagues being formed for those clubs not strong enough to gain entry to the top competition. Lancashire was particularly quick in providing alternatives and many of the major towns where the game was popular soon had their own leagues. However the principle league for Lancashire clubs outside the Football League was the county-wide Lancashire League which was formed in 1889 and it was this competition to which non-League clubs in the county initially aspired. However the Lancashire League had an implacable policy of not allowing reserve sides to enter and this led to the formation of the Lancashire Combination. Blackburn Rovers, Bolton Wanderers and Preston North End were not to be thwarted in finding a suitable competition for their second string sides, so in 1891 and with the willing help of a number of other clubs, the rival Lancashire Combination was formed.

The founder members were Blackburn Rovers Reserves, Bolton Wanderers Reserves, Halliwell, Hindley, North Meols (Southport), Preston North End Reserves, Royton, Skelmersdale United and Stanley (Liverpool). Blackburn Rovers Reserves had previously played in the North-East Lancashire League, Hindley in the Lancashire Alliance and Stanley in the West Lancashire League in 1889-90. Any leagues that the other founder members may have previously played in have not been traced.

Table errors

A number of the tables published at the time contained errors. Additional research has resulted in most of these being corrected; those remaining are noted below.

1892-93	Goals for 1 higher than goals against.
1893-94	Total wins 2 less than total losses.
1893-94	Goals for 2 lower than goals against.
1894-95	Goals for 4 lower than goals against.
1896-97	Goals for 2 higher than goals against.
1897-98	Goals for 2 higher than goals against.
1898-99	1 point too many.
1900-01	Goals for 1 lower than goals against.
1902-03	4 points too many.
1903-04	Division One: 2 points too many.
1903-04	Division Two: 4 points too many.
1905-06	Div. Two: Goals for 2 higher than against.
1936-37	Goals for 9 lower than goals against.
1945-46	1 point too many.
1948-49	Division Two: Goals for 1 higher than goals against
1972-73	Goals for 1 lower than goals against.
1977-78	Goals for 1 higher than goals against.
1978-79	Goals for 4 higher than goals against.

LANCASHIRE COMBINATION

1891-92

Blackburn Rovers Reserves	14	10	3	1	44	17	23
Hindley	14	9	0	5	28	22	18
Royton	14	7	2	5	39	25	16
Bolton Wanderers Reserves	14	7	1	6	42	25	15
Preston North End Reserves	13	6	3	4	44	33	15
North Meols (Southport)	14	6	0	8	27	37	12
Skelmersdale United	13	3	1	9	26	53	7
Stanley (Liverpool)	14	1	2	11	13	51	4

Halliwell were unable to fulfil their fixtures and so were expelled and their record was expunged.   One game was not played.

1892-93

Blackburn Rovers Reserves	20	14	1	5	59	30	29
Darwen Reserves	20	11	3	6	84	42	25
Newton Heath Reserves	20	10	5	5	47	30	25
Bolton Wanderers Reserves	20	12	0	8	42	42	24
Turton	20	9	3	8	50	41	21
North Meols (Southport)	20	8	4	8	42	38	20
Royton	20	8	4	8	44	42	20
Ardwick Reserves	20	8	3	9	49	46	19
Preston North End Reserves	20	6	4	10	40	44	16
Skelmersdale United	20	5	2	13	28	78	12
Tranmere Rovers	20	4	1	15	30	81	9

1893-94

Blackburn Rovers Reserves	16	13	2	1	62	13	28
Bolton Wanderers Reserves	16	11	2	3	72	26	24
Darwen Reserves	14	8	1	5	47	22	17
Tranmere Rovers	16	6	2	8	30	54	14
Lostock Hall	14	6	1	7	49	43	13
Newton Heath Reserves	16	5	2	9	37	36	12
Turton	16	5	2	9	28	43	12
Preston North End Reserves	16	4	1	11	24	63	9
Ardwick Reserves	16	3	3	10	18	69	9

Royton failed to fulfil their fixtures and were expelled, their record was expunged. Games between Darwen Reserves & Lostock Hall cancelled.

1894-95

Everton Reserves	24	20	3	1	137	33	43
Preston North End Reserves	24	16	2	6	84	34	34
Darwen Reserves	24	13	3	8	85	61	29
Oswaldtwistle Rovers	24	13	1	10	59	56	27
Rawtenstall	24	12	2	10	57	70	26
Bolton Wanderers Reserves	24	12	3	9	78	55	25
Burnley Reserves	24	10	4	10	64	45	24
Blackburn Rovers Reserves	24	10	2	12	45	49	22
Turton	24	10	2	12	48	69	22
Padiham	24	8	3	13	41	82	17
Newton Heath Reserves	24	5	8	11	41	75	16
Manchester City Reserves	24	6	1	17	50	95	13
Bell's Temperance	24	3	2	19	34	103	6

Bolton Wanderers Reserves, Padiham, Newton Heath Reserves and Bell's Temperance had 2 points deducted for fielding ineligible players.

1895-96

Preston North End Reserves	26	20	3	3	93	28	43
Blackburn Rovers Reserves	26	15	6	5	61	34	36
Newton Heath Reserves	26	14	2	10	61	57	30
Bolton Wanderers Reserves	26	13	3	10	66	47	29
Oswaldtwistle Rovers	26	12	5	9	53	42	29
Burnley Reserves	26	11	7	8	66	54	29
Turton	26	13	3	10	57	57	29
Bury Reserves	26	7	10	9	51	47	24
Manchester City Reserves	26	10	4	12	54	53	24
Little Lever	26	11	2	13	51	70	24
Padiham	26	9	5	12	51	58	23
Rawtenstall	26	10	2	14	41	65	22
Darwen Reserves	26	6	4	16	49	77	16
Lostock Hall	26	1	4	21	18	88	6

Accrington and Tonge failed to complete their fixtures and their records were excluded from the final table.

1896-97

Liverpool Reserves	28	23	1	4	78	30	47
Preston North End Reserves	28	18	6	4	82	34	42
Bury Reserves	28	15	5	8	70	36	35
Manchester City Reserves	28	17	1	10	75	40	35
Blackburn Rovers Reserves	28	15	5	8	59	44	35
Rochdale	28	16	2	10	79	54	34
Burnley Reserves	28	12	6	10	64	44	30
Turton	28	10	9	9	58	64	29
Bolton Wanderers Reserves	28	12	2	14	66	49	26
Padiham	28	9	8	11	55	56	26
Newton Heath Reserves	28	8	8	12	49	53	24
Darwen Reserves	28	9	5	14	65	89	23
Blackpool Reserves	28	7	3	18	41	88	17
Rawtenstall	28	3	3	22	33	113	9
Oswaldtwistle Rovers	28	3	2	23	27	105	8

1897-98

Preston North End Reserves	30	24	3	3	121	26	51
Liverpool Reserves	30	20	1	9	100	48	41
Bury Reserves	30	17	4	9	70	43	38
Bolton Wanderers Reserves	30	15	5	10	69	51	35
Blackburn Rovers Reserves	30	14	7	9	67	51	35
Fleetwood Rangers	30	16	2	12	69	54	34
Manchester City Reserves	30	15	4	11	67	68	34
Turton	30	16	2	12	68	71	34
Newton Heath Reserves	30	14	2	14	65	42	30
Skerton	30	11	7	12	58	71	29
Berry's Association	30	12	4	14	71	78	28
Blackburn Park Road	30	9	5	16	54	90	23
Burnley Reserves	30	9	4	17	61	82	22
Padiham	30	10	2	18	51	79	22
Prescot	30	6	5	19	43	99	17
Darwen Reserves	30	3	1	26	37	116	7

1898-99

Preston North End Reserves	28	21	3	4	99	42	45
Manchester City Reserves	28	19	3	6	83	37	41
Bolton Wanderers Reserves	28	19	3	6	88	40	41
Burnley Reserves	28	17	5	6	75	30	39
Newton Heath Reserves	28	14	6	8	62	43	34
Blackburn Rovers Reserves	28	14	5	9	72	55	33
Berry's Association	28	14	4	10	71	53	32
Skerton	28	13	3	12	67	55	29
Turton	28	12	3	13	41	56	27
Hurst Ramblers	28	11	3	14	58	75	25
Bury Reserves	28	9	4	15	55	58	22
Blackburn Park Road	28	5	5	18	36	96	15
Leyland	28	5	4	19	28	70	14
Fleetwood Rangers	28	2	8	18	36	87	12
Rossendale United	28	4	4	20	25	99	12

1899-1900

Liverpool Reserves	30	23	2	5	76	26	48
Preston North End Reserves	30	22	1	7	83	29	45
Everton Reserves	30	20	4	6	78	28	44
Burnley Reserves	30	18	4	8	66	49	40
Manchester City Reserves	30	18	4	8	63	49	40
Blackburn Rovers Reserves	30	14	4	12	78	48	32
Newton Heath Reserves	30	13	4	13	63	56	30
Berry's Association	30	10	8	12	49	60	28
Bury Reserves	30	12	2	16	54	56	26
Blackburn Park Road	30	9	7	14	48	65	25
Turton	30	8	7	15	41	72	23
Glossop Reserves	30	9	4	17	46	65	22
Bolton Wanderers Reserves	30	10	2	18	38	56	22
Leyland	30	5	9	16	31	74	19
Astley Bridge Wanderers	30	8	2	20	41	76	18
St. Helens Recreation	30	7	4	19	37	83	18

Hurst Ramblers and Skerton both disbanded during the season and their records were expunged.

1900-1901

	P	W	D	L	F	A	Pts
Everton Reserves	34	29	2	3	114	22	60
Liverpool Reserves	34	28	4	2	117	29	60
Manchester City Reserves	34	22	4	8	108	60	48
Bury Reserves	34	19	5	10	64	55	43
St. Helens Recreation	34	16	8	10	79	60	40
Preston North End Reserves	34	16	6	12	89	61	38
New Brighton Tower Reserves	34	16	6	12	73	56	38
Stockport County Reserves	34	16	6	12	60	66	38
Accrington Stanley	34	17	2	15	55	51	36
Padiham	34	14	6	14	60	63	34
Burnley Reserves	34	13	7	14	61	56	33
Turton	34	10	5	19	44	84	25
Glossop Reserves	34	11	2	21	42	81	24
Berry's Association	34	9	3	22	55	92	21
Leyland	34	7	6	21	37	79	20
Blackburn Park Road	34	6	7	21	38	90	19
Oswaldtwistle Rovers	34	7	4	23	39	93	18
Newton Heath Reserves	34	5	7	22	40	78	17

1901-02

	P	W	D	L	F	A	Pts
Manchester City Reserves	34	29	0	5	125	30	58
Everton Reserves	34	24	3	7	86	35	51
Accrington Stanley	34	21	5	8	79	48	47
Bolton Wanderers Reserves	34	19	5	10	81	58	43
Liverpool Reserves	34	16	7	11	83	54	39
Bury Reserves	34	17	4	13	84	46	38
St. Helens Recreation	34	17	3	14	80	64	37
Preston North End Reserves	34	17	2	15	91	73	36
Nelson	34	13	7	14	60	64	33
Rossendale United	34	13	5	16	62	89	31
Oswaldtwistle Rovers	34	12	6	16	55	62	30
Turton	34	12	6	16	50	67	30
Blackburn Rovers Reserves	34	11	7	16	56	77	29
Newton Heath Reserves	34	11	5	18	54	97	27
Stockport County Reserves	34	10	6	18	63	77	26
Burnley Reserves	34	9	5	20	42	99	23
Padiham	34	5	9	20	36	85	19
Glossop Reserves	34	4	7	23	36	98	15

St. Helens Recreation refused to play Nelson. Nelson were awarded a win and the 2 points.

1902-03

	P	W	D	L	F	A	Pts
Accrington Stanley	34	26	2	6	114	36	54
Manchester City Reserves	34	23	7	4	84	36	53
Bury Reserves	34	22	6	6	85	39	50
Manchester United Reserves	34	20	8	6	83	45	48
Bolton Wanderers Reserves	34	19	3	12	81	58	41
Everton Reserves	34	16	7	11	74	54	39
Liverpool Reserves	34	15	8	11	70	64	38
Blackburn Rovers Reserves	34	13	9	12	66	53	35
Padiham	34	15	4	15	71	70	34
Black Lane Temperance	34	12	4	18	50	79	28
Preston North End Reserves	34	11	5	18	68	80	27
Heywood	34	10	7	17	49	66	27
Oswaldtwistle Rovers	34	11	5	18	53	84	27
Trawden Forest	34	9	8	17	38	66	26
Rossendale United	34	10	6	18	49	87	26
Heywood United	34	7	9	18	46	72	23
Nelson	34	7	7	20	43	80	21
Turton	34	6	7	21	43	98	19

1903-04

Division One

	P	W	D	L	F	A	Pts
Everton Reserves	34	26	6	2	114	32	58
Accrington Stanley	34	24	4	6	89	36	52
Manchester City Reserves	34	21	7	6	90	36	49
Manchester United Reserves	34	19	8	7	72	35	46
Darwen	34	19	7	8	79	45	45
Blackburn Rovers Reserves	34	17	6	11	75	64	40
Bury Reserves	34	17	5	12	81	66	39
Nelson	34	16	4	14	66	61	36
Liverpool Reserves	34	12	10	12	75	65	34
Rossendale United	34	13	7	14	45	57	33
Bolton Wanderers Reserves	34	13	6	15	79	58	32
Preston North End Reserves	34	11	10	13	70	59	32
Colne	34	11	4	19	59	78	26
Oswaldtwistle Rovers	34	7	9	18	50	84	23
Heywood	34	9	4	21	51	112	22
Turton	34	6	6	22	57	108	18
Padiham	34	6	5	23	31	94	17
Black Lane Temperance	34	3	6	25	39	132	12

Division Two

	P	W	D	L	F	A	Pts
Southport Central	34	23	6	5	82	30	52
Earlestown	34	23	5	6	94	49	51
Stalybridge Rovers	34	19	8	7	79	39	46
Stockport County Reserves	34	21	3	10	81	60	45
St. Helens Town	34	16	9	9	64	52	41
Ashton Town	34	16	8	10	51	42	40
Hyde St. George's	34	15	9	10	59	50	39
Bolton St. Luke's	34	12	9	13	79	71	33
Barrow	34	12	9	13	51	54	33
Newton-le-Willows	34	13	6	15	71	69	32
St. Helens Recreation	34	12	8	14	47	47	32
Atherton Church House	34	13	3	18	62	72	29
Chorley	34	11	7	16	53	62	29
Brynn Central	34	13	3	18	62	80	29
Skelmersdale United	34	9	9	16	52	75	27
Clitheroe Central	34	11	3	20	63	89	25
Chorley St. George's	34	5	10	19	46	82	20
Bacup	34	5	3	26	36	109	13

Atherton Church House took over the fixtures of Rochdale Town in December 1903 when Rochdale had played 14 games for 6 points.

1904-05

Division One

	P	W	D	L	F	A	Pts
Stockport County	34	21	7	6	63	27	49
Liverpool Reserves	34	18	6	10	88	54	42
Southport Central	34	17	8	9	59	41	42
Manchester United Reserves	34	19	1	14	74	50	39
Darwen	34	14	10	10	55	49	38
Manchester City Reserves	34	13	11	10	64	56	37
Accrington Stanley	34	16	5	13	57	55	37
Bury Reserves	34	15	5	14	58	63	35
Everton Reserves	34	13	8	13	49	41	34
Nelson	34	13	7	14	57	53	33
Bolton Wanderers Reserves	34	13	7	14	67	65	33
Preston North End Reserves	34	12	8	14	50	48	32
Rossendale United	34	12	8	14	54	68	32
Earlestown	34	12	5	17	50	71	29
Blackburn Rovers Reserves	34	11	6	17	53	75	28
Ashton Town	34	7	11	16	36	50	25
Stalybridge Rovers	34	10	4	20	34	63	24
St. Helens Town	34	7	9	18	38	77	23

Division Two

St. Helens Recreation	34	22	6	6	91	32	50
Barrow	34	22	2	10	73	43	46
Oldham Athletic	34	19	6	9	80	38	44
Atherton Church House	34	20	4	10	81	55	44
Brynn Central	34	17	8	9	69	44	42
Hyde St. George's	34	14	12	8	86	49	40
Oswaldtwistle Rovers	34	17	6	11	81	56	40
Chorley	34	15	7	12	68	56	37
Workington	34	15	7	12	56	60	37
Turton	34	15	6	13	80	69	36
Blackpool Reserves	34	13	6	15	62	63	32
Skelmersdale United	34	12	7	15	56	53	31
Colne	34	13	3	18	59	66	29
Padiham	34	11	7	16	53	85	29
Newton-le-Willows	34	7	7	20	54	84	21
Bacup	34	6	7	21	43	92	19
Bolton St. Luke's	34	7	4	23	38	98	18
Lytham	34	8	1	25	38	125	17

1905-06

Division One

Accrington Stanley	38	22	10	6	88	33	54
Darwen	38	19	9	10	81	64	47
Manchester United Reserves	38	17	10	11	86	62	44
St. Helens Recreation	38	17	10	11	74	69	44
Bolton Wanderers Reserves	38	15	13	10	72	50	43
Liverpool Reserves	38	17	8	13	72	57	42
Bury Reserves	38	15	12	11	82	69	42
Everton Reserves	38	14	10	14	64	63	38
Blackburn Rovers Reserves	38	13	12	13	65	69	38
Stalybridge Rovers	38	14	10	14	50	71	38
Manchester City Reserves	38	14	9	15	72	63	37
Rossendale United	38	14	8	16	68	73	36
Nelson	38	16	4	18	66	76	36
Oldham Athletic	38	14	8	16	45	52	36
Preston North End Reserves	38	14	7	17	67	65	35
Barrow	38	14	7	17	78	78	35
Southport Central	38	11	10	17	70	96	32
Atherton Church House	38	11	9	18	55	72	31
Stockport County Reserves	38	9	9	20	57	77	27
Earlestown	38	9	7	22	64	96	25

Division Two

Colne	36	24	6	6	95	40	54
Blackpool Reserves	36	23	4	9	92	66	50
Workington	36	21	7	8	102	50	49
St. Helens Town	36	17	10	9	51	39	44
Chorley	36	18	6	12	88	62	42
Failsworth	36	19	3	14	86	62	41
Brynn Central	36	16	9	11	76	55	41
Ashton Town	36	17	6	13	70	60	40
Clitheroe Central	36	16	5	15	86	58	37
Burnley Reserves	36	16	5	15	69	55	37
Lancaster	36	12	11	13	54	70	35
Skelmersdale United	36	14	6	16	75	77	34
Carlisle United	36	14	6	16	70	73	34
Padiham	36	14	2	20	63	82	30
Bacup	36	9	9	18	45	87	27
Oswaldtwistle Rovers	36	10	4	22	56	77	24
Newton-le-Willows	36	10	4	22	45	89	24
Haslingden	36	10	3	23	64	115	23
Hyde St. George's	36	7	4	25	50	118	18

1906-07

Division One

Oldham Athletic	38	26	5	7	105	33	57
Liverpool Reserves	38	25	7	6	108	64	57
Everton Reserves	38	24	5	9	90	47	53
Bury Reserves	38	19	9	10	90	57	47
Accrington Stanley	38	18	7	13	76	60	43
Manchester United Reserves	38	18	6	14	80	67	42
Darwen	38	17	8	13	60	55	42
Bolton Wanderers Reserves	38	17	7	14	66	52	41
Southport Central	38	14	13	11	50	50	41
Atherton	38	15	10	13	67	59	40
Blackpool Reserves	38	16	8	14	70	64	40
Manchester City Reserves	38	16	7	15	70	86	39
Rossendale United	38	13	10	15	71	70	36
St. Helens Recreation	38	15	6	17	75	75	36
Preston North End Reserves	38	15	3	20	81	86	33
Barrow	38	12	4	22	73	95	28
Blackburn Rovers Reserves	38	11	5	22	67	85	27
Nelson	38	10	5	23	53	113	25
Colne	38	7	5	26	56	92	19
Stalybridge Rovers	38	5	4	29	39	137	14

Division Two

Carlisle United	38	23	10	5	113	46	56
Earlestown	38	24	5	9	124	57	53
Chorley	38	23	5	10	96	60	51
Workington	38	23	3	12	100	52	49
St. Helens Town	38	21	6	11	88	72	48
Bacup	38	21	5	12	109	63	47
Glossop Reserves	38	18	8	12	85	63	44
Burnley Reserves	38	20	2	16	93	68	42
Lancaster	38	15	8	15	60	64	38
Stockport County Reserves	38	14	9	15	71	58	37
Failsworth	38	12	11	15	77	90	35
Port Sunlight	38	14	6	18	64	74	34
Clitheroe Central	38	11	12	15	65	81	34
Brynn Central	38	13	8	17	48	67	34
Haslingden	38	15	3	20	70	85	33
Hyde	38	13	6	19	63	79	32
Newton-le-Willows	38	14	3	21	76	97	31
Oswaldtwistle Rovers	38	12	6	20	72	114	30
Ashton Town	38	6	7	25	40	107	19
Skelmersdale United	38	6	1	31	39	156	13

1907-08

Division One

Everton Reserves	38	26	7	5	109	38	59
Carlisle United	38	23	8	7	79	55	54
Workington	38	20	8	10	68	47	48
Liverpool Reserves	38	20	7	11	81	57	47
Rossendale United	38	18	7	13	69	64	43
Southport Central	38	18	7	13	60	63	43
Accrington Stanley	38	16	9	13	77	66	41
Bury Reserves	38	17	6	15	83	72	40
Preston North End Reserves	38	16	8	14	60	53	40
Bolton Wanderers Reserves	38	17	4	17	69	57	38
Atherton	38	14	9	15	60	64	37
Oldham Athletic Reserves	38	15	6	17	74	70	36
Manchester United Reserves	38	14	7	17	58	54	35
St. Helens Recreation	38	14	6	18	67	73	34
Blackpool Reserves	38	12	8	18	47	71	32
Darwen	38	11	8	19	52	85	30
Manchester City Reserves	38	11	7	20	55	70	29
Chorley	38	9	9	20	68	89	27
Earlestown	38	8	8	22	43	88	24
Barrow	38	8	7	23	55	102	23

Division Two

Blackburn Rovers Reserves	38	30	3	5	141	34	63
Burnley Reserves	38	26	4	8	130	52	56
Colne	38	23	10	5	123	50	56
Nelson	38	26	3	9	124	48	55
St. Helens Town	38	23	7	8	100	71	53
Lancaster	38	22	8	8	80	47	52
Haslingden	38	22	2	14	87	63	46
Pendlebury	38	16	5	17	74	79	37
Ashton Town	38	16	4	18	63	89	36
Hyde	38	13	8	17	72	63	34
Bacup	38	14	6	18	63	89	34
Glossop Reserves	38	11	10	17	54	67	32
Heywood United	38	14	3	21	72	96	31
Brynn Central	38	11	8	19	44	64	30
Turton	38	13	4	21	68	107	30
Clitheroe Central	38	12	5	21	64	86	29
Oswaldtwistle Rovers	38	11	5	22	58	100	27
Failsworth	38	8	10	20	57	99	26
Wigan Town	38	9	5	24	43	104	23
Newton-le-Willows	38	3	4	31	29	138	10

1908-09

Division One

Everton Reserves	38	23	8	7	104	51	54
Liverpool Reserves	38	23	3	12	91	60	49
Oldham Athletic Reserves	38	22	3	13	75	45	47
St. Helens Recreation	38	20	7	11	73	60	47
Burnley Reserves	38	17	12	9	92	66	46
Carlisle United	38	18	8	12	79	70	44
Blackburn Rovers Reserves	38	15	10	13	85	61	40
Nelson	38	15	9	14	62	63	39
Bury Reserves	38	16	7	15	76	78	39
Bolton Wanderers Reserves	38	16	7	15	90	93	39
Manchester United Reserves	38	13	11	14	63	70	37
Accrington Stanley	38	15	6	17	88	87	36
Workington	38	14	8	16	69	79	36
Southport Central	38	13	8	17	61	67	34
Preston North End Reserves	38	13	7	18	74	60	33
Colne	38	14	5	19	68	97	33
Darwen	38	13	5	20	41	85	31
Rossendale United	38	11	7	20	58	94	29
Blackpool Reserves	38	11	3	24	60	90	25
Atherton	38	8	6	24	61	94	22

Division Two

Manchester City Reserves	38	24	8	6	131	50	56
Chorley	38	25	2	11	125	58	52
St. Helens Town	38	23	6	9	98	53	52
Hyde	38	23	5	10	93	59	51
Stockport County Reserves	38	21	8	9	101	47	50
Eccles Borough	38	22	6	10	86	46	50
Haslingden	38	19	7	12	102	79	45
Lancaster	38	17	6	15	71	66	40
Barrow	38	18	4	16	80	85	40
Rochdale	38	16	5	17	58	60	37
Glossop Reserves	38	15	5	18	72	70	35
Earlestown	38	16	3	19	65	90	35
Heywood United	38	14	6	18	76	99	34
Clitheroe Central	38	12	8	18	72	88	32
Ashton Town	38	10	12	16	53	72	32
Bacup	38	13	6	19	60	85	32
Turton	38	14	3	21	98	89	31
Pendlebury	38	9	6	23	54	111	24
Oswaldtwistle Rovers	38	8	3	27	42	137	19
Great Harwood	38	6	1	31	55	148	13

Great Harwood took over the fixtures of Brynn Central who disbanded.

1909-10

Division One

Everton Reserves	38	22	8	8	87	39	52
Bolton Wanderers Reserves	38	21	9	8	83	49	51
Accrington Stanley	38	20	7	11	71	62	47
Chorley	38	18	11	9	61	55	47
Bury Reserves	38	20	4	14	81	66	44
Manchester City Reserves	38	17	9	12	65	58	43
Carlisle United	38	14	11	13	69	60	39
Nelson	38	14	10	14	61	59	38
Burnley Reserves	38	13	11	14	66	69	37
Preston North End Reserves	38	15	6	17	53	54	36
Blackburn Rovers Reserves	38	14	8	16	59	77	36
Workington	38	14	8	16	67	58	36
Colne	38	13	9	16	69	68	35
Manchester United Reserves	38	15	5	18	71	75	35
Oldham Athletic Reserves	38	14	6	18	47	59	34
St. Helens Recreation	38	13	8	17	58	69	34
Liverpool Reserves	38	12	9	17	73	80	33
Southport Central	38	13	7	18	61	67	33
Hyde	38	10	7	21	54	94	27
St. Helens Town	38	10	3	25	48	86	23

Division Two

Glossop Reserves	38	29	5	4	120	35	63
Stockport County Reserves	38	28	4	6	133	41	60
Blackpool Reserves	38	27	5	6	118	31	59
Rochdale	38	23	8	7	92	33	54
Haslingden	38	25	3	10	113	45	53
Rossendale United	38	21	4	13	105	69	46
Atherton	38	20	5	13	78	60	45
Earlestown	38	18	7	13	80	71	43
Heywood United	38	16	6	16	72	76	38
Eccles Borough	38	17	4	17	61	52	38
Darwen	38	15	6	17	71	68	36
Great Harwood	38	14	6	18	74	77	34
Ashton Town	38	12	9	17	67	84	33
Lancaster	38	13	6	19	71	88	32
Barrow	38	12	8	18	60	78	32
Bacup	38	11	1	26	63	111	23
Walkden Central	38	10	3	25	65	128	23
Clitheroe Central	38	9	4	25	52	101	22
Turton	38	7	7	24	45	126	21
Denton	38	1	3	34	23	189	5

Denton took over Pendlebury's fixtures.

1910-11

Division One

Rochdale	38	25	6	7	87	45	56
Everton Reserves	38	21	7	10	82	35	49
Bolton Wanderers Reserves	38	19	10	9	72	59	48
Liverpool Reserves	38	19	8	11	76	59	46
Blackburn Rovers Reserves	38	16	8	14	66	63	40
Colne	38	17	5	16	67	56	39
Accrington Stanley	38	15	8	15	82	78	38
Nelson	38	15	8	15	64	63	38
Manchester United Reserves	38	15	7	16	75	69	37
Chorley	38	11	15	12	55	60	37
Southport Central	38	11	15	12	55	61	37
Preston North End Reserves	38	14	9	15	43	55	37
St. Helens Recreation	38	15	6	17	60	57	36
Blackpool Reserves	38	14	8	16	52	62	36
Bury Reserves	38	14	7	17	61	67	35
Burnley Reserves	38	15	5	18	62	69	35
Glossop Reserves	38	14	7	17	49	62	35
Manchester City Reserves	38	11	9	18	49	76	31
Stockport County Reserves	38	11	15	12	42	78	26
Oldham Athletic Reserves	38	9	6	23	42	73	24

Chorley vs Liverpool Reserves was abandoned after 25 minutes on the last day of the season with Liverpool leading 1-0. The result stood.

Division Two

Haslingden	38	26	5	7	98	47	57
Barrow	38	27	2	9	102	47	56
Chester	38	26	4	8	104	51	56
St. Helens Town	38	25	4	9	89	38	54
Hyde	38	24	5	9	99	49	53
Bacup	38	17	12	9	98	70	46
Rossendale United	38	19	7	12	124	64	45
Denton	38	21	3	14	100	76	45
Earlestown	38	15	8	15	73	76	38
Walkden Central	38	14	9	15	72	71	37
Eccles Borough	38	13	9	16	67	81	35
Heywood United	38	14	6	18	75	73	34
Tranmere Rovers	38	14	6	18	60	69	34
Fleetwood	38	14	6	18	72	83	34
Great Harwood	38	12	6	20	54	78	30
Atherton	38	11	7	20	55	73	29
Darwen	38	13	3	22	59	91	29
Hindley Central	38	9	4	25	48	103	22
Padiham	38	5	5	28	31	120	15
Ashton Town	38	2	7	29	21	141	11

Ashton Town's fixtures were taken over by Tyldesley Albion late in the season.

1911-12

Division One

Rochdale	32	23	4	5	81	24	50
St. Helens Recreation	32	19	6	7	69	49	44
Hyde	32	17	5	10	68	41	39
Barrow	32	15	9	8	66	48	39
Colne	32	16	6	10	59	43	38
Chester	32	15	7	10	74	50	37
Chorley	32	14	7	11	50	43	35
Rossendale United	32	12	9	11	58	48	33
Accrington Stanley	32	12	6	14	70	66	30
Haslingden	32	11	8	13	54	53	30
Eccles Borough	32	12	6	14	49	51	30
Heywood United	32	11	5	16	40	68	27
St. Helens Town	32	9	8	15	45	56	26
Nelson	32	9	7	16	58	66	25
Denton	32	11	3	18	52	77	25
Walkden Central	32	6	7	19	37	74	19
Bacup	32	6	5	21	41	114	17

Earlestown disbanded in October 1911 and Heywood United took over their fixtures.

Division Two

Stalybridge Celtic	30	23	2	5	110	39	48
Altrincham	30	23	2	5	92	37	48
Tranmere Rovers	30	18	6	6	83	41	42
Fleetwood	30	16	4	10	64	31	36
South Liverpool	30	17	2	11	85	49	36
Macclesfield	30	14	6	10	57	40	34
Padiham	30	14	4	12	58	61	32
Oswestry United	30	13	5	12	75	64	31
Tyldesley Albion	30	11	5	14	61	66	27
Hindley Central	30	12	3	15	67	69	27
Barnoldswick United	30	10	5	15	53	79	25
Atherton	30	11	3	16	49	77	25
Darwen	30	9	3	18	34	84	21
Great Harwood	30	7	5	18	50	72	19
Portsmouth Rovers	30	6	5	19	51	86	17
Lancaster Town	30	4	4	22	29	123	12

Barnoldswick United took over Heywood United's fixtures in October 1911.

1912-13

Division One

Eccles Borough	34	23	4	7	96	49	50
Accrington Stanley	34	21	3	10	75	54	45
Nelson	34	19	4	11	82	59	42
Chorley	34	18	5	11	67	51	41
Barrow	34	17	6	11	73	34	40
Tranmere Rovers	34	16	6	12	92	58	38
Chester	34	12	13	9	89	64	37
St. Helens Recreation	34	16	4	14	72	56	36
Fleetwood	34	14	7	13	71	69	35
Haslingden	34	16	2	16	77	78	34
Altrincham	34	13	6	15	81	84	32
Hyde	34	13	5	16	76	70	31
Walkden Central	34	13	5	16	54	80	31
St. Helens Town	34	12	5	17	49	75	29
Heywood United	34	13	2	19	76	100	28
Denton	34	9	6	19	55	101	24
Rossendale United	34	8	7	19	63	105	23
Colne	34	6	4	24	49	110	16

Division Two

South Liverpool	34	24	5	5	94	24	53
Stalybridge Celtic Reserves	34	21	5	8	74	45	47
Atherton	34	20	7	7	87	59	47
Northwich Victoria	34	18	9	7	101	43	45
Hurst	34	19	6	9	93	62	44
Macclesfield	34	17	8	9	75	40	42
Hindley Central	34	17	6	11	89	56	40
Witton Albion	34	17	5	12	81	57	39
Great Harwood	34	16	7	11	62	62	39
Oswestry United	34	17	3	14	79	80	37
Padiham	34	14	4	16	61	76	32
Nantwich	34	12	7	15	64	70	31
Rochdale Reserves	34	10	5	19	52	63	25
Darwen	34	9	5	20	53	85	23
Barnoldswick United	34	7	6	21	50	99	20
Portsmouth Rovers	34	8	3	23	53	101	19
Bacup	34	8	1	25	43	116	17
Lancaster Town	34	3	6	25	27	100	12

1913-14

Division One

Tranmere Rovers	34	25	4	5	85	32	54
Barrow	34	21	5	8	92	39	47
Northwich Victoria	34	21	5	8	65	36	47
Eccles Borough	34	19	5	10	70	49	43
Atherton	34	18	6	10	82	57	42
South Liverpool	34	17	7	10	78	62	41
Accrington Stanley	34	15	8	11	76	66	38
Hurst	34	12	8	14	58	54	32
Chorley	34	12	8	14	48	60	32
Nelson	34	14	4	16	47	64	32
Fleetwood	34	10	9	15	54	57	29
Chester	34	9	10	15	59	62	28
Altrincham	34	10	7	17	61	80	27
Hyde	34	10	7	17	59	82	27
Heywood United	34	10	6	18	41	57	26
Haslingden	34	11	4	19	52	77	26
St. Helens Town	34	9	8	17	47	83	26
Walkden Central	34	5	5	24	40	97	15

Division Two

Witton Albion	34	22	5	7	107	44	49
Macclesfield	34	21	4	9	79	39	46
Rossendale United	34	19	4	11	84	42	42
Denton	34	18	4	12	62	56	40
Great Harwood	34	18	3	13	74	56	39
Stalybridge Celtic Reserves	34	17	4	13	77	47	38
Lancaster Town	34	16	6	12	70	54	38
Darwen	34	15	6	13	66	65	36
Crewe Alexandra Reserves	34	14	7	13	60	50	35
Nantwich	34	15	4	15	75	75	34
Padiham	34	13	7	14	61	67	33
Oswestry United	34	14	4	16	47	60	32
Barnoldswick United	34	13	5	16	61	72	31
Hindley Central	34	11	6	17	61	83	28
Rochdale Reserves	34	11	5	18	44	72	27
Newton Heath Athletic	34	10	5	19	44	89	25
Portsmouth Rovers	34	11	2	21	52	81	24
Bacup	34	5	5	24	40	112	15

1914-15

Division One

Eccles Borough	32	18	8	6	77	41	44
Hurst	32	17	8	7	76	48	42
Tranmere Rovers	32	19	3	10	84	52	41
Macclesfield	32	19	3	10	68	49	41
Northwich Victoria	32	16	6	10	71	50	38
Accrington Stanley	32	15	7	10	75	59	37
Altrincham	32	15	4	13	68	55	34
Atherton	32	15	4	13	69	59	34
South Liverpool	32	13	7	12	72	67	33
Witton Albion	32	13	6	13	61	63	32
Nelson	32	13	4	15	66	64	30
Denton	32	13	2	17	72	98	28
Barrow	32	11	6	15	59	89	28
Fleetwood	32	9	5	18	65	94	23
Rossendale United	32	11	0	21	42	64	22
Hyde	32	8	5	19	65	93	21
Chorley	32	6	4	22	46	91	16

Chester withdrew from the league in March 1915 due to war-time difficulties and their record was deleted.

Division Two

Rochdale Reserves	24	15	4	5	53	22	34
Lancaster Town	24	16	1	7	78	31	33
Haslingden	24	13	5	6	52	34	31
Nantwich	24	12	5	7	64	43	29
Heywood United	24	12	5	7	55	44	29
Great Harwood	24	12	4	8	62	36	28
Newton Heath Athletic	24	11	3	10	40	51	25
Walkden Central	24	9	5	10	45	44	23
Padiham	24	10	2	12	43	45	22
Glossop Reserves	24	9	4	11	39	55	22
Portsmouth Rovers	24	7	3	14	49	68	17
Hebden Bridge	24	7	1	16	31	62	15
Bacup	24	1	2	21	21	97	4

1915-16

Northern Division – First League

Accrington Stanley	18	12	4	2	48	20	28
Blackburn Trinity	18	10	4	4	45	27	24
Haslingden	18	8	4	6	42	31	20
Rossendale United	18	8	3	7	41	30	19
Chorley	18	8	3	7	26	32	19
Nelson	17	7	4	6	24	35	18
Padiham	18	7	3	8	35	30	17
Great Harwood	18	7	3	8	30	26	17
Leyland	17	6	1	10	43	49	13
Adlington	18	1	1	16	18	72	3

Nelson v Leyland not played due to bad weather.

Southern Division – First League

South Liverpool	18	11	2	5	53	26	24
Eccles Borough	18	11	2	5	44	26	24
Atherton	18	10	3	5	38	22	23
Hyde	18	11	1	6	47	28	23
Altrincham	18	9	2	7	36	35	20
Stalybridge Celtic	18	6	7	5	35	23	19
Tranmere Rovers	18	6	4	8	37	37	16
Walkden Central	18	6	1	11	30	62	13
Glossop Reserves	18	5	2	11	29	45	12
Denton	18	2	2	14	12	57	6

Northern Division – Subsidiary Competition

Great Harwood	12	8	3	1	27	14	19
Blackburn Trinity	12	7	2	3	43	20	16
Leyland	12	7	2	3	30	25	16
Accrington Stanley	12	4	2	6	21	19	10
Padiham	12	4	1	7	20	29	9
Rossendale United	12	4	1	7	21	33	9
Nelson	12	2	1	9	13	35	5

Southern Division – Subsidiary Competition

Stalybridge Celtic	18	12	1	5	46	24	25
Atherton	18	12	0	6	38	19	24
Eccles Borough	18	11	1	6	36	25	23
South Liverpool	18	10	1	7	35	16	21
Tranmere Rovers	18	9	2	7	36	28	20
Altrincham	18	7	3	8	28	29	17
Hyde	17	8	1	8	33	41	17
Warrington Town	18	7	1	10	38	37	15
Walkden Central	17	3	3	11	14	42	9
Glossop Reserves	18	3	1	14	22	65	7

Hyde v Walkden Central not played due to bad weather.

1916-17

First Competition

Hurst	19	13	4	2	52	24	30
Stalybridge Celtic	19	12	2	5	48	32	26
Tranmere Rovers	19	11	1	7	43	30	23
South Liverpool	17	9	2	6	37	22	20
Warrington Town	20	7	5	8	31	45	19
Atherton	18	7	4	7	29	34	18
Altrincham	17	8	1	8	41	30	17
Walkden Central	18	5	5	8	33	40	15
Eccles Borough	15	3	4	8	23	38	10
Barrow	14	3	2	9	23	32	8
Hyde	14	0	4	10	15	48	4

Some games were not completed due to bad weather or lack of official permission.

Second Competition

Tranmere Rovers	9	5	3	1	15	8	13
South Liverpool	11	5	2	4	21	14	12
Warrington Town	7	4	1	2	19	11	9
Altrincham	8	2	1	5	11	21	5
Stalybridge Celtic	4	1	1	2	3	5	3
Barrow	2	1	1	0	6	4	3
Atherton	3	1	1	1	1	3	3
Lancaster United	4	0	0	4	2	12	0

1917-18

South Liverpool	22	12	3	7	39	38	27
Tranmere Rovers	20	10	4	6	43	21	24
Brynn	16	7	6	3	26	25	20
St. Helens Association	14	3	1	10	15	34	7
Horwich RMI	12	2	2	8	17	22	6

1918-19

Liverpool Section

Tranmere Rovers	22	17	1	4	69	26	35
Prescot	22	16	0	6	53	34	32
South Liverpool	22	12	5	5	49	38	29
Liverpool Reserves	22	12	1	9	67	38	25
Runcorn	21	11	1	9	46	35	23
Bolton Wanderers Reserves	22	9	3	10	49	47	21
Garswood Hall	22	8	3	11	35	40	19
Brynn	20	8	3	9	30	38	19
Everton Reserves	22	9	0	13	35	61	18
Plank Lane	22	6	1	15	34	65	13
Horwich RMI	21	4	3	14	34	53	11
Blackpool RAMC	18	5	1	12	26	52	11

Manchester Section

Stalybridge Celtic	14	12	0	2	46	15	24
Mossley	14	10	2	2	28	18	22
Altrincham	14	9	2	3	46	16	20
Hurst	14	6	1	7	28	29	13
Monk's Hall	14	6	1	7	30	40	13
Witton Albion	12	3	0	9	14	22	6
Northwich Victoria	12	3	0	9	15	29	6
Marple	10	0	0	10	6	44	0

Auxiliary Section

Chorley	19	4	7	8	26	39	15
South Liverpool	10	5	3	2	26	14	13
Lancaster United	12	5	3	4	21	26	13
Tranmere Rovers	8	5	2	1	24	11	12
Rylands Recreation	23	4	4	15	31	76	12
Runcorn	4	4	0	0	15	0	8
Plank Lane	4	4	0	0	17	3	8
Garswood Hall	6	3	2	1	11	11	8
Brynn	6	3	1	2	22	8	7
Horwich RMI	6	2	3	1	17	10	7
Prescot	5	3	1	1	11	8	7
Monk's Hall	10	3	1	6	21	25	7
Everton Reserves	3	2	0	1	10	5	4
Bolton Wanderers Reserves	4	2	0	2	6	10	4
Liverpool Reserves	3	1	1	1	3	3	3
Barrow	5	1	1	3	9	10	3
Blackpool RAMC	4	0	1	3	4	15	1

1919-20

Chorley	34	25	2	7	101	30	52
Lancaster Town	34	21	6	7	83	38	48
Eccles United	34	19	6	9	86	46	44
Tranmere Rovers Reserves	34	20	4	10	91	62	44
Barrow	34	20	3	11	58	37	43
Horwich RMI	34	20	0	14	72	59	40
Accrington Stanley	34	18	4	12	86	73	40
Great Harwood	34	17	3	14	78	57	37
Hurst	34	16	4	14	72	57	36
Rossendale United	34	16	3	15	64	71	35
South Liverpool	34	15	4	15	67	69	34
Fleetwood	34	15	3	16	67	63	33
Glossop	34	15	2	17	59	74	32
Stalybridge Celtic Reserves	34	11	3	20	60	95	25
Plank Lane	34	8	5	21	46	101	21
Dick Kerr's	34	6	5	23	61	89	17
Prescot	34	8	1	25	41	106	17
Rochdale Reserves	34	5	4	25	32	97	14

1920-21

Barrow	34	23	6	5	79	28	52
Eccles United	34	21	4	9	90	40	46
Fleetwood	34	21	2	11	86	51	44
Darwen	34	17	10	7	79	51	44
Lancaster Town	34	17	8	9	67	40	42
Accrington Stanley	34	16	9	9	63	41	41
Hurst	34	14	9	11	61	56	37
Chorley	34	15	7	12	47	44	37
Atherton	34	14	9	11	59	57	37
South Liverpool	34	14	5	15	70	75	33
Leyland	34	12	9	13	58	66	33
Great Harwood	34	11	11	12	42	51	33
Morecambe	34	10	5	19	58	83	25
Rossendale United	34	10	5	19	52	76	25
Dick Kerr's	34	9	6	19	65	89	24
Bacup Borough	34	8	6	20	42	75	22
Wigan Borough	34	6	8	20	41	79	20
Horwich RMI	34	4	9	21	34	91	17

1921-22

Lancaster Town	34	22	7	5	67	33	51
Chorley	34	22	4	8	79	43	48
New Brighton	34	22	3	9	72	38	47
Darwen	34	21	3	10	75	51	45
Fleetwood	34	19	5	10	76	43	43
Stockport County Reserves	34	18	7	9	71	49	43
Bacup Borough	34	15	6	13	57	48	36
Eccles United	34	15	5	14	57	48	35
Atherton	34	15	5	14	52	48	35
Rossendale United	34	13	8	13	66	51	34
Leyland	34	13	7	14	55	69	33
Horwich RMI	34	12	6	16	45	59	30
Skelmersdale United	34	13	4	17	45	62	30
Morecambe	34	10	6	18	36	56	26
Hurst	34	11	3	20	50	82	25
Great Harwood	34	7	6	21	44	87	20
Rochdale Reserves	34	6	5	23	47	83	17
Dick Kerr's	34	4	6	24	38	82	14

1922-23

Chorley	34	19	9	6	78	38	47
Lancaster Town	34	17	10	7	55	30	44
Darwen	34	17	9	8	77	60	43
New Brighton	34	16	9	9	69	32	41
Rossendale United	34	19	3	12	85	55	41
Fleetwood	34	17	6	11	67	54	40
New Cross	34	16	7	11	66	51	39
Leyland	34	14	7	13	55	47	35
Atherton	34	12	9	13	62	58	33
Eccles United	34	14	5	15	59	56	33
Rochdale Reserves	34	13	7	14	50	64	33
Hurst	34	12	7	15	58	63	31
Bacup Borough	34	13	5	16	44	59	31
Skelmersdale United	34	12	4	18	54	84	28
Morecambe	34	9	8	17	41	60	26
Dick Kerr's	34	6	13	15	38	68	25
Horwich RMI	34	7	10	17	54	76	24
Great Harwood	34	5	8	21	32	89	18

1923-24

Fleetwood	38	29	4	5	100	40	62
Southport Reserves	38	21	6	11	71	59	48
Darwen	38	19	8	11	84	63	46
Horwich RMI	38	20	4	14	72	49	44
Rossendale United	38	18	8	12	69	56	44
Bacup Borough	38	19	4	15	84	70	42
Eccles United	38	19	4	15	78	72	42
Lancaster Town	38	17	8	13	61	67	42
Wigan Borough Reserves	38	16	9	13	76	54	41
Chorley	38	17	7	14	77	66	41
Manchester North End	38	17	7	14	71	63	41
Accrington Stanley Reserves	38	17	6	15	72	67	40
Atherton	38	17	5	16	56	44	39
Nelson Reserves	38	14	7	17	65	65	35
Morecambe	38	15	5	18	60	63	35
Leyland	38	10	9	19	55	75	29
Great Harwood	38	9	6	23	55	102	24
Dick Kerr's	38	8	7	23	48	89	23
Rochdale Reserves	38	9	3	26	69	94	21
Skelmersdale United	38	7	7	24	52	117	21

1924-25

Morecambe	36	24	7	5	88	31	55
Rochdale Reserves	36	24	6	6	105	38	54
Darwen	36	17	11	8	64	35	45
Dick Kerr's	36	20	5	11	81	60	45
Atherton	36	19	7	10	62	40	45
Rossendale United	36	16	9	11	76	67	41
Fleetwood	36	14	11	11	74	59	39
Southport Reserves	36	15	8	13	60	46	38
Horwich RMI	36	14	8	14	74	60	36
Barnoldswick Town	36	15	5	16	72	84	35
Lancaster Town	36	13	8	15	60	54	34
Eccles United	36	13	7	16	68	90	33
Nelson Reserves	36	12	8	16	60	77	32
Bacup Borough	36	11	10	15	65	82	32
Accrington Stanley Reserves	36	12	7	17	71	61	31
Chorley	36	10	8	18	49	77	28
Wigan Borough Reserves	36	12	4	20	45	82	28
Great Harwood	36	7	4	25	38	104	18
Leyland	36	6	3	27	40	105	15

1927-28

Chorley	38	28	3	7	128	49	59
Lancaster Town	38	26	3	9	148	58	55
Horwich RMI	38	23	9	6	111	61	55
Accrington Stanley Reserves	38	25	2	11	100	64	52
Rossendale United	38	21	7	10	110	60	49
Dick Kerr's	38	19	4	15	115	93	42
Clitheroe	38	17	8	13	86	81	42
Morecambe	38	17	6	15	92	72	40
Wigan Borough Reserves	38	16	8	14	79	72	40
Southport Reserves	38	16	7	15	94	91	39
Burscough Rangers	38	13	9	16	88	99	35
Great Harwood	38	12	9	17	97	128	33
Atherton	38	12	6	20	87	114	30
Preston North End "A"	38	10	10	18	80	108	30
Nelson Reserves	38	12	6	20	80	113	30
Prescot Cables	38	12	6	20	63	128	30
Barnoldswick Town	38	12	3	23	77	114	27
Hindley Green Athletic	38	11	4	23	71	108	26
Darwen	38	10	6	22	68	104	26
Bacup Borough	38	7	6	25	52	109	20

Fleetwood resigned after playing 22 matches and Prescot Cables took over their fixtures.

1925-26

Nelson Reserves	38	27	5	6	123	51	59
Morecambe	38	21	10	7	103	58	52
Rossendale United	38	23	4	11	119	89	50
Fleetwood	38	19	7	12	87	69	45
Bacup Borough	38	20	3	15	71	82	43
Dick Kerr's	38	18	6	14	100	70	42
Horwich RMI	38	19	3	16	87	84	41
Lancaster Town	38	17	6	15	107	81	40
Darwen	38	18	4	16	93	75	40
Atherton	38	17	5	16	85	79	39
Chorley	38	16	7	15	103	101	39
Southport Reserves	38	16	5	17	82	75	37
Hindley Green Athletic	38	16	5	17	92	101	37
Barnoldswick Town	38	15	5	18	90	112	35
Accrington Stanley Reserves	38	14	5	19	83	106	33
Colne Town	38	14	4	20	77	101	32
Preston North End "A"	38	12	6	20	73	94	30
Wigan Borough Reserves	38	11	7	20	74	102	29
Clitheroe	38	9	7	22	76	103	25
Great Harwood	38	5	2	31	50	142	12

1928-29

Chorley	38	29	3	6	125	52	61
Horwich RMI	38	24	2	12	152	87	50
Rossendale United	38	23	4	11	126	74	50
Prescot Cables	38	20	8	10	87	49	48
Lancaster Town	38	20	8	10	91	65	48
Clitheroe	38	21	4	13	93	79	46
Manchester Central	38	21	3	14	106	87	45
Southport Reserves	38	21	2	15	98	63	44
Accrington Stanley Reserves	38	19	5	14	77	72	43
Morecambe	38	20	2	16	89	73	42
Darwen	38	17	5	16	84	82	39
Burscough Rangers	38	15	9	14	66	78	39
Dick Kerr's	38	13	8	17	77	82	34
Atherton	38	13	3	22	80	109	29
Nelson Reserves	38	12	5	21	55	85	29
Bacup Borough	38	10	5	23	69	109	25
Wigan Borough Reserves	38	9	6	23	69	99	24
Barnoldswick Town	38	10	4	24	66	139	24
Preston North End "A"	38	8	4	26	67	126	20
Great Harwood	38	8	4	26	65	132	20

1926-27

Rossendale United	38	27	6	5	129	65	60
Chorley	38	25	9	4	111	45	59
Morecambe	38	23	4	11	105	58	50
Barnoldswick Town	38	21	6	11	125	79	48
Dick Kerr's	38	21	6	11	105	68	48
Accrington Stanley Reserves	38	19	9	10	109	75	47
Lancaster Town	38	21	5	12	96	76	47
Southport Reserves	38	20	3	15	93	82	43
Clitheroe	38	17	8	13	100	91	42
Horwich RMI	38	18	5	15	106	76	41
Darwen	38	15	6	17	89	98	36
Fleetwood	38	14	5	19	63	82	33
Bacup Borough	38	12	8	18	82	92	32
Nelson Reserves	38	12	7	19	72	90	31
Preston North End "A"	38	10	8	20	77	93	28
Atherton	38	12	4	22	76	122	28
Hindley Green Athletic	38	10	5	23	93	146	25
Wigan Borough Reserves	38	9	6	23	73	120	24
Colne Town	38	11	1	26	55	127	23
Great Harwood	38	5	5	28	55	129	15

1929-30

Lancaster Town	38	28	4	6	138	49	60
Manchester Central	38	25	9	4	99	38	59
Bacup Borough	38	24	3	11	101	82	51
Darwen	38	22	4	12	93	62	48
Chorley	38	19	9	10	89	53	47
Prescot Cables	38	21	5	12	93	56	47
Horwich RMI	38	20	6	12	112	70	46
Rossendale United	38	18	7	13	83	82	43
Dick Kerr's	38	18	5	15	87	70	41
Southport Reserves	38	17	6	15	94	74	40
Accrington Stanley Reserves	38	14	12	12	77	76	40
Nelson Reserves	38	15	8	15	86	82	38
Atherton	38	15	3	20	72	105	33
Morecambe	38	12	7	19	74	111	31
Wigan Borough Reserves	38	12	6	20	66	96	30
Burscough Rangers	38	12	4	22	71	92	28
Clitheroe	38	12	3	23	74	100	27
Barnoldswick Town	38	6	9	23	63	117	21
Lytham	38	6	6	26	56	120	18
Great Harwood	38	3	6	29	50	143	12

1930-31

	P	W	D	L	F	A	Pts
Darwen	38	23	7	8	116	55	53
Prescot Cables	38	22	6	10	112	56	50
Lytham	38	23	4	11	94	64	50
Lancaster Town	38	20	9	9	85	64	49
Horwich RMI	38	21	5	12	119	73	47
Barnoldswick Town	38	21	5	12	111	92	47
Dick Kerr's	38	20	6	12	102	71	46
Southport Reserves	38	21	4	13	94	70	46
Manchester Central	38	19	6	13	97	60	44
Chorley	38	15	9	14	86	68	39
Bacup Borough	38	17	4	17	93	105	38
Burscough Rangers	38	19	0	19	84	96	38
Accrington Stanley Reserves	38	16	5	17	83	99	37
Clitheroe	38	16	4	18	87	85	36
Rossendale United	38	15	6	17	80	89	36
Morecambe	38	12	8	18	76	97	32
Great Harwood	38	9	5	24	67	106	23
Wigan Borough Reserves	38	10	2	26	63	120	22
Nelson Reserves	38	8	3	27	72	119	19
Rochdale Reserves	38	4	0	34	62	194	8

1931-32

	P	W	D	L	F	A	Pts
Darwen	36	24	7	5	104	43	55
Prescot Cables	36	21	6	9	91	48	48
Barrow Reserves	36	19	8	9	87	45	46
Lancaster Town	36	18	9	9	77	52	45
Nelson	36	19	6	11	74	53	44
Rossendale United	36	18	6	12	86	74	42
Fleetwood	36	17	7	12	98	78	41
Southport Reserves	36	18	4	14	87	60	40
Chorley	36	17	5	14	85	71	39
Barnoldswick Town	36	13	10	13	68	78	36
Clitheroe	36	14	7	15	65	77	35
Lytham	36	13	7	16	77	93	33
Dick Kerr's	36	14	4	18	85	83	32
Bacup Borough	36	15	2	19	71	83	32
Great Harwood	36	13	5	18	68	80	31
Burscough Rangers	36	11	8	17	60	82	30
Horwich RMI	36	10	3	23	73	108	23
Morecambe	36	6	6	24	41	93	18
Accrington Stanley Reserves	36	5	4	27	40	136	14

Wigan Borough disbanded in November 1931 and their reserves' record was deleted.

1932-33

	P	W	D	L	F	A	Pts
Chorley	38	28	6	4	113	44	62
Prescot Cables	38	25	3	10	127	66	53
Southport Reserves	38	22	6	10	96	61	50
Darwen	38	22	5	11	119	67	49
Fleetwood	38	21	7	10	97	58	49
Barrow Reserves	38	21	6	11	100	55	48
Horwich RMI	38	21	5	12	107	82	47
Lancaster Town	38	18	8	12	86	72	44
Clitheroe	38	18	4	16	95	73	40
Accrington Stanley Reserves	38	16	5	17	86	94	37
Nelson	38	14	8	16	83	81	36
Dick Kerr's	38	14	6	18	72	106	34
Lytham	38	13	7	18	94	116	33
Morecambe	38	11	10	17	68	84	32
Rossendale United	38	10	11	17	65	89	31
Rochdale Reserves	38	13	4	21	73	111	30
Great Harwood	38	12	4	22	86	114	28
Burscough Rangers	38	9	9	20	59	100	27
Bacup Borough	38	7	5	26	62	125	19
Barnoldswick Town	38	3	5	30	42	132	11

1933-34

	P	W	D	L	F	A	Pts
Chorley	38	29	3	6	133	53	61
Fleetwood	38	27	4	7	109	60	58
Lancaster Town	38	23	8	7	130	71	54
Clitheroe	38	21	6	11	129	86	48
Darwen	38	20	7	11	122	72	47
Barrow Reserves	38	22	3	13	92	70	47
Southport Reserves	38	17	10	11	73	70	44
Nelson	38	16	8	14	97	86	40
Accrington Stanley Reserves	38	15	7	16	85	102	37
Bacup Borough	38	15	6	17	86	83	36
Dick Kerr's	38	14	7	17	76	79	35
Rochdale Reserves	38	14	6	18	69	81	34
Lytham	38	13	6	19	83	94	32
Rossendale United	38	13	6	19	70	98	32
Great Harwood	38	11	9	18	72	103	31
Horwich RMI	38	13	4	21	85	107	30
Leyland Motors	38	12	3	23	94	129	27
Morecambe	38	9	9	20	65	101	27
Northern Nomads	38	10	3	25	77	114	23
Barnoldswick Town	38	6	5	27	54	142	17

1934-35

	P	W	D	L	F	A	Pts
Lancaster Town	38	28	4	6	143	60	60
Fleetwood	38	25	5	8	99	44	55
Chorley	38	25	2	11	94	54	52
Clitheroe	38	22	8	8	99	65	52
Rossendale United	38	22	6	10	103	65	50
Nelson	38	17	10	11	88	61	44
Darwen	38	19	6	13	119	83	44
Morecambe	38	17	5	16	63	60	39
Rochdale Reserves	38	15	8	15	86	82	38
Horwich RMI	38	16	3	19	91	88	35
New Brighton Reserves	38	14	7	17	79	97	35
Dick Kerr's	38	13	8	17	82	73	34
Bacup Borough	38	13	8	17	88	90	34
Southport Reserves	38	15	4	19	81	88	34
Barrow Reserves	38	12	10	16	65	78	34
Accrington Stanley Reserves	38	13	5	20	65	92	31
Northern Nomads	38	11	6	21	77	127	28
Lytham	38	10	3	25	58	117	23
Leyland Motors	38	8	4	26	66	142	20
Great Harwood	38	8	2	28	62	142	18

1935-36

	P	W	D	L	F	A	Pts
Lancaster Town	40	29	5	6	142	60	63
Barrow Reserves	40	30	2	8	138	53	62
Fleetwood	40	23	6	11	117	64	52
South Liverpool	40	22	4	14	93	71	48
Chorley	40	22	4	14	100	82	48
Morecambe	40	19	9	12	78	65	47
Clitheroe	40	19	8	13	123	103	46
Darwen	40	21	3	16	104	77	45
Bacup Borough	40	20	5	15	96	83	45
Nelson	40	16	9	15	86	84	41
New Brighton Reserves	40	17	5	18	111	98	39
Accrington Stanley Reserves	40	17	5	18	76	90	39
Leyland Motors	40	15	7	18	73	104	37
Marine	40	14	8	18	94	86	36
Horwich RMI	40	14	8	18	103	111	36
Northern Nomads	40	15	4	21	79	101	34
Southport Reserves	40	12	9	19	76	97	33
Rochdale Reserves	40	13	6	21	91	133	32
Rossendale United	40	10	9	21	77	108	29
Great Harwood	40	6	7	27	55	129	19
Lytham	40	2	5	33	46	159	9

Dick Kerr's disbanded in December 1935 and their record was deleted.

1936-37

South Liverpool	40	29	2	9	125	55	60
Accrington Stanley Reserves	40	26	7	7	105	51	59
Darwen	40	24	7	9	106	63	55
Barrow Reserves	40	21	8	11	100	72	50
Chorley	40	22	5	13	120	74	49
Clitheroe	40	20	9	11	122	85	49
Fleetwood	40	22	5	13	99	82	49
Marine	40	20	6	14	107	81	46
Lancaster Town	40	21	4	15	105	107	46
Morecambe	40	17	10	13	95	75	44
Southport Reserves	40	17	10	13	84	75	44
Bacup Borough	40	14	7	19	60	83	35
New Brighton Reserves	40	12	8	20	77	102	32
Leyland Motors	40	9	13	18	77	105	31
Horwich RMI	40	11	8	21	82	91	30
Great Harwood	40	10	10	20	80	114	30
Droylsden	40	13	3	24	88	118	29
Prescot Cables	40	11	7	22	70	112	29
Rossendale United	40	11	6	23	81	134	28
Rochdale Reserves	40	9	6	25	82	123	24
Northern Nomads	40	9	3	28	71	143	21

1937-38

South Liverpool	42	33	3	6	177	53	69
Clitheroe	42	25	9	8	139	82	59
Oldham Athletic Reserves	42	26	6	10	131	62	58
Accrington Stanley Reserves	42	23	7	12	103	63	53
Lancaster City	42	21	11	10	93	72	53
Morecambe	42	21	10	11	90	70	52
Darwen	42	19	9	14	103	85	47
Prescot Cables	42	17	11	14	82	72	45
Rossendale United	42	18	7	17	74	73	43
Leyland Motors	42	16	10	16	82	99	42
Bacup Borough	42	15	11	16	82	88	41
New Brighton Reserves	42	16	9	17	78	89	41
Chorley	42	18	4	20	93	104	40
Droylsden	42	13	13	16	91	98	39
Southport Reserves	42	16	7	19	80	96	39
Marine	42	15	7	20	80	105	37
Fleetwood	42	13	8	21	91	94	34
Horwich RMI	42	14	5	23	92	123	33
Barrow Reserves	42	13	5	24	66	99	31
Great Harwood	42	10	8	24	66	89	28
Rochdale Reserves	42	9	5	28	62	128	23
Northern Nomads	42	8	1	33	42	153	17

1938-39

South Liverpool	42	29	4	9	137	61	62
Bangor City	42	27	7	8	126	75	61
Clitheroe	42	25	7	10	121	74	57
Accrington Stanley Reserves	42	23	8	11	109	64	54
Chorley	42	23	7	12	118	62	53
Rossendale United	42	19	12	11	110	95	50
New Brighton Reserves	42	20	7	15	107	83	47
Marine	42	22	3	17	107	92	47
Oldham Athletic Reserves	42	18	10	14	108	94	46
Fleetwood	42	18	8	16	85	92	44
Lancaster City	42	19	6	17	95	103	44
Rochdale Reserves	42	17	9	16	91	90	43
Darwen	42	18	6	18	116	87	42
Leyland Motors	42	16	7	19	94	101	39
Morecambe	42	14	10	18	67	76	38
Barrow Reserves	42	16	5	21	87	116	37
Southport Reserves	42	14	8	20	81	99	36
Bacup Borough	42	13	6	23	81	99	32
Prescot Cables	42	12	7	23	79	131	31
Great Harwood	42	7	8	27	72	156	22
Horwich RMI	42	7	7	28	80	143	21
Droylsden	42	7	4	31	79	157	18

1945-46

Chorley	22	14	4	4	78	42	32
Netherfield	22	13	3	6	64	39	29
Barrow Reserves	22	12	4	6	62	43	28
Bacup Borough	22	12	3	7	49	41	27
Darwen	22	9	7	6	50	48	25
Rossendale United	22	9	4	9	53	47	22
Leyland Motors	22	9	3	10	50	56	21
Rochdale Reserves	22	9	2	11	52	53	20
Morecambe	22	6	6	10	54	68	18
Prescot Cables	22	6	5	11	57	81	17
Lancaster City	22	6	4	12	53	75	16
Accrington Stanley Reserves	22	3	4	15	38	67	10

1946-47

Bacup Borough	42	26	9	7	111	54	61
Marine	42	25	6	11	121	72	56
Netherfield	42	22	8	12	100	64	52
Morecambe	42	23	5	14	133	85	51
Rochdale Reserves	42	23	3	16	116	72	49
Prescot Cables	42	21	6	15	116	99	48
Lancaster City	42	22	3	17	104	66	47
Oldham Athletic Reserves	42	20	7	15	95	94	47
Clitheroe	42	19	7	16	107	105	45
Barrow Reserves	40	15	14	11	77	76	44
Nelson	42	18	7	17	100	85	43
Fleetwood	42	18	7	17	78	72	43
New Brighton Reserves	42	20	2	20	80	92	42
Horwich RMI	42	17	6	19	83	93	40
Bangor City	40	14	9	17	84	94	37
Southport Reserves	42	15	6	21	76	84	36
Chorley	42	13	9	20	84	92	35
Darwen	42	14	6	22	84	122	34
Leyland Motors	42	13	7	22	66	90	33
Rossendale United	42	11	10	21	76	113	32
Accrington Stanley Reserves	42	11	7	24	70	122	29
Great Harwood	42	6	4	32	63	178	16

Bangor City & Barrow Reserves did not meet due to travelling problems

1947-48

Division One

Wigan Athletic	42	25	9	8	72	37	59
Nelson	42	24	9	9	84	62	57
Barrow Reserves	42	24	7	11	88	55	55
Morecambe	42	24	6	12	98	59	54
Fleetwood	42	23	7	12	73	52	53
Marine	42	23	6	13	103	64	52
Netherfield	42	23	6	13	83	58	52
Lancaster City	42	21	7	14	80	69	49
Bacup Borough	42	20	6	16	96	67	46
Oldham Athletic Reserves	42	19	8	15	76	71	46
Chorley	42	19	7	16	89	74	45
Prescot Cables	42	19	6	17	87	80	44
Rochdale Reserves	42	14	8	20	79	76	36
Bangor City	42	14	8	20	62	77	36
Rossendale United	42	11	12	19	80	90	34
Darwen	42	12	9	21	60	91	33
Accrington Stanley Reserves	42	12	7	23	71	106	31
Clitheroe	42	13	5	24	70	110	31
New Brighton Reserves	42	11	8	23	56	85	30
Leyland Motors	42	11	7	24	73	115	29
Horwich RMI	42	10	7	25	58	104	27
Southport Reserves	42	9	7	26	57	93	25

Division Two

Stubshaw Cross Rovers	32	23	4	5	88	43	50
Nelson Reserves	32	23	4	5	79	42	50
Astley & Tyldesley Collieries	32	18	3	11	88	76	39
Darwen Reserves	31	14	7	10	85	72	35
Great Harwood	32	9	10	13	61	69	28
Belle Vue	31	10	5	16	72	85	25
Bacup Borough Reserves	32	8	8	16	76	90	24
Barnoldswick and District	31	10	3	18	70	85	23
Oldham Athletic "A"	29	1	6	22	37	94	8

Rossendale United Reserves resigned during October and Horwich RMI Reserves resigned during February. Both of their records were deleted. Oldham Athletic "A" failed to complete their fixtures.

1948-49

Division One

	P	W	D	L	F	A	Pts
Netherfield	42	26	10	6	112	46	62
Chorley	42	23	12	7	72	55	58
Morecambe	42	22	6	14	80	60	50
Nelson	42	20	9	13	87	68	49
Darwen	42	21	7	14	81	65	49
Wigan Athletic	42	19	9	14	73	68	47
Bangor City	42	18	10	14	75	71	46
Prescot Cables	42	19	7	16	89	72	45
Lancaster City	42	15	14	13	58	50	44
Rochdale Reserves	42	17	10	15	75	71	44
Fleetwood	42	17	8	17	81	66	42
Rossendale United	42	17	8	17	85	78	42
Barrow Reserves	42	16	10	16	73	69	42
Oldham Athletic Reserves	42	13	15	14	80	71	41
Ashton United	42	14	13	15	73	79	41
Southport Reserves	42	17	7	18	60	69	41
Marine	42	14	10	18	73	83	38
Clitheroe	42	13	9	20	74	99	35
Accrington Stanley Reserves	42	14	6	22	69	86	34
New Brighton Reserves	42	9	13	20	53	82	31
Leyland Motors	42	7	9	26	49	94	23
Bacup Borough	42	7	6	29	49	119	20

Division Two

	P	W	D	L	F	A	Pts
Bootle	24	19	2	3	77	29	40
Horwich RMI	24	19	1	4	75	28	39
Belle Vue	24	16	3	5	78	32	35
Stubshaw Cross Rovers	24	15	3	6	58	53	33
Lytham	24	15	2	7	61	42	32
Great Harwood	24	9	4	11	55	59	22
ACI Horwich	24	9	2	13	47	62	20
Nelson Reserves	24	7	5	12	44	53	19
Lancaster City Reserves	24	6	5	13	39	64	17
Darwen Reserves	24	5	4	15	33	55	14
Barnoldswick and District	24	4	6	14	29	55	14
Oldham Athletic "A"	24	6	2	16	47	90	14
Bolton Wanderers "B"	24	4	5	15	33	53	13

1949-50

Division One

	P	W	D	L	F	A	Pts
Nelson	42	30	4	8	125	63	64
Wigan Athletic	42	24	8	10	79	47	56
Prescot Cables	42	22	12	8	102	64	56
Chorley	42	20	9	13	71	67	49
Ashton United	42	20	7	15	90	62	47
Rochdale Reserves	42	19	8	15	87	79	46
Bangor City	42	18	9	15	96	70	45
Fleetwood	42	18	9	15	76	67	45
Morecambe	42	17	11	14	62	55	45
Netherfield	42	20	5	17	88	83	45
Accrington Stanley Reserves	42	16	10	16	64	75	42
Southport Reserves	42	14	13	15	67	67	41
Oldham Athletic Reserves	42	15	10	17	77	72	40
Lancaster City	42	14	10	18	67	74	38
Barrow Reserves	42	14	10	18	63	81	38
Bootle	42	14	9	19	61	71	37
Darwen	42	13	11	18	55	66	37
Rossendale United	42	13	8	21	73	85	34
Clitheroe	42	13	8	21	66	90	34
New Brighton Reserves	42	13	6	23	63	102	32
Marine	42	11	9	22	74	104	31
Horwich RMI	42	8	6	28	52	114	22

Division Two

	P	W	D	L	F	A	Pts
Blackpool "B"	38	29	3	6	139	38	61
Earlestown	38	29	2	7	149	60	60
Leyland Motors	38	26	4	8	111	50	56
Bacup Borough	38	26	3	9	101	51	55
Stubshaw Cross Rovers	38	21	4	13	81	76	46
Droylesden United	38	20	5	13	103	80	45
St. Helens Town	38	16	11	11	84	77	43
Lytham	38	19	3	16	86	73	41
Nelson Reserves	38	20	1	17	100	89	41
Bolton Wanderers "B"	38	16	7	15	73	64	39
Chorley Reserves	38	16	5	17	96	88	37
Wigan Athletic Reserves	38	13	10	15	58	70	36
ACI Horwich	38	15	4	19	95	122	34
Lomax	38	13	6	19	84	107	32
Lancaster City Reserves	38	12	8	18	65	93	32
Padiham	38	12	4	22	91	106	28
Great Harwood	38	11	3	24	68	113	25
Barnoldswick and District	38	11	1	26	55	113	24
Darwen Reserves	38	7	5	26	64	117	19
De Havilland	38	2	2	34	43	160	6

1950-51

Division One

	P	W	D	L	F	A	Pts
Wigan Athletic	42	27	7	8	98	43	61
Nelson	42	29	3	10	120	64	61
Netherfield	42	26	7	9	107	57	59
Fleetwood	42	21	10	11	100	70	52
Rochdale Reserves	42	20	10	12	87	69	50
Bootle	42	22	5	15	89	61	49
Southport Reserves	42	19	8	15	98	81	46
Chorley	42	17	10	15	91	93	44
Oldham Athletic Reserves	42	16	11	15	88	78	43
Barrow Reserves	42	17	9	16	68	63	43
Lancaster City	42	17	9	16	75	89	43
Ashton United	42	16	9	17	85	88	41
New Brighton Reserves	42	15	8	19	53	56	38
Darwen	42	12	12	18	62	79	36
Morecambe	42	12	12	18	56	73	36
Clitheroe	42	15	6	21	69	90	36
Earlestown	42	16	3	23	91	115	35
Blackpool "B"	42	13	8	21	69	87	34
Rossendale United	42	13	7	22	63	102	33
Marine	42	11	8	23	68	87	30
Prescot Cables	42	10	10	22	57	89	30
Accrington Stanley Reserves	42	7	10	25	44	104	24

Division Two

	P	W	D	L	F	A	Pts
St. Helens Town	42	29	6	7	132	49	64
Horwich RMI	42	30	4	8	154	60	64
Bacup Borough	42	26	4	12	109	65	56
Lytham	42	23	6	13	99	67	52
Nelson Reserves	42	22	8	12	84	60	52
Hindsford	42	23	6	13	87	83	52
Padiham	42	21	9	12	100	59	51
Bolton Wanderers "B"	42	22	6	14	117	72	50
Leyland Motors	42	18	8	16	93	78	44
Stubshaw Cross Rovers	42	18	8	16	85	83	44
Wigan Athletic Reserves	42	17	9	16	77	74	43
Netherfield Reserves	42	17	9	16	75	98	43
Droylesden United	42	18	5	19	95	97	41
ACI Horwich	42	18	5	19	88	91	41
Morecambe Reserves	42	13	10	19	75	106	36
Atherton Collieries	42	15	4	23	98	113	34
Lomax	42	12	7	22	105	125	33
Great Harwood	42	13	6	23	99	124	32
Chorley Reserves	42	12	7	23	77	126	31
Barnoldswick and District	42	10	6	26	65	130	26
Lancaster City Reserves	42	7	4	31	64	139	18
Darwen Reserves	42	6	5	31	63	142	17

1951-52

Division One

Nelson	42	30	3	9	139	59	63
Lancaster City	42	24	7	11	89	69	55
Netherfield	42	22	10	10	108	63	54
Wigan Athletic	42	21	9	12	73	57	51
Morecambe	42	21	7	14	74	72	49
Ashton United	42	21	6	15	96	87	48
Rochdale Reserves	42	20	6	16	104	79	46
Barrow Reserves	42	19	8	15	73	66	46
Fleetwood	42	20	5	17	94	87	45
Bootle Athletic	42	17	8	17	73	73	42
Chorley	42	16	10	16	66	72	42
Horwich RMI	42	17	7	18	99	97	41
New Brighton	42	16	8	18	73	85	40
Blackpool "B"	42	18	4	20	72	88	40
Marine	42	13	12	17	77	85	38
Darwen	42	16	5	21	60	83	37
Oldham Athletic Reserves	42	13	9	20	87	91	35
Clitheroe	42	13	9	20	59	79	35
Southport Reserves	42	12	12	10	20	70	76	34
Rossendale United	42	13	5	24	77	95	31
St. Helens Town	42	12	5	25	86	119	29
Earlestown	42	6	11	25	68	135	23

Division Two

Prescot Cables	42	32	5	5	151	44	69
Nelson Reserves	42	30	6	6	123	49	66
Droylsden	42	28	7	7	172	78	63
Accrington Stanley Reserves	42	27	6	9	115	56	60
Leyland Motors	42	26	6	10	104	56	58
Bacup Borough	42	22	8	12	107	72	52
Lytham	42	20	7	15	100	68	47
Great Harwood	42	22	3	17	115	107	47
Barnoldswick and District	42	19	8	15	89	86	46
Bolton Wanderers "B"	42	18	6	18	107	75	42
Netherfield Reserves	42	15	11	16	79	87	41
Wigan Athletic Reserves	42	18	5	19	85	108	41
Astley Bridge	42	14	5	23	80	110	33
Hindsford	42	13	7	22	76	106	33
Stubshaw Cross Rovers	42	14	4	24	76	110	32
Padiham	42	12	7	23	81	112	31
Morecambe Reserves	42	13	4	25	68	139	30
Lomax	42	11	6	25	83	124	28
Chorley Reserves	42	11	5	26	72	120	27
ACI Horwich	42	11	5	26	76	137	27
Atherton Collieries	42	11	5	26	65	123	27
Darwen Reserves	42	10	4	28	64	121	24

1952-53

Division One

Wigan Athletic	42	27	13	2	124	45	67
Prescot Cables	42	25	5	12	83	46	55
Darwen	42	19	11	12	88	65	49
Marine	42	19	11	12	91	72	49
Nelson	42	20	8	14	86	72	48
Lancaster City	42	21	6	15	81	72	48
Horwich RMI	42	17	13	12	109	105	47
Ashton United	42	18	9	15	105	85	45
Netherfield	42	20	4	18	82	81	44
Southport Reserves	42	17	8	17	78	80	42
Morecambe	42	16	9	17	60	61	41
Bootle Athletic	42	16	8	18	64	64	40
Oldham Athletic Reserves	42	16	7	19	84	89	39
Rossendale United	42	16	7	19	84	92	39
Fleetwood	42	16	7	19	76	105	39
Chorley	42	16	5	21	81	87	37
New Brighton	42	14	9	19	61	70	37
Accrington Stanley Reserves	42	13	11	18	64	78	37
Rochdale Reserves	42	11	9	22	61	76	31
Barrow Reserves	42	10	11	21	57	80	31
Clitheroe	42	11	9	22	69	115	31
Blackpool "B"	42	11	6	25	49	97	28

Division Two

Bolton Wanderers "B"	42	32	4	6	135	43	68
South Liverpool	42	32	2	8	164	61	66
Droylsden	42	28	6	8	145	66	62
St. Helens Town	42	26	5	11	137	75	57
Earlestown	42	23	6	13	110	69	52
Barnoldswick and District	42	23	6	13	125	108	52
Leyland Motors	42	21	9	12	84	67	51
Lytham	42	18	9	15	81	77	45
Crompton's Recreation	42	17	11	14	98	101	45
Astley Bridge	42	17	10	15	99	97	44
Bacup Borough	42	17	8	17	100	77	42
Lomax	42	17	6	19	82	103	40
Great Harwood	42	15	9	18	95	112	39
Padiham	42	15	8	19	87	101	38
Wigan Athletic Reserves	42	14	9	19	81	91	37
Chorley Reserves	42	14	9	19	94	112	37
Nelson Reserves	42	13	5	24	69	105	31
Netherfield Reserves	42	10	11	21	78	119	31
Stubshaw Cross Rovers	42	11	5	26	71	114	27
Darwen Reserves	42	6	10	26	52	105	22
Morecambe Reserves	42	7	8	27	68	141	22
Hindsford	42	5	6	31	70	181	16

1953-54

Division One

Wigan Athletic	40	31	4	5	110	48	66
Netherfield	40	20	11	9	104	73	51
Nelson	40	21	6	13	91	68	48
Horwich RMI	40	21	5	14	95	65	47
Darwen	40	18	9	13	80	49	45
Marine	40	17	6	17	70	77	40
South Liverpool	40	15	9	16	77	73	39
Oldham Athletic Reserves	40	17	5	18	77	81	39
Lancaster City	40	16	7	17	79	84	39
Southport Reserves	40	16	7	17	56	67	39
Accrington Stanley Reserves	40	17	3	20	91	88	37
Bolton Wanderers "B"	40	16	5	19	62	71	37
Rossendale United	40	14	8	18	87	89	36
Ashton United	40	17	2	21	74	85	36
Rochdale Reserves	40	14	8	18	61	80	36
Barrow Reserves	40	15	6	19	57	79	36
Fleetwood	40	14	7	19	78	88	35
Chorley	40	12	10	18	51	60	34
Morecambe	40	14	6	20	58	83	34
New Brighton	40	13	7	20	70	94	33
Prescot Cables	40	13	7	20	63	89	33

Bootle Athletic disbanded and their record was deleted.

Division Two

Burscough	42	33	4	5	155	38	70
Blackpool "B"	42	29	6	7	132	53	64
Burnley "A"	42	29	4	9	146	66	62
Earlestown	42	26	8	8	121	74	60
Droylsden	42	26	7	9	116	50	59
Nelson Reserves	42	25	4	13	101	85	54
Barnoldswick and District	42	21	8	13	120	95	50
Bacup Borough	42	20	8	14	99	86	48
Clitheroe	42	21	4	17	113	107	46
Leyland Motors	42	20	3	19	87	84	43
Lytham	42	17	9	16	66	78	43
Crompton's Recreation	42	19	3	20	88	111	41
Darwen Reserves	42	18	3	21	90	94	39
Prescot Cables Reserves	42	16	6	20	101	90	38
St. Helens Town	42	16	6	20	86	98	38
Chorley Reserves	42	12	8	22	81	111	32
Wigan Athletic Reserves	42	12	7	23	83	107	31
Padiham	42	12	3	27	60	118	27
Great Harwood	42	10	6	26	82	120	26
Lomax	42	12	1	29	73	139	25
Astley Bridge	42	7	4	31	65	160	18
Stubshaw Cross Rovers	42	4	2	36	51	152	10

1954-55

Division One

Accrington Stanley Reserves	42	29	10	3	110	46	68
Rossendale United	42	24	6	12	123	84	54
Wigan Athletic	42	21	10	11	93	56	52
Burscough	42	22	8	12	75	49	52
Oldham Athletic Reserves	42	21	10	11	98	74	52
Blackpool "B"	42	22	5	15	101	59	49
Fleetwood	42	19	11	12	73	69	49
Horwich RMI	42	20	8	14	81	62	48
Morecambe	42	18	8	16	68	65	44
Marine	42	19	5	18	91	84	43
Netherfield	42	20	3	19	92	94	43
Darwen	42	15	13	14	64	79	43
Chorley	42	17	7	18	78	91	41
Lancaster City	42	16	9	17	68	84	41
Barrow Reserves	42	14	9	19	87	90	37
Nelson	42	14	8	20	82	84	36
Ashton United	42	13	9	20	75	107	35
Southport Reserves	42	12	9	21	74	79	33
Bolton Wanderers "B"	42	12	8	22	62	68	32
South Liverpool	42	12	8	22	67	105	32
Rochdale Reserves	42	8	9	25	58	92	25
New Brighton	42	6	3	33	48	147	15

Division Two

Burnley "A"	38	33	1	4	137	39	67
Prescot Cables	38	31	2	5	173	53	64
Droylsden	38	29	3	6	128	54	61
Crompton's Recreation	38	23	6	9	119	71	52
Wigan Athletic Reserves	38	22	3	13	111	67	47
Bacup Borough	38	22	3	13	105	75	47
Clitheroe	38	19	4	15	86	75	42
Lytham	38	16	7	15	87	75	39
Leyland Motors	38	16	3	19	78	85	35
Blackburn Rovers "A"	38	15	5	18	84	93	35
Earlestown	38	14	7	17	81	93	35
Barnoldswick and District	38	14	6	18	78	89	34
Preston North End "A"	38	12	10	16	82	107	34
Nelson Reserves	38	10	8	20	56	87	28
Chorley Reserves	38	11	4	23	64	93	26
Great Harwood	38	11	4	23	67	114	26
Darwen Reserves	38	9	7	22	55	107	25
St. Helens Town	38	10	5	23	48	115	25
Lomax	38	9	3	26	63	117	21
Padiham	38	5	7	26	53	146	17

1955-56

Division One

Burscough	38	26	7	5	96	37	59
Horwich RMI	38	24	9	5	104	49	57
Accrington Stanley Reserves	38	20	10	8	87	56	50
Netherfield	38	21	7	10	95	55	49
Lancaster City	38	19	11	8	83	59	49
Wigan Athletic	38	18	10	10	80	56	46
New Brighton	38	18	8	12	78	57	44
Prescot Cables	38	19	6	13	104	92	44
Chorley	38	17	5	16	78	68	39
Marine	38	14	8	16	71	83	36
Southport Reserves	38	13	9	16	54	60	35
Ashton United	38	14	7	17	62	75	35
Darwen	38	13	8	17	66	85	34
Fleetwood	38	12	8	18	65	79	32
Nelson	38	12	8	18	60	89	32
Bacup Borough	38	10	9	19	58	76	29
Morecambe	38	12	5	21	62	94	29
South Liverpool	38	12	3	23	69	98	27
Rossendale United	38	8	9	21	61	89	25
St. Helens Town	38	3	3	32	34	110	9

Division Two

Skelmersdale United	34	21	9	4	110	54	51
Droylsden	34	23	4	7	111	71	50
Wigan Athletic Reserves	34	21	6	7	102	44	48
Burscough Reserves	34	23	1	10	91	49	47
Crompton's Recreation	34	20	7	7	94	55	47
Lytham	34	19	7	8	81	46	45
Clitheroe	34	19	4	11	82	69	42
Lomax	34	15	2	17	81	91	32
Chorley Reserves	34	11	6	17	59	76	28
Earlestown	34	10	6	18	60	77	26
Leyland Motors	34	10	6	18	65	87	26
Nelson Reserves	34	11	4	19	72	102	26
Prescot Cables Reserves	34	11	4	19	60	99	26
Great Harwood	34	9	7	18	65	74	25
St. Annes Athletic	34	10	5	19	63	97	25
Rolls Royce	34	10	4	20	77	109	24
Padiham	34	9	5	20	63	101	23
Darwen Reserves	34	6	9	19	43	78	21

1956-57

Division One

Prescot Cables	38	26	5	7	123	52	57
New Brighton	38	25	4	9	94	50	54
Morecambe	38	20	7	11	81	53	47
Horwich RMI	38	22	3	13	93	70	47
Burscough	38	19	7	12	86	58	45
Accrington Stanley Reserves	38	18	8	12	82	61	44
Ashton United	38	19	5	14	89	74	43
Chorley	38	15	8	15	74	74	38
Netherfield	38	15	8	15	73	73	38
Wigan Athletic	38	17	3	18	73	61	37
Lancaster City	38	14	8	16	71	91	36
Bacup Borough	38	12	11	15	80	88	35
Nelson	38	15	5	18	53	59	35
Skelmersdale United	38	14	6	18	67	82	34
South Liverpool	38	14	5	19	71	82	33
Fleetwood	38	13	7	18	56	70	33
Marine	38	12	8	18	62	84	32
Southport Reserves	38	12	7	19	62	88	31
Darwen	38	11	5	22	62	88	27
Droylsden	38	4	6	28	59	153	14

Division Two

Rossendale United	34	25	3	6	111	34	53
Crompton's Recreation	34	19	7	8	72	45	45
Clitheroe	34	17	10	7	90	56	44
Rolls Royce	34	20	4	10	100	74	44
Earlestown	34	20	1	13	95	86	41
St. Helens Town	34	15	9	10	87	67	39
Nelson Reserves	34	14	10	10	72	52	38
Lytham	34	15	8	11	73	59	38
Lomax	34	15	7	12	86	89	37
Prescot Cables Reserves	34	15	5	14	67	75	35
Burscough Reserves	34	14	4	16	72	75	32
Wigan Athletic Reserves	34	14	3	17	62	71	31
St. Annes Athletic	34	10	6	18	78	97	26
Darwen Reserves	34	10	5	19	48	101	25
Leyland Motors	34	10	3	21	57	81	23
Great Harwood	34	9	5	20	57	84	23
Chorley Reserves	34	9	4	21	52	95	22
Padiham	34	6	4	24	57	95	16

1957-58

Division One

Horwich RMI	42	28	7	7	109	47	63
Prescot Cables	42	26	9	7	117	49	61
New Brighton	42	23	8	11	85	61	54
Wigan Athletic	42	21	11	10	95	60	53
Accrington Stanley Reserves	42	23	6	13	92	71	52
Netherfield	42	20	9	13	87	70	49
Morecambe	42	18	12	12	66	50	48
Rossendale United	42	19	10	13	104	88	48
Chorley	42	20	7	15	123	85	47
Marine	42	17	7	18	74	103	41
Nelson	42	17	6	19	65	71	40
Ashton United	42	17	5	20	96	108	39
Lancaster City	42	15	7	20	74	93	37
Southport Reserves	42	16	5	21	69	102	37
Burscough	42	14	8	20	80	79	36
South Liverpool	42	15	6	21	94	102	36
Skelmersdale United	42	15	6	21	77	92	36
Darwen	42	14	6	22	71	104	34
Droylsden	42	13	7	22	75	99	33
Bacup Borough	42	12	8	22	88	115	32
Fleetwood	42	11	10	21	57	82	32
Crompton's Recreation	42	5	6	31	51	118	16

Division Two

Oldham Athletic Reserves	38	28	4	6	135	45	60
Clitheroe	38	27	6	5	137	48	60
Earlestown	38	21	10	7	130	79	52
Padiham	38	20	9	9	84	64	49
Northern Nomads	38	21	6	11	88	58	48
Lytham	38	18	10	10	89	75	46
Chorley Reserves	38	19	7	12	103	64	45
Glossop	38	19	6	13	92	81	44
Wigan Athletic Reserves	38	18	7	13	101	64	43
St. Helens Town	38	17	7	14	87	67	41
Horwich RMI Reserves	38	17	6	15	80	87	40
Morecambe Reserves	38	13	8	17	68	86	34
Leyland Motors	38	14	4	20	81	98	32
Lomax	38	10	10	18	63	92	30
Rolls Royce	38	10	9	19	69	93	29
Prescot Cables Reserves	38	8	10	20	63	90	26
Nelson Reserves	38	6	11	21	65	134	23
St. Annes Athletic	38	7	8	23	68	117	22
Great Harwood	38	6	10	22	59	125	22
Darwen Reserves	38	6	2	30	36	131	14

1958-59

Division One

New Brighton	42	29	6	7	127	53	64
Prescot Cables	42	27	6	9	111	57	60
Horwich RMI	42	25	9	8	95	57	59
Skelmersdale United	42	22	10	10	107	69	54
Morecambe	42	22	9	11	77	44	53
Chorley	42	22	7	13	109	82	51
Netherfield	42	22	5	15	91	73	49
Bacup Borough	42	19	10	13	104	88	48
Nelson	42	19	9	14	82	74	47
Fleetwood	42	20	4	18	72	87	44
Marine	42	16	8	18	80	97	40
Burscough	42	15	9	18	60	69	39
South Liverpool	42	16	6	20	81	94	38
Darwen	42	16	6	20	75	93	38
Lancaster City	42	13	12	17	69	95	38
Rossendale United	42	16	5	21	88	89	37
Oldham Athletic Reserves	42	13	8	21	80	98	34
Wigan Athletic	42	12	7	23	60	84	31
Ashton United	42	12	6	24	69	103	30
Southport Reserves	42	10	8	24	70	104	28
Clitheroe	42	11	3	28	71	105	25
Droylsden	42	6	5	31	43	106	17

Division Two

Netherfield Reserves	34	23	7	4	110	46	53
Chorley Reserves	34	21	5	8	86	53	47
Earlestown	34	21	4	9	109	62	46
Lytham	34	18	8	8	89	72	44
Padiham	34	19	5	10	95	60	43
Northern Nomads	34	17	6	11	76	70	40
Leyland Motors	34	14	8	12	85	69	36
Crompton's Recreation	34	14	7	13	80	75	35
Glossop	34	14	6	14	75	64	34
St. Helens Town	34	15	3	16	73	62	33
Horwich RMI Reserves	34	13	4	17	71	73	30
Rossendale United Reserves	34	9	10	15	59	78	28
Lomax	34	12	4	18	71	105	28
Wigan Athletic Reserves	34	10	7	17	46	69	27
Great Harwood	34	10	6	18	62	100	26
Morecambe Reserves	34	10	5	19	56	86	25
Nelson Reserves	34	8	8	18	52	84	24
Rolls Royce	34	3	7	24	35	102	13

1959-60

Division One

Chorley	42	31	5	6	133	48	67
Wigan Athletic	42	27	6	9	101	51	60
New Brighton	42	28	4	10	103	54	60
Morecambe	42	28	2	12	103	54	58
Rossendale United	42	21	7	14	116	95	49
Burscough	42	20	8	14	94	73	48
Nelson	42	22	4	16	78	68	48
Netherfield	42	20	7	15	88	70	47
Marine	42	19	6	17	92	98	44
Horwich RMI	42	17	8	17	82	76	42
Prescot Cables	42	16	9	17	74	68	41
Oldham Athletic Reserves	42	16	7	19	64	66	39
Ashton United	42	13	12	17	61	86	38
Fleetwood	42	16	5	21	63	71	37
Bacup Borough	42	11	12	19	71	99	34
Earlestown	42	13	7	22	79	113	33
Lancaster City	42	12	9	21	73	107	33
Lytham	42	10	12	20	60	88	32
Skelmersdale United	42	13	6	23	59	97	32
Darwen	42	10	11	21	57	86	31
Southport Reserves	42	9	10	23	57	92	28
South Liverpool	42	7	9	26	54	102	23

Division Two

Clitheroe	34	26	3	5	81	28	55
Droylsden	34	25	3	6	106	55	53
Chorley Reserves	34	24	4	6	92	37	52
Glossop	34	19	3	12	75	57	41
St. Helens Town	34	17	7	10	63	52	41
Wigan Athletic Reserves	34	18	4	12	93	69	40
Morecambe Reserves	34	16	4	14	88	75	36
Crompton's Recreation	34	14	7	13	78	61	35
Padiham	34	16	3	15	74	65	35
Netherfield Reserves	34	13	8	13	77	74	34
Nelson Reserves	34	13	7	14	58	61	33
Horwich RMI Reserves	34	13	4	17	90	84	30
Rolls Royce	34	12	2	20	61	109	26
Leyland Motors	34	8	8	18	51	80	24
Lancaster City Reserves	34	9	4	21	48	88	22
Northern Nomads	34	8	3	23	52	91	19
Lomax	34	7	5	22	48	107	19
Great Harwood	34	7	3	24	44	86	17

1960-61

Division One

Chorley	42	31	7	4	125	33	69
Nelson	42	29	7	6	106	47	65
Wigan Athletic	42	25	8	9	108	56	58
Burscough	42	25	8	9	76	49	58
Netherfield	42	24	8	10	123	71	56
Morecambe	42	23	5	14	96	76	51
Lancaster City	42	17	14	11	75	53	48
Prescot Cables	42	20	7	15	70	78	47
New Brighton	42	20	6	16	80	65	46
Marine	42	17	10	15	79	75	44
Clitheroe	42	17	7	18	84	88	41
Ashton United	42	18	5	19	78	88	41
Horwich RMI	42	14	7	21	75	94	35
Lytham	42	13	8	21	69	85	34
Skelmersdale United	42	12	9	21	71	85	33
Rossendale United	42	13	7	22	92	139	33
Oldham Athletic Reserves	42	13	6	23	71	84	32
Earlestown	42	12	8	22	74	103	32
Bacup Borough	42	11	9	22	76	96	31
Fleetwood	42	12	5	25	82	110	29
Droylsden	42	10	5	27	73	132	25
Darwen	42	7	2	33	45	121	16

Division Two

Chorley Reserves	34	24	6	4	120	56	54
Morecambe Reserves	34	21	8	5	92	46	50
Padiham	34	21	6	7	94	55	48
Wigan Athletic Reserves	34	22	3	9	105	47	47
Southport Reserves	34	21	5	8	86	50	47
South Liverpool	34	21	4	9	116	60	46
Northern Nomads	34	16	6	12	91	80	38
Netherfield Reserves	34	16	5	13	89	81	37
St. Helens Town	34	15	5	14	69	67	35
Glossop	34	13	5	16	64	86	31
Nelson Reserves	34	13	3	18	55	78	29
Leyland Motors	34	10	7	17	66	86	27
Crompton's Recreation	34	10	6	18	67	93	26
Horwich RMI Reserves	34	10	6	18	67	106	26
Prescot Cables Reserves	34	10	4	20	66	74	24
Great Harwood	34	8	5	21	56	104	21
Rolls Royce	34	6	1	27	50	117	13
Lancaster City Reserves	34	4	5	25	44	111	13

1961-62

Division One

Morecambe	42	32	6	4	143	51	70
Netherfield	42	27	10	5	143	67	64
Horwich RMI	42	26	9	7	110	48	61
Burscough	42	26	8	8	122	68	60
Chorley	42	24	9	9	107	71	57
Rossendale United	42	22	6	14	114	89	50
Oldham Athletic Reserves	42	21	8	13	89	71	50
New Brighton	42	23	3	16	105	57	49
Lancaster City	42	18	12	12	75	65	48
Southport Reserves	42	18	9	15	102	77	45
Nelson	42	20	5	17	86	71	45
Clitheroe	42	18	9	15	85	83	45
Earlestown	42	17	6	19	89	102	40
Marine	42	15	7	20	94	99	37
Prescot Cables	42	14	9	19	66	83	37
Fleetwood	42	11	11	20	84	89	33
Skelmersdale United	42	12	7	23	62	103	31
Lytham	42	9	7	26	67	127	25
Darwen	42	8	9	25	56	119	25
Leyland Motors	42	6	8	28	67	126	20
Bacup Borough	42	6	4	32	52	149	16
Padiham	42	4	8	30	51	154	16

Division Two

Ashton United	36	29	4	3	124	32	62
South Liverpool	36	25	4	7	110	41	54
Droylsden	36	25	3	8	126	46	53
Morecambe Reserves	36	24	3	9	91	63	51
Glossop	36	20	5	11	85	62	45
Barrow Reserves	36	20	4	12	81	46	44
Chorley Reserves	36	17	7	12	79	58	41
Netherfield Reserves	36	16	8	12	92	66	40
Nelson Reserves	36	16	6	14	87	62	38
St. Helens Town	36	13	8	15	67	62	34
Wigan Rovers	36	14	6	16	67	82	34
Lancaster City Reserves	36	14	2	20	77	80	30
Rolls Royce	36	12	6	18	100	108	30
Horwich RMI Reserves	36	13	3	20	77	85	29
Crompton's Recreation	36	12	3	21	73	109	27
Northern Nomads	36	10	6	20	68	94	26
Prescot Cables Reserves	36	10	4	22	63	107	24
Great Harwood	36	9	2	25	76	129	20
Lucas Sports Club	36	1	0	35	28	239	2

Accrington Stanley Reserves withdrew and their record was deleted.

1962-63

Division One

Morecambe	42	31	6	5	153	40	68
Chorley	42	31	6	5	137	59	68
Ashton United	42	25	8	9	101	57	58
Horwich RMI	42	25	5	12	107	59	55
Netherfield	42	23	7	12	125	69	53
Lancaster City	42	23	6	13	96	61	52
Marine	42	22	6	14	92	73	50
Nelson	42	22	4	16	95	81	48
Fleetwood	42	23	1	18	97	71	47
South Liverpool	42	20	3	19	76	65	43
New Brighton	42	18	5	19	83	76	41
Southport Reserves	42	17	7	18	80	76	41
Clitheroe	42	17	6	19	80	81	40
Rossendale United	42	17	6	19	103	138	40
Skelmersdale United	42	15	5	22	73	90	35
Burscough	42	15	5	22	68	93	35
Bacup Borough	42	14	6	22	81	110	34
Earlestown	42	14	3	25	88	132	31
Prescot Cables	42	13	5	24	71	108	31
Leyland Motors	42	9	7	26	54	106	25
Darwen	42	5	6	31	41	117	16
Lytham	42	5	3	34	34	173	13

Division Two

Crompton's Recreation	38	29	5	4	138	52	63
Droylsden	38	27	6	5	124	31	60
Morecambe Reserves	38	23	6	9	93	46	52
Barrow Reserves	38	24	3	11	91	52	51
Great Harwood	38	22	7	9	121	77	51
Horwich RMI Reserves	38	21	6	11	100	58	48
Chorley Reserves	38	21	5	12	94	63	47
Accrington Stanley	38	19	7	12	99	66	45
Glossop	38	15	9	14	75	73	39
St. Helens Town	38	16	6	16	59	58	38
Blackpool Mechanics	38	14	10	14	67	84	38
Rolls Royce	38	13	8	17	82	101	34
Netherfield Reserves	38	11	10	17	72	84	32
Wigan Rovers	38	10	10	18	73	98	30
Northern Nomads	38	10	8	20	64	93	28
Padiham	38	11	6	21	70	109	28
Lancaster City Reserves	38	9	6	23	67	111	24
Nelson Reserves	38	8	4	26	47	114	20
Vulcan Institute	38	9	1	28	74	137	19
Prescot Cables Reserves	38	5	3	30	40	143	13

1963-64
Division One

Chorley	42	27	7	8	114	51	61
Netherfield	42	26	8	8	123	64	60
New Brighton	42	24	10	8	83	45	58
Horwich RMI	42	24	8	10	91	51	56
Ashton United	42	20	10	12	91	65	50
Lancaster City	42	21	8	13	90	69	50
Droylsden	42	21	7	14	80	58	49
Nelson	42	23	3	16	84	73	49
South Liverpool	42	19	9	14	88	62	47
Morecambe	42	19	8	15	93	71	46
Skelmersdale United	42	21	4	17	88	76	46
Southport Reserves	42	17	6	19	68	75	40
Bacup Borough	42	17	5	20	59	68	39
Marine	42	15	8	19	73	83	38
Burscough	42	11	11	20	80	84	33
Rossendale United	42	12	9	21	70	114	33
Fleetwood	42	10	13	19	54	88	33
Prescot Cables	42	11	9	22	66	98	31
Clitheroe	42	10	10	22	59	88	30
Leyland Motors	42	11	7	24	57	118	29
Barrow Reserves	42	8	9	25	56	109	25
Crompton's Recreation	42	8	5	29	58	115	21

Division Two

Accrington Stanley	34	23	6	5	90	40	52
Chorley Reserves	34	21	7	6	102	45	49
Great Harwood	34	21	4	9	117	48	46
St. Helens Town	34	21	3	10	95	52	45
Netherfield Reserves	34	20	4	10	73	48	44
Wigan Rovers	34	18	6	10	81	61	42
Horwich RMI Reserves	34	17	6	11	93	47	40
Glossop	34	17	5	12	73	61	39
Darwen	34	14	10	10	77	59	38
Northern Nomads	34	15	4	15	73	64	34
Morecambe Reserves	34	13	7	14	63	47	33
Radcliffe Borough	34	13	7	14	84	74	33
Lancaster City Reserves	34	11	4	19	57	80	26
Blackpool Mechanics	34	10	6	18	54	94	26
Lytham	34	8	7	19	48	108	23
Kirkby Town	34	9	2	23	59	110	20
Vulcan Institute	34	4	5	25	49	134	13
Padiham	34	4	1	29	38	154	9

1964-65
Division One

Netherfield	42	30	6	6	143	53	66
Chorley	42	27	9	6	130	55	63
Morecambe	42	30	2	10	132	50	62
Horwich RMI	42	24	13	5	128	53	61
South Liverpool	42	27	5	10	97	67	59
Droylsden	42	23	6	13	81	67	52
New Brighton	42	21	9	12	82	48	51
Marine	42	21	6	15	90	69	48
Barrow Reserves	42	19	9	14	80	77	47
Great Harwood	42	19	7	16	85	83	45
Lancaster City	42	18	6	18	75	65	42
Fleetwood	42	14	12	16	68	93	40
Nelson	42	15	7	20	68	108	37
Skelmersdale United	42	15	6	21	83	84	36
Bacup Borough	42	16	2	24	61	94	34
Leyland Motors	42	13	7	22	74	105	33
Clitheroe	42	13	6	23	60	90	32
Rossendale United	42	13	6	23	75	114	32
Southport Reserves	42	11	5	26	51	99	27
Burscough	42	11	3	28	68	90	25
Accrington Stanley	42	7	4	31	48	127	18
Prescot Town	42	4	6	32	44	132	14

Division Two

Netherfield Reserves	32	22	6	4	103	32	50
Chorley Reserves	32	22	3	7	90	36	47
St. Helens Town	32	21	4	7	77	36	46
Guinness Exports	32	18	9	5	88	35	45
Kirkby Town	32	17	9	6	90	45	43
Radcliffe Borough	32	17	6	9	77	44	40
Horwich RMI Reserves	32	17	4	11	101	58	38
Wigan Rovers	32	15	8	9	65	54	38
Blackpool Mechanics	32	16	3	13	62	47	35
Morecambe Reserves	32	13	9	10	68	62	35
Darwen	32	15	5	12	63	58	35
Lytham	32	14	4	14	58	52	32
Glossop	32	10	2	20	49	80	22
Fleetwood Reserves	32	5	2	25	42	121	12
Lancaster City Reserves	32	5	2	25	33	102	12
Padiham	32	3	2	27	30	122	8
Accrington Stanley Reserves	32	2	2	28	30	142	6

1965-66
Division One

South Liverpool	42	29	6	7	128	56	64
Chorley	42	24	12	6	121	56	60
Skelmersdale United	42	28	4	10	120	62	60
Marine	42	27	4	11	129	66	58
Horwich RMI	42	26	3	13	100	58	55
Netherfield	42	20	13	9	104	70	53
Morecambe	42	19	12	11	105	65	50
Lancaster City	42	19	10	13	77	59	48
Clitheroe	42	20	8	14	77	73	48
Great Harwood	42	18	10	14	81	73	46
Barrow Reserves	42	19	8	15	88	85	46
Droylsden	42	15	12	15	80	78	42
Fleetwood	42	18	5	19	95	101	41
Guinness Exports	42	14	5	23	74	103	33
Leyland Motors	42	14	5	23	52	99	33
Burscough	42	13	6	23	76	89	32
St. Helens Town	42	11	5	26	65	125	27
Rossendale United	42	9	9	24	48	97	27
Bacup Borough	42	11	5	26	57	126	27
Southport Reserves	42	9	7	26	65	98	25
Nelson	42	10	5	27	56	121	25
Prescot Town	42	8	8	26	66	104	24

Division Two

Wigan Rovers	26	20	5	1	91	22	45
Chorley Reserves	26	17	4	5	60	31	38
Darwen	26	15	2	9	52	33	32
Glossop	26	12	5	9	42	40	29
Radcliffe Borough	26	11	7	8	54	54	29
Netherfield Reserves	26	10	6	10	51	45	26
Kirkby Town	26	8	10	8	36	35	26
Horwich RMI Reserves	26	11	2	13	53	53	24
Morecambe Reserves	26	9	5	12	52	54	23
Fleetwood Reserves	26	8	6	12	53	65	22
Blackpool Mechanics	26	6	8	12	33	48	20
Lytham	26	7	6	13	35	54	20
Lancaster City Reserves	26	5	6	15	42	70	16
Padiham	26	5	4	17	34	84	14

Accrington Stanley disbanded and their record was deleted.

1966-67

Division One

Morecambe	41	30	9	2	90	24	69
Horwich RMI	42	27	9	6	88	37	63
Netherfield	42	27	8	7	122	54	62
Chorley	42	23	9	10	97	59	55
Fleetwood	42	22	10	10	103	62	54
South Liverpool	42	24	6	12	94	61	54
Marine	42	20	9	13	84	69	49
Wigan Rovers	42	16	15	11	78	64	47
Skelmersdale United	41	20	5	16	99	77	45
Lancaster City	42	18	6	18	66	72	42
Southport Reserves	42	16	8	18	72	77	40
Bacup Borough	42	15	9	18	53	57	39
Droylsden	42	14	9	19	59	68	37
Burscough	42	16	5	21	55	85	37
St. Helens Town	42	13	9	20	66	76	35
Guinness Exports	42	12	11	19	62	87	35
Barrow Reserves	42	13	8	21	80	84	34
Rossendale United	42	12	8	22	64	90	32
Clitheroe	42	10	10	22	56	93	30
Great Harwood	42	11	5	26	56	101	27
Darwen	42	6	12	24	56	102	24
Leyland Motors	42	4	4	34	28	129	12

Skelmersdale United suffered from fixture congestion as they reached the F.A. Amateur Cup Final and they were not able to play their final fixture against Morecambe.

Division Two

Kirkby Town	30	22	7	1	84	26	51
Prescot Town	30	20	4	6	67	35	44
Ashton United	30	17	4	9	74	61	38
Netherfield Reserves	30	15	7	8	74	55	37
Radcliffe Borough	30	14	8	8	77	65	36
Morecambe Reserves	30	16	2	12	56	48	34
Oldham Athletic Reserves	30	12	8	10	68	40	32
Horwich RMI Reserves	30	13	5	12	52	52	31
Chorley Reserves	30	11	6	13	52	55	28
Blackpool Mechanics	30	11	4	15	42	61	26
Dukinfield Town	30	10	5	15	56	69	25
Lancaster City Reserves	30	6	10	14	48	73	22
Nelson	30	8	5	17	44	73	21
Lytham	30	8	3	19	36	58	19
Fleetwood Reserves	30	8	3	19	38	66	19
Padiham	30	6	5	19	52	83	17

1967-68

Division One

Morecambe	42	28	9	5	112	41	65
Guinness Exports	42	29	6	7	85	37	64
Skelmersdale United	42	23	10	9	94	49	56
Fleetwood	42	22	10	10	72	43	54
Marine	42	21	10	11	78	60	52
Great Harwood	42	20	11	11	71	50	51
South Liverpool	42	21	7	14	76	53	49
Netherfield	42	20	9	13	103	88	49
Horwich RMI	42	19	9	14	79	52	47
Lancaster City	42	18	11	13	72	67	47
Chorley	42	17	9	16	72	65	43
St. Helens Town	42	16	8	18	68	65	40
Kirkby Town	42	13	13	16	54	60	39
Burscough	42	13	10	19	53	64	36
Droylsden	42	13	10	19	52	84	36
Wigan Rovers	42	14	6	22	56	69	34
Clitheroe	42	14	6	22	58	86	34
Southport Reserves	42	12	9	21	59	66	33
Barrow Reserves	42	13	4	25	55	78	30
Prescot Town	42	12	1	29	53	109	25
Bacup Borough	42	8	6	28	34	105	22
Rossendale United	42	6	6	30	50	115	18

Division Two

Oldham Athletic Reserves	32	23	7	2	102	21	53
Darwen	32	21	6	5	72	35	48
Morecambe Reserves	32	17	7	8	77	50	41
Ashton United	32	17	5	10	67	52	39
Radcliffe Borough	32	17	4	11	62	52	38
Leyland Motors	32	15	5	12	55	66	35
Dukinfield Town	32	14	5	13	69	54	33
Chorley Reserves	32	13	7	12	68	55	33
Fleetwood Reserves	32	13	7	12	71	71	33
Blackpool Mechanics	32	11	8	13	62	58	30
Wigan Athletic Reserves	32	13	3	16	67	66	29
Nelson	32	12	5	15	63	67	29
Netherfield Reserves	32	8	6	18	63	92	22
Lancaster City Reserves	32	8	6	18	45	85	22
Lytham	32	7	7	18	42	82	21
Horwich RMI Reserves	32	5	9	18	50	82	19
Padiham	32	7	5	20	43	90	19

1968-69

Great Harwood	42	33	6	3	115	35	72
Kirkby Town	42	27	11	4	126	36	65
Lancaster City	42	28	3	11	120	58	59
Burscough	42	23	11	8	110	51	57
Prestwich Heys	42	24	7	11	109	58	55
St. Helens Town	42	22	10	10	84	44	54
Marine	42	22	9	11	95	48	53
Darwen	42	17	9	16	59	64	43
Blackpool Mechanics	42	16	10	16	76	68	42
Formby	42	17	7	18	82	72	41
Wigan Rovers	42	17	7	18	68	82	41
Radcliffe Borough	42	16	8	18	86	72	40
Rossendale United	42	16	8	18	68	83	40
Clitheroe	42	15	8	19	68	74	38
Wigan Athletic Reserves	42	13	9	20	73	80	35
Prescot Town	42	12	11	19	49	80	35
Barrow Reserves	42	11	10	21	51	82	32
Nelson	42	12	8	22	66	110	32
Dukinfield Town	42	9	11	22	63	98	29
Leyland Motors	42	9	11	22	44	90	29
Bacup Borough	42	9	3	30	33	109	21
Lytham	42	3	5	34	23	174	11

1969-70

Burscough	38	30	4	4	116	35	64
Prestwich Heys	38	28	5	5	127	46	61
Chorley	38	27	6	5	112	35	60
Kirkby Town	38	25	9	4	98	38	59
Radcliffe Borough	38	22	7	9	84	45	51
Lancaster City	38	22	6	10	84	43	50
Rossendale United	38	22	4	12	96	50	48
St. Helens Town	38	21	4	13	69	42	46
Blackpool Mechanics	38	20	4	14	78	56	44
Darwen	38	15	11	12	78	67	41
Bacup Borough	38	18	5	15	78	72	41
Formby	38	13	7	18	48	71	33
Wigan Athletic Reserves	38	10	9	19	44	61	29
Prescot Town	38	10	6	22	58	85	26
Dukinfield Town	38	6	11	21	49	96	23
Nelson	38	8	5	25	60	106	21
Clitheroe	38	6	7	25	40	107	19
Leyland Motors	38	5	8	25	37	96	18
Lytham	38	6	4	28	29	109	16
Wigan Rovers	38	1	8	29	22	147	10

1970-71

Prestwich Heys	30	23	3	4	85	35	49
Dukinfield Town	30	19	7	4	65	36	45
Radcliffe Borough	30	16	9	5	64	35	41
Wigan Athletic Reserves	30	18	3	9	68	35	39
Formby	30	15	7	8	47	35	37
Accrington Stanley (1968)	30	15	5	10	65	52	35
Blackpool Mechanics	30	14	6	10	49	38	34
Clitheroe	30	11	8	11	52	63	30
Prescot Town	30	11	6	13	37	40	28
Nelson	30	9	8	13	55	59	26
Darwen	30	10	6	14	44	57	26
St. Helens Town	30	8	9	13	36	42	25
Bacup Borough	30	9	4	17	48	66	22
Leyland Motors	30	8	5	17	39	69	21
Lytham	30	5	5	20	38	78	15
Wigan Rovers	30	2	3	25	26	78	7

1971-72

St. Helens Town	28	20	7	1	56	16	47
Accrington Stanley (1968)	28	18	5	5	81	40	41
Blackpool Mechanics	28	17	4	7	63	31	38
Clitheroe	28	16	5	7	52	45	37
Ashton Town	28	15	4	9	59	45	34
Dukinfield Town	28	12	9	7	57	41	33
Nelson	28	13	5	10	69	49	31
Prescot Town	28	9	9	10	39	35	27
Darwen	28	10	6	12	48	57	26
Atherton Collieries	28	9	7	12	45	51	25
Leyland Motors	28	8	5	15	54	66	21
Bacup Borough	28	9	1	18	55	74	19
Kirkby Town Reserves	28	6	6	16	32	59	18
Wigan Rovers	28	6	3	19	34	65	15
Corinthians	28	3	2	23	24	94	8

1972-73

Darwen	38	30	4	4	105	39	64
Bacup Borough	38	27	5	6	101	36	59
Accrington Stanley (1968)	38	26	7	5	96	36	59
St. Helens Town	38	22	9	7	55	29	53
Skelmersdale United Reserves	38	24	5	9	76	46	53
Wren Rovers	38	18	10	10	62	46	46
Blackpool Mechanics	38	15	14	9	62	45	44
Dukinfield Town	38	19	3	16	63	65	41
Ashton Town	38	16	5	17	60	60	37
Clitheroe	38	14	8	16	73	79	36
Leyland Motors	38	13	8	17	41	56	34
Nelson	38	12	7	19	60	76	31
Prescot Town	38	10	9	19	46	72	29
Kirkby Town	38	11	7	20	43	68	29
Maghull	38	9	9	20	49	64	27
Ford Motors	38	11	5	22	49	83	27
Atherton Collieries	38	10	7	21	46	84	27
Lomond	38	6	12	20	28	73	24
Great Harwood Reserves	38	7	7	24	55	77	21
Wigan Rovers	38	5	9	24	41	78	19

1973-74

Accrington Stanley (1968)	38	29	5	4	80	26	63
Darwen	38	24	10	4	89	38	58
Bacup Borough	38	24	10	4	76	35	58
Skelmersdale United Reserves	38	22	6	10	76	34	50
St. Helens Town	38	24	2	12	73	34	50
Wren Rovers	38	17	11	10	68	47	45
Maghull	38	18	8	12	59	42	44
Blackpool Mechanics	38	18	7	13	52	47	43
Dukinfield Town	38	14	12	12	59	56	40
Leyland Motors	38	14	11	13	60	55	39
Clitheroe	38	16	6	16	73	53	38
Atherton Collieries	38	14	10	14	68	63	38
Great Harwood Reserves	38	12	8	18	54	68	32
Kirkby Town	38	10	9	19	54	70	29
Ashton Town	38	10	9	19	46	64	29
Ellesmere Port Town	38	10	9	19	40	67	29
Lomond	38	6	9	23	25	72	21
Prescot Town	38	6	6	26	34	89	18
Ford Motors	38	5	8	25	30	81	18
Nelson	38	6	6	26	36	111	18

1974-75

Darwen	38	26	8	4	97	36	60
Blackpool Mechanics	38	25	9	4	70	21	59
Bootle	38	19	14	5	75	30	52
Bacup Borough	38	20	12	6	69	31	52
St. Helens Town	38	22	5	11	69	40	49
Nelson	38	19	8	11	77	50	46
Kirkby Town	38	17	10	11	65	49	44
Leyland Motors	38	19	5	14	76	51	43
Clitheroe	38	17	8	13	70	51	42
Accrington Stanley (1968)	38	17	7	14	75	55	41
Maghull	38	16	8	14	60	58	40
Wren Rovers	38	13	8	17	47	72	34
Great Harwood Reserves	38	14	5	19	58	75	33
Ford Motors	38	10	12	16	49	71	32
Skelmersdale United Reserves	38	10	7	21	52	77	27
Atherton Collieries	38	8	10	20	46	80	26
Dukinfield Town	38	10	5	23	49	86	25
Ellesmere Port Town	38	8	9	21	27	57	25
Prescot Town	38	7	6	25	53	107	20
Ashton Town	38	3	4	31	38	125	10

1975-76

Bootle	34	28	3	3	82	29	59
Accrington Stanley (1968)	34	25	5	4	104	36	55
Kirkby Town	34	18	9	7	69	38	45
Blackpool Mechanics	34	18	9	7	48	32	45
Nelson	34	18	5	11	59	35	41
Colne Dynamoes	34	13	10	11	59	55	36
Maghull	34	14	6	14	54	62	34
Lytham	34	11	9	14	53	54	31
Clitheroe	34	11	9	14	51	54	31
Bacup Borough	34	9	12	13	44	59	30
Ford Motors	34	10	10	14	37	50	30
Wren Rovers	34	10	10	14	37	51	30
Skelmersdale United Reserves	34	11	8	15	35	56	30
Morecambe Reserves	34	12	3	19	50	57	27
Leyland Motors	34	9	9	16	46	54	27
Wigan Athletic Reserves	34	11	3	20	37	57	25
Atherton Collieries	34	6	8	20	48	72	20
Ashton Town	34	6	4	24	33	95	16

1976-77

Bootle	34	30	2	2	100	21	62
Kirkby Town	34	28	3	3	89	18	59
Accrington Stanley (1968)	34	25	7	2	86	20	57
Wren Rovers	34	17	11	6	49	33	45
Lytham	34	17	7	10	58	42	41
Maghull	34	13	11	10	55	50	37
Colne Dynamoes	34	14	6	14	54	53	34
Nelson	34	15	3	16	48	46	33
Blackpool Mechanics	34	13	6	15	53	49	32
Skelmersdale United	34	11	8	15	43	49	30
Bacup Borough	34	9	8	17	46	65	26
Atherton Collieries	34	9	8	17	50	79	26
Wigan Athletic Reserves	34	9	7	18	43	53	25
Clitheroe	34	10	5	19	43	63	25
Ford Motors	34	7	9	18	34	68	23
Ashton Town	34	9	2	23	37	91	20
Morecambe Reserves	34	7	5	22	46	87	19
Leyland Motors	34	7	4	23	43	90	18

1977-78

Accrington Stanley (1968)	34	25	7	2	99	32	57
Wren Rovers	34	22	8	4	64	27	52
Bootle	34	19	9	6	74	32	47
Kirkby Town	34	19	6	9	72	38	44
Colne Dynamoes	34	18	5	11	80	42	41
Maghull	34	15	11	8	57	41	41
Leyland Motors	34	15	10	9	63	47	40
Skelmersdale United	34	14	10	10	53	41	38
Atherton Collieries	34	14	8	12	63	52	36
Lytham	34	13	8	13	54	66	34
Ford Motors	34	11	8	15	57	64	30
Padiham	34	12	6	16	51	60	30
Bacup Borough	34	12	5	17	43	63	29
Blackpool Mechanics	34	10	6	18	38	65	26
Morecambe Reserves	34	6	9	19	36	69	21
Clitheroe	34	7	6	21	41	87	20
Ashton Town	34	4	5	25	32	89	13
Nelson	34	4	5	25	33	94	13

1978-79

Wren Rovers	28	21	5	2	51	10	47
Leyland Motors	28	18	6	4	63	26	42
Whitworth Valley	28	15	8	5	49	35	38
Colne Dynamoes	28	13	8	7	50	32	34
Bacup Borough	28	14	6	8	48	36	34
Padiham	28	14	5	9	40	35	33
Lytham	28	11	8	9	41	34	30
Nelson	28	7	10	11	31	33	24
Blackpool Mechanics	28	7	10	11	21	33	24
Chorley Reserves	28	6	11	11	34	37	23
Wigan Rovers	28	6	9	13	25	40	21
Barrow Reserves	28	6	8	14	25	39	20
Daisy Hill	28	5	10	13	26	45	20
Clitheroe	28	7	5	16	31	46	19
Ashton Athletic	28	3	5	20	17	67	11

1979-80

Clitheroe	32	17	12	3	55	25	46
Colne Dynamoes	32	18	8	6	54	35	44
Barrow Reserves	32	16	9	7	56	30	41
Great Harwood Town	32	15	11	6	53	29	41
Vulcan Newton	32	14	12	6	60	34	40
Bacup Borough	32	16	8	8	63	41	40
Padiham	32	15	8	9	49	34	38
Chorley Reserves	32	11	13	8	42	38	35
Whitworth Valley	32	13	9	10	52	53	35
Leyland Motors	32	10	14	8	50	36	34
Lytham	32	10	9	13	42	63	29
Daisy Hill	32	11	6	15	35	40	28
Wren Rovers	32	9	8	15	38	48	26
Nelson	32	7	8	17	46	67	22
Blackpool Mechanics	32	5	9	18	27	56	19
Ashton Athletic	32	7	3	22	25	68	17
Wigan Rovers	32	2	5	25	29	79	9

1980-81

Wren Rovers	34	24	7	3	75	25	55
Colne Dynamoes	34	21	5	8	57	30	47
Great Harwood Town	34	18	7	9	68	42	43
Padiham	34	16	11	7	57	40	41
Chorley Reserves	34	15	11	8	53	42	41
Caernarfon Town	34	15	7	12	55	37	37
Vulcan Newton	34	15	6	13	53	44	36
Lytham	34	14	8	12	51	45	36
Clitheroe	34	14	7	13	42	36	35
Chadderton	34	14	7	13	58	64	35
Whitworth Valley	34	13	8	13	50	54	34
Wigan Rovers	34	13	8	13	50	60	34
Daisy Hill	34	12	9	13	52	48	33
Bacup Borough	34	9	11	14	47	57	29
Ashton Athletic	34	9	6	19	47	73	24
Blackpool Mechanics	34	6	11	17	32	57	23
Nelson	34	7	3	24	29	60	17
Manchester Polytechnic	34	2	6	26	24	86	10

Padiham had 2 points deducted

1981-82

Caernarfon Town	34	23	8	3	71	27	54
Colne Dynamoes	34	24	4	6	72	33	52
Nelson	34	19	7	8	66	44	45
Wren Rovers	34	18	7	9	67	47	43
Clitheroe	34	13	16	5	67	40	42
Great Harwood Town	34	16	8	10	61	47	40
Chadderton	34	17	5	12	62	43	39
Blackpool Mechanics	34	14	9	11	47	34	37
Vulcan Newton	34	13	8	13	61	56	34
Padiham	34	14	6	14	47	47	34
Lytham	34	11	11	12	74	66	33
Oldham Dew	34	12	6	16	48	61	30
Wigan Rovers	34	11	7	16	44	53	29
Bacup Borough	34	9	8	17	47	77	26
Whitworth Valley	34	5	12	17	42	68	22
Daisy Hill	34	5	9	20	31	64	19
Bolton ST	34	7	4	23	40	86	18
Ashton Athletic	34	4	7	23	22	76	15

FORMATION

Following the successful formation of the Football League in 1888, other areas were quick to copy the idea. Several leagues began operating in Lancashire in 1889-90 but none of them specifically catered for senior clubs in the Manchester district, or in Cheshire where the game had been popular for many years.

Therefore in the spring of 1890 moves began to start a league centred on that area and following a meeting in Manchester in May, 12 clubs were proposed as potential members. The 12 were Ardwick (reformed in 1894 as Manchester City), Burslem Port Vale, Bury, Chester, Gorton Villa, Halliwell, Heywood Central, Kidderminster, Leek, Northwich Victoria, South Shore (from Blackpool) and Witton (from Blackburn). However Burslem Port Vale and Kidderminster were elected to the Midland League instead and Bury and Heywood Central preferred to stay in the Lancashire League. Halliwell and South Shore also declined to join and so it was necessary to find suitable replacements. Another meeting was held in Manchester – at the Brunswick Hotel in Piccadilly, on Tuesday 3rd June – and a revised list was drawn up. This time the proposed membership was: Ardwick, Burton Swifts, Chester, Denton, Derby St. Luke's, Gorton Villa, Hyde, Leek, Macclesfield, Northwich Victoria, Stafford County and Witton. Buxton and Manchester also attended the meeting but were not elected while Witton were elected despite not attending. Ardwick later withdrew and Wrexham – who had also missed the meeting – were elected in their place.

Of the 12 who became founder members, Hyde and Leek already had experience of league football, Hyde having played in the Lancashire League in 1889-90 and Leek in the Midland League.

TABLE ERRORS

A number of the tables published at the time contained errors. Additional research has resulted in all but one of these being corrected as noted below.

1890-91   Goals for 4 higher than goals against.

THE COMBINATION

1890-91

Gorton Villa	16	10	2	4	47	26	22
Macclesfield	16	9	3	4	44	27	21
Chester	16	8	4	4	42	30	20
Burton Swifts	14	9	0	5	55	28	18
Denton	16	8	1	7	39	32	17
Northwich Victoria	16	5	7	4	28	30	17
Hyde	14	3	4	7	25	39	10
Wrexham	16	4	4	8	25	47	10
Leek	16	1	1	14	18	60	3

Two games were not played.
Wrexham had 2 points deducted for fielding an ineligible player.
Derby St. Luke's, Stafford County and Witton all resigned and their
records were deleted.

1891-92

Everton Reserves	22	17	2	3	99	20	36
Northwich Victoria	22	15	1	6	84	25	31
Macclesfield	22	15	0	7	52	38	30
Stoke Swifts	22	13	1	8	49	29	27
Buxton	22	11	3	8	35	30	25
Wrexham	22	9	2	11	45	65	20
Chirk	22	7	5	10	48	56	19
Chester	22	8	3	11	52	61	19
Gorton Villa	22	8	3	11	41	51	19
Leek	22	8	0	14	46	62	16
Stockport County	22	7	2	13	29	44	16
Denton	22	2	2	18	25	124	6

1892-93

Everton Reserves	22	18	2	2	107	13	38
Stoke Swifts	22	14	4	4	48	23	32
Chester	22	12	2	8	52	41	26
Chirk	22	10	3	9	63	43	23
Buxton	22	8	7	7	37	33	23
Stockport County	22	8	6	8	38	35	22
Dresden United	22	8	3	11	34	43	19
Wrexham	22	9	1	12	41	66	19
Macclesfield	22	6	6	10	45	55	18
Leek	22	6	3	13	31	60	15
Nantwich	22	6	3	13	36	81	15
Gorton Villa	22	6	2	14	29	68	14

1893-94

Everton Reserves	18	15	2	1	77	19	32
Stoke Swifts	18	10	1	7	57	31	21
Leek	18	9	2	7	32	27	20
Stockport County	18	7	6	5	33	32	20
Dresden United	18	7	5	6	34	28	19
Chester	18	6	6	6	24	26	18
Macclesfield	18	5	7	6	36	35	17
Wrexham	18	5	5	7	36	46	16
Buxton	18	5	4	9	28	41	14
Nantwich	18	1	1	16	12	84	3

Gorton Villa resigned and their record was deleted.

1894-95

Ashton North End	20	14	3	3	62	32	31
Glossop North End	20	14	2	4	49	19	30
Chester	20	12	2	6	53	35	26
Dresden United	20	9	7	4	52	35	25
Stalybridge Rovers	20	8	5	7	41	35	21
Macclesfield	20	8	3	9	44	38	19
Leek	20	7	4	9	36	47	18
Hurst Ramblers	20	7	1	12	35	61	15
Hanley Town	20	6	2	12	37	62	12
Buxton	20	4	3	13	22	48	11
Northwich Victoria	20	4	2	14	26	55	10

Hanley Town had 2 points deducted for fielding an ineligible player.

1895-96

Everton Reserves	14	11	2	1	54	12	24
Macclesfield	14	11	2	1	37	13	24
Glossop North End	14	9	3	2	33	13	21
Oldham County	14	5	1	8	24	39	11
Chester	14	4	2	8	27	29	10
Northwich Victoria	14	4	1	9	14	35	9
Leek	14	3	3	8	15	35	7
Buxton	14	1	2	11	15	43	4

Leek had 2 points deducted for fielding an ineligible player.

1896-97

Everton Reserves	18	14	3	1	61	14	31
Rock Ferry	18	12	3	3	57	18	27
Chester	18	11	3	4	41	25	25
Northwich Victoria	18	8	2	8	31	41	18
Buxton	18	7	3	8	39	34	17
Wrexham	18	7	2	9	41	40	16
Middleton	18	7	3	8	40	32	15
Macclesfield	18	5	2	11	34	60	12
Crewe Alexandra	18	5	1	12	35	53	9
Barnton Rovers	18	2	2	14	18	80	4

Middleton, Crewe Alexandra and Barnton Rovers all had 2 points
deducted for fielding ineligible players.

1897-98

Everton Reserves	24	15	5	4	65	25	35
Crewe Alexandra	24	12	6	6	53	34	30
Chirk	24	11	4	9	38	27	26
Wrexham	24	10	6	8	45	44	26
Stoke Swifts	24	10	5	9	42	35	25
Buxton	24	9	7	8	44	44	25
Rock Ferry	24	8	8	8	34	30	24
White Star Wanderers	24	8	7	9	41	42	23
Garston Copper Works	24	8	7	9	37	60	23
Druids	24	9	3	12	43	46	21
Chester	24	7	5	12	39	50	19
Tranmere Rovers	24	9	3	12	35	45	19
Northwich Victoria	24	6	2	16	40	74	14

Tranmere Rovers had 2 points deducted for fielding an ineligible player.
Dresden United resigned in January 1898 due to financial difficulties
and their record was deleted.

1898-99

Everton Reserves	28	23	4	1	112	18	50
Liverpool Reserves	28	21	3	4	87	22	45
Tranmere Rovers	28	15	4	9	54	33	34
Druids	28	16	1	11	64	31	33
Wrexham	28	15	3	10	55	48	33
Chester	28	13	5	10	60	57	31
Bangor	28	12	6	10	63	78	30
Chirk	28	12	3	13	44	48	27
Llandudno Swifts	28	12	3	13	48	58	27
White Star Wanderers	28	11	6	11	68	54	26
South Liverpool	28	9	4	15	36	52	22
Oswestry United	28	9	2	17	49	73	20
Buxton	28	7	2	19	43	102	16
Garston Copper Works	28	5	2	21	31	77	12
Rhyl	28	6	0	22	35	98	12

White Star Wanderers had 2 points deducted for fielding an ineligible
player.

1899-1900

Chirk	16	10	4	2	36	12	24
Wrexham	16	11	1	4	58	25	23
Druids	16	9	3	4	38	22	21
Bangor	16	8	1	7	37	36	17
Birkenhead	16	4	5	7	27	37	13
Newtown	16	6	1	9	34	56	13
Aberystwyth	16	4	4	8	23	36	12
Oswestry United	16	5	2	9	30	38	10
Rhyl	16	2	5	9	26	47	9

Oswestry United had 2 points deducted for fielding an ineligible player.

1900-1901

Wrexham	22	16	3	3	62	20	35
Rhyl United	22	15	2	5	49	33	32
Bangor	22	13	3	6	62	45	29
Oswestry United	22	10	8	4	57	28	28
Chirk	22	10	5	7	46	40	25
White Star Wanderers	22	8	6	8	45	40	22
Hudson's (Liverpool)	22	7	3	12	39	42	17
Tranmere Rovers	22	6	5	11	32	37	17
Birkenhead	22	6	4	12	37	52	16
Warrington	22	7	2	13	27	57	16
Buckley Victoria	22	6	4	12	32	68	16
Newton-le-Willows	22	3	5	14	38	64	11

1901-1902

Wrexham	26	17	7	2	80	21	41
Burslem Port Vale Reserves	26	14	7	5	61	43	33
Oswestry United	26	12	6	8	55	33	30
Nantwich	26	13	4	9	68	47	30
Wellington Town	26	11	5	10	39	36	27
Bangor	26	11	5	10	51	74	27
Birkenhead	26	9	8	9	42	40	26
Witton Albion	26	11	3	12	47	52	25
Newton-le-Willows	26	9	6	11	40	71	24
Tranmere Rovers	26	8	7	11	46	49	23
Rhyl United	26	6	8	12	45	53	20
White Star Wanderers	26	9	2	15	50	63	20
Chirk	26	8	1	17	48	69	17
Chester	26	6	7	13	46	67	17

Burslem Port Vale Reserves and Chester both had 2 points deducted for fielding an ineligible player.

1902-03

Wrexham	26	19	5	2	80	23	43
Nantwich	26	15	4	7	69	43	34
Birkenhead	26	15	4	7	53	36	34
Burslem Port Vale Reserves	26	12	7	7	63	35	31
Oswestry United	26	14	2	10	57	42	30
Witton Albion	26	11	8	7	52	49	30
Chester	26	9	8	9	48	49	26
Middlewich	26	9	8	9	43	62	26
Bangor	26	9	8	9	53	72	24
Winsford United	26	8	5	13	51	54	19
Newton-le-Willows	26	8	3	15	52	74	19
Rhyl	26	8	4	14	52	64	18
Tranmere Rovers	26	4	5	17	30	64	13
Chirk	26	4	3	19	34	70	11

Bangor, Winsford United and Rhyl all had 2 points deducted for fielding ineligible players.
White Star Wanderers resigned in March, 1903 and their record was deleted.

1903-04

Birkenhead	24	17	3	4	49	22	37
Chester	24	15	3	6	65	29	33
Nantwich	24	14	3	7	60	30	31
Tranmere Rovers	24	14	1	9	54	42	29
Wrexham	24	12	4	8	54	34	28
Bangor	24	12	2	10	60	55	26
Oswestry United	24	11	2	11	42	55	24
Rhyl	24	10	1	13	52	52	21
Broughton United	24	8	3	13	38	55	19
Middlewich Athletic Rangers	24	7	5	12	40	63	19
Winsford United	24	6	6	12	40	46	18
Witton Albion	24	4	8	12	30	61	16
Chirk	24	3	5	16	36	76	11

1904-05

Wrexham	26	21	1	4	70	16	43
Chester	26	17	3	6	69	35	37
Broughton United	26	14	5	7	43	44	33
Nantwich	26	11	7	8	66	39	29
Port Sunlight	26	11	5	10	56	50	27
Tranmere Rovers	26	10	7	9	41	37	27
Rhyl	26	11	5	10	40	44	27
Whitchurch	26	11	4	11	60	58	26
Middlewich Athletic Rangers	26	10	2	14	44	55	22
Oswestry United	26	10	2	14	43	62	22
Birkenhead	26	7	6	13	35	47	20
Bangor	26	8	3	15	55	61	19
Druids	26	7	5	14	29	54	19
Chirk	26	4	5	17	32	81	13

1905-06

Whitchurch	28	18	5	5	87	32	41
Chester	28	16	4	8	72	29	36
Glossop Reserves	28	15	4	9	53	37	34
Druids	28	14	5	9	52	46	33
Tranmere Rovers	28	13	8	7	40	36	32
Crewe Alexandra Reserves	28	14	3	11	53	42	31
Nantwich	28	14	2	12	47	53	30
Port Sunlight	28	11	6	11	43	42	28
Oswestry United	28	13	1	14	72	56	27
Bangor	28	9	6	13	38	63	24
Rhyl	28	10	3	15	61	70	23
Chirk	28	8	7	13	48	71	23
Broughton United	28	11	2	15	46	61	22
Birkenhead	28	9	3	16	38	54	21
Wigan Town	28	4	3	21	32	90	7

Middlewich resigned in January 1906 and Wigan Town took over their fixtures.
Tranmere Rovers and Broughton United both had 2 points deducted for fielding ineligible players.
Wigan Town had 4 points deducted for fielding ineligible players.

1906-07

Whitchurch	26	20	5	1	84	30	45
Chester	26	19	3	4	75	27	41
Wigan Town	26	12	6	8	44	45	30
Nantwich	26	12	3	11	49	46	27
Wrexham Reserves	26	11	4	11	50	45	26
Birkenhead	26	12	4	10	64	63	26
Crewe Alexandra Reserves	26	10	5	11	66	61	25
Tranmere Rovers	26	10	5	11	35	39	25
Oswestry United	26	9	6	11	49	41	24
Bangor	26	8	5	13	36	51	21
Chirk	26	8	4	14	39	61	20
Rhyl	26	8	2	16	38	64	18
Druids	26	6	6	14	29	70	18
Wrexham Victoria	26	8	0	18	29	44	16

Birkenhead had 2 points deducted for fielding an ineligible player.

1907-08

Tranmere Rovers	26	20	4	2	83	21	44
Chester	26	21	2	3	87	29	44
Oswestry United	26	16	4	6	62	38	36
Crewe Alexandra Reserves	26	14	3	9	69	50	31
Whitchurch	26	13	4	9	66	42	30
Nantwich	26	12	5	9	65	57	29
Connah's Quay	26	13	3	10	55	57	29
Druids	26	9	5	12	53	58	23
Bangor	26	8	3	15	38	68	19
Chirk	26	9	0	17	41	63	18
Rhyl	26	7	2	17	49	80	16
Wrexham Reserves	26	6	4	16	42	74	16
Birkenhead	26	5	5	16	33	61	15
Welshpool	26	5	4	17	34	79	14

1908-09

Chester	30	21	7	2	91	34	49
Saltney	30	16	9	5	93	42	41
Tranmere Rovers	30	15	5	10	86	48	35
Welshpool	30	13	8	9	63	53	34
Crewe Alexandra Reserves	30	13	7	10	95	56	33
Connah's Quay	30	13	7	10	60	63	33
Bangor	30	13	6	11	71	81	32
Nantwich	30	12	7	11	59	61	31
Oswestry United	30	13	4	13	74	55	30
Whitchurch	30	11	8	11	53	64	30
Wrexham Reserves	30	10	6	14	48	59	26
Chirk	30	9	8	13	48	62	26
Middlewich	30	8	8	14	67	84	24
Druids	30	10	4	16	51	74	24
Birkenhead	30	7	2	21	48	95	16
Rhyl	30	6	4	20	37	113	16

1909-10

Crewe Alexandra Reserves	30	24	3	3	105	33	51
Saltney	30	22	4	4	81	32	48
Chester	30	20	2	8	85	47	42
Tranmere Rovers	30	18	2	10	92	50	38
Bangor	30	16	3	11	79	66	35
Whitchurch	30	16	3	11	61	53	35
Wrexham Reserves	30	15	5	10	64	58	35
Nantwich	30	14	4	12	57	56	32
Connah's Quay	30	14	1	15	65	67	29
Middlewich	30	12	3	15	58	61	27
Oswestry United	30	9	7	14	44	62	25
Rhyl	30	7	6	17	54	83	20
Chirk	30	8	3	19	57	91	19
Druids	30	7	3	20	44	83	17
Denbigh Town	30	6	4	20	52	93	16
Brymbo Victoria	30	5	1	24	42	105	11

Birkenhead resigned in December 1909 and their fixtures were taken over by Brymbo Victoria.

1910-11

Whitchurch	20	12	3	5	56	25	27
Bangor	20	12	3	5	72	38	27
Oswestry United	20	11	3	6	44	27	25
Brymbo Victoria	20	11	2	7	55	34	24
Wrexham Reserves	20	11	2	7	53	40	24
Chester Reserves	20	9	3	8	57	44	21
Saltney	20	8	2	10	50	43	18
Connah's Quay	20	7	3	10	35	35	17
Rhyl United	20	8	1	11	33	65	17
Flint	20	6	2	12	32	76	14
Denbigh Town	20	2	2	16	24	84	6

FORMATION

For almost 50 years the best non-League clubs in the north-west played in either the Cheshire League or the Lancashire Combination. There were few transfers between the two leagues, only 10 clubs moving from Lancashire to Cheshire between 1920 and 1968 with 5 going in the opposite direction. Generally speaking, the two competitions were of roughly equal status although the Cheshire League probably became slightly the stronger after the Second World War. However the formation of the Northern Premier League (NPL) in 1968 not only added an extra layer above the two older leagues, it also fundamentally changed the relationship between them. Instead of being roughly equal, the Cheshire League very quickly became the more senior as the Lancashire Combination rapidly declined in strength, as the movements of its clubs shows very clearly.

In 1968 the Lancashire Combination lost 5 of its 22 clubs to the new NPL, theoretically still leaving 17 strong clubs to continue in the competition. Yet by the start of the 1970-71 season, 12 of those 17 had left, 3 more to the NPL and 7 to the Cheshire League. After 1970, no Lancashire Combination club was good enough to be promoted to the NPL but the Cheshire League had another 8 clubs good enough to be promoted. To a large extent the Cheshire League made up its losses in this period by recruiting from the Lancashire Combination, taking 5 clubs between 1970 and 1977 and 8 more to help to form its new Second Division in 1978. The very fact that 8 Lancashire Combination clubs preferred Division Two of the Cheshire League shows that they recognised that in effect their own competition had now become a feeder to its neighbour.

It therefore made perfect sense when in 1982, the management committees of the Cheshire League and the Lancashire Combination decided to recognise the position formally and merge the two competitions. A three division structure was put in place and 57 of the 58 clubs in the two leagues applied to join the new North-West Counties League, the exception being Middlewich Athletic of Division Two of the Cheshire League who applied initially but then withdrew their application and rejoined the Mid-Cheshire League instead. A points system was devised to decide which division of the new league the 57 clubs should play in and the results of this were recorded on 3rd June, 1982.

The scoring system was as follows. The previous two seasons, that is 1980-81 and 1981-82, were considered and for each of those two seasons the top team in Division One of the Cheshire League was awarded 40 points, the second team 39, and so on down the league table. The top teams of the Lancashire Combination and Cheshire League Division Two were each awarded 20 points, the second team 19 and so on down the league tables. Champions and runners-up in the Lancashire Combination and Cheshire League Division Two were awarded 5 bonus points each.

Having calculated the points the three Divisions were split as follows:

Division One – Included all clubs with ground grades of A to C with 35 points or more. The number of clubs was made up to 20 by adding the necessary number of D graded clubs with the most points.

Division Two – Included all remaining A to D clubs, all E clubs and the number of clubs was made up to 20 by adding the necessary number of F graded clubs with the most points.

Division Three – Included all remaining F graded clubs and all G graded clubs. The number was made even by electing new applicants.

The exceptions were that any club whose pitch size failed to meet the standards laid down was not considered for Division One and any club not playing on their own ground (i.e. ground-sharing) was also not considered for Division One. The results of all these deliberations are shown below.

However Hyde United and Chorley did not take up their places in the North-West Counties League as they were later elected to the NPL. Their places were taken by Lancaster City who dropped down from the NPL due to financial difficulties and Penrith who were elected from the Northern League. Division Three was made up to 18 clubs by the election of Newton from the Mid-Cheshire League where they had been known as HB & H Newton.

Meanwhile across the Pennines, the Midland League and Yorkshire League were also merging to form the Northern Counties (East) League and thus the second layer of the non-League pyramid covering most of the northern half of the country was then in place.

Grading System for North-West Counties League

Club	Ground Grade	Points Awarded 1980-81	Points Awarded 1981-82	Points Awarded Bonus	Total	Previous League	NWLC Division	See Notes
Hyde United	A	39	40		79	CL – 1	1	N
Chorley	A	35	39		74	CL – 1	1	N
Stalybridge Celtic	A	36	31		67	CL – 1	1	
Horwich RMI	A	32	25		57	CL – 1	1	
Winsford United	B	38	37		75	CL – 1	1	
Prescot Cables	B	33	32		65	CL – 1	1	
Burscough	B	25	38		63	CL – 1	1	
Leek Town	B	31	26		57	CL – 1	1	
Accrington Stanley	B	20	28	5	53	CL – 1	1	
Rhyl	B	14	19	5	38	CL – 2	1	
Kirkby Town	B	22	14		36	CL – 2	2	G
Curzon Ashton	C	29	33		62	CL – 1	1	
Ashton United	C	30	22		52	CL – 1	1	
St. Helens Town	C	28	23		51	CL – 1	1	
Droylsden	C	23	21		44	CL – 1	2	P
Congleton Town	C	11	20	5	36	CL – 2	1	
Leyland Motors	C	18	17		35	CL – 2	1	
Nantwich Town	D	40	27		67	CL – 1	1	
Formby	D	37	29		66	CL – 1	1	
Glossop	D	19	35	5	59	CL – 1	1	
Bootle	D	34	24		58	CL – 1	1	
Darwen	D	24	34		58	CL – 1	1	
Fleetwood Town	D	27	30		57	CL – 1	2	
Ellesmere Port & Neston	A	0	7		7	CL – 2	2	
Great Harwood Town	B	18	15		33	Lancs.	2	P

Club	Ground Grade	Points Awarded 1980-81	1981-82	Bonus	Total	Previous League	NWLC Division	See Notes
Ford Motors	C	12	9		21	CL – 2	2	
Salford	C	6	5		11	CL – 2	2	
Skelmersdale United	C	4	6		10	CL – 2	2	
Padiham	D	17	11		28	Lancs.	2	
Atherton Laburnum Rovers	D	16	10		26	CL – 2	2	
Chadderton	D	11	14		25	Lancs.	2	
Radcliffe Borough	D	10	15		25	CL – 2	2	
Eastwood Hanley	D	5	12		17	CL – 2	2	
Rossendale United	E	26	36		62	CL – 1	2	
Caernarfon Town	E	15	20	5	40	Lancs.	2	
Irlam Town	E	9	18		27	CL – 2	2	
Lytham	E	13	10		23	Lancs.	2	
New Mills	E	21	2		23	CL – 2	2	
Prescot BI	E	15	8		23	CL – 2	2	
Wren Rovers	F	20	17	5	42	Lancs.	2	
Maghull	F	13	16		29	CL – 2	3	
Clitheroe	F	12	16		28	Lancs.	3	
Vulcan Newton	F	14	12		26	Lancs.	3	
Nelson	F	4	18		22	Lancs.	3	
Warrington Town	F	8	13		21	CL – 2	3	
Bacup Borough	F	7	7		14	Lancs.	3	
Oldham Dew	F	0	9		9	Lancs.	3	
Atherton Collieries	F	3	4		7	CL – 2	3	
Ashton Town	F	2	3		5	CL – 2	3	
Colne Dynamoes	G	19	19	10	48	Lancs.	3	
Blackpool Mechanics	G	5	13		18	Lancs.	3	
Wigan Rovers	G	9	8		17	Lancs.	3	
Whitworth Valley	G	10	6		16	Lancs.	3	
Daisy Hill	G	8	5		13	Lancs.	3	
Ashton Athletic	G	6	3		9	Lancs.	3	
Prestwich Heys	G	7	1		8	CL – 2	3	
Bolton ST	G	0	4		4	Lancs.	3	

Notes

N – Subsequently elected to the Northern Premier League.

G – Ground-sharing at Prescot Cables.

P – Under-sized pitch.

NORTH-WEST COUNTIES LEAGUE

1982-83

Division One

Prescot Cables	42	30	6	6	110	38	96
Clitheroe	42	28	8	6	97	38	92
Mossley	42	27	7	8	100	41	88
Newcastle Town	42	23	12	7	83	52	81
Skelmersdale United	42	22	8	12	91	51	74
Nantwich Town	42	19	11	12	90	74	68
St. Helens Town	42	17	14	11	77	60	65
Congleton Town	42	19	8	15	72	62	65
Salford City	42	17	12	13	84	63	63
Fleetwood Town	42	17	9	16	73	70	60
Alsager Town	42	15	11	16	61	67	56
Squires Gate	42	13	12	17	58	71	51
Abbey Hey	42	12	13	17	56	73	49
Atherton Laburnum Rovers	42	11	12	19	65	86	45
Ramsbottom United	42	11	11	20	73	83	44
Warrington Town	42	11	11	20	48	66	44
Woodley Sports	42	11	9	22	62	85	42
Curzon Ashton	42	11	9	22	60	87	42
Atherton Collieries	42	11	7	24	52	85	40
Glossop North End	42	10	9	23	55	104	39
Flixton	42	10	8	24	44	112	38
Winsford United	42	10	7	25	48	91	37

Division Two

Bacup Borough	34	25	2	7	91	32	77
Stone Dominoes	34	24	3	7	94	34	75
Maine Road	34	23	2	9	74	55	71
Padiham	34	20	5	9	69	42	65
Holker Old Boys	34	18	7	9	65	42	61
Great Harwood Town	34	15	7	12	64	61	52
Nelson	34	13	12	9	50	40	51
Darwen	34	14	7	13	59	64	49
Norton United	34	14	6	14	50	52	48
Colne	34	14	5	15	65	53	47
Ashton Town	34	12	9	13	49	53	45
Castleton Gabriels	34	10	8	16	43	60	38
Cheadle Town	34	10	8	16	39	56	38
Blackpool Mechanics	34	9	10	15	39	52	37
Leek County School Old Boys	34	8	9	17	46	57	33
Daisy Hill	34	7	5	22	42	93	26
Oldham Town	34	4	12	18	40	86	24
Chadderton	34	5	5	24	33	80	20

Division Two

Fleetwood Town	34	24	8	2	73	24	56
Eastwood Hanley	34	21	6	7	69	35	48
Irlam Town	34	19	8	7	67	41	46
Warrington Town	34	18	7	9	65	45	43
Droylsden	34	19	5	10	59	42	43
Colne Dynamoes	34	16	9	9	55	37	41
Ellesmere Port & Neston	34	12	10	12	49	38	34
Chadderton	34	14	6	14	56	46	34
Atherton Laburnum Rovers	34	11	11	12	37	41	33
Wren Rovers	34	11	10	13	45	47	32
Skelmersdale United	34	13	6	15	60	63	32
Ford Motors	34	9	9	16	38	53	27
Prescot BI	34	9	9	16	50	66	27
Lytham	34	13	3	18	56	81	27
Rossendale United	34	10	6	18	53	84	26
Great Harwood Town	34	5	12	17	36	60	22
Salford	34	5	11	18	24	60	21
Nantwich Town	34	8	2	24	44	73	18

Lytham had 2 points deducted.

Division Three

Clitheroe	34	22	7	5	79	29	51
Padiham	34	19	8	7	58	34	46
Ashton Town	34	19	7	8	54	42	45
Oldham Dew	34	17	9	8	63	37	43
Daisy Hill	34	19	3	12	54	40	41
Maghull	34	16	8	10	60	50	40
Blackpool Mechanics	34	17	5	12	70	49	39
Atherton Collieries	34	14	9	11	54	50	37
Vulcan Newton	34	15	8	11	64	54	36
Prestwich Heys	34	15	5	14	61	59	33
Whitworth Valley	34	11	8	15	45	53	30
Bolton ST	34	10	10	14	49	64	30
Bacup Borough	34	11	9	14	65	60	27
Nelson	34	8	10	16	49	55	26
Cheadle Town	34	9	8	17	39	67	26
Urmston Town	34	7	9	18	35	67	23
Newton	34	8	4	22	33	63	20
Ashton Athletic	34	4	3	27	30	89	11

Vulcan Newton and Prestwich Heys had 2 points deducted.
Bacup Borough had 4 points deducted.

1983-84

Division One

Stalybridge Celtic	38	26	8	4	81	30	60
Penrith	38	23	9	6	88	39	55
Radcliffe Borough	38	26	3	9	79	41	55
Burscough	38	22	8	8	87	47	52
Curzon Ashton	38	21	5	12	74	51	47
Lancaster City	38	21	3	14	76	56	43
Accrington Stanley	38	17	8	13	67	60	42
St. Helens Town	38	17	7	14	69	55	41
Congleton Town	38	18	5	15	64	50	41
Prescot Cables	38	17	6	15	72	45	40
Leek Town	38	14	10	14	56	64	38
Winsford United	38	12	12	14	49	54	36
Formby	38	14	7	17	48	61	35
Caernarfon Town	38	11	12	15	46	55	34
Glossop	38	11	11	16	38	61	33
Bootle	38	11	7	20	46	69	27
Leyland Motors	38	9	9	20	44	79	27
Netherfield	38	5	11	22	27	73	21
Ashton United	38	7	9	22	47	86	19
Darwen	38	2	2	34	29	111	6

Lancaster City and Bootle had 2 points deducted.
Ashton United had 4 points deducted.

1984-85

Division One

Radcliffe Borough	38	24	10	4	67	33	58
Caernarfon Town	38	23	9	6	73	40	55
Burscough	38	23	7	8	81	46	53
Stalybridge Celtic	38	21	10	7	89	40	52
Eastwood Hanley	38	20	12	6	72	42	52
Curzon Ashton	38	21	6	11	85	60	48
Winsford United	38	20	7	11	58	37	47
Fleetwood Town	38	18	8	12	84	57	44
Leek Town	38	16	11	11	52	38	43
Congleton Town	38	13	11	14	43	46	37
Leyland Motors	38	13	8	17	52	67	34
St. Helens Town	38	12	9	17	64	75	33
Prescot Cables	38	13	7	18	64	68	31
Bootle	38	10	11	17	34	48	31
Accrington Stanley	38	11	8	19	45	59	30
Glossop	38	8	11	19	46	70	27
Formby	38	9	9	20	41	79	25
Netherfield	38	7	9	22	42	80	23
Lancaster City	38	8	5	25	46	90	21
Penrith	38	4	4	30	36	99	12

Prescot Cables and Formby had 2 points deducted.

Division Two

Clitheroe	34	19	13	2	70	33	51
Irlam Town	34	21	9	4	60	24	51
Warrington Town	34	17	14	3	59	29	48
Ashton United	34	17	7	10	56	55	41
Droylsden	34	15	10	9	51	47	40
Wren Rovers	34	15	9	10	53	41	39
Great Harwood Town	34	17	4	13	49	44	38
Chadderton	34	13	9	12	47	46	35
Colne Dynamoes	34	9	14	11	45	40	32
Atherton Laburnum Rovers	34	13	6	15	42	43	32
Nantwich Town	34	13	5	16	50	47	31
Ford Motors	34	11	8	15	44	45	30
Skelmersdale United	34	11	8	15	39	56	30
Rossendale United	34	10	9	15	51	53	29
Salford	34	11	5	18	46	64	27
Darwen	34	7	6	21	32	62	20
Padiham	34	8	5	21	42	74	19
Ellesmere Port & Neston	34	5	7	22	34	67	15

Padiham and Ellesmere Port & Neston both had 2 points deducted.

Division Two

Kirkby Town	34	24	7	3	85	30	55
Rossendale United	34	20	8	6	81	36	48
Wren Rovers	34	18	8	8	60	46	44
Warrington Town	34	17	9	8	62	48	43
Colwyn Bay	34	17	8	9	74	53	42
Chadderton	34	15	12	7	66	48	42
Colne Dynamoes	34	15	9	10	59	43	39
Great Harwood Town	34	13	10	11	38	45	36
Skelmersdale United	34	14	5	15	58	53	33
Droylsden	34	13	7	14	48	56	33
Atherton Laburnum Rovers	34	12	6	16	49	61	30
Lancaster City	34	10	9	15	57	66	29
Ellesmere Port & Neston	34	9	9	16	45	61	27
Ashton United	34	11	5	18	46	64	25
Darwen	34	8	8	18	48	57	24
Salford	34	9	4	21	38	72	22
Ford Motors	34	5	10	19	36	64	20
Nantwich Town	34	5	8	21	31	78	18

Ashton United had 2 points deducted.

Division Three

Kirkby Town	34	26	5	3	83	30	57
Colwyn Bay	34	22	10	2	75	32	54
Newton	34	16	10	8	56	33	42
Urmston Town	34	14	10	10	42	39	38
Blackpool Mechanics	34	15	7	12	61	48	37
Lytham	34	14	7	13	54	45	35
Atherton Collieries	34	13	8	13	44	44	34
Ashton Town	34	13	7	14	62	56	33
Oldham Dew	34	11	10	13	51	44	32
Bolton ST	34	12	8	14	55	73	32
Maghull	34	12	7	15	56	51	31
Cheadle Town	34	12	7	15	46	62	31
Bacup Borough	34	11	8	15	54	59	30
Ashton Athletic	34	12	6	16	45	61	30
Daisy Hill	34	10	9	15	51	61	27
Whitworth Valley	34	10	7	17	51	71	27
Nelson	34	9	4	21	43	80	22
Prestwich Heys	34	7	4	23	35	75	16

Daisy Hill and Prestwich Heys both had 2 points deducted.

Division Three

Blackpool Mechanics	28	22	2	4	77	33	44
Oldham Town	28	14	9	5	56	29	37
Maghull	28	15	6	7	62	36	36
Daisy Hill	28	13	7	8	62	45	33
Atherton Collieries	28	13	7	8	48	37	33
Bolton ST	28	12	7	9	42	34	29
Cheadle Town	28	9	10	9	42	26	28
Bacup Borough	28	10	8	10	36	40	28
Padiham	28	8	10	10	44	45	26
Prestwich Heys	28	10	6	12	53	66	26
Newton	28	7	10	11	43	48	24
Whitworth Valley	28	7	8	13	42	48	22
Huyton Town	28	7	7	14	41	71	21
Nelson	28	7	7	14	36	65	19
Ashton Athletic	28	1	6	21	24	85	8

Blackpool Mechanics, Bolton ST and Nelson all had 2 points deducted.

1985-86

Division One

Clitheroe	38	20	14	4	61	30	54
Congleton Town	38	22	10	6	51	29	54
Eastwood Hanley	38	22	9	7	68	45	53
Stalybridge Celtic	38	21	10	7	62	39	52
Fleetwood Town	38	21	10	7	70	34	50
Irlam Town	38	16	14	8	66	45	46
Leek Town	38	20	6	12	64	44	46
Curzon Ashton	38	18	9	11	52	50	45
Burscough	38	15	10	13	45	35	40
St. Helens Town	38	15	8	15	65	55	38
Accrington Stanley	38	13	11	14	62	60	37
Leyland Motors	38	13	8	17	62	67	34
Winsford United	38	14	6	18	55	68	34
Radcliffe Borough	38	12	9	17	48	49	33
Bootle	38	11	7	20	46	54	29
Penrith	38	9	8	21	46	63	26
Netherfield	38	8	10	20	38	76	26
Glossop	38	7	10	21	37	69	24
Prescot Cables	38	5	9	24	33	68	19
Formby	38	5	8	25	35	86	18

Fleetwood Town had 2 points deducted.

1986-87

Division One

Stalybridge Celtic	38	25	8	5	74	39	58
Accrington Stanley	38	19	15	4	63	32	53
Clitheroe	38	20	12	6	76	47	52
Kirkby Town	38	22	4	12	71	48	48
Bootle	38	19	10	9	52	38	48
St. Helens Town	38	19	9	10	65	37	47
Winsford United	38	19	8	11	55	39	46
Fleetwood Town	38	16	13	9	61	49	45
Penrith	38	16	10	12	62	59	42
Rossendale United	38	14	11	13	66	59	39
Congleton Town	38	13	11	14	38	39	37
Burscough	38	11	11	16	58	54	33
Leyland Motors	38	13	7	18	52	56	33
Eastwood Hanley	38	10	11	17	40	50	31
Radcliffe Borough	38	11	8	19	46	57	30
Leek Town	38	9	12	17	42	55	30
Netherfield	38	12	5	21	45	73	29
Irlam Town	38	4	13	21	36	74	21
Curzon Ashton	38	4	12	22	35	78	20
Glossop	38	5	8	25	33	87	18

Division Two

Droylsden	34	20	8	6	79	42	48
Warrington Town	34	16	13	5	48	34	45
Ashton United	34	19	6	9	73	45	44
Wren Rovers	34	18	8	8	65	39	44
Colwyn Bay	34	17	9	8	61	43	43
Darwen	34	15	8	11	45	47	38
Chadderton	34	14	9	11	52	47	37
Colne Dynamoes	34	14	8	12	57	44	36
Skelmersdale United	34	13	10	11	52	53	36
Ellesmere Port & Neston	34	15	5	14	68	54	35
Formby	34	13	7	14	54	55	33
Blackpool Mechanics	34	12	8	14	56	64	32
Lancaster City	34	12	7	15	55	53	31
Prescot Cables	34	12	6	16	46	48	28
Great Harwood Town	34	9	8	17	36	59	24
Oldham Town	34	7	9	18	38	57	23
Atherton Laburnum Rovers	34	8	5	21	32	61	21
Salford	34	1	8	25	17	89	10

Prescot Cables and Great Harwood Town both had 2 points deducted.

Division Three

Atherton Collieries	24	16	4	4	46	22	36
Flixton	24	15	5	4	58	29	35
Maghull	24	14	2	8	44	29	30
Nelson	24	12	6	6	37	29	30
Newton	24	11	5	8	42	36	27
Ford Motors	24	9	8	7	38	27	26
Bacup Borough	24	10	6	8	27	27	26
Cheadle Town	24	9	5	10	33	44	23
Daisy Hill	24	6	7	11	21	42	17
Padiham	24	4	8	12	35	39	16
Nantwich Town	24	5	6	13	26	42	16
Ashton Town	24	4	9	11	29	39	15
Whitworth Valley	24	3	5	16	17	48	11

Daisy Hill and Ashton Town both had 2 points deducted.

1987-88

Division One

Colne Dynamoes	34	24	7	3	71	14	55
Rossendale United	34	24	7	3	68	23	55
Clitheroe	34	18	10	6	51	20	46
Colwyn Bay	34	20	7	7	60	42	45
St. Helens Town	34	18	6	10	61	36	42
Ellesmere Port & Neston	34	17	5	12	55	48	39
Darwen	34	14	10	10	55	45	38
Warrington Town	34	16	5	13	68	47	37
Kirkby Town	34	11	13	10	57	54	35
Burscough	34	14	7	13	45	51	35
Leyland Motors	34	10	11	13	53	53	31
Prescot Cables	34	10	11	13	34	45	29
Bootle	34	12	5	17	43	61	29
Formby	34	6	10	18	32	63	22
Salford	34	8	6	20	33	66	22
Skelmersdale United	34	4	11	19	34	64	19
Atherton Laburnum Rovers	34	4	7	23	31	78	15
Glossop	34	5	4	25	30	71	14

Colwyn Bay and Prescot Cables both had 2 points deducted.

Division Two

Ashton United	42	32	6	4	107	30	70
Flixton	42	27	10	5	94	38	64
Wren Rovers	42	26	9	7	92	51	61
Newcastle Town	42	26	7	9	81	39	59
Maine Road	42	23	4	15	74	48	50
Maghull	42	18	11	13	73	66	47
Vauxhall GM	42	15	16	11	58	50	46
Atherton Collieries	42	20	6	16	63	63	46
Whitworth Valley	42	15	12	15	50	60	42
Ashton Town	42	17	8	17	64	70	40
Oldham Town	42	13	11	18	44	51	37
Cheadle Town	42	13	11	18	47	62	35
Chadderton	42	13	9	20	55	71	35
Great Harwood Town	42	14	8	20	52	66	34
Blackpool Mechanics	42	12	10	20	57	77	34
Nelson	42	12	10	20	49	76	34
Ford Motors	42	12	9	21	59	70	33
Daisy Hill	42	12	8	22	55	66	32
Padiham	42	10	14	18	53	76	32
Newton	42	10	12	20	47	84	30
Nantwich Town	42	8	13	21	41	68	29
Bacup Borough	42	8	8	26	38	71	22

Ashton Town, Cheadle Town, Great Harwood Town, Padiham, Newton and Bacup Borough all had 2 points deducted.

1988-89

Division One

Rossendale United	34	24	8	2	84	27	56
Knowsley United	34	21	8	5	85	43	50
St. Helens Town	34	20	8	6	60	25	48
Colwyn Bay	34	19	9	6	77	45	47
Darwen	34	19	9	6	64	36	47
Warrington Town	34	16	10	8	47	37	42
Flixton	34	15	8	11	61	44	38
Leyland Motors	34	15	8	11	53	44	38
Bootle	34	14	4	16	49	54	32
Burscough	34	11	10	13	40	51	32
Ellesmere Port & Neston	34	9	12	13	36	42	30
Clitheroe	34	8	12	14	38	41	28
Skelmersdale United	34	8	9	17	39	68	25
Atherton Laburnum Rovers	34	9	6	19	47	74	24
Prescot Cables	34	7	9	18	36	60	23
Salford	34	7	8	19	33	70	22
Ashton United	34	7	6	21	37	72	18
Formby	34	3	4	27	24	77	10

Ashton United had 2 points deducted.

Division Two

Vauxhall GM	34	25	8	1	68	17	58
Maine Road	34	22	7	5	96	40	51
Chadderton	34	20	9	5	71	29	49
Wren Rovers	34	19	10	5	77	45	48
Nantwich Town	34	20	4	10	66	28	44
Newcastle Town	34	15	10	9	53	37	40
Great Harwood Town	34	16	6	12	52	40	38
Maghull	34	12	13	9	46	44	37
Bacup Borough	34	11	12	11	55	57	34
Daisy Hill	34	12	6	16	36	49	30
Atherton Collieries	34	9	11	14	52	58	29
Padiham	34	9	10	15	39	57	28
Glossop	34	10	7	17	42	60	27
Cheadle Town	34	10	7	17	46	67	27
Oldham Town	34	6	11	17	46	66	23
Blackpool Mechanics	34	9	5	20	46	72	23
Ashton Town	34	4	11	19	31	68	19
Newton	34	1	5	28	23	111	7

1989-90

Division One

Warrington Town	34	22	6	6	69	31	72
Knowsley United	34	21	6	7	68	45	69
Colwyn Bay	34	16	12	6	79	50	60
Vauxhall GM	34	16	9	9	50	42	57
Clitheroe	34	17	6	11	48	47	57
Darwen	34	15	9	10	40	34	54
Nantwich Town	34	13	5	16	50	52	44
St. Helens Town	34	10	13	11	50	48	43
Ashton United	34	11	10	13	39	45	43
Prescot Cables	34	10	11	13	49	54	41
Bootle	34	11	8	15	44	58	41
Flixton	34	11	7	16	37	47	40
Leyland Motors	34	10	7	17	55	64	37
Atherton Laburnum Rovers	34	8	13	13	43	58	37
Skelmersdale United	34	8	11	15	48	59	35
Salford	34	8	11	15	31	47	35
Burscough	34	8	12	14	38	41	33
Chadderton	34	7	12	15	39	55	33

Burscough had 3 points deducted.

Division Two

Maine Road	30	22	4	4	84	35	70
Bacup Borough	30	21	5	4	76	30	68
Blackpool Mechanics	30	17	6	7	59	30	57
Wren Rovers	30	16	7	7	72	38	55
Great Harwood Town	30	16	6	8	52	29	54
Cheadle Town	30	13	8	9	54	45	47
Maghull	30	13	6	11	40	43	45
Atherton Collieries	30	12	7	11	34	38	43
Oldham Town	30	11	5	14	47	51	38
Ashton Town	30	9	7	14	42	57	34
Padiham	30	9	6	15	44	53	33
Formby	30	7	7	16	33	57	28
Newcastle Town	30	8	4	18	38	65	28
Glossop	30	8	3	19	34	58	27
Westhoughton Town	30	8	3	19	36	62	27
Newton	30	5	6	19	29	83	21

1990-91

Division One

Knowsley United	36	25	8	3	95	37	83
Colwyn Bay	36	22	10	4	85	32	76
Ashton United	36	20	7	9	80	45	67
Eastwood Hanley	36	16	12	8	42	29	60
Vauxhall GM	36	15	10	11	42	36	55
Prescot	36	13	12	11	57	55	51
Flixton	36	14	7	15	48	72	49
St. Helens Town	36	13	9	14	52	47	48
Maine Road	36	13	9	14	58	61	48
Skelmersdale United	36	12	11	13	56	49	47
Nantwich Town	36	13	8	15	43	56	47
Leyland DAF-SGL	36	12	10	14	51	53	46
Bootle	36	10	9	17	55	64	39
Bacup Borough	36	9	12	15	38	47	39
Clitheroe	36	10	8	18	50	63	38
Darwen	36	9	11	16	44	62	38
Penrith	36	10	8	18	41	65	38
Atherton Laburnum Rovers	36	9	11	16	42	68	38
Salford City	36	6	10	20	30	68	28

Division Two

Great Harwood Town	34	27	5	2	81	22	86
Blackpool Rovers	34	25	4	5	84	33	78
Bradford Park Avenue	34	20	9	5	72	41	69
Bamber Bridge	34	20	6	8	78	46	66
Blackpool Mechanics	34	18	7	9	51	30	61
Newcastle Town	34	16	12	6	48	30	60
Cheadle Town	34	17	3	14	55	54	54
Glossop	34	12	10	12	47	42	46
Burscough	34	12	8	14	39	51	44
Westhoughton Town	34	11	10	13	50	64	43
Castleton Gabriels	34	11	9	14	42	47	42
Chadderton	34	10	6	18	51	61	36
Maghull	34	9	8	17	37	54	35
Kidsgrove Athletic	34	7	10	17	37	65	31
Ashton Town	34	9	2	23	43	86	29
Oldham Town	34	8	4	22	35	66	27
Formby	34	5	9	20	46	63	24
Atherton Collieries	34	6	4	24	37	78	22

Blackpool Rovers and Oldham Town both had 1 point deducted.

1991-92

Division One

Ashton United	34	24	5	5	61	31	77
Great Harwood Town	34	22	8	4	68	38	74
Eastwood Hanley	34	18	9	7	54	35	63
Blackpool Rovers	34	16	7	11	73	57	55
Prescot	34	15	6	13	48	43	51
Penrith	34	15	5	14	57	58	50
Skelmersdale United	34	11	11	12	48	52	44
Flixton	34	11	9	14	46	50	42
Clitheroe	34	11	9	14	44	55	42
Darwen	34	10	11	13	56	55	41
Atherton Laburnum Rovers	34	11	8	15	38	45	41
Nantwich Town	34	11	10	13	44	49	40
Vauxhall GM	34	10	10	14	42	51	40
Bacup Borough	34	9	11	14	41	45	38
St. Helens Town	34	9	9	16	49	55	36
Maine Road	34	9	9	16	40	60	36
Bradford Park Avenue	34	10	5	19	57	68	35
Bootle	34	9	8	17	41	61	35

Nantwich Town had 3 points deducted.

Division Two

Bamber Bridge	34	25	3	6	97	39	78
Newcastle Town	34	23	6	5	69	26	75
Blackpool Mechanics	34	20	9	5	75	34	69
Burscough	34	19	7	8	82	46	64
Formby	34	17	5	12	49	39	56
Glossop	34	15	9	10	61	44	54
Salford City	34	14	9	11	57	41	51
Castleton Gabriels	34	14	9	11	54	43	51
Cheadle Town	34	15	6	13	53	50	51
Kidsgrove Athletic	34	14	7	13	44	45	49
Chadderton	34	14	6	14	50	48	48
Oldham Town	34	11	8	15	49	62	41
Atherton Collieries	34	12	4	18	51	64	40
Squires Gate	34	11	5	18	45	60	38
Holker Old Boys	34	10	6	18	37	53	36
Maghull	34	7	2	25	38	90	23
Ashton Town	34	4	7	23	47	101	19
Westhoughton Town	34	5	4	25	33	106	19

1992-93

Division One

Atherton Laburnum Rovers	42	33	7	2	75	25	106
Bamber Bridge	42	24	11	7	81	37	83
Chadderton	42	24	11	7	99	64	83
Prescot	42	20	12	10	68	44	72
Newcastle Town	42	20	8	14	70	57	68
Bradford Park Avenue	42	19	8	15	54	43	65
Clitheroe	42	17	8	17	61	40	59
St. Helens Town	42	16	11	15	79	62	59
Salford City	42	15	13	14	58	61	58
Burscough	42	16	10	16	58	68	58
Flixton	42	14	15	13	50	42	57
Blackpool Rovers	42	16	9	17	66	64	57
Nantwich Town	42	14	15	13	60	60	57
Penrith	42	15	11	16	62	67	56
Bacup Borough	42	14	13	15	66	59	55
Glossop North End	42	16	9	17	70	67	54
Darwen	42	14	10	18	54	61	52
Eastwood Hanley	42	14	10	18	45	57	52
Maine Road	42	12	9	21	55	63	45
Kidsgrove Athletic	42	9	8	25	53	94	35
Skelmersdale United	42	7	10	25	45	84	31
Blackpool Mechanics	42	2	4	36	27	137	10

Glossop North End had 3 points deducted.

Division Two

Maghull	34	21	9	4	77	26	72
Bootle	34	20	8	6	89	49	68
Oldham Town	34	20	6	8	79	47	66
Ellesmere Port Town	34	16	9	9	65	46	57
Stantondale	34	16	9	9	59	49	57
Castleton Gabriels	34	15	10	9	61	48	55
North Trafford	34	14	9	11	67	63	51
Formby	34	14	9	11	49	49	51
Atherton Collieries	34	14	7	13	63	67	49
Burnley Bank Hall	34	14	4	16	87	77	46
Westhoughton Town	34	14	3	17	65	75	42
Cheadle Town	34	12	7	15	44	48	40
Squires Gate	34	11	5	18	56	73	38
K Chell	34	10	8	16	52	72	38
Holker Old Boys	34	8	13	13	57	60	37
Ashton Town	34	8	8	18	51	74	32
Nelson	34	7	7	20	47	82	28
Irlam Town	34	4	5	25	47	110	17

Westhoughton Town and Cheadle Town both had 3 points deducted.

1993-94

Division One

Atherton Laburnum Rovers	42	25	13	4	83	34	88
Rossendale United	42	25	9	8	76	46	84
Burscough	42	22	13	7	107	50	79
Nantwich Town	42	22	11	9	80	54	77
Eastwood Hanley	42	22	11	9	75	52	77
Bootle	42	21	10	11	77	61	73
Penrith	42	20	11	11	62	44	71
Blackpool Rovers	42	19	10	13	64	57	67
Clitheroe	42	19	9	14	75	58	66
Kidsgrove Athletic	42	16	10	16	70	61	58
St. Helens Town	42	14	13	15	60	55	55
Prescot	42	14	13	15	46	47	55
Maine Road	42	14	13	15	58	64	55
Newcastle Town	42	14	10	18	66	67	52
Bradford Park Avenue	42	12	12	18	54	79	48
Darwen	42	12	8	22	38	61	44
Glossop North End	42	12	8	22	58	86	44
Salford City	42	11	10	21	50	67	43
Chadderton	42	10	8	24	49	85	38
Bacup Borough	42	9	9	24	57	85	36
Skelmersdale United	42	8	8	26	55	92	32
Flixton	42	9	5	28	35	90	32

Division Two

Haslingden	34	26	5	3	117	39	83
North Trafford	34	24	2	8	95	36	74
Holker Old Boys	34	23	3	8	75	40	72
Stantondale	34	20	8	6	88	45	68
Castleton Gabriels	34	19	6	9	55	46	63
Nelson	34	16	8	10	75	52	56
Atherton Collieries	34	15	9	10	58	40	54
Maghull	34	15	8	11	70	46	53
Ellesmere Port Town	34	14	8	12	62	63	50
Formby	34	12	11	11	59	50	47
Oldham Town	34	13	6	15	61	68	45
Cheadle Town	34	11	9	14	69	62	42
Blackpool Mechanics	34	10	5	19	50	69	35
Westhoughton Town	34	9	3	22	53	100	30
Ashton Town	34	7	8	19	42	91	29
Irlam Town	34	8	4	22	41	73	28
K Chell	34	4	6	24	35	97	18
Squires Gate	34	1	9	24	20	108	12

1994-95

Division One

Bradford Park Avenue	42	30	4	8	96	43	94
Clitheroe	42	27	9	6	104	49	90
St. Helens Town	42	27	8	7	86	42	89
Trafford	42	27	5	10	98	50	86
Newcastle Town	42	24	7	11	75	57	79
Glossop North End	42	23	8	11	88	59	77
Blackpool Rovers	42	22	7	13	81	64	73
Burscough	42	19	15	8	102	65	72
Prescot	42	16	8	18	47	47	56
Penrith	42	16	7	19	72	72	55
Chadderton	42	15	7	20	56	70	52
Maine Road	42	14	9	19	68	81	51
Eastwood Hanley	42	14	8	20	75	81	50
Holker Old Boys	42	13	11	18	63	72	50
Kidsgrove Athletic	42	14	8	20	66	78	50
Nantwich Town	42	14	7	21	85	83	49
Darwen	42	14	5	23	65	82	47
Rossendale United	42	12	11	19	60	82	47
Bootle	42	11	10	21	46	68	43
Skelmersdale United	42	10	7	25	67	118	37
Salford City	42	9	9	24	45	85	36
Bacup Borough	42	3	6	33	35	132	15

Division Two

Flixton	30	21	6	3	98	32	69
Oldham Town	30	20	6	4	83	34	66
Tetley Walker	30	18	5	7	75	46	59
Atherton Collieries	30	18	4	8	67	41	58
Stantondale	30	18	3	9	58	43	57
Nelson	30	13	8	9	64	44	47
Haslingden	30	14	4	12	76	64	46
Blackpool Mechanics	30	12	8	10	72	57	44
Maghull	30	11	8	11	58	46	41
Formby	30	11	6	13	57	53	39
Cheadle Town	30	10	7	13	48	52	37
Castleton Gabriels	30	9	9	12	56	75	36
Daisy Hill	30	6	8	16	53	73	26
Ashton Town	30	6	2	22	39	92	20
Irlam Town	30	5	3	22	30	98	18
Squires Gate	30	2	5	23	30	114	11

1995-96

Division One

Flixton	42	28	8	6	85	30	92
Newcastle Town	42	26	7	9	88	42	85
Trafford	42	26	5	11	89	45	83
Mossley	42	24	8	10	87	59	80
Burscough	42	23	8	11	77	40	77
Bootle	42	23	5	14	74	55	74
Clitheroe	42	20	12	10	63	44	72
St. Helens Town	42	19	13	10	71	53	70
Nantwich Town	42	20	7	15	64	59	67
Prescot	42	17	11	14	70	66	62
Holker Old Boys	42	19	4	19	77	72	61
Glossop North End	42	15	15	12	55	48	60
Kidsgrove Athletic	42	15	9	18	61	64	54
Eastwood Hanley	42	12	15	15	60	57	51
Maine Road	42	12	14	16	60	71	50
Chadderton	42	14	8	20	52	69	50
Blackpool Rovers	42	11	9	22	49	74	42
Penrith	42	9	12	21	57	69	39
Darwen	42	9	10	23	57	77	37
Salford City	42	10	5	27	49	93	35
Rossendale United	42	6	10	26	32	114	28
Skelmersdale United	42	5	3	34	45	121	18

Division Two

Vauxhall GM	34	28	4	2	112	25	88
Atherton Collieries	34	25	5	4	90	44	80
Tetley Walker	34	22	7	5	76	35	73
Castleton Gabriels	34	19	5	10	77	52	62
Nelson	34	17	9	8	78	55	60
Cheadle Town	34	17	5	12	67	49	56
Haslingden	34	15	9	10	69	45	54
Maghull	34	16	3	15	55	42	51
Oldham Town	34	14	8	12	75	74	50
Middlewich Athletic	34	12	7	15	45	74	43
Daisy Hill	34	12	4	18	46	66	40
Ramsbottom United	34	11	6	17	60	65	39
Formby	34	10	7	17	59	76	37
Stantondale	34	11	4	19	47	75	37
Blackpool Mechanics	34	8	8	18	56	74	32
Ashton Town	34	8	3	23	53	102	27
Squires Gate	34	5	7	22	37	82	22
Bacup Borough	34	4	3	27	35	102	15

Division Two

Ramsbottom United	38	27	6	5	100	34	87
Haslingden	38	27	6	5	90	32	87
Garswood United	38	26	5	7	90	38	83
Tetley Walker	38	24	5	9	105	58	77
Castleton Gabriels	38	22	8	8	78	39	74
Leek County School Old Boys	38	22	7	9	67	49	73
Formby	38	21	6	11	86	57	69
Maghull	38	17	7	14	52	50	58
Cheadle Town	38	15	8	15	59	63	53
Skelmersdale United	38	14	10	14	72	66	52
Nelson	38	14	10	14	64	72	52
Stantondale	38	11	12	15	59	69	45
Middlewich Athletic	38	13	6	19	54	65	45
Squires Gate	38	12	4	22	44	79	40
Daisy Hill	38	10	5	23	47	76	35
Bacup Borough	38	9	6	23	48	83	33
Ashton Town	38	6	14	18	53	77	32
Blackpool Mechanics	38	7	5	26	48	88	26
Oldham Town	38	6	7	25	48	113	25
Colne	38	6	5	27	35	91	23

1997-98

Division One

Kidsgrove Athletic	42	32	3	7	127	50	99
Burscough	42	29	7	6	101	30	94
Newcastle Town	42	23	16	3	82	32	85
Vauxhall GM	42	24	9	9	91	52	81
St. Helens Town	42	22	12	8	91	59	78
Clitheroe	42	21	10	11	72	51	73
Prescot Cables	42	19	11	12	72	57	68
Glossop North End	42	19	7	16	78	69	64
Mossley	42	16	14	12	67	52	62
Nantwich Town	42	17	6	19	71	79	57
Maine Road	42	15	10	17	56	70	55
Chadderton	42	15	8	19	63	59	53
Rossendale United	42	15	6	21	61	80	51
Blackpool Rovers	42	13	9	20	68	84	48
Atherton Laburnum Rovers	42	12	11	19	54	73	47
Haslingden	42	12	10	20	68	95	46
Ramsbottom United	42	12	9	21	58	85	45
Salford City	42	13	4	25	64	92	43
Warrington Town	42	10	10	22	56	72	40
Holker Old Boys	42	7	12	23	46	96	33
Darwen	42	6	13	23	42	93	31
Atherton Collieries	42	7	9	26	42	100	30

1996-97

Division One

Trafford	42	29	7	6	99	38	94
Newcastle Town	42	27	7	8	71	31	88
Clitheroe	42	23	14	5	75	36	83
Penrith	42	23	10	9	75	49	79
Burscough	42	22	9	11	68	48	75
Eastwood Hanley	42	20	10	12	64	51	70
Mossley	42	20	8	14	79	58	68
Blackpool Rovers	42	17	16	9	70	47	67
Prescot Cables	42	17	11	14	68	60	62
Vauxhall GM	42	14	15	13	70	69	57
Nantwich Town	42	14	11	17	74	74	53
Bootle	42	15	8	19	62	73	53
Glossop North End	42	14	11	17	56	67	53
St. Helens Town	42	14	6	22	65	79	48
Atherton Collieries	42	12	9	21	63	85	45
Kidsgrove Athletic	42	10	14	18	53	73	44
Rossendale United	42	11	9	22	51	76	42
Chadderton	42	10	11	21	49	80	41
Holker Old Boys	42	10	9	23	60	80	39
Maine Road	42	9	11	22	49	85	38
Darwen	42	9	10	23	49	82	37
Salford City	42	8	12	22	53	82	36

Division Two

Oldham Town	40	27	8	5	118	49	89
Skelmersdale United	40	26	7	7	111	50	85
Leek County School Old Boys	40	26	7	7	76	38	85
Cheadle Town	40	24	9	7	108	58	81
Woodley Sports	40	22	7	11	118	56	73
Formby	40	22	7	11	90	63	73
Bootle	40	19	15	6	82	60	72
Garswood United	40	19	10	11	98	62	67
Tetley Walker	40	19	9	12	98	62	66
Castleton Gabriels	40	18	7	15	86	59	61
Maghull	40	16	10	14	67	62	58
Fleetwood Freeport	40	15	11	14	73	55	56
Nelson	40	17	5	18	69	76	56
Bacup Borough	40	13	8	19	58	83	47
Squires Gate	40	11	9	20	72	88	42
Daisy Hill	40	11	9	20	60	86	42
Middlewich Athletic	40	11	8	21	48	90	41
Colne	40	8	7	25	48	91	31
Ashton Town	40	6	6	28	73	137	24
Stantondale	40	4	4	32	50	146	16
Blackpool Mechanics	40	2	5	33	33	165	11

1998-99

Division One

Workington	40	27	9	4	86	28	90
Mossley	40	27	7	6	91	38	88
Vauxhall GM	40	26	7	7	92	40	85
Newcastle Town	40	25	9	6	86	33	84
Kidsgrove Athletic	40	24	7	9	90	47	79
Prescot Cables	40	21	9	10	78	44	72
Skelmersdale United	40	21	8	11	82	48	71
St. Helens Town	40	22	5	13	77	58	71
Leek County School Old Boys	40	14	11	15	52	58	53
Salford City	40	15	7	18	63	73	52
Ramsbottom United	40	14	8	18	54	64	50
Clitheroe	40	14	6	20	68	58	48
Maine Road	40	14	6	20	50	71	48
Rossendale United	40	14	5	21	59	81	47
Nantwich Town	40	12	6	22	54	68	42
Glossop North End	40	12	6	22	53	81	42
Cheadle Town	40	12	6	22	56	97	42
Atherton Laburnum Rovers	40	10	9	21	45	73	39
Atherton Collieries	40	9	7	24	50	88	34
Bootle	40	9	7	24	41	84	34
Holker Old Boys	40	4	3	33	21	116	15

Division Two

Fleetwood Freeport	36	21	8	7	102	34	71
Abbey Hey	36	20	6	10	70	35	66
Squires Gate	36	17	14	5	53	31	65
Warrington Town	36	18	9	9	82	46	63
Woodley Sports	36	17	10	9	60	38	61
Castleton Gabriels	36	17	10	9	71	56	61
Formby	36	17	7	12	81	59	58
Darwen	36	13	12	11	64	53	51
Chadderton	36	11	17	8	42	38	50
Tetley Walker	36	14	8	14	62	64	50
Bacup Borough	36	11	14	11	47	61	47
Daisy Hill	36	12	9	15	51	63	45
Nelson	36	11	11	14	51	49	44
Curzon Ashton	36	12	7	17	56	58	43
Maghull	36	11	10	15	50	70	43
Colne	36	11	7	18	53	70	40
Ashton Town	36	11	6	19	35	59	39
Oldham Town	36	5	7	24	35	99	22
Blackpool Mechanics	36	4	6	26	40	122	18

1999-2000

Division One

Vauxhall Motors	42	29	7	6	101	32	94
Newcastle Town	42	26	7	9	82	35	85
Ramsbottom United	42	23	10	9	87	53	79
Mossley	42	23	10	9	80	50	79
Rossendale United	42	23	9	10	77	46	78
Skelmersdale United	42	22	9	11	91	53	75
Fleetwood Freeport	42	21	10	11	75	45	73
Prescot Cables	42	21	10	11	83	55	73
St. Helens Town	42	20	13	9	81	59	73
Clitheroe	42	21	7	14	75	49	70
Salford City	42	17	7	18	70	69	58
Atherton Collieries	42	16	6	20	58	68	54
Kidsgrove Athletic	42	14	9	19	47	66	51
Abbey Hey	42	14	8	20	50	75	50
Nantwich Town	42	13	9	20	60	73	48
Great Harwood Town	42	12	9	21	55	81	45
Glossop North End	42	10	11	21	52	73	41
Cheadle Town	42	8	13	21	49	85	37
Maine Road	42	9	10	23	59	100	37
Leek County School Old Boys	42	8	10	24	49	101	34
Bootle	42	6	8	28	29	90	26
Atherton Laburnum Rovers	42	4	12	26	51	103	24

Division Two

Woodley Sports	34	24	6	4	85	29	78
Curzon Ashton	34	24	6	4	78	26	78
Nelson	34	21	8	5	77	31	71
Darwen	34	20	6	8	69	35	66
Bacup Borough	34	15	11	8	68	42	56
Squires Gate	34	16	7	11	70	49	55
Tetley Walker	34	16	4	14	56	70	52
Castleton Gabriels	34	15	6	13	67	67	51
Warrington Town	34	14	8	12	66	44	50
Chadderton	34	12	12	10	52	57	48
Formby	34	12	8	14	52	68	44
Alsager	34	11	8	15	48	64	41
Colne	34	12	2	20	44	70	38
Holker Old Boys	34	8	11	15	59	73	35
Blackpool Mechanics	34	9	6	19	49	74	33
Daisy Hill	34	7	5	22	41	75	26
Oldham Town	34	4	6	24	43	86	18
Ashton Town	34	5	2	27	30	94	17

2000-2001

Division One

Rossendale United	42	29	5	8	114	44	92
Clitheroe	42	27	8	7	105	47	89
Ramsbottom United	42	28	4	10	85	44	88
St. Helens Town	42	26	9	7	98	40	87
Fleetwood Freeport	42	26	4	12	90	50	82
Kidsgrove Athletic	42	24	10	8	81	46	82
Salford City	42	23	10	9	87	41	79
Prescot Cables	42	24	5	13	94	54	77
Newcastle Town	42	20	7	15	69	45	67
Mossley	42	19	7	16	73	56	64
Curzon Ashton	42	18	9	15	67	66	63
Skelmersdale United	42	17	8	17	69	69	59
Woodley Sports	42	16	9	17	69	69	57
Abbey Hey	42	15	6	21	76	92	51
Maine Road	42	15	3	24	75	102	48
Nantwich Town	42	10	9	23	46	79	39
Atherton Collieries	42	11	6	25	43	88	39
Glossop North End	42	9	4	29	41	111	31
Great Harwood Town	42	7	9	26	44	93	30
Flixton	42	5	13	24	47	100	28
Leek County School Old Boys	42	5	12	25	39	89	27
Cheadle Town	42	5	9	28	42	129	24

Division Two

Warrington Town	38	24	7	7	90	31	79
Tetley Walker	38	24	5	9	83	41	77
Atherton Laburnum Rovers	38	24	3	11	88	50	75
Nelson	38	21	11	6	89	44	74
Squires Gate	38	21	7	10	75	47	70
Blackpool Mechanics	38	21	6	11	85	47	69
Alsager	38	19	8	11	48	42	65
Padiham	38	20	4	14	83	71	64
Daisy Hill	38	18	6	14	78	80	60
Chadderton	38	17	7	14	68	58	58
Darwen	38	16	7	15	72	66	55
Formby	38	15	8	15	65	56	53
Stone Dominoes	38	15	6	17	62	63	51
Bacup Borough	38	13	9	16	59	60	48
Holker Old Boys	38	14	5	19	67	79	47
Bootle	38	11	8	19	70	76	41
Castleton Gabriels	38	10	7	21	52	90	37
Ashton Town	38	8	3	27	46	98	27
Colne	38	4	4	30	37	107	16
Oldham Town	38	3	3	32	38	149	12

2001-2002

Division One

Kidsgrove Athletic	44	31	9	4	125	47	102
Prescot Cables	44	29	10	5	110	42	97
Salford City	44	29	10	5	91	40	97
St. Helens Town	44	28	6	10	101	44	90
Newcastle Town	44	22	11	11	97	66	77
Clitheroe	44	22	10	12	73	53	76
Winsford United	44	19	12	13	72	71	69
Mossley	44	18	14	12	82	63	68
Skelmersdale United	44	19	5	20	87	89	62
Woodley Sports	44	16	12	16	58	65	60
Warrington Town	44	16	11	17	78	72	59
Ramsbottom United	44	15	10	19	75	73	55
Curzon Ashton	44	16	7	21	74	72	55
Fleetwood Freeport	44	13	13	18	70	86	52
Nantwich Town	44	12	15	17	63	90	51
Congleton Town	44	13	11	20	71	79	50
Atherton Collieries	44	13	8	23	66	91	47
Abbey Hey	44	12	11	21	62	101	47
Glossop North End	44	13	7	24	78	105	46
Atherton Laburnum Rovers	44	11	11	22	62	88	44
Flixton	44	11	9	24	61	112	42
Maine Road	44	8	7	29	68	115	31
Great Harwood Town	44	5	11	28	39	99	26

Division Two

Stand Athletic	40	30	5	5	110	47	95
Alsager Town	40	24	9	7	77	31	81
Squires Gate	40	24	9	7	103	60	81
Stone Dominoes	40	25	3	12	71	40	78
Formby	40	21	14	5	76	39	77
Bootle	40	19	7	14	82	64	64
Norton United	40	19	7	14	56	51	64
Blackpool Mechanics	40	18	9	13	69	48	63
Nelson	40	18	9	13	73	63	63
Leek County School Old Boys	40	17	8	15	62	65	59
Darwen	40	15	10	15	77	73	55
Bacup Borough	40	13	13	14	52	66	52
Padiham	40	14	8	18	69	66	50
Colne	40	14	8	18	61	72	50
Chadderton	40	15	5	20	65	81	50
Ashton Town	40	13	6	21	65	85	45
Cheadle Town	40	10	8	22	66	85	38
Castleton Gabriels	40	10	3	27	61	95	33
Holker Old Boys	40	7	9	24	43	79	30
Daisy Hill	40	8	4	28	49	114	28
Oldham Town	40	7	4	29	50	113	25

Division Two

Bacup Borough	34	25	2	7	91	32	77
Stone Dominoes	34	24	3	7	94	34	75
Maine Road	34	23	2	9	74	55	71
Padiham	34	20	5	9	69	42	65
Holker Old Boys	34	18	7	9	65	42	61
Great Harwood Town	34	15	7	12	64	61	52
Nelson	34	13	12	9	50	40	51
Darwen	34	14	7	13	59	64	49
Norton United	34	14	6	14	50	52	48
Colne	34	14	5	15	65	53	47
Ashton Town	34	12	9	13	49	53	45
Castleton Gabriels	34	10	8	16	43	60	38
Cheadle Town	34	10	8	16	39	56	38
Blackpool Mechanics	34	9	10	15	39	52	37
Leek County School Old Boys	34	8	9	17	46	57	33
Daisy Hill	34	7	5	22	42	93	26
Oldham Town	34	4	12	18	40	86	24
Chadderton	34	5	5	24	33	80	20

2002-2003

Division One

Prescot Cables	42	30	6	6	110	38	96
Clitheroe	42	28	8	6	97	38	92
Mossley	42	27	7	8	100	41	88
Newcastle Town	42	23	12	7	83	52	81
Skelmersdale United	42	22	8	12	91	51	74
Nantwich Town	42	19	11	12	90	74	68
St. Helens Town	42	17	14	11	77	60	65
Congleton Town	42	19	8	15	72	62	65
Salford City	42	17	12	13	84	63	63
Fleetwood Town	42	17	9	16	73	70	60
Alsager Town	42	15	11	16	61	67	56
Squires Gate	42	13	12	17	58	71	51
Abbey Hey	42	12	13	17	56	73	49
Atherton Laburnum Rovers	42	11	12	19	65	86	45
Ramsbottom United	42	11	11	20	73	83	44
Warrington Town	42	11	11	20	48	66	44
Woodley Sports	42	11	9	22	62	85	42
Curzon Ashton	42	11	9	22	60	87	42
Atherton Collieries	42	11	7	24	52	85	40
Glossop North End	42	10	9	23	55	104	39
Flixton	42	10	8	24	44	112	38
Winsford United	42	10	7	25	48	91	37

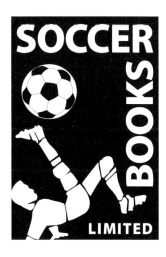

SOCCER BOOKS LIMITED

72 ST. PETERS AVENUE (Dept. SBL)
CLEETHORPES
N.E. LINCOLNSHIRE
DN35 8HU
ENGLAND

Tel. 01472 696226   Fax 01472 698546

Web site http://www.soccer-books.co.uk
e-mail – info@soccer-books.co.uk

Established in 1982, Soccer Books Limited has the biggest range of English-Language soccer books and videos available. We are now expanding our stocks even further to include many more titles including German, French, Spanish and Italian-language books.

With over 100,000 satisfied customers already, we supply books to virtually every country in the world but have maintained the friendliness and accessibility associated with a small family-run business. The range of titles we sell includes:

YEARBOOKS – All major yearbooks including Rothmans (many editions), Calcios (many editions), Supporters' Guides, Playfair Annuals, North & Latin American Guides (all editions), African Guides, Non-League Directories.

CLUB HISTORIES – Complete Records, Official Histories, 25 Year Records, Definitive Histories plus many more.

WORLD FOOTBALL – World Cup books, International Line-up & Statistics Series, European Championships History, International Statistical Histories (many titles) and much more.

BIOGRAPHIES & WHO'S WHOS – on Managers and Players plus Who's Whos etc.

ENCYCLOPEDIAS & GENERAL TITLES – Books on Stadia, Hooligan studies, Histories and dozens of others.

VIDEOS & DVDs – Season's highlights, histories, big games, World Cup, player profiles, F.A. Cup Finals – including many back items.

For a current listing of our titles, please contact us using the information at the top of the page.

Supporters' Guides & Other Titles

This top-selling series has been published annually since 1982 and contains 2002/2003 Season's results and tables, Directions, Photographs, Phone numbers, Parking information, Admission details, Disabled information and much more.

THE SUPPORTERS' GUIDE TO PREMIER & FOOTBALL LEAGUE CLUBS 2004

The 20th edition featuring all Premiership and Football League clubs.   *Price £6.99*

THE SUPPORTERS' GUIDE TO NON-LEAGUE FOOTBALL 2004

The 11th edition featuring all Conference, Unibond Premier, Rymans Premier and Dr. Martens Premier clubs.   *Price £6.99*

THE SUPPORTERS' GUIDE TO SCOTTISH FOOTBALL 2004

The 11th edition featuring all Scottish League and Highland League clubs.   *Price £6.99*

THE SUPPORTERS' GUIDE TO WELSH FOOTBALL 2004

The 4th edition featuring all League of Wales, Cymru Alliance & Welsh Football League Clubs + results, tables & much more.   *Price £6.99*

THE SUPPORTERS' GUIDE TO FOOTBALL PROGRAMMES 2004

Produced in conjunction with *Programme Monthly* magazine, this book contains an appraisal of the programmes of all 92 Premier and Football League Clubs during the 2002/2003 Season.   *Price £6.99*

FOOTBALL LEAGUE TABLES 1888-2003

The 6th edition contains every Football League, Premier League, Scottish League and Scottish Premier League Final Table from 1888-2003 together with Cup Final information.   *Price £9.99*

These books are available UK & Surface post free from –

Soccer Books Limited (Dept. SBL)
72 St. Peter's Avenue
Cleethorpes
N.E. Lincolnshire
DN35 8HU